SMALL SAMPLE SIZE SOLUTIONS

Researchers often have difficulties collecting enough data to test their hypotheses, either because target groups are small or hard to access, or because data collection entails prohibitive costs. Such obstacles may result in data sets that are too small for the complexity of the statistical model needed to answer the research question. This unique book provides guidelines and tools for implementing solutions to issues that arise in small sample research. Each chapter illustrates statistical methods that allow researchers to apply the optimal statistical model for their research question when the sample is too small.

This essential book will enable social and behavioral science researchers to test their hypotheses even when the statistical model required for answering their research question is too complex for the sample sizes they can collect. The statistical models in the book range from the estimation of a population mean to models with latent variables and nested observations, and solutions include both classical and Bayesian methods. All proposed solutions are described in steps researchers can implement with their own data and are accompanied with annotated syntax in R.

The methods described in this book will be useful for researchers across the social and behavioral sciences, ranging from medical sciences and epidemiology to psychology, marketing, and economics.

Prof. Dr. Rens van de Schoot works as a Full Professor teaching Statistics for Small Data Sets at Utrecht University in the Netherlands and as an Extra-ordinary Professor at North-West University in South Africa. He obtained his PhD *cum laude* on the topic of applying Bayesian statistics to empirical data.

Dr. Milica Miočević is an Assistant Professor in the Department of Psychology at McGill University. She received her PhD in Quantitative Psychology from Arizona State University in 2017. Dr. Miočević's research evaluates optimal ways to use Bayesian methods in the social sciences, particularly for mediation analysis.

EUROPEAN ASSOCIATION OF METHODOLOGY

The European Association of Methodology (EAM) serves to promote research and development of empirical research methods in the fields of the Behavioural, Social, Educational, Health and Economic Sciences as well as in the field of Evaluation Research.
Homepage: www.eam-online.org.

The purpose of the EAM book series is to advance the development and application of methodological and statistical research techniques in social and behavioral research. Each volume in the series presents cutting-edge methodological developments in a way that is accessible to a broad audience. Such books can be authored, monographs, or edited volumes.

Sponsored by the European Association of Methodology, the EAM book series is open to contributions from the Behavioral, Social, Educational, Health and Economic Sciences. Proposals for volumes in the EAM series should include the following: (1) title; (2) authors/editors; (3) a brief description of the volume's focus and intended audience; (4) a table of contents; (5) a timeline including planned completion date. Proposals are invited from all interested authors. Feel free to submit a proposal to one of the members of the EAM book series editorial board by visiting the EAM website http://eam-online.org. Members of the EAM editorial board are Manuel Ato (University of Murcia), Pamela Campanelli (Survey Consultant, UK), Edith de Leeuw (Utrecht University) and Vasja Vehovar (University of Ljubljana).

Volumes in the series include

Van de Schoot/Miočević: *Small Sample Size Solutions: A Guide for Applied Researchers and Practitioners*, 2020

Davidov/Schmidt/Billiet/Meuleman: *Cross-Cultural Analysis: Methods and Applications*, 2nd edition, 2018

Engel/Jann/Lynn/Scherpenzeel/Sturgis: *Improving Survey Methods: Lessons from Recent Research*, 2015

Das/Ester/Kaczmirek: *Social and Behavioral Research and the Internet: Advances in Applied Methods and Research Strategies*, 2011

Hox/Roberts: *Handbook of Advanced Multilevel Analysis*, 2011

De Leeuw/Hox/Dillman: *International Handbook of Survey Methodology*, 2008

Van Montfort/Oud/Satorra: *Longitudinal Models in the Behavioral and Related Sciences*, 2007

SMALL SAMPLE SIZE SOLUTIONS

A Guide for Applied Researchers and Practitioners

Edited by Rens van de Schoot and Milica Miočević

LONDON AND NEW YORK

First published 2020
by Routledge
2 Park Square, Milton Park, Abingdon, Oxon, OX14 4RN

52 Vanderbilt Avenue, New York, NY 10017
and by Routledge

Routledge is an imprint of the Taylor & Francis Group, an informa business

© 2020 selection and editorial matter, Rens van de Schoot and Milica Miočević; individual chapters, the contributors

The right of Rens van de Schoot and Milica Miočević to be identified as the authors of the editorial material, and of the authors for their individual chapters, has been asserted in accordance with sections 77 and 78 of the Copyright, Designs and Patents Act 1988.

The Open Access version of this book, available at www.taylorfrancis.com, has been made available under a Creative Commons Attribution-Non Commercial-No Derivatives 4.0 license.

Trademark notice: Product or corporate names may be trademarks or registered trademarks, and are used only for identification and explanation without intent to infringe.

Library of Congress Cataloging-in-Publication Data
A catalog record for this title has been requested

ISBN: 978-0-367-22189-8 (hbk)
ISBN: 978-0-367-22222-2 (pbk)
ISBN: 978-0-429-27387-2 (ebk)

Typeset in Bembo
by Swales & Willis, Exeter, Devon, UK

CONTENTS

Introduction viii
Rens van de Schoot and Milica Miočević
List of symbols xi

PART I
Bayesian solutions 1

1 Introduction to Bayesian statistics 3
 Milica Miočević, Roy Levy, and Rens van de Schoot

2 The role of exchangeability in sequential updating of findings from small studies and the challenges of identifying exchangeable data sets 13
 Milica Miočević, Roy Levy, and Andrea Savord

3 A tutorial on using the WAMBS checklist to avoid the misuse of Bayesian statistics 30
 Rens van de Schoot, Duco Veen, Laurent Smeets, Sonja D. Winter, and Sarah Depaoli

4 The importance of collaboration in Bayesian analyses with small samples 50
 Duco Veen and Marthe Egberts

5 A tutorial on Bayesian penalized regression with shrinkage priors for small sample sizes 71
Sara van Erp

PART II
n = 1 85

6 One by one: the design and analysis of replicated randomized single-case experiments 87
Patrick Onghena

7 Single-case experimental designs in clinical intervention research 102
Marija Maric and Vera van der Werff

8 How to improve the estimation of a specific examinee's ($n = 1$) math ability when test data are limited 112
Kimberley Lek and Ingrid Arts

9 Combining evidence over multiple individual analyses 126
Fayette Klaassen

10 Going multivariate in clinical trial studies: a Bayesian framework for multiple binary outcomes 139
Xynthia Kavelaars

PART III
Complex hypotheses and models 155

11 An introduction to restriktor: evaluating informative hypotheses for linear models 157
Leonard Vanbrabant and Yves Rosseel

12 Testing replication with small samples: applications to ANOVA 173
Mariëlle Zondervan-Zwijnenburg and Dominique Rijshouwer

13 Small sample meta-analyses: exploring heterogeneity using MetaForest 186
Caspar J. van Lissa

14 Item parcels as indicators: why, when, and how to use them in small sample research 203
    Charlie Rioux, Zachary L. Stickley, Omolola A. Odejimi, and Todd D. Little

15 Small samples in multilevel modeling 215
    Joop Hox and Daniel McNeish

16 Small sample solutions for structural equation modeling 226
    Yves Rosseel

17 SEM with small samples: two-step modeling and factor score regression versus Bayesian estimation with informative priors 239
    Sanne C. Smid and Yves Rosseel

18 Important yet unheeded: some small sample issues that are often overlooked 255
    Joop Hox

Index *266*

INTRODUCTION

Rens van de Schoot and Milica Miočević

Researchers often have difficulties collecting enough data to test their hypotheses, either because target groups are small (e.g., patients with severe burn injuries); data are sparse (e.g., rare diseases), hard to access (e.g., infants of drug-dependent mothers), or data collection entails prohibitive costs (e.g., fMRI, measuring phonological difficulties of babies); or the study participants come from a population that is prone to drop-out (e.g., because they are homeless or institutionalized). Such obstacles may result in data sets that are too small for the complexity of the statistical model needed to answer the research question. Researchers could reduce the required sample size for the analysis by simplifying their statistical models. However, this may leave the "true" research questions unanswered. As such, limitations associated with small data sets can restrict the usefulness of the scientific conclusions and might even hamper scientific breakthroughs.

The field of methodological solutions for issues due to small sample sizes is developing rapidly, and fast software implementations of these methods are becoming increasingly available. However, the selection of texts on statistical methods for small sample research with complex models is sparse. In March 2018, we organized the first edition of the Small Sample Size Solutions conference (S4; www.uu.nl/s4) with the goal of bringing together applied researchers who encounter issues due to small samples, and statisticians working on solutions to such issues. The aim of the S4 Conference was to share information, learn about new developments, and discuss solutions for typical small sample size problems. The chapters in the current volume describe some of the solutions to small sample size issues presented at the first S4 Conference. The list of contributors includes both established authors who provide an overview of available methods in a particular field, and early-career researchers working on promising innovative solutions. The authors of the chapters reviewed at least one other chapter in this volume, and each chapter was written with the goal of being accessible for applied researchers and students with a basic knowledge of statistics. Note that collecting more data, if at all possible, is always preferred, and that the methods described in the current book are a last resort.

The current book provides guidelines and tools for implementing a variety of solutions to issues that arise in small sample research, along with references for further (technical) details. The book includes solutions for estimation of population means, regression analyses, meta-analyses, factor analyses, advanced structural equation models with latent variables, and models for nested observations. The types of solutions consist of Bayesian estimation with informative priors, various classical and Bayesian methods for synthesizing data with small samples, constrained statistical inference, two-step modeling, and data analysis methods for one participant at a time. All methods require a strong justification of the choice of analytic strategy and complete transparency about all steps in the analysis. The book is accompanied by state-of-the-art software solutions, some of which will only be released next year. All proposed solutions are described in steps researchers can implement with their own data and are accompanied with annotated syntax in R available on the Open Science Framework (osf.io/am7pr/). The content of the substantive applications spans a variety of disciplines, and we expect the book to be of interest to researchers within and outside academia who are working with small samples sizes.

The book is split into three parts:

Part I contains several chapters that describe and make use of Bayesian statistics. Chapter 1 offers a gentle introduction to the main ingredients in Bayesian analyses and provides necessary information for understanding Bayesian parameter estimation and Bayes Factors. Chapter 2 offers a discussion of exchangeability and its role in the choice of sources of prior information in Bayesian analyses, which is relevant when combining datasets. Chapter 3 provides an extension of the When-to-Worry-and-How-to-Avoid-the-Misuse-of-Bayesian-Statistics (WAMBS) checklist, which is a 10-point checklist used to ensure optimal practices when applying Bayesian methods, extended to include prior and posterior predictive checking. Chapter 4 illustrates difficulties that can arise when implementing Bayesian solutions to a complex model and offers suggestions for avoiding these issues by making use of the effective sample size and divergent transitions. Chapter 5 provides a tutorial on Bayesian penalized regression for scenarios with a small sample size relative to the complexity of the statistical model by applying so-called "shrinkage priors" that shrink small effects towards zero while leaving substantial effects large.

Part II is composed of chapters on methods for analyzing data from a single participant. Chapter 6 introduces single-case experimental designs ($n = 1$) and provides background information for analyzing a single-case experimental design (SCED) using unilevel design-based analysis. Chapter 7 discusses SCEDs in detail and provides an example of tests of effectiveness and change processes. Chapter 8 introduced a shiny app that allows researchers to supplement test scores of a single participant with teacher input or scores from other students in order to obtain a more accurate estimate of a given student's ability. Chapter 9 presents a Bayesian method to evaluate hypotheses for each person in a sample and aggregate these results to find out whether a hypothesis holds for everyone in the sample, rather than for sample participants on average. Chapter 10 introduces a Bayes decision-making strategy for clinical trials, such that decisions can be made with smaller samples without increasing the risk of making an error.

Part III deals with complex hypotheses and models fit to small sample data. Chapter 11 provides examples and software for increasing power to detect mean differences by testing informative hypotheses within the framework of constrained statistical inference. Chapter 12 discusses several Bayesian methods for evaluating whether a finding was replicated across studies, which is extremely important in small sample research. Chapter 13 introduces software based on a machine-learning approach for identifying relevant moderators in meta-analysis. Chapter 14 provides an overview of the psychometric and model estimation benefits of parceling, and discusses how parcels can be particularly beneficial for small sample research. Chapter 15 offers an in-depth discussion of issues and potential solutions for multilevel models fit to small samples, from both frequentist and Bayesian perspectives. Chapter 16 describes several potential solutions for point estimation in structural equation models, including penalized likelihood estimation, a method based on model-implied instrumental variables, two-step estimation, and factor score regression. Chapter 17 compares, by means of a simulation study, two-step modeling, factor score regression, maximum likelihood, and Bayesian estimation with three prior specifications for latent variable regression analysis with small samples. Finally, Chapter 18 offers a number of unique conclusions regarding data analysis with small samples.

The S4 Conference is a reoccurring event, and the research on optimal solutions to small sample size issues is ongoing. This book represents a much-needed collection of currently available solutions, and we hope that it aids applied researchers in their endeavors and inspires methodological researchers to expand the field of small sample size solutions. We would like to thank all contributors for sharing their work, and give a special thanks to Evelien Schat and Gerbrich Ferdinands for their assistance with compiling this book. We hope to meet you, reader of this book, at our next conference.

SYMBOLS

Symbol	Definition (A superscript after a symbol definition indicates the chapter number where the symbol appears *if* the symbol appears in only one chapter)
α	Maximum Type I error probability
α_1	Group mean of the latent intercept[4]
BF	Bayes Factor
β	Regression coefficient, e.g. $\beta_{intercept}$ is the regression intercept
$\hat{\beta}_{BAYES}$	Posterior mode of regression coefficient[5]
$\hat{\beta}_{LASSO}$	Ordinary least squares with lasso penalty regression coefficient[5]
$\hat{\beta}_{OLS}$	Ordinary least squares estimate of regression coefficient[5]
$\beta_{intercept.0}$	Subscript zero indicates it concerns the prior mean for the corresponding regression coefficient (here the intercept)
$\beta_{intercept.p}$	Subscript p indicates it concerns the posterior mean of the regression coefficient (here the intercept)
β_1^i	Regression coefficient at the individual level[9]
β^Z	Standardized regression coefficient
C	Control treatment[6]
d	Cohen's d (effect size)
Δ	Difference

E	Experimental treatment[6]
ε	Random error
fs_{33}	Factor score of mother and child pair no. 33[4]
H_0	Null hypothesis
H_{alt}	Alternative hypothesis
H_{inf}	Informative hypothesis
H_{unc}	Unconstrained hypothesis
H_1^i	Individual hypothesis 1 for person i[9]
H_{1c}	Complement of hypothesis 1[9]
H_{RF}	Relevant finding hypothesis (in original study)[12]
H_{A0}	Null hypothesis test Type A: parameters constrained to be equal[11]
H_{A1}	Hypothesis test Type A: order-constrained hypothesis[11]
H_{B0}	Null hypothesis test Type B: all restrictions hold[11]
H_{B1}	Hypothesis test Type B: parameters unconstrained[11]
H_2^d	Hypothesis including effect sizes[11]
$H_{(\cdot)}^{\forall i}$	Hypothesis for all individuals i[9]
$H\mathcal{N}$	Half-normal distribution[4]
η^2	Effect size, partial eta squared
G	Gamma distribution
g	Effect size, Hedge's g
Θ	Covariance matrix
θ	The population value used for data generation[17]
$\boldsymbol{\theta}$	Parameter or set of parameters (in Bayesian statistics)
$\theta_{8,6}$	Covariance between random errors
IG	Inverse Gamma distribution
i	Individual
j	Draw from the posterior distribution
K	Number of columns
k	Thinning parameter
$\lambda_{7,1}$	Factor loading
ℓ	Penalty
ℓ_1	Lasso penalty
ℓ_2	Ridge penalty
lp	Indication of the likelihood of the data given all posterior parameters[4]

MD	Mean difference
m	Count (e.g. m groups, m movies)
min/max	Minimum and maximum sampled value
μ	Mean
μ_0	Prior mean
μ_p	Posterior mean
N	Population size
$\mathcal{N}$	Normal distribution
n	Sample size
n_{max}	Sample size to terminate the trial if the data do *not* provide sufficient evidence for superiority[10]
n_{min}	Sample size at first interim analysis[10]
P	Number of variables
R^2	Explained variance
R^2_{cv}	Predictive performance obtained during cross validation[13]
R^2_{oob}	Out-of-bag predictive performance[13]
R^2_{test}	Predictive performance on test set[13]
r	Correlation coefficient
r_{xy}	Correlation between variables x and y
r_{yy}	Reliability of measure y[18]
r^2	Explained variance per predictor
s	Specific variance
σ	Standard deviation
σ_0	Prior standard deviation
σ_ε	Error standard deviation
σ_p	Posterior standard deviation
σ_{pooled}	Pooled standard deviation
σ_0^2	Prior variance
$\sigma^2_{\hat{T}_i}$	Error variance of $\hat{T}_i$[8]
σ_p^2	Posterior variance
σ^2	Variance
σ_ε^2	Error variance
T	True score
T_i	True score for individual i
$\hat{T}_i$	Estimate of $\hat{T}_i$[8]
τ_0^2	Prior precision

τ_p^2	Posterior precision
X, Y	Latent variable
x, y	Independent and dependent variables
x_i, y_i	Sample observations
$\bar{x}$, $\bar{y}$	Sample mean
$y_1, \ldots, y_n$	Sample of data with n observations
y_{rep}	Prior or posterior replicated y values
ψ	Variance of a construct or covariance between two constructs
w_m	The level-probabilities (chi-bar-square weights)[11]
ω^2	Effect size, generalized omega squared
$x_{00}^{obs}, x_{10}^{obs}, x_{01}^{obs}, x_{11}^{obs}$	Observed frequencies in binary outcome data[10]
$x_{11}^{prior}, x_{10}^{prior}, x_{01}^{prior}, x_{00}^{prior}$	Prior frequencies in binary outcome data[10]
$x_{00}^{post}, x_{10}^{post}, x_{01}^{post}, x_{11}^{post}$	Posterior frequencies in binary outcome data[10]

PART I
Bayesian solutions

1

INTRODUCTION TO BAYESIAN STATISTICS

Milica Miočević

DEPARTMENT OF PSYCHOLOGY, MCGILL UNIVERSITY, MONTREAL, CANADA

Roy Levy

T. DENNY SANFORD SCHOOL OF SOCIAL AND FAMILY DYNAMICS, ARIZONA STATE UNIVERSITY, ARIZONA, UNITED STATES OF AMERICA

Rens van de Schoot

DEPARTMENT OF METHODOLOGY AND STATISTICS, UTRECHT UNIVERSITY, UTRECHT, THE NETHERLANDS & OPTENTIA RESEARCH PROGRAM, FACULTY OF HUMANITIES, NORTH-WEST UNIVERSITY, VANDERBIJLPARK, SOUTH AFRICA

Introduction

Bayesian statistics are becoming more popular in many fields of science. See, for example, the systematic reviews published in various fields from educational science (König & Van de Schoot, 2017), epidemiology (Rietbergen, Debray, Klugkist, Janssen, & Moons, 2017), health technology (Spiegelhalter, Myles, Jones, & Abrams, 2000), medicine (Ashby, 2006), and psychology (Van de Schoot, Winter, Ryan, Zondervan-Zwijnenburg, & Depaoli, 2017) to psychotraumatology (Van de Schoot, Schalken, & Olff, 2017). Bayesian methods appeal to researchers who only have access to a relatively small number of participants because Bayesian statistics are not based on large samples (i.e., the central limit theorem) and hence may produce reasonable results even with small to moderate sample sizes. This is especially the case when background knowledge is available. In general, the more information a researcher can specify before seeing the data, the smaller the sample size required to obtain the same certainty compared to an analysis without specifying any prior knowledge.

In this chapter, we describe Bayes' theorem, which is the foundation of Bayesian statistics. We proceed to discuss Bayesian estimation and Bayes Factors (BFs). The chapter concludes with a brief summary of take-home messages that will allow readers who are new to Bayesian statistics to follow subsequent chapters in this book that make use of Bayesian methods. The applications of Bayesian statistics described in this volume cover the following topics: the role of exchangeability between prior and data (Chapter 2, Miočević et al.), applying the WAMBS checklist (Chapter 3, Van de

Schoot et al.) using informative priors when fitting complex statistical models to small samples (Chapter 4, Veen & Egberts), regression analysis with small sample sizes relative to the number of predictors (Chapter 5, Van Erp), data analysis with few observations from a single participant (Chapter 8, Lek & Arts), updating results participant by participant (Chapter 9, Klaassen), clinical trials with small sample sizes and informative priors based on findings from other trials (Chapter 10, Kavelaars), tests for evaluating whether a finding was replicated (Chapter 12, Zondervan-Zwijnenburg & Rijshouwer), and a comparison between frequentist two-step modeling and Bayesian methods with informative priors (Chapter 17, Smid & Rosseel). Due to space considerations, this chapter does not offer an exhaustive discussion of Bayesian statistics and the differences between Bayesian and classical (frequentist) statistics; for approachable texts on Bayesian statistics in the social sciences, we refer readers to books by Kaplan (2014) and Kruschke (2014), and the chapter by Gigerenzer (1993).

Bayes' theorem

Bayesian statistics are a branch of statistics that implements Bayes' theorem to update prior beliefs with new data:

$$p(\boldsymbol{\theta}|data) = \frac{p(data|\boldsymbol{\theta})p(\boldsymbol{\theta})}{p(data)} \propto p(data|\boldsymbol{\theta})p(\boldsymbol{\theta}) \qquad (1.1)$$

where $\boldsymbol{\theta}$ denotes a set of parameters (e.g., regression coefficients), $p(\boldsymbol{\theta}|data)$ is the posterior distribution of the parameters, which was obtained by updating the prior distribution of the parameters, $p(\boldsymbol{\theta})$, with the observed data represented by the likelihood function, $p(data|\boldsymbol{\theta})$. The term $p(data)$ is the marginal probability of the data that can be considered a normalizing constant that ensures that the posterior distribution integrates to 1. As the right-hand side of Equation 1.1 shows, excluding this term yields a result that is proportional to the posterior distribution.

In the Bayesian framework, the updated (posterior) beliefs about the parameters in a statistical model are used for inference. The posterior distribution can be summarized to report the probability that a parameter lies within a given range. Bayes' theorem stems from the laws of conditional probabilities, which are not controversial. The controversial elements surrounding Bayesian statistics are *whether* to engage in Bayesian analysis and accept the requirement of specifying a prior distribution, and once the researcher chooses to use Bayesian inference, *how* to specify the prior distribution, $p(\boldsymbol{\theta})$. Applied researchers are often advised to base their prior distributions on previous findings, meta-analyses, and/or expert opinion; for considerations related to the choice of source of prior information, see Chapter 2. The exact influence of the prior is often not well understood, and priors will have a larger impact on the results when sample size is small (see Chapter 3). Bayesian analyses of small data sets using priors chosen by the researcher can sometimes lead to worse estimates than those obtained using uninformative priors or classical methods (Smid, McNeish, Miočević, & Van de Schoot, 2019). Thus, priors should be chosen carefully.

To illustrate a Bayesian statistical analysis, consider a normally distributed variable y (for example, IQ, used to illustrate Bayesian inference in the shiny application example from www.rensvandeschoot.com/fbi/; see also the Center for Open Science (OSF): https://osf.io/vg6bw/) with unknown mean μ and a known variance σ^2. In the frequentist framework, one would collect a sample of data (IQ scores), $y_1, \ldots y_n$, compute the sample mean $\bar{y}$, and use it as the estimate of the population mean of IQ. The standard error is a measure of the uncertainty surrounding the estimate.

In the Bayesian framework, the researcher would start the analysis by specifying a prior distribution for μ (population mean of IQ). When specifying a prior distribution, researchers have to select a distributional form (e.g., normal distribution, t-distribution, beta distribution), and specify the parameters of the prior distribution, known as hyperparameters. A common choice of prior distribution for the population mean μ is the normal distribution, which is described by the prior mean (μ_0) and prior variance (σ_0^2) or prior standard deviation (σ_0) or prior precision (τ_0^2) hyperparameters. The mean hyperparameter (μ_0) may be seen as encoding the researcher's best guess about the population mean being estimated, and the variance hyperparameter (σ_0^2) encodes the informativeness (or uncertainty) of the prior distribution. The smaller the variance hyperparameter, the more informative the prior distribution, and the more weight it carries in the analysis. Visually, this analysis is presented in Figure 1.1, where we observe three different situations: panel A depicts an analysis with a sample size of 20 participants from a population where the mean is 100, and the standard deviation is 15; panel B represents the analysis with a sample of 50 participants from that same population; and panel C represents the analysis with a sample of 200 participants from the same population. The prior distribution is the same in all three analyses. Notice how the density of the posterior distribution "moves" closer to the likelihood function as sample size increases from 20–200.

This example has an analytical solution; that is, under the specifications just described, the posterior $p(\mu|y)$ has a known form. It can be shown (Gelman et al., 2013) that the posterior $p(\mu|y)$ is a normal distribution with posterior mean:

$$\mu_p = \frac{\frac{1}{\sigma_0^2}\mu_0 + \frac{n}{\sigma^2}\bar{y}}{\frac{1}{\sigma_0^2} + \frac{n}{\sigma^2}} \qquad (1.2)$$

and posterior variance

$$\sigma_p^2 = \left(\frac{1}{\sigma_0^2} + \frac{n}{\sigma^2}\right)^{-1} \qquad (1.3)$$

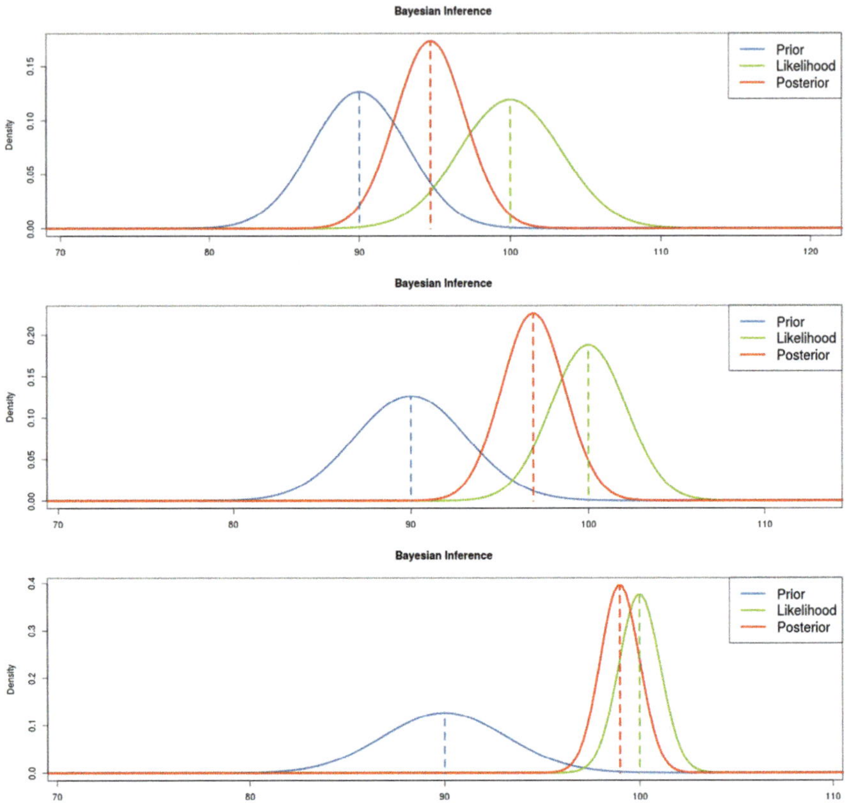

FIGURE 1.1 Plots of the Bayesian computation of a mean parameter with a known variance obtained using the shiny application available at www.rensvandeschoot.com/tutorials/fbi/ (see also the OSF: https://osf.io/vg6bw/)

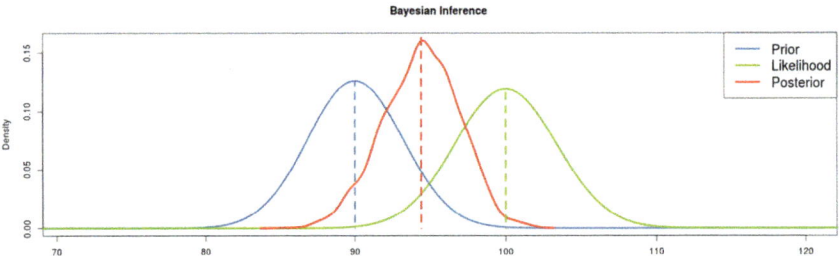

FIGURE 1.2 Plots of the Bayesian computation of a mean parameter with an unknown variance obtained using the shiny application available at www.rensvandeschoot.com/tutorials/fbi/ (see also the OSF: https://osf.io/vg6bw/)

where μ_0 denotes the mean of the normal prior distribution, $\bar{y}$ denotes the observed mean in the sample, n is the sample size, σ_0^2 is the variance hyperparameter in the prior, and σ^2 is the variance in the observed sample. Both the prior and posterior are normal distributions; this is the case because the normal prior distribution is a conjugate prior for the mean parameter. All conjugate prior distributions, when multiplied by the likelihood function, yield posterior distributions from the same distributional family. We can use Equations 1.2 and 1.3 to obtain the analytical solution for the mean and variance of the posterior for the mean of IQ. If we select the prior mean of IQ to be $\mu_0 = 90$ and the prior variance equal to $\sigma_0^2 = 10$, and we observe a sample of 20 participants for which the sample mean of IQ is $\bar{y} = 100$ and the sample variance is $\sigma^2 = 225$, we end up with a posterior distribution centered around $\mu_p = \frac{\frac{1}{10}90 + \frac{20}{225}100}{\frac{1}{10} + \frac{20}{225}} = 94.71$ with a posterior variance equal to $\sigma_p^2 = \left(\frac{1}{10} + \frac{20}{225}\right)^{-1} = 5.29$. Notice how the posterior mean, μ_p, is a "compromise" between the prior mean μ_0, and the mean of the variable in the observed data set, $\bar{y}$. Notice also how decreasing the prior variance (σ_0^2) gives the prior mean more weight, and how increasing the sample size n gives the observed data more weight in determining the posterior mean.

Bayesian estimation

In the example where it is of interest to estimate the mean of a population with a known variance, it is possible to obtain the posterior distribution analytically. However, most statistical models in the social sciences are more complex, and the posterior distribution cannot be obtained analytically. In these situations, results are obtained by progressively approximating the posterior distribution using Markov Chain Monte Carlo (MCMC; Brooks, Gelman, Jones, & Meng, 2011). MCMC is an iterative procedure, like maximum likelihood (ML). However, unlike ML, which seeks to maximize the likelihood function, MCMC seems to approximate the entire posterior distribution. Figure 1.2 illustrates an approximation of the posterior for the same analysis as in panel A of Figure 1.1 obtained using MCMC instead of using the analytical solution; note that the distribution is no longer smooth because it is an approximation of the posterior. In the following paragraphs, we briefly survey some of the practical aspects involved in utilizing MCMC for Bayesian analyses.

In a Bayesian analysis, MCMC proceeds by simulating values from distributions such that, in the limit, the values may be seen as draws from the posterior distribution (for visual representations of multiple chains, see Figure 3.4 in Chapter 3). A properly constructed chain will eventually converge to the point where the subsequent simulated values may be seen as samples from the posterior; however, there is no guarantee as to *when* that will happen. Though there is no way of definitively knowing that a chain has converged to the posterior distribution, there are several techniques one can use to find evidence of convergence (Cowles & Carlin, 1996).

In the social sciences literature, the most commonly encountered convergence diagnostics are those offered by the majority of software packages, which include the Potential Scale Reduction factor (Gelman & Rubin, 1992), Geweke's diagnostic (1992), and trace plots of draws plotted against the iteration number for each parameter (Brooks, 1998; see Chapter 3 for information about how to obtain and interpret trace plots). Several convergence diagnostics rely on running multiple chains from dispersed starting values for different chains in order to assist with the monitoring of convergence (Gelman & Shirley, 2011). The generated values from the chain prior to convergence are referred to as burn-in iterations and are discarded; values from the chain after convergence are taken to be draws from the posterior and can be summarized to represent the posterior. In theory, the more draws are taken from the posterior, the better it is approximated.

A complicating factor for MCMC is the within-chain correlation of the draws (see Figure 3.8 in Chapter 3); for a more detailed discussion on autocorrelation and possible solutions see Chapter 3. It is often recommended to use thinning[1] to reduce the autocorrelation between the retained draws (Gelman & Shirley, 2011). However, some researchers argue that thinning can be problematic for obtaining precise summaries of the posterior (Link & Eaton, 2012) and that it is better to run longer chains than to thin. *Stopping time* refers to ending the sampling and depends on time constraints, how long the chain(s) ran before convergence, the researcher's confidence that convergence was reached, and the autocorrelation between draws (see Chapter 3). The number of draws to retain after convergence (i.e., post burn-in) should be determined in part by the precision with which the researcher wants to estimate the posterior, or its features. Estimating broad summaries, such as the posterior mean, tends to require fewer draws than features out in the tails, such as extreme percentiles (Kruschke, 2014).

To summarize the posterior, all non-discarded draws (i.e., all draws after burn-in) from all chains should be mixed together (Gelman & Shirley, 2011). Features of these draws (e.g., mean, standard deviation, intervals) are seen as estimates of the corresponding features of the posterior distribution. Common point summaries of the posterior are the mean, median, and mode. Common interval summaries are $(1-\alpha)\%$ equal-tail credibility intervals, which are constructed from the $(\alpha/2)^{th}$ and $(1-\alpha/2)^{th}$ percentiles of the posterior distribution, and highest posterior density credibility intervals which have the property that no values outside the interval are more probable than any values inside the interval.

Bayes Factors

Null hypothesis significance testing (NHST) has been the dominant approach to statistical inference in the social sciences since the 1940s (Gigerenzer, 1993). NHST belongs to the family of frequentist statistics, which define probability as the frequency of an event. Two quantities that stem from this school of statistics and rely on the above definition of probability are *p*-values and confidence intervals. The *p*-value quantifies the probability of finding the observed or a more extreme result given that the null hypothesis is true, and the $(1-\alpha)\%$ confidence intervals tell us that upon repeated sampling, $(1-\alpha)\%$ of the confidence intervals will contain the true value of the parameter (Jackman, 2009). The reliance on NHST and *p*-values has been criticized for decades (Bakan, 1966; Ioannidis, 2005; Rozeboom, 1960). Some researchers advocate for the replacement of *p*-values with alternatives such as effect size measures and confidence intervals (Cumming, 2014). Others have argued for abandoning the frequentist paradigm altogether because the *p*-value does not quantify the probability of the hypothesis given the data (Wagenmakers, Wetzels, Borsboom, & Van der Maas, 2011), nor does it provide any measure of whether the finding is replicable (Cohen, 1994), and confidence intervals do not have the properties they are ascribed to have and are easily misunderstood (Morey, Hoekstra, Rouder, Lee, & Wagenmakers, 2016).

In the Bayesian framework, it is possible to calculate the probability of a hypothesis given the data, and to compute the posterior odds in favor of one hypothesis (or model) relative to another hypothesis (or model; Kass & Raftery, 1995). The ratio of posterior probabilities is equal to the ratio of prior probabilities multiplied by the ratio of marginal likelihoods under each hypothesis:

$$\frac{p(H_2|data)}{p(H_1|data)} = \frac{p(H_2)}{p(H_1)} \times \frac{\int_{\theta_{(2)}} p(data|\theta_{(2)}) p(\theta_{(2)}|data) d\theta_{(2)}}{\int_{\theta_{(1)}} p(data|\theta_{(1)}) p(\theta_{(1)}|data) d\theta_{(1)}} \quad (1.4)$$

The last term on the right-hand side, the ratio of marginal likelihoods, is also called the Bayes Factor (Kass & Raftery, 1995; Raftery, 1993). BFs are a way of comparing two competing hypotheses (H_1 and H_2) and are calculated by dividing the integrated likelihoods of the two models (Jeffreys, 1998). Chapters 9 and 12 make use of *BF*; the readers will notice that there are notational differences between chapters, and this is the case in the literature as well. However, the meaning and interpretations of *BF* are the same as described in this chapter, unless the authors indicate otherwise. If the prior probabilities of the two models are both set to 0.5, then the posterior odds equal the BF. If the prior probabilities are not .5, then the BF is not equal to the posterior odds. However, the BF still captures the weight of evidence from the data in favor of one hypothesis. A BF of 1 indicates that the data do not support one hypothesis more than the other, a BF below 1 indicates that the data provide support for H_1 over H_2, and a BF above 1 indicates that the data support H_2 over H_1. The computation of the BF does not require nesting of the models being compared. Unlike classical hypothesis tests, BFs can support a null hypothesis. In the words of Dienes (2014, p. 1), BFs "allow accepting and rejecting the null hypothesis to be put on an equal footing", but as indicated by Konijn, Van de Schoot, Winter, & Ferguson (2015), we should avoid BF-hacking (cf., "God would love a Bayes Factor of 3.01 nearly as much as a BF of 2.99"). Especially when BF values are small, replication studies and Bayesian updating are still necessary to draw conclusions (see Chapter 12 for more on this topic).

Conclusion

In this brief introductory chapter, we sought to inform readers about the fundamental concepts in Bayesian statistics. The most important take-home messages to remember are that in Bayesian statistics, the analysis starts with an explicit formulation of prior beliefs that are updated with the observed data to obtain a posterior distribution. The posterior distribution is then used to make inferences about probable values of a given parameter (or set of parameters). Furthermore, BFs allow for comparison of non-nested models, and it is possible to compute the amount of support for the null hypothesis, which cannot be done in the frequentist framework. Subsequent chapters in this volume make use of Bayesian methods for obtaining posteriors of parameters of interest, as well as BFs.

Note

1 Thinning is the practice of retaining only every k^{th} draw, where the thinning parameter k is chosen so that the retained draws are approximately independent. However, thinning represents a loss of information and is not necessary, and "as long as a sequence has converged and the number of iterations retained is substantial, it makes no practical difference if we keep all or every 25th or every 50th iteration" (Scheines, Hoijtink, & Boomsma, 1999, p. 42).

References

Ashby, D. (2006). Bayesian statistics in medicine: A 25 year review. *Statistics in Medicine, 25* (21), 3589–3631. doi:doi.org/10.1002/sim.2672.

Bakan, D. (1966). The test of significance in psychological research. *Psychological Bulletin, 66*(6), 423–437. doi:10.1037/h0020412.

Brooks, S. P. (1998). Markov chain Monte Carlo method and its application. *Journal of the Royal Statistical Society. Series D (the Statistician), 47*(1), 69–100. doi:10.1111/1467-9884.00117.

Brooks, S. P., Gelman, A., Jones, G. L., & Meng, X.-L. (Eds.). (2011). *Handbook of Markov Chain Monte Carlo.* Boca Raton, FL: Chapman & Hall/CRC Press.

Cohen, J. (1994). The earth is round (p <. 05). *American Psychologist, 49*(12), 997–1003. doi:10.1037/0003-066X.49.12.997.

Cowles, M. K., & Carlin, B. P. (1996). Markov chain Monte Carlo convergence diagnostics: A comparative review. *Journal of the American Statistical Association, 91*(434), 883–904. doi:10.2307/2291683.

Cumming, G. (2014). The new statistics: Why and how. *Psychological Science, 25*(1), 7–29. doi:10.1177/0956797613504966.

Dienes, Z. (2014). Using Bayes to get the most out of non-significant results. *Frontiers in Psychology, 5*, 781.

Gelman, A., Carlin, J. B., Stern, H. S., Dunson, D. B., Vehtari, A., & Rubin, D. B. (2013). *Bayesian data analysis* (3rd ed.). Boca Raton: FL: CRC Press.

Gelman, A., & Rubin, D. B. (1992). Inference from iterative simulation using multiple sequences. *Statistical Science, 7*(4), 457–472. doi:10.1214/ss/1177011136.

Gelman, A., & Shirley, K. (2011). Inference from simulations and monitoring convergence. In S. P. Brooks, A. Gelman, G. L. Jones, and X.-L. Meng (Eds.), *Handbook of Markov Chain Monte Carlo* (pp. 116–162). Boca Raton, FL: Chapman & Hall/CRC Press.

Geweke, J. (1992). Evaluating the accuracy of sampling-based approaches to the calculation of posterior moments. In J. M. Bernardo, A. F. M. Smith, A. P. Dawid, and J. O. Berger (Eds.), *Bayesian Statistics 4* (pp. 169–193). Oxford: Oxford University Press.

Gigerenzer, G. (1993). The superego, the ego, and the id in statistical reasoning. In G. Keren and C. Lewis (Eds.), *A handbook for data analysis in the behavioral sciences: Methodological issues* (pp. 311–339). Hillsdale, NJ: Erlbaum.

Ioannidis, J. P. (2005). Why most published research findings are false. *PLoS Medicine, 2*(8), e124. doi:10.1371/journal.pmed.0020124.

Jackman, S. (2009). *Bayesian analysis for the social sciences* (Vol. 846). Chichester: John Wiley & Sons.

Jeffreys, H. (1998). *The theory of probability.* Oxford: Oxford University Press.

Kaplan, D. (2014). *Bayesian statistics for the social sciences.* New York, NY: Guilford.

Kass, R. E., & Raftery, A. E. (1995). Bayes factors. *Journal of the American Statistical Association, 90*(430), 773–795. doi:10.1080/01621459.1995.10476572.

König, C., & Van de Schoot, R. (2017). Bayesian statistics in educational research: A look at the current state of affairs. *Educational Review,* 1–24. doi:10.1080/00131911.2017.1350636.

Konijn, E. A., Van de Schoot, R., Winter, S. D., & Ferguson, C. J. (2015). Possible solution to publication bias through Bayesian statistics, including proper null hypothesis testing. *Communication Methods and Measures, 9*(4), 280–302.

Kruschke, J. K. (2014). *Doing Bayesian data analysis: A tutorial with R, JAGS, and stan* (2nd ed.). Boston, MA: Academic Press.

Link, W. A., & Eaton, M. J. (2012). On thinning of chains in MCMC. *Methods in Ecology and Evolution, 3*(1), 112–115.

Morey, R. D., Hoekstra, R., Rouder, J. N., Lee, M. D., & Wagenmakers, E.-J. (2016). The fallacy of placing confidence in confidence intervals. *Psychonomic Bulletin & Review, 23*(1), 103–123. doi:10.3758/s13423-015-0947-8.

Raftery, A. E. (1993). Bayesian model selection in structural equation models. *Sage Focus Editions, 154,* 163.

Rietbergen, C., Debray, T. P. A., Klugkist, I., Janssen, K. J. M., & Moons, K. G. M. (2017). Reporting of Bayesian analysis in epidemiologic research should become more transparent. *Journal of Clinical Epidemiology, 86,* 51–58.e52. doi:10.1016/j.jclinepi.2017.04.008.

Rozeboom, W. W. (1960). The fallacy of the null-hypothesis significance test. *Psychological Bulletin, 57*(5), 416–428. doi:10.1037/h0042040.

Scheines, R., Hoijtink, H., & Boomsma, A. (1999). Bayesian estimation and testing of structural equation models. *Psychometrika, 64*(1), 37–52. doi:10.1007/BF02294318.

Smid, S. C., McNeish, D., Miočević, M., & Van de Schoot, R. (2019). Bayesian versus frequentist estimation for structural equation models in small sample contexts: A systematic review. *Structural Equation Modeling: A Multidisciplinary Journal.* doi:10.1080/10705511.2019.1577140.

Spiegelhalter, D. J., Myles, J. P., Jones, D. R., & Abrams, K. R. (2000). Bayesian methods in health technology assessment: A review. *Health Technology Assessment, 4*(38), 1–130.

Van de Schoot, R., Schalken, N., & Olff, M. (2017). Systematic search of Bayesian statistics in the field of psychotraumatology. *European Journal of Psychotraumatology*, *8*(sup1). doi:10.1080/20008198.2017.1375339.

Van de Schoot, R., Winter, S. D., Ryan, O., Zondervan-Zwijnenburg, M., & Depaoli, S. (2017). A systematic review of Bayesian articles in psychology: The last 25 years. *Psychological Methods*, *22*(2), 217–239. doi:10.1037/met0000100.

Wagenmakers, E.-J., Wetzels, R., Borsboom, D., & Van der Maas, H. (2011). Why psychologists must change the way they analyze their data: The case of psi. *Journal of Personality and Social Psychology*, *100*(3), 426–432. doi:10.1037/a0022790.

2

THE ROLE OF EXCHANGEABILITY IN SEQUENTIAL UPDATING OF FINDINGS FROM SMALL STUDIES AND THE CHALLENGES OF IDENTIFYING EXCHANGEABLE DATA SETS

Milica Miočević

DEPARTMENT OF PSYCHOLOGY, MCGILL UNIVERSITY, MONTREAL, CANADA

Roy Levy

T. DENNY SANFORD SCHOOL OF SOCIAL AND FAMILY DYNAMICS, ARIZONA STATE UNIVERSITY, ARIZONA, UNITED STATES OF AMERICA

Andrea Savord

DEPARTMENT OF PSYCHOLOGY, ARIZONA STATE UNIVERSITY, ARIZONA, UNITED STATES OF AMERICA

Introduction

In a scientific setting, we can think of the observations from the same experiment as exchangeable events, and we can also extend this logic to groups of observations (i.e., samples from the same population). Conceptually, variables (data sets, studies, or any other units of analysis) are exchangeable to a researcher if the researcher holds the same beliefs about them for their purposes at hand (Levy & Mislevy, 2016). Thus, if we say that two samples or two studies are exchangeable, we are also saying that the order in which they were collected or executed does not matter because we cannot distinguish between them based on any relevant characteristics. Somewhat formally, a collection of random variables is exchangeable if the joint distribution is invariant to any permutation (reordering, relabeling) of the random variables (de Finetti, 1974; see also Bernardo & Smith, 2000). In de Finetti's example, the exchangeable events are coin tosses, and the goal is to compute the probability of getting "heads" on the toss of a coin. Exchangeability amounts to saying that if we have five tosses of the coin the salient information is the number of heads; it does not matter *which* tosses were heads (Diaconis & Freedman, 1980). De Finetti (1931, 1937/1964) showed that if a collection of variables is deemed exchangeable, then the joint distribution can be represented as a product of conditional distributions of each variable, conditional on some parameter, marginalized over the distribution of that parameter (Bernardo & Smith, 2000). The upshot of this is that deeming variables to be exchangeable warrants treating them as conditionally independent given some parameter. As we will see in the next section, this facilitates a particular form of Bayesian inference. The following sections illustrate how Bayesian inference proceeds with exchangeable data sets, discuss relevant characteristics for evaluating whether two studies are exchangeable, illustrate the challenges in deciding whether two real studies differ on relevant characteristics, and discuss potential ways of calibrating findings from non-exchangeable data sets in order to use them as prior distributions in Bayesian inference. In the remainder of the chapter, we assume familiarity with Bayesian statistics, and for readers new to Bayesian statistics we recommend reading Chapter 1 (Miočević, Levy, & Van de Schoot) first. Annotated R code to reproduce the results can be found on the Open Science Framework (https://osf.io/am7pr/).

Bayesian inference for exchangeable data sets

We now consider the situation where there are two data sets. If we deem the data sets to be exchangeable, we can:

1. conduct Bayesian inference after obtaining the first data set and some (original) prior distribution to yield a posterior distribution for the set of parameters $\boldsymbol{\theta}$;
2. utilize that posterior distribution as the prior distribution in another Bayesian analysis for the second data set.

The resulting posterior distribution from the second analysis is equivalent to what would be obtained if both data sets were analyzed in a single Bayesian analysis using the original prior distribution. In this chapter we argue that exchangeability justifies the use of the Bayesian machinery described here, where the result of the analysis of one data set is the prior distribution for the analysis of another data set[1]. Furthermore, given the symmetry of the roles of the data sets in the factorization in Equation 2.2 below, it does not matter in what order we analyze the data sets; the end result will be the same final posterior distribution. Thus, if we can assume exchangeability of a series of studies, Bayesian methods allow for the synthesis of the results from all of the studies in any order, as we have no way of distinguishing which study should be first (i.e., qualitatively distinguishing; we can be aware of the temporal ordering of the studies and distinguish between them based on which one was carried out first). In this case, Bayes' theorem states that the posterior distribution is:

$$p(\boldsymbol{\theta}|data_1, data_2) \propto p(data_1, data_2|\boldsymbol{\theta})p(\boldsymbol{\theta}) \qquad (2.1)$$

where $data_1$ and $data_2$ are the two data sets, respectively. If the data sets are exchangeable and we can treat them as conditionally independent given $\boldsymbol{\theta}$, we can factor the first term on the right-hand side accordingly:

$$p(\boldsymbol{\theta}|data_1, data_2) \propto p(data_2|\boldsymbol{\theta})p(data_1|\boldsymbol{\theta})p(\boldsymbol{\theta}). \qquad (2.2)$$

Note the last two terms on the right-hand side present an opportunity to invoke Bayes' theorem. Doing so yields:

$$p(\boldsymbol{\theta}|data_1, data_2) \propto p(data_2|\boldsymbol{\theta})p(\boldsymbol{\theta}|data_1). \qquad (2.3)$$

Formally, the posterior distribution after observing *two* data sets may be seen by taking the posterior distribution after observing *one* data set and having that serve as the prior distribution in an instance of Bayes' theorem, updated by the *second* data set (readers interested in methods for updating information about participants *within* a data set should see Chapter 9 by Klaassen). This expression also reveals how Bayesian inference is a mechanism for accumulating evidence as new data arrive. More philosophically, it reveals that our beliefs about the parameter(s) are relative to a certain state of knowledge (e.g., based on whatever data have been incorporated so far), and subject to being revised or updated (e.g., based on whatever new data comes our way). This feature of Bayesian inference supports the common Bayesian refrain that "today's posterior is tomorrow's prior." Studies with small samples are often underpowered, and sequentially updating findings from multiple exchangeable studies can increase power to detect the effect of interest and provide a more precise interval around the effect of interest.

Example of two exchangeable data sets

Consider the following example: in the 1930s, the Rothamsted Experimental Station was testing the efficacy of a variety of nitrogen-rich fertilizers, including sulphate of ammonia (Rothamsted Experimental Station, 1936)[2]. For the 1935 growing season, the fertilizer was added to the Great Harpenden field with the intention of increasing wheat yield. The field was divided into 36 equal-sized plots and the plots were randomly assigned to receive anywhere from zero to five doses of sulphate of ammonia throughout the growing year (October–August) such that each treatment condition was applied to six plots. The overall yield of grain in pounds for each plot was measured at the end of the year (Rothamsted Experimental Station, 1936). In 1936, the same study was carried out on the Great Knott field (Rothamsted Experimental Station, 1937).

Though a different field was studied each year, these two data sets can be considered exchangeable: both fields are located on the Rothamsted campus, they had the same six treatment conditions applied at approximately equal time points throughout the year, and the fields were split into equal-sized plots and had the same previous-year crop (beans) and the same variety of wheat planted during the fertilizer experiment.

Bayesian multiple regression analysis with exchangeable data sets

A brief overview of Bayesian multiple regression analysis illustrated using a study of the effectiveness of the different applications of fertilizer in two data sets highlights the benefits of exchangeability when considering the prior distributions for an analysis. The Bayesian multiple regression analysis presented below has five dummy coded predictors corresponding to the five treatment groups (one to five doses of sulphate of ammonia) with the zero-dose control as the reference group, and a continuous outcome variable (pounds of grain harvested from each plot):

$$y_i = \beta_{intercept} + \beta_1 x_{1i} + \beta_2 x_{2i} + \beta_3 x_{3i} + \beta_4 x_{4i} + \beta_5 x_{5i} + \varepsilon_i. \quad (2.4)$$

When considering the 1935 data set, as we have no strong prior beliefs regarding the situation, it is suitable to assume diffuse (non-informative) prior distributions for all unknown parameters: the regression coefficients, intercept, and residual variance. Additionally, we chose to specify conditionally conjugate priors for the unknown parameters, which ease the computations involved in fitting the model using Markov chain Monte Carlo (MCMC) estimation (Gelman et al., 2013). Conjugate priors yield posterior distributions from the same distributional family. Finally, we chose values for the diffuse priors based on the scale of the variables themselves rather than the default specifications of the software because the prior variances in the default specifications of the software (i.e., 1,000 in normal priors for intercepts and 100 in normal priors for regression coefficients) were too small for these priors to be uninformative (i.e., the variance of the dependent variable was equal to 93.24 in 1935 and to 41.43 in 1936).

We employed the following conjugate diffuse priors: normal distributions with mean 0 and variance of 10^{10} for the intercept ($\beta_{intercept}$) and regression coefficients ($\beta_1, \ldots, \beta_5$), and an inverse-gamma distribution with shape 1 and scale 1000 for the residual variance (σ_ε^2). We conducted an analysis using the R package blavaan (Merkle & Rosseel, 2018) running a Markov chain for 26,000 iterations, discarding the first 6,000 as adaptation and burn-in following an assessment of convergence (Gelman et al., 2013). Before interpreting results,

TABLE 2.1 Posterior distribution summaries for the 1935 and 1936 data analyses

	1935 analyses	1936 analyses		
Parameter	Diffuse priors (Posterior mean, Posterior SD) [95% HPDI]	Informed prior specification 1936 prior specification	Diffuse priors (Posterior mean, Posterior SD) [95% HPDI]	Results under informed priors (Posterior mean, Posterior SD) [95% HPDI]
$\beta_{intercept}$	(85.933, 3.959) [78.196, 93.765]	N(85.933, 15.674)	(85.744, 2.591) [80.670, 90.838]	(85.449, 1.911) [81.694, 89.181]
β_1	(1.120, 5.674) [-10.120, 12.223]	N(1.120, 32.194)	(3.682, 3.654) [-3.250, 11.147]	(3.245, 3.171) [-2.885, 9.508]
β_2	(-5.838, 5.623) [-16.657, 5.677]	N(-5.838, 31.618)	(-3.701, 3.629) [-10.852, 3.506]	(-4.015, 3.158) [-10.193, 2.139]
β_3	(-3.274, 5.608) [-14.156, 7.749]	N(-3.274, 31.450)	(-3.505, 3.649) [-10.895, 3.552]	(-3.251, 3.171) [-9.716, 2.740]
β_4	(1.035, 5.604) [-10.387, 11.768]	N(1.035, 31.405)	(-3.044, 3.648) [-10.375, 4.035]	(-1.805, 3.178) [-8.129, 4.350]
β_5	(5.174, 5.593) [-5.801, 16.138]	N(5.174, 31.282)	(0.555, 3.675) [-6.804, 7.641]	(1.972, 3.162) [-4.156, 8.246]
σ_ε^2	(83.670[a], 25.234) [52.132, 144.312]	IG(18, 1506.06)	(35.91[a], 10.675) [21.903, 61.100]	(63.01[a], 11.322) [44.010, 87.075]

Note: N stands for *normal distribution*, and *IG* stands for *inverse-gamma*. The first parameter in the normal distribution is the mean, and the second parameter is the variance. HPDI denotes a Highest Posterior Density Interval.
[a] Denotes posterior mode instead of posterior mean reported.

convergence of the chains should be examined through trace plots, autocorrelation plots, and other diagnostic criteria; these checks will not be discussed for this example, but see Chapter 3 (Van de Schoot, Veen, Smeets, Winter, & Depaoli) for more information. The second column of Table 2.1 contains numerical summaries of the marginal posterior distributions for each parameter. Because of the asymmetry of the residual variance's posterior distribution, the mode is reported instead of the mean, as this value is a better summary of our beliefs about the residual variance.

Turning to the 1936 data set, we have a few options. We could conduct an analysis as we did with the 1935 data set, using the specified diffuse priors outlined above. Alternatively, we could leverage our view that the 1935 and 1936 data sets are exchangeable, and build a prior distribution for the 1936 analysis using the results from the analysis of the 1935 data set. Adopting this approach, we once again employed conjugate prior distributions for the parameters, and based them on results from the analysis of the 1935 data set. For the intercepts and coefficients, we employed normal distributions with means and variances defined by the posterior means and posterior variances from the marginal posterior distributions from the analysis of the 1935 data set. For the residual variance, we employed an inverse-gamma prior distribution with shape parameters equal to half the sample size of the 1935 data set ($36/2 = 18$), and scale parameters equal to the half of the product of the sample size of the 1935 data set and the posterior mode from the analysis of the 1935 data set (Gelman et al., 2013). These distributions are listed in the second column of Table 2.1. Note that the use of these prior distributions only approximates the ideal case of using the true posterior distribution from the 1935 analysis. It is approximate for two reasons. First, the results of the 1935 analysis were obtained using MCMC, which approximates the posterior distribution. This approximation can be improved by running more iterations during estimation. Second, the true posterior distribution is a multivariate distribution over all the unknown parameters. In the analysis of the 1936 data, we use the marginal posteriors as the basis for the univariate priors for the parameters. Any dependence among the parameters in the posterior distribution from the 1935 analysis is neglected by specifying univariate priors for the 1935 analysis. Furthermore, the marginal posteriors for the coefficients depart slightly from normality, though exhibit its main features (unimodal, symmetric, bell-shaped).

We conducted two analyses of the 1936 data set: one using the diffuse prior distributions, and the second using the priors which are informed by the results from the analysis of the 1935 data set. The results for these two analyses are summarized in Table 2.1. Consider first the comparison between the results for the 1935 and 1936 analyses using diffuse priors. Though all of the highest posterior density intervals (HPDIs) contain 0 in both analyses, the coefficients themselves reflect different rates of change. With the exception of β_3, the regression slope coefficients are all different by at least two units (pounds of grain) with the largest differences being β_4 (a 4.079-unit decrease, changing the value from positive to negative), and β_5 (a 4.620-unit decrease) from 1935 to 1936, respectively. The intercepts are fairly similar, but the residual variances are quite different.

In summary, different stories emerge from consideration of the 1935 data set and the 1936 data set individually. This is not altogether surprising; each data set only had 36 observations, and uncertainty abounds. By treating the data sets as exchangeable and using the results from the analysis of one as the basis for the prior for the analysis of the other, we accumulate evidence over multiple data sets, which yields different (and arguably more accurate) results than evaluating either single data set with no known prior information. While both analyses seem to indicate that no sulphate of ammonia dosage seems to produce more grain than the control plots, the combined analysis makes this more salient. This is manifest when looking at the posterior standard deviations of the regression coefficients and intercept, all of which are smaller in the analysis with informed priors. Additionally, when comparing the 1936 analyses with diffuse and informed priors, we again observe large differences between the β_4 and β_5 coefficients: the analysis with diffuse priors indicated a steeper slope for β_4, and weaker slope for β_5 relative to the analysis with informed priors. What results should we trust the most at this point: those from the 1935 analysis using diffuse priors, those from the 1936 analysis using diffuse priors, or those from the 1936 analysis using the informed priors? Following the logic of Bayesian inference under exchangeable data sets, we argue that we should prefer the results from the latter. In this way, exchangeability allows researchers to use more information with each subsequent analysis, thereby obtaining what are ideally more accurate posterior distributions.

The preceding characterization is an idealized case where exchangeability between data sets is warranted, and an illustration of such was given. The example outlined is a simplified one: five dummy coded predictors were used in a multiple regression model to examine wheat yield of field plots. More complicated models (e.g., including possible covariates, using a longitudinal model) are possible, and could potentially yield new or different insights into the data sets. However, in many practical situations, researchers might not judge the prior and current study to be precisely exchangeable. Accordingly, the following sections take up this issue of judging exchangeability, review relevant characteristics on which two studies may differ, and propose extensions of already available criteria.

Relevant characteristics for establishing exchangeability

When thinking about exchangeability, it is helpful to think about the concept of replication, and to borrow some ideas from the literature on replication (readers interested in evaluating whether findings from one study were replicated in a second study should see Chapter 12 by Zondervan-Zwijnenburg & Rijshouwer). According to the scientists in the "Many Labs" Replication Project, in order to replicate an experiment, the conditions of the initial experiment ought to be recreated (Klein et al., 2014; Klein et al., 2018). Even though the literature on replication does not use the term "exchangeable," when replicating a study researchers are essentially trying to make the new study identical to the original study on all relevant characteristics. In the "Many Labs" project, researchers standardized the procedural characteristics (i.e., experiment protocol), but varied the sample and setting in order to evaluate whether 13 effects from the literature replicate across different samples and settings. Findings from this project indicate that in social and cognitive psychology, "variability in observed effect sizes was more attributable to the effect being studied than the sample or setting [country and in-person vs. online] which it was studied" (Klein et al., 2018, p. 446), which will be relevant for compiling a list of relevant characteristics for establishing exchangeability. The authors caution the reader that "the generalizability of these results to other psychological findings is unknown" (Klein et al., 2018, p. 483), thus the finding that country and setting do not account for considerable variability in the observed effect may not generalize across other research questions and areas of social and behavioral sciences.

Schmidt (2009) distinguishes between *direct* replication, i.e., repetition of an experimental procedure, and conceptual replication, which consists of testing the same hypothesis as a prior study, but intentionally using different methods. For the definition of exchangeability posited in this chapter, *conceptual* replication automatically does not lead to an exchangeable sample, whereas direct replication is a necessary, but not sufficient, requirement for exchangeability.

Patil, Peng, & Leek (2016) define replicability as re-performing the experiment and collecting new data. When reflecting on exchangeability, we do not focus on the research question or the findings from the studies, but on the characteristics of the sample and the data collection procedure. Findings from two exchangeable studies with the same research question and data analysis technique can still differ due to sampling variability, and this is not an issue, because in the long run collecting a large number of exchangeable random samples will presumably lead to the truth regarding the phenomenon under study. Inspired by the visual model in the paper by Patil, Peng, & Leek (2016), we construct a similar table of relevant characteristics for diagnosing whether two intervention studies are exchangeable, and we demonstrate some of the considerations and challenges in the evaluation of exchangeability.

Empirical example of challenges to exchangeability

We consider two related, but not exchangeable studies called SHIELD (Kuehl et al., 2016) and PHLAME (Elliot et al., 2004, 2007). The health promotion study SHIELD was designed to increase the health of law enforcement officers. Before SHIELD, a comparable intervention program was tested in a sample of firefighters in a study called PHLAME. The two studies were carried out by the same team of principal investigators and the interventions in the two studies targeted the same health outcomes. The similarity of the study design is a reason for using prior information from PHLAME in the analysis of SHIELD results. However, the qualitative difference in participants would be a good reason to temper, to some degree, beliefs arising from the analysis of one set of participants when translating to another set of participants. We start with an effort to evaluate the degree of exchangeability between these two studies (Table 2.2).

Table 2.2 presents an attempt to catalogue aspects on which SHIELD and PHLAME are exchangeable. However, there are several challenges and multiple occasions where subjective judgment is necessary in the evaluation of exchangeability of two studies on a given criterion. First, the list in Table 2.2 is designed by the authors of this chapter, and different groups of researchers might come up with different lists. Second, the relevance of different study aspects changes depending on the research question. For example, in a study of diabetes patients, criteria related to medical history may deserve more weight than criteria related to occupation and education. Thus, the relative contribution of each criterion to the extent to which two studies are exchangeable will depend on the nature of the research question and the variables that correlate the highest with the

TABLE 2.2 Exchangeability criteria for SHIELD and PHLAME

	SHIELD	PHLAME	Exchangeable
		Population	
Location	One police department and two sheriff's offices from Oregon and Southwest Washington	Fire departments close to Oregon Health & Science University, Portland, Oregon	Yes
Nationality	NR	NR	NR
Age (mean, SD)	Control 41.6 (9.37) Treatment 44.3 (9.67)	Mean age of 41 years (range 20–60 years old)	Yes
SES:			No
• Profession	• Law enforcement officers	• Firefighters	
• Education	• NR	• NR	
• Income	• NR	• Annual household income of ≥$50,000 (79%)	
• Family background	• Control: married (67%); treatment: married (77%)	• Married (79%)	
Gender	Control: 140 men (69%) Treatment: 114 men (56%)	579 men (97%) 20 women (3%)	No
Other demographics characteristics	Control: White (91%) Treatment: White (92%) Years in law enforcement: Control 13.5 (7.67) Treatment 14.7 (8.89)	White (91%)	Yes
Medical history	NA	NA	NA
		Experimental procedure	
Location of data collection (e.g., research lab, workplace, online)	NR	NR	NR

(*Continued*)

TABLE 2.2 (Cont).

	SHIELD	PHLAME	Exchangeable
		"Individuals were evaluated at approximately 8:00 AM and, after obtaining baseline informed consent, participants proceeded to questionnaire completion and physical testing."	No
Experimental manipulation (instructions, materials, events; Schmidt, 2009)	NA	"Reflecting the three 24-h shift structure, each site was assessed over 3 days in late spring 2010, during which consents were obtained, surveys completed, limited physiological data acquired (height, weight), and group interviews conducted. Following data collection, PHLAME materials were distributed, and shifts were oriented to conducting the program. Technical support was available to all sites throughout the study. Approximately 6 months later, the initial data gathering activities were repeated during a second round of 3-day visits. Follow-up assessments included program exposure indexed as the participant self-reported session completion, using cued recall of session content; the survey and group interviews included additional items relating to the program's characteristics and use."	
Equipment	NR	NR	NR
Experimenter	NR	NR	NR

Self-report measurement instruments and procedures	***Nutrition*** National Cancer Institute's fruit and vegetable all day screener, a standardized instrument of daily servings ***Sleep/fatigue*** National Institutes of Health Patient-Reported Outcomes Information System (PROMIS) sleep disturbance, the Pittsburgh Sleep Quality Index (PSQI), and the Karolinska Sleepiness Scale ***Health perceptions*** General health status was assessed with the SF-36 ***Musculo-skeletal discomfort*** 18 of the 54 items of the Cornell Musculo-skeletal Discomfort Questionnaire (CMDQ) ***Stress, healthy eating, and physical activity*** "Constructs with established reliability from our previous studies were used." ***Burnout*** Maslach Burnout Inventory (MBI)	***Questionnaires*** assessing demographics; knowledge, behaviors, and beliefs concerning nutrition; exercise; body weight; and other potentially influential factors, including workgroup characteristics and overall health. Most questions were answered using an anchored seven-point Likert-type agreement scale (strongly agree to strongly disagree). ***Dietary instruments*** assessing "daily servings of fruits and vegetables and percentage of total calories from fat. The final instrument contained 116 items. Firefighters completed the surveys while receiving light refreshments during the hour between specimen collection and physical testing; completed surveys were reviewed by research staff to minimize missing items."	Yes
Other measurement instruments and procedures (e.g., physiological measures or coding of behavior from videos)	NA	***Physiological measures*** "Research staff, different from those performing the MI counseling and implementing the team program, obtained fitness indices and anthropometric measures (height, weight, body composition, and body mass index). Oxygen uptake was measured during Bruce protocol treadmill exercise to maximal exertion using a SensorMedics 2900 (Viasys Healthcare,	No

(Continued)

TABLE 2.2 (Cont).

	SHIELD	PHLAME	Exchangeable
		Yorba Linda, CA) or a MedGraphics TEEM 100 metabolic cart (Aerosport, Inc., Ann Arbor, MI), with the same instrument used for an individual's pretesting and testing at one year. Maximal exertion was defined as volitional exhaustion, a plateau in heart rate, or a respiratory exchange ratio greater than 1.10. Body composition was calculated from seven-site skin folds, assessed using Harpenden calipers on one side of the body, with values recorded to the nearest 0.1 mm. Strength and flexibility measures [...] also were obtained, including sit-ups/one minute and sit-and-reach."	
Frequency of measurement	Baseline, 6 months, 12 months	NA	No
Duration of the study	NA	"Data were collected in 2002 through 2004, with analyses in 2005."	No
Data analysis*			
Data cleaning procedure	NR	NR	NR
Statistical model	NR	NR	NR
Covariates	NR	NR	NR

Note: NR indicates that this criterion is not relevant for the phenomenon being studied. *NA* indicates that the information is relevant, but not available.

* All aspects of the data analyses were indicated as irrelevant for evaluating exchangeability because it was assumed that the analysts would have access to raw data based on which they could construct the prior, and not only published results. If analysts are basing their priors on published results from a previous study, then the data cleaning procedure, model, and covariates need to be exchangeable between studies.

predictors and outcomes in the statistical model. Third, in this chapter, we erred on the side of concluding the studies are exchangeable when the relevant information was missing for one of the studies because the same team of researchers conducted both studies. However, we do not know whether the experimental manipulations and measurement instruments were indeed identical. Thus, another researcher evaluating the exchangeability between SHIELD and PHLAME could have come up with a different set of answers in the last column of Table 2.2. Fourth, notice that even studies conducted by the same team of researchers differ in the reporting of descriptive statistics and study procedures: in SHIELD the demographic information is reported for the entire sample and the self-report measurement instruments are described without listing the scale names, whereas in PHLAME the demographic information is reported by treatment group and the self-report measurement instruments are described by type of question. We suspect that this issue is almost ubiquitous, and even greater for two studies conducted by different teams of researchers. Finally, we want to emphasize that exchangeability is not a property of the external world, but a feature of the analyst. We considered the 1935 and 1936 studies from the Rothamsted Experimental Station exchangeable, because to our knowledge there were no relevant differences in farming practices and environmental setting that would allow us to distinguish between these two studies. We are not certain that a farmer from the 1930s would agree with this assumption. This issue can be remedied by consulting experts on the subject matter when trying to establish whether two studies are exchangeable, but one can never be 100% certain that two studies are completely exchangeable.

Conclusions and next steps

Even though Bayesian statistics offer a promising framework for sequentially accumulating scientific knowledge with each new research study, there are still concerns about using informative prior distributions in Bayesian analysis. When the bulk of the prior distribution lies around the true value of the parameter, then Bayesian methods with informative prior distributions have less bias (e.g., Depaoli, 2013), and more power and precision than classical methods and Bayesian methods with diffuse priors (Miočević, MacKinnon, & Levy, 2017). However, when the bulk of the prior distribution lies further away from the population value of the parameter, then such a prior distribution can produce biased findings (e.g., Depaoli, 2014). Knowing whether a researcher's best guess about the parameter encoded in the prior distribution is close to the population value of the parameter is possible only in simulation studies; in real life, applied researchers have no way of knowing whether they are specifying a prior distribution that reflects the true values of the parameters in their model. When using results from a non-exchangeable previous study to construct priors for the current study, the lack of exchangeability between the two studies can cause inaccuracy in the prior. Applied researchers who still wish to use non-exchangeable prior information in the analysis of a new study have several options:

1. Use the posteriors from PHLAME as priors for SHIELD without any adjustment and assume that the two studies are exchangeable. However, if there are any relevant differences between two studies, and in this example there are at least a few, using uncalibrated findings from the previous study is likely to yield a less accurate informative prior than a prior that downweighs the influence of the non-exchangeable previous study.
2. Use power prior distributions to downweigh the information from the previous study based on the assumed level of exchangeability between the previous and current studies. Power priors are a class of informative prior distributions that are constructed by raising the likelihood function from a previous study to a power between 0 and 1 (Ibrahim & Chen, 2000). Values closer to 0 give the previous study less weight, and values closer to 1 give the previous study more weight. Values of the power parameter closer to 1 communicate the assumption that the data sets are exchangeable. In light of the ambiguity associated with the evaluation of exchangeability, researchers may wish to use several different values between 0 and 1 as the power parameter and evaluate them all in a sensitivity analysis.
3. Account for the differences between the studies using the hierarchical replication model described by de Leeuw and Klugkist (2012). This method allows each study to have a different regression coefficient and includes study-level predictors. This is a good solution if we can assume that the observations within each study are exchangeable, but the studies are not exchangeable, and if the same model is fit using both data sets, and both studies have the same predictors and outcome.
4. Use the downweighed posteriors from the previous study as priors for the current study by basing the priors on the posterior from the previous study but make the prior variances larger than what the posterior from the previous study would suggest. The idea here is to build in some additional uncertainty by inflating the variance in the prior. However, exactly how to do that in a broad class of situations is unclear, as there is no universal number that will be appropriate as a multiplier of the posterior variance from the initial study. Some distributional forms (e.g., inverse-gamma) allow for selecting the desired sample size for the prior through the choice of hyperparameters, which gives researchers the option of designing informative priors that carry only a fraction of the weight of the likelihood function from the current study. Unfortunately, most commonly used distributions do not have this feature (e.g., normal distribution), which makes it difficult to translate the prior variance into an approximate sample size allocated to the prior distribution.

The example of SHIELD and PHLAME concerns a lack of exchangeability among people, and we assumed exchangeability in terms of measurement instruments. Options 2–4 here are ways to address a lack of exchangeability among people. A lack of exchangeability in measurement instruments may lead to non-exchangeability among variables in the two data sets, e.g., if the same construct is measured using different scales in the two studies, then a one-unit change on one scale may not be comparable to a one-unit change on the other scale. When faced with non-exchangeability of variables, we propose two potential solutions:

1. If the variables are about the same construct, then use the standardized solution from one data set to form the prior for the other data set.
2. Use latent variable modeling (factor analysis, or Item Response Theory – IRT) to handle different measures (at least some of which have to exhibit measurement invariance across studies), as described in the literature on integrative data analysis (Curran & Hussong, 2009; Curran et al., 2008; McArdle, Grimm, Hamagami, Bowles, & Meredith, 2009).

Despite the increasing availability of relevant prior information that can be used in a Bayesian analysis, there are still no clear guidelines for how non-exchangeable information ought to be calibrated to create informative prior distributions. In this chapter we highlighted some of the challenges in evaluating the extent to which two studies are exchangeable and some ideas for dealing with the conversion of a non-exchangeable prior study into an informative prior distribution for the current study. Different methods for incorporating non-exchangeable prior information need to be tested in simulation studies, which will hopefully yield guidelines for applied researchers who wish to specify informative priors based on previous studies. For now, it is prudent to proceed with caution when specifying informative prior distributions, and to remain mindful about the kinds of non-exchangeability that might exist between the prior and current studies.

Notes

1 Lindley and Phillips (1976) go further and argue that exchangeability justifies the use of *all* Bayesian machinery – as they see it, there is no assumption of the prior, only the assumption of exchangeability, and from that assumption arises the notion of a prior and the subsequent Bayesian calculations.
2 We are using this classic data set from the same institution where the mathematician and geneticist Ronald Aylmer Fisher developed the analysis of variance a decade earlier, in the 1920s.

References

Bernardo, J. M., & Smith, A. F. M. (2000). *Bayesian theory*. Chichester: John Wiley & Sons.
Curran, P. J., & Hussong, A. M. (2009). Integrative data analysis: The simultaneous analysis of multiple data sets. *Psychological Methods*, *14*(2), 81–100. doi:10.1037/a0015914.
Curran, P. J., Hussong, A. M., Cai, L., Huang, W., Chassin, L., Sher, K. J., & Zucker, R. A. (2008). Pooling data from multiple longitudinal studies: The role of item response theory in integrative data analysis. *Developmental Psychology*, *44*(2), 365–380. doi:10.1037/0012-1649.44.2.365.

De Finetti, B. (1931). Funzione caratteristica di un fenomeno aleatorio. *Atti Della R. Academia Nazionale Dei Lincei, Serie 6. Memorie, Classe Di Scienze Fisiche, Mathematice E Naturale, 4*, 251–299.

De Finetti, B. (1964). Studies in subjective probability. In H. E. Kyburg & H. E. Smokler (Ed.), *Annales de l'Institut Henri Poincaré 7* (pp. 1–68). New York, NY: John Wiley & Sons. (Original work published 1937).

De Finetti, B. (1974). *Theory of probability*, Vol. 1. New York, NY: John Wiley & Sons.

De Leeuw, C., & Klugkist, I. (2012). Augmenting data with published results in Bayesian linear regression. *Multivariate Behavioral Research, 47*(3), 369–391. doi:10.1080/00273171.2012.673957.

Depaoli, S. (2013). Mixture class recovery in GMM under varying degrees of class separation: Frequentist versus Bayesian estimation. *Psychological Methods, 18*(2), 186–219. doi:10.1037/a0031609.

Depaoli, S. (2014). The impact of inaccurate "informative" priors for growth parameters in Bayesian growth mixture modeling. *Structural Equation Modeling: A Multidisciplinary Journal, 21*(2), 239–252. doi:10.1080/10705511.2014.882686.

Diaconis, P., & Freedman, D. (1980). De Finetti's generalizations of exchangeability. In R. C. Jeffrey (Ed.), *Studies in inductive logic and probability*, Vol. 2 (pp. 233–249). Berkeley, CA: University of California Press.

Elliot, D. L., Goldberg, L., Duncan, T. E., Kuehl, K. S., Moe, E. L., Breger, R. K. R., Stevens, V. J. (2004). The PHLAME firefighters' study: Feasibility and findings. *American Journal of Health Behavior, 28*(1), 13–23. doi:10.5993/AJHB.28.1.2.

Elliot, D. L., Goldberg, L., Kuehl, K. S., Moe, E. L., Breger, R. K. R., & Pickering, M. A. (2007). The PHLAME (Promoting Healthy Lifestyles: Alternative Models' Effects) firefighter study: Outcomes of two models of behavior change. *Journal of Occupational and Environmental Medicine, 49*(2), 204–213. doi:10.1097/JOM.0b013e3180329a8d.

Gelman, A., Carlin, J. B., Stern, H. S., Dunson, D. B., Vehtari, A., & Rubin, D. B. (2013). *Bayesian data analysis* (3rd ed.). Boca Raton: FL: CRC Press.

Ibrahim, J. G., & Chen, M.-H. (2000). Power prior distributions for regression models. *Statistical Science, 15*(1), 46–60. doi:10.1214/ss/1009212673.

Klein, R. A., Ratliff, K. A., Vianello, M., Adams, R. B., Jr, Bahník, Š., Bernstein, M. J., … Nosek, B. A. (2014). Investigating variation in replicability: A "many labs" replication project. *Social Psychology, 45*(3), 142–152. doi:10.1027/1864-9335/a000178.

Klein, R. A., Vianello, M., Hasselman, F., Adams, B. G., Adams, R. B., Jr., Alper, S., & Bahník, Š. (2018). Many labs 2: Investigating variation in replicability across samples and settings. *Advances in Methods and Practices in Psychological Science, 1*(4), 443–490. doi:10.1177/2515245918810225.

Kuehl, K. S., Elliot, D. L., MacKinnon, D. P., O'Rourke, H. P., DeFrancesco, C., Miočević, M., … McGinnis, W. (2016). The SHIELD (Safety & Health Improvement: Enhancing Law Enforcement Departments) study: Mixed methods longitudinal findings. *Journal of Occupational and Environmental Medicine/American College of Occupational and Environmental Medicine, 58*(5), 492–498. doi:10.1097/JOM.0000000000000716.

Levy, R., & Mislevy, R. J. (2016). *Bayesian psychometric modeling*. Boca Raton, FL: Chapman & Hall/CRC Press.

Lindley, D. V., & Phillips, L. D. (1976). Inference for a Bernoulli process (a Bayesian view). *The American Statistician, 30*(3), 112–119. doi:10.1080/00031305.1976.10479154.

McArdle, J. J., Grimm, K. J., Hamagami, F., Bowles, R. P., & Meredith, W. (2009). Modeling life-span growth curves of cognition using longitudinal data with multiple samples and changing scales of measurement. *Psychological Methods*, *14*(2), 126–149. doi:10.1037/a0015857.

Merkle, E. C., & Rosseel, Y. (2018). blavaan: Bayesian structural equation models via parameter expansion. *Journal of Statistical Software*, *85*(4), 30. doi:10.18637/jss.v085.i04.

Miočević, M., MacKinnon, D. P., & Levy, R. (2017). Power in Bayesian mediation analysis for small sample research. *Structural Equation Modeling: A Multidisciplinary Journal*, *24*(5), 666–683.

Patil, P., Peng, R. D., & Leek, J. T. (2016). A statistical definition for reproducibility and replicability. *bioRxiv*, 066803. doi:10.1101/066803.

Rothamsted Experimental Station. (1936). Other experiments at Rothamsted. In *Rothamsted Report for 1935* (pp. 174–193): Lawes Agricultural Trust.

Rothamsted Experimental Station. (1937). Other experiments at Rothamsted. In *Rothamsted Report for 1936* (pp. 205–223): Lawes Agricultural Trust.

Schmidt, S. (2009). Shall we really do it again? The powerful concept of replication is neglected in the social sciences. *Review of General Psychology*, *13*(2), 90–100.

3

A TUTORIAL ON USING THE WAMBS CHECKLIST TO AVOID THE MISUSE OF BAYESIAN STATISTICS

Rens van de Schoot
DEPARTMENT OF METHODOLOGY AND STATISTICS, UTRECHT UNIVERSITY, UTRECHT, THE NETHERLANDS & OPTENTIA RESEARCH PROGRAM, FACULTY OF HUMANITIES, NORTH-WEST UNIVERSITY, VANDERBIJLPARK, SOUTH AFRICA

Duco Veen
DEPARTMENT OF METHODOLOGY AND STATISTICS, UTRECHT UNIVERSITY, UTRECHT, THE NETHERLANDS

Laurent Smeets
DEPARTMENT OF METHODOLOGY AND STATISTICS, UTRECHT UNIVERSITY, UTRECHT, THE NETHERLANDS

Sonja D. Winter
PSYCHOLOGICAL SCIENCES, UNIVERSITY OF CALIFORNIA, MERCED, CA, UNITED STATES OF AMERICA

Sarah Depaoli
PSYCHOLOGICAL SCIENCES, UNIVERSITY OF CALIFORNIA, MERCED, CA, UNITED STATES OF AMERICA

Introduction

The current chapter guides the reader through the steps of the When-to-Worry-and-How-to-Avoid-the-Misuse-of-Bayesian-Statistics checklist (the WAMBS checklist), in order to provide background for the other chapters in this book. New in comparison to the original WAMBS checklist is that we include prior and posterior predictive model checking. We also compare the performance of two popular Bayesian software packages: RStan (Carpenter et al., 2017) and rjags (Plummer, Stukalov, & Denwood, 2018) ran via blavaan (Merkle & Rosseel, 2018). We show why using the Hamiltonian Monte Carlo (HMC) procedure (Betancourt, 2017), available in RStan, is more efficient when sample size is small. Note that for a full explanation of each step we refer to the paper in which the checklist was published (Depaoli & Van de Schoot, 2017). For a more detailed introduction to

Bayesian modeling, we refer the novice reader to Chapter 1 (Miočević, Levy, & Van de Schoot), among many other resources. The checklist is extended in Chapter 4 (Veen & Egberts) with some additional tools and debugging options. All data and the annotated R code to reproduce the results are available on the Open Science Framework (https://osf.io/am7pr/).

Example data

The data we use throughout the chapter is based on a study of PhD delays (Van de Schoot, Yerkes, Mouw, & Sonneveld, 2013). Among many other questions, the researchers asked the PhD recipients how long it had taken them to finish their PhD thesis ($n = 333$). It appeared that PhD recipients took an average of 59.8 months (five years and four months) to complete their PhD trajectory. The variable of interest measures the difference between planned and actual project time in months ($\overline{delay} = 9.97$, $min/max = -31/91$, $\sigma = 14.43$).

Let us assume we are interested in the question of whether age ($\overline{age} = 31.68$, $min/max = 26/69$) of the PhD recipients is related to delay in their project. Also, assume we expect this relation to be non-linear. So, in our model the gap between planned and actual project time is the dependent variable and age and age² are the predictors, resulting in a regression model with four parameters:

- the intercept denoted by $\beta_{intercept}$
- two regression parameters:
    - β_{age} or β_1 for the linear relation with age
    - β_{age^2} or β_2 for the quadratic relation with age

- variance of the residuals denoted by σ_ε^2

WAMBS checklist

Do you understand the priors?

Since we know that at least some degree of information is necessary to properly estimate small data (Smid, McNeish, Miočević, & Van de Schoot, 2019), the next question is: How to assess and use such information? There are many ways to specify subjective priors—for example, based on expert elicitation or previous data (Van de Schoot et al., 2018)—and none are inherently right or wrong. For more details on where to get the priors from, see Zondervan-Zwijnenburg, Peeters, Depaoli, & Van de Schoot (2017).

In the current chapter we propose to use background information to specify priors that cover a plausible parameter space. That is, we define a range of possible parameter values considered to be reasonable, thereby excluding impossible values and assigning only a limited density mass to implausible values. Note that in the sensitivity analyses presented in Steps 7–9 of the checklist, we investigate the extent of "wiggle room" for these values. Stated differently, whether different specifications of the plausible parameter space lead to different conclusions.

Define parameter space

We developed a free online app that can help with specifying the plausible parameter space for the PhD delay example (see the OSF for source code (https://osf.io/am7pr/), and for the online version go to www.rensvandeschoot.com/pps or https://utrecht-university.shinyapps.io/priors_phd/)[1]; for a screenshot, see Figure 3.1. If useful background knowledge is available and you are therefore unsure about your prior beliefs, trying to infer a plausible parameter space is to be preferred over just relying on software defaults.

First, define what you believe to be a reasonable range for age (in years). Think about what you believe to be the youngest age someone can acquire a PhD (delay included) and what the oldest age might be. This yields an age range of, for example, 18–70. Then, define the delay (in months) you believe to be reasonable. A negative delay indicates that someone finished their PhD ahead of schedule. Think about how many months someone can finish ahead of schedule and what you believe to be the maximum time that someone can be delayed; for example, -25–120 (Figure 3.1).

Second, think about what you consider plausible estimates for the intercept, the linear effect, and the quadratic effect. The data is not centered, which means that the intercept represents the expected delay of a zero-year-old. The linear effect is the expected increase in delay (in months) over time. For example, a linear effect of 3 means that for a one-year increase in age, the expected delay increases by three months. The quadratic effect is the deviation from linearity. Let us assume we expect a positive linear increase of 2.5 starting at a delay of -35 months (note this is possible because it is the delay of a zero-year old PhD candidate) and a small negative quadratic effect of -.03, so that this effect would look like a negative parabola (n-shaped) with the maximum delay occurring around the fifties (Figure 3.1).

Priors for regression coefficients (or any prior for that matter) are never just a point estimate, but always follow a distribution. In this example, only normal distributions are used, but most Bayesian software will allow many different types of distributions. The variances of a normally distributed the prior, denoted by σ_0^2, resemble a measure of uncertainty; see also Chapter 1. It is important to note that these variances are measured on the same scale as the regression coefficients. A variance that is small for the intercept might be relatively large for the quadratic effect. This means that you always have to be careful with the default prior of any Bayesian software package. For our model, a small change in the variance of the quadratic effect has a large influence on the plausible parameter space. This becomes clear in the app because any small adjustment of the variance (note that the scales of variance sliders are different) for the quadratic effect leads to a large widening of the ribbon of the quadratic effect over time.

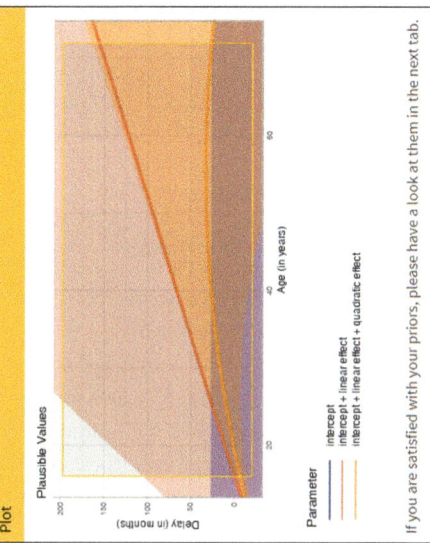
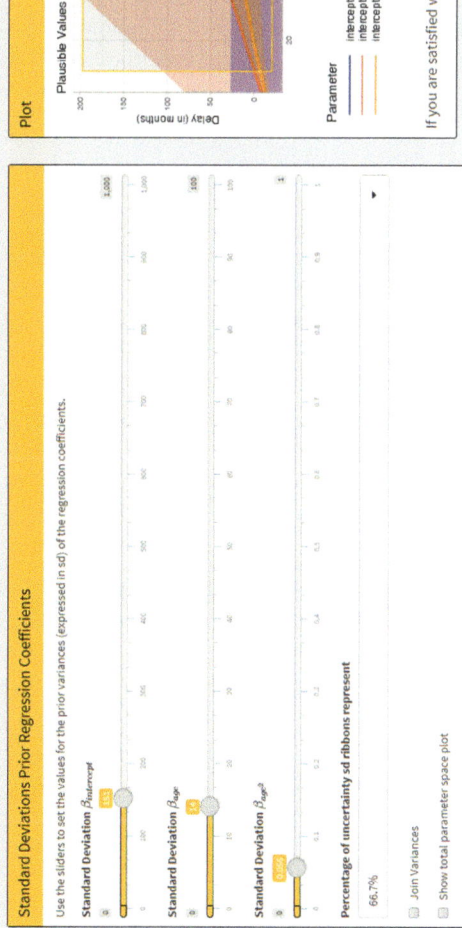

FIGURE 3.1 Screenshots of the app to specify the plausible parameter space for the PhD delay example

The following hyperparameters cover the entire plausible parameter space, with $\mathcal{N}(\mu_0, \sigma_0^2)$, and $IG(shape, scale)^2$:

- $\beta_{intercept} \sim \mathcal{N}(-35, 20)$
- $\beta_{age} \sim \mathcal{N}(.8, 5)$
- $\beta_{age^2} \sim \mathcal{N}(0, 10)$
- $\sigma_\varepsilon^2 \sim IG(.5, .5)$

Load data and define the model

Now that the hyperparameter values of the priors are specified, the data can be uploaded into R (or any other software for Bayesian estimation) and the statistical model can be specified. We ran the model using RStan. For an introduction, see for instance Carpenter et al. (2017). We also include some results obtained with rjags via blavaan (Merkle et al., 2019; Plummer et al., 2018) to show why using RStan might be preferred over rjags even though the syntax is more complicated. See the online supplementary materials for all annotated code (https://osf.io/am7pr/).

Prior predictive checking

Now that the model has been specified, we can investigate the priors further by computing prior predictive checks which allow for inspecting the implications of all univariate priors together. To get the prior predictive results we ignore the sample data. In the top panel of Figure 3.2, the 95% prior predictive intervals are shown for generated observations based on the priors for each individual, denoted by y_{rep}, and the observations from the sample, denoted by y. That is, values of y_{rep} are based on the prior specifications for each individual and represent possible values for PhD delay implied by the priors. In general, for all cases the prior intervals imply delays possible from approximately -100 to +100 months (with some extreme values up to ± 250) and the entire plausible parameter space (and more) is covered.

We can also look at the possible data sets generated by the priors. In the top panel of Figure 3.3, distributions of PhD delay are plotted based on the set of priors. It appears that a wide variety of data sets is plausible, though still ruling out delays larger or smaller than +300/-300. In general, we can at least be confident that when using our priors we do not exclude potential scenarios, but at the same time are able to rule out large parts of the parameters space, which is what is needed when sample sizes are small.

Does the trace-plot exhibit convergence?

To obtain estimates for the parameters in our model we make use of Monte Carlo simulations; see also Chapter 1. Traditionally a very successful and often-used algorithm is the Gibbs Sampler, a method of Markov chain Monte Carlo simulation

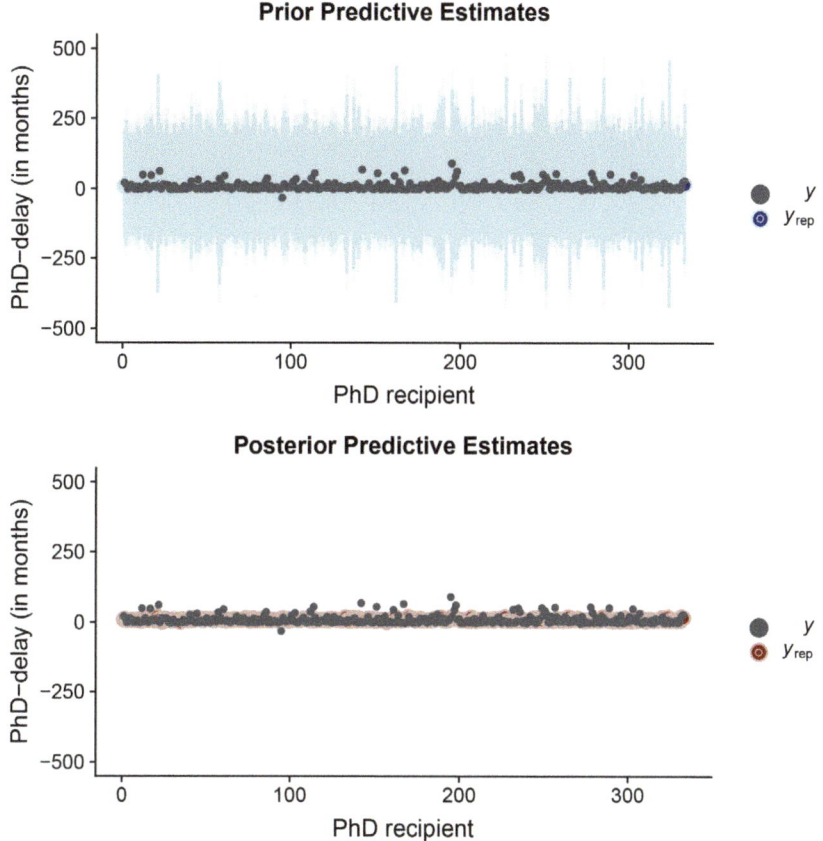

FIGURE 3.2 The 95% prior predictive intervals (top panel) and posterior predictive intervals (bottom panel) for each observation in the sample ($n = 333$)

(MCMC). This is the algorithm used by `rjags`. `RStan` uses a different MCMC algorithm, namely HMC and specifically the No-U-Turn-Sampler (Hoffman & Gelman, 2014); see also Chapter 4. For a conceptual introduction to HMC see Betancourt (2017) or the very accessible blog post by McElreath (2017). One of the benefits of this algorithm, and of the specific way it is implemented in `Stan`, is that these Monte Carlo samples suffer less from autocorrelation between the samples in the chains of samples (see Chapter 1 for an explanation of these terms). Thus, fewer Monte Carlo samples are needed to accurately describe the posterior distributions. In other words, the effective number of samples relative to our total amount of samples increases; see Chapter 4 for an extensive discussion on this topic. As a result, usually, convergence is obtained faster with the more efficient HMC.

To determine whether the sampling algorithm has converged, one should check the stability of the generated parameter values. A visual check of the

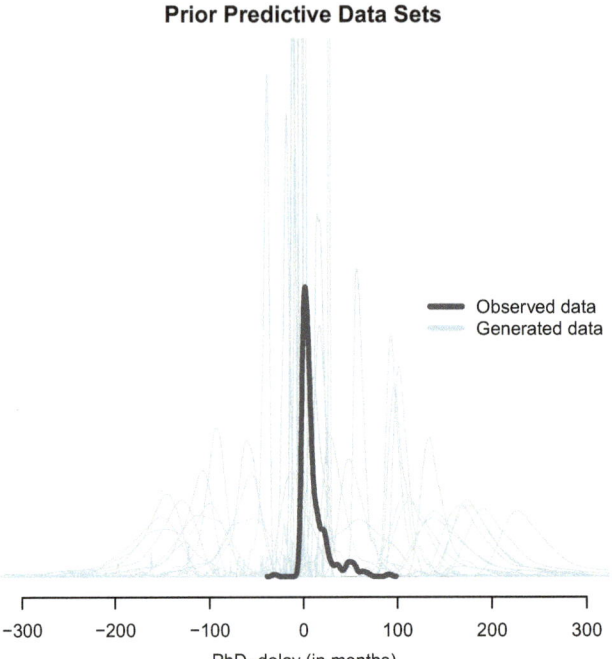
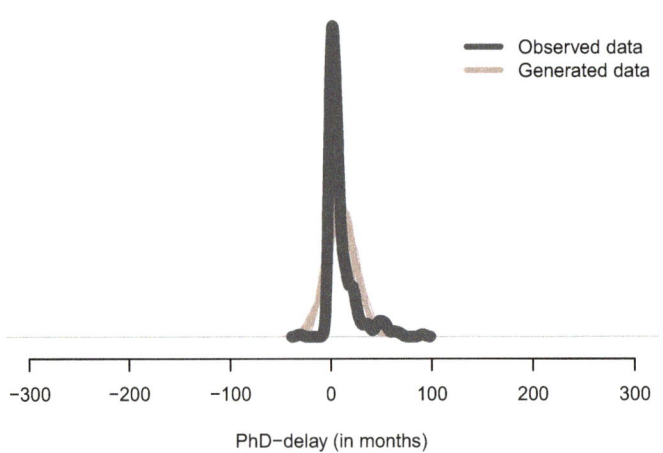

FIGURE 3.3 Generated data sets based on the prior (top panel) and posterior predictives (bottom panel)

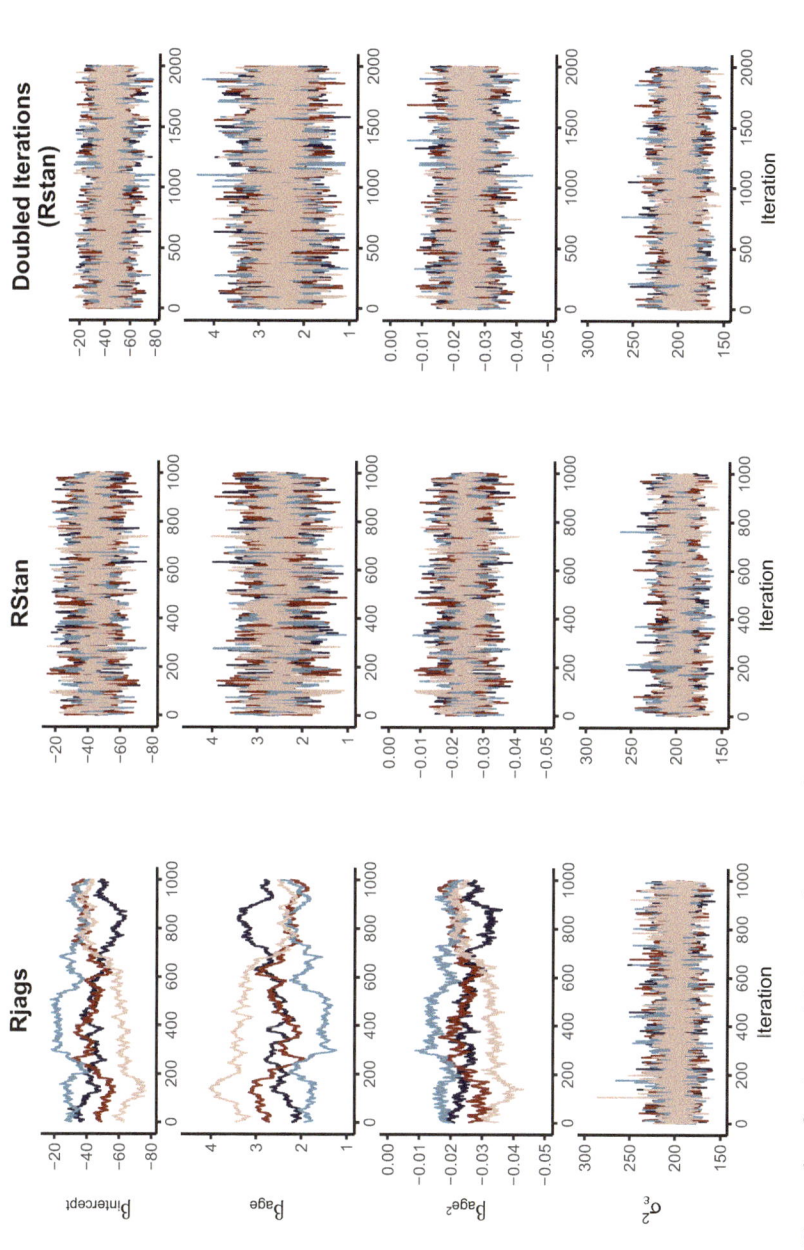

FIGURE 3.4 Trace plots for rjags and RStan with 1,000 and 2,000 iterations for each parameter in the regression model

stability of the generated parameter values implies estimating multiple chains and then plotting the results in so-called trace plots. Figure 3.4 shows the trace plots for all parameters obtained by RStan and rjags, based on four chains of 1,000 samples per chain for both samplers and 1,000 iterations burn-in. When comparing the results for RStan and rjags, it becomes clear that RStan is more efficient than rjags: we see in the plots that the chains of the MCMC sampler rjags move more slowly from one step to the next than in the HMC sampler RStan. This is caused by autocorrelation between the samples, as we show in Step 5 of the WAMBS checklist.

Next to inspecting trace plots there are several diagnostic tools to determine convergence. We discuss two completely different diagnostic tools.

First, the Gelman–Rubin statistic compares the amount of variance within the individual chains to the amount of variance between the chains up to the last iteration in the chains (Gelman & Rubin, 1992). If this ratio is close to 1—for example, if the value is smaller than 1.1 for all parameters (Gelman & Shirley, 2011)—we can be more confident that the chains describe the same distribution and that we have reached convergence. Figure 3.5 shows the development of the statistic as the number of samples increases using Gelman–Rubin diagnostic plots for both rjags and RStan.

Another convergence diagnostic is the Geweke diagnostic (Geweke, 1992), which is based on testing equality of means between the first 10% and last 50% parts of each chain. The test statistic is a standard Z-score: the difference between the two sample means divided by its estimated standard error. In

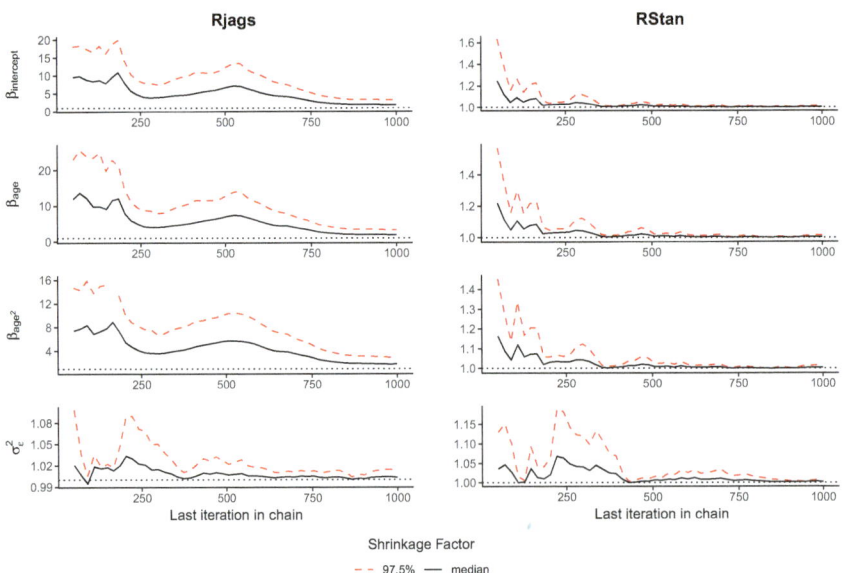

FIGURE 3.5 Gelman–Rubin statistics for RStan and rjags

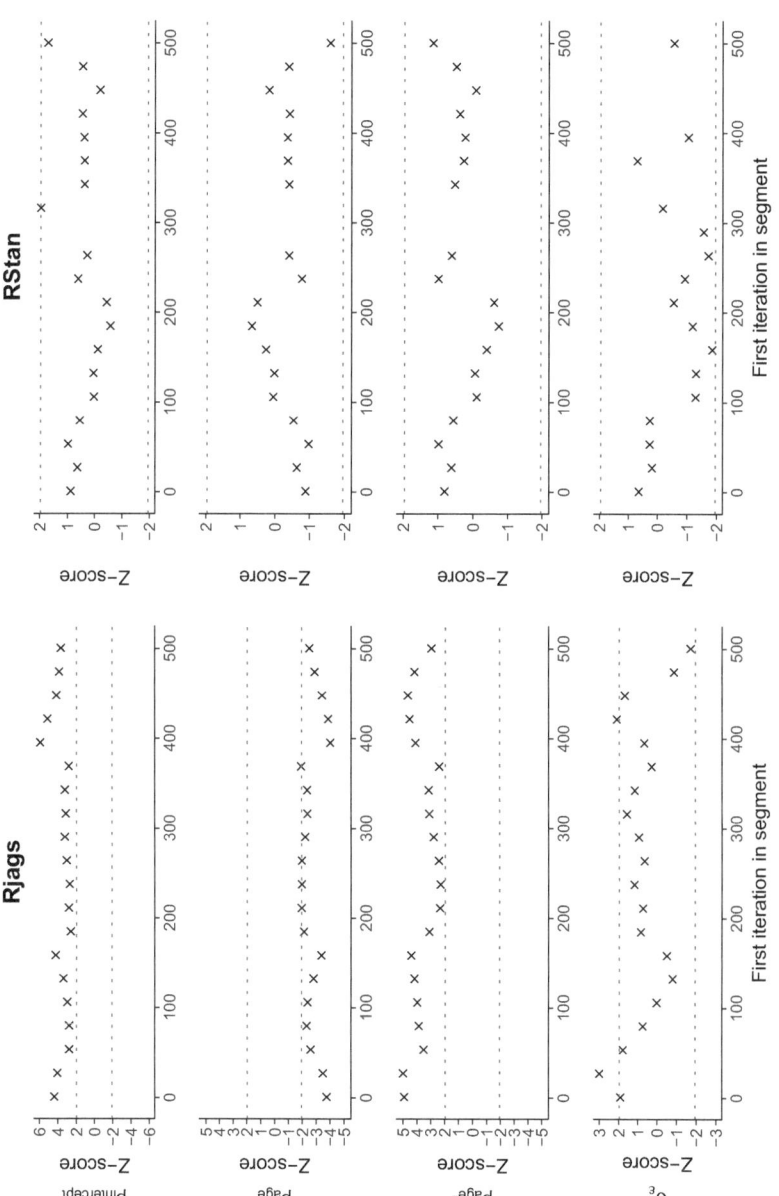

FIGURE 3.6 Geweke statistics for RStan and rjags

Figure 3.6, it could be checked how often values exceed the boundary lines of the Z-scores. Scores above 1.96 or below -1.96 indicate that the two portions of the chain differ significantly, and full chain convergence is not reached.

All results in Figures 3.4–3.6 point to convergence in the case of `RStan`, but not in the case of `rjags`. We continue using only `RStan`, with the exception of Step 5 in the checklist, where we compare the levels of autocorrelation between both packages to demonstrate the added value of `RStan` once more.

Does convergence remain after doubling the number of iterations?

As is recommended in the WAMBS checklist, we double the amount of iterations to check for local convergence. According to the checklist:

> Local convergence can be thought of as the case where convergence appears to be visually obtained – often with a smaller number of iterations – but when the chain is left to run longer, then the chain shifts and converges to another location.
>
> *(Depaoli & Van de Schoot, 2017)*

We re-ran the model with 2,000 samples per chain.

Next to inspecting the trace plots (see Figure 3.4) and the convergence diagnostics (available on the OSF) we can also compute the relative bias, in order to inspect if doubling the number of iterations influences the posterior parameter estimates. One can use the following equation by filling in a posterior estimate:

$$relative\ bias = 100 * \frac{|posterior\ estimate_{initial\ model}| - |posterior\ estimate_{new\ model}|}{|posterior\ estimate_{initial\ model}|}$$

If the relative bias is $> |5|\%^3$, then it is advised to rerun the initial model with four times the number of iterations, and again up till the relative bias is small enough; see also Chapter 4. As can be seen in the first column of Table 3.1, all

TABLE 3.1 Results of relative bias (in %) for different models

	Step 3: Double iterations	Step 7: Different variance priors	Step 8: Non-informative priors
$\beta_{intercept}$	−1.029	1.052	−6.349
β_{age}	−0.811	0.880	−5.312
β_{age^2}	−0.778	0.967	−5.578
σ_ε^2	−0.149	−0.345	0.248

values of relative bias are < 1.03%, which means doubling the number of iterations hardly changes the posterior estimates.

Does the histogram contain enough information?

The parameter estimates of all chains (after burn-in) can be plotted in a histogram. The amount of information, or smoothness, of the histogram should be checked to ensure that the posterior is represented using a large enough number of samples. There should be no gaps or other abnormalities in the histogram. The histograms in Figure 3.7 all look smooth, thus suggesting that adding more iterations is not necessary.

Do the chains exhibit a strong degree of autocorrelation?

The dependence between the samples of a Monte Carlo simulation can be summarized by autocorrelation. If samples are less correlated, we need fewer Monte Carlo samples to get an accurate description of our posterior distribution. High autocorrelation can be a sign that there was a problem with the functioning of the MCMC sampling algorithm or in the initial setup of the model. Also, if convergence is not obtained with an extreme number of iterations, then these issues can be indicative of a model specification problem, multicollinearity, *or* the sampling algorithm. In our case, the sampling algorithm itself solves the high amount of autocorrelation in the model. Compare

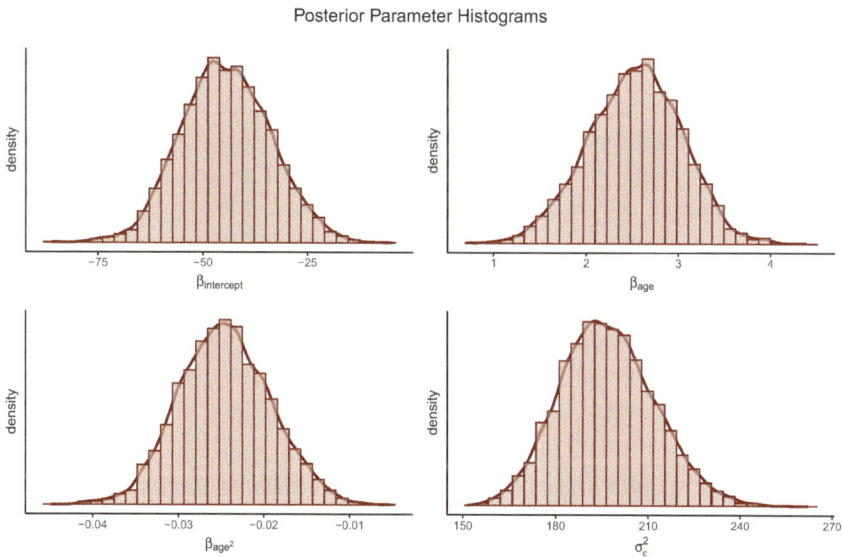

FIGURE 3.7 Plots with histograms

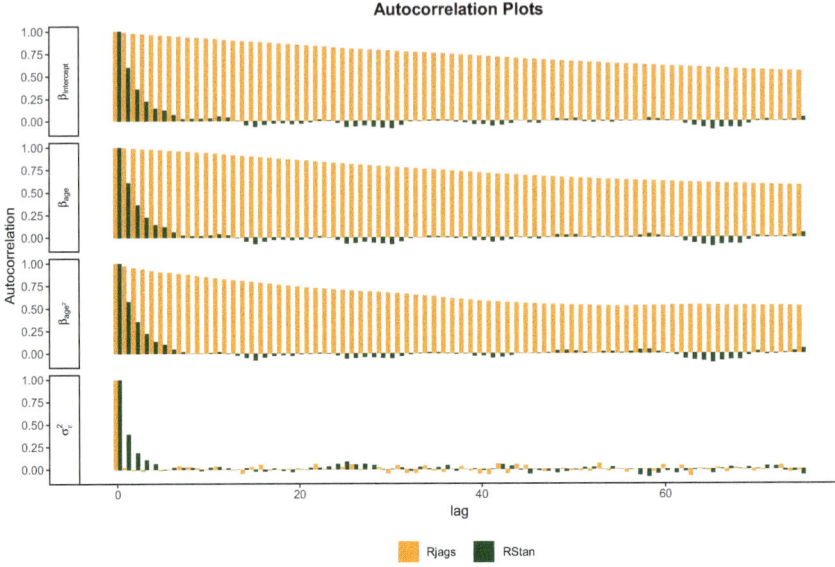

FIGURE 3.8 Plots with levels of autocorrelation for both `RStan` and `rjags`

the plots in Figure 3.8 showing high degrees of correlation across iterations obtained in `rjags` (orange) with those obtained in `RStan` (green). The results obtained in `RStan` show less dependency between iterations when compared to `rjags`.

Do the posterior distributions make substantive sense?

Plotting a smoothed line through the histogram can be used as an approximation of the posterior distribution. In Figure 3.7 we plotted these to check if they are unimodal (i.e., have one peak), are clearly centered around one value, give a realistic estimate, and make substantive sense compared to our prior beliefs. As can be seen in Figure 3.7, there are no such issues with the posterior distributions obtained for our parameters. The posterior distributions of our regression coefficients fall within the range we specified above, and the peak of our posterior distributions is within reasonable distance from the means of our prior specifications. Substantive interpretations of these posteriors will follow in Step 10 of the checklist.

Do different specifications of the priors for variance parameters influence the results?

To understand the influence of the priors as specified in Step 1, it is recommended to conduct a sensitivity analysis (Van Erp, Mulder, & Oberski,

2018). It is essential that researchers report results of a sensitivity analysis, even if there is no substantive impact on results. Do not despair if there are differences between posterior results! Such findings are actually very interesting (and even fun). In such situations, we recommend dedicating considerable space in the discussion section to the description of the discrepancy between results obtained using informative versus non-informative priors and the implications of this discrepancy. The discussion could then illustrate the mismatch between theory (i.e., priors should reflect the current state of affairs) and data, and it is up to the researcher to come up with an explanation for such a mismatch.

Although a sensitivity analysis needs you to play around with some of the prior settings, it is important to note that this can only be an exercise to improve the understanding of the priors. It is not a method for changing the original prior. That is, if a researcher actually changes the prior after seeing the results of Steps 7–9, then this is considered as manipulating the results, related to questionable research practices or even fraud.

To understand how the prior for the residual variance impacts the posterior, we compared the current results with a model that uses different hyperparameters for the Inverse Gamma prior for the residual variance. So far we used $\sigma_\varepsilon^2 \sim IG(.5, .5)$, but we can also use $\sigma_\varepsilon^2 \sim IG(.01, .01)$ and see if doing so makes a difference (many other variations are possible). To quantify the impact of the prior, we again calculated the relative bias (computed the same way as in Step 3); see the second column of Table 3.1. The results are robust, because there is only a minimum amount of relative bias for the residual variance.

Is there a notable effect of the prior when compared to non-informative priors?

In order to understand the impact of our informative priors on the posterior results, we also compare our subjective priors with non-informative priors:

- $\beta_{intercept} \sim \mathcal{N}(0, 10^6)$
- $\beta_{age} \sim \mathcal{N}(0, 1000)$
- $\beta_{age^2} \sim \mathcal{N}(0, 1000)$
- $\sigma_\varepsilon^2 \sim IG(1, .5)$

We computed the relative bias, and as can be seen in the third column of Table 3.1, there is some bias between the two models. To understand the impact of our informative priors, we plotted the priors and posteriors for both models and for all parameters in Figure 3.9. In the last column the two posteriors are plotted in the same graph, and, as can be seen, the informative priors do impact the posterior results when compared to the non-informative priors.

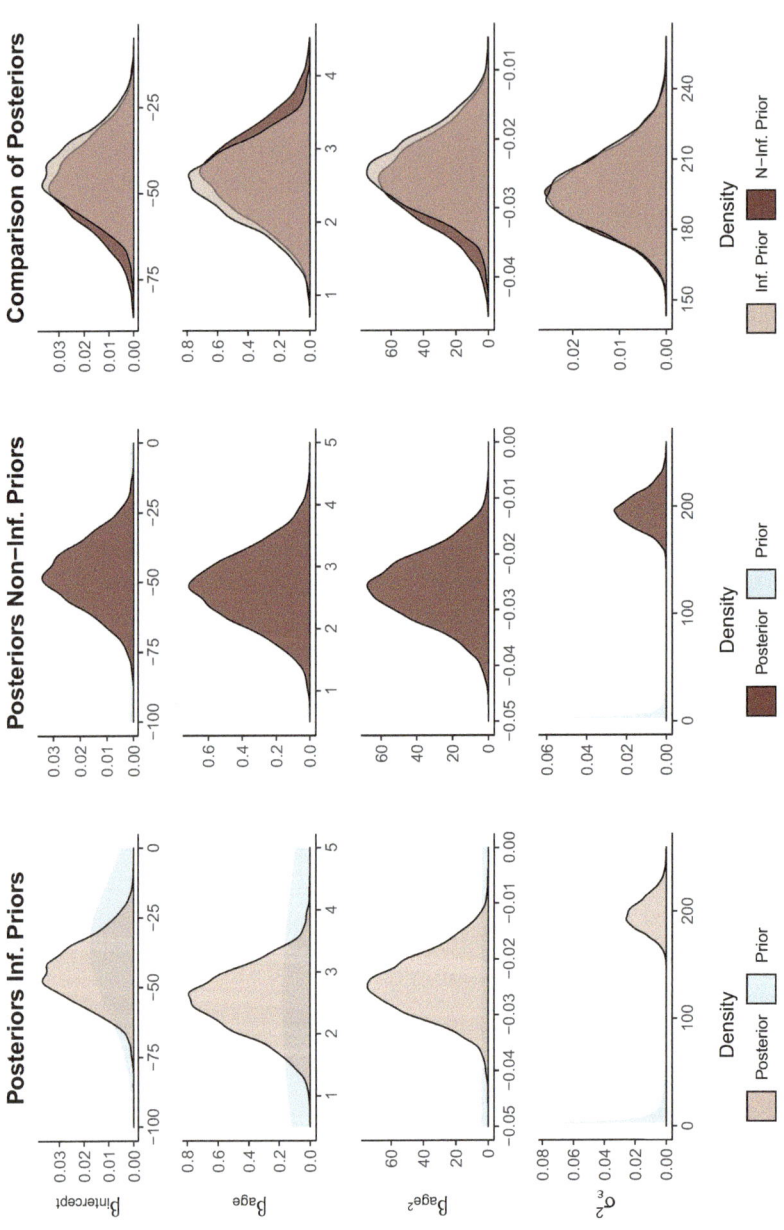

FIGURE 3.9 Priors and posteriors for the models with and without informative priors

Are the results stable with a sensitivity analysis?

In addition to the previous steps, we not only checked the sensitivity of the results to different prior specifications (our informative priors, a factor 10 times more informative, and non-informative), but we also checked the stability of the posterior estimates across participants by sequential updating. That is, with Bayesian statistics the priors can be updated with a sample size of $n = 1, \ldots, n = N$. Thus, in each step the original prior is updated with more and more data so that the posterior becomes more dominated by the data and less by the prior. The stability of the results is indicative of how small the sample size could have been with different prior settings.

As we assume our data to be exchangeable (see Chapter 2, Miočević, Levy, and Savord), it should not matter in which order the data points were observed if our posterior distributions are to pass this second sensitivity analysis. Therefore, we created five permutations of the data in which only the order of the participants was randomly changed. For each of these five data sets, we ran the model with the three different prior specifications, resulting in 15 different models. After the first update with the first participant, the posteriors were updated again with adding the second participant to the data, and so on.

As can be seen in Figure 3.10, updating the model 333 times results in similar posterior results for all the five different data sets, which makes sense since the data is exchangeable and the order in which the data is analyzed should not matter. But when inspecting, for example, the results for the intercept with the priors as specified in Step 1, it can be seen that only after roughly 100 participants are the results stable. Stated differently, if we had included only 50 PhD recipients in our data, the uncertainty in the posterior would have been much larger, even allowing zero plausibility (grey line; the blue line resembles the prior mean). This effect is much lager for the non-informative priors and a much larger data set is needed to obtain stable results. It is not surprising, however, that with precise priors (small prior variance) our data does not change the estimates much: after a few samples our posterior estimates from the permuted data sets are highly similar.

In conclusion, the data, with $n = 333$, could have been a bit smaller with our informative priors, but not much. Only with highly informative priors, the sample size could have been smaller.

TABLE 3.2 Results for the model using our informative priors

	Mean	SD	2.5%	50%	97.5%
$\beta_{intercept}$	-44.425	10.579	-64.325	-44.668	-23.387
β_{age}	2.532	.503	1.522	2.544	3.477
β_{age^2}	-.025	.005	-.034	-.025	-.014
σ_ε^2	196.923	15.266	168.758	196.255	228.166

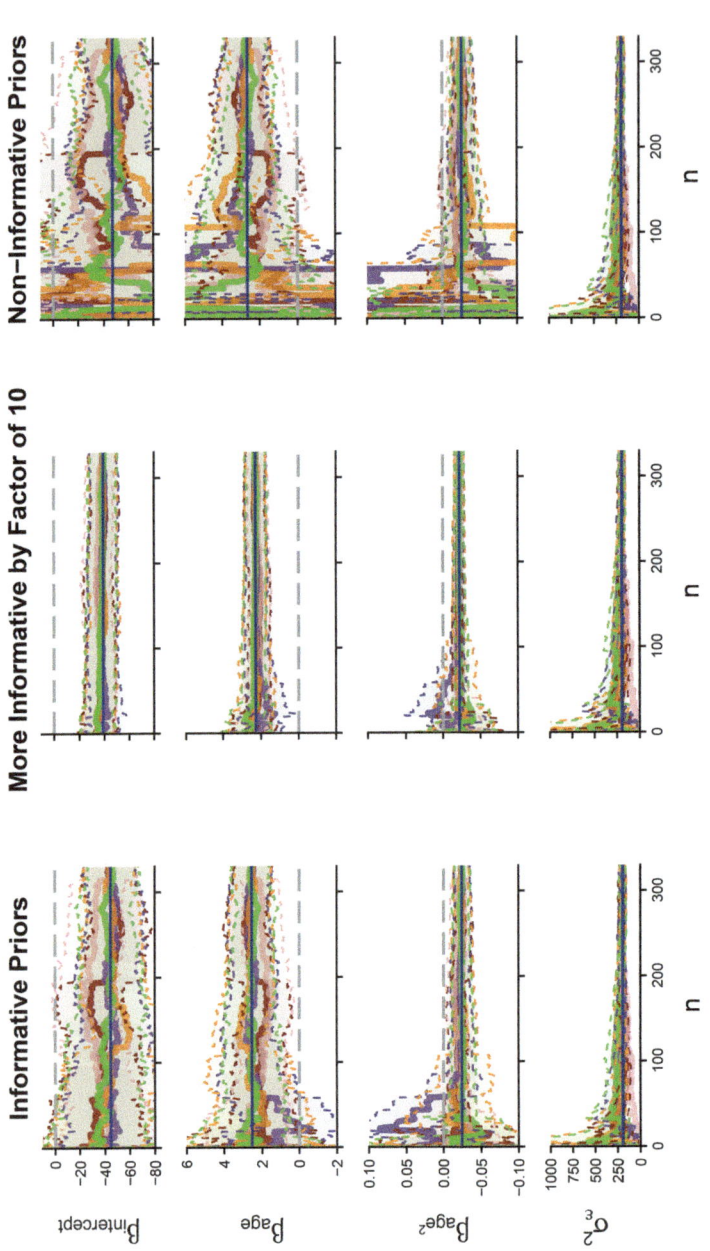

FIGURE 3.10 Results sensitivity analysis

Is the Bayesian way of interpreting and reporting model results used?

The posterior parameter estimates can be summarized using, for example, the median of the posterior distributions, and can be found in Table 3.2. Based on these point summaries, it appears the delay peaks at around the age of 50 $(2.532/-(2*.025))$. Considering that 0 is not included in the 95% interval of the linear effect and the quadratic effect, we can conclude that there is a small positive linear effect and a small negative quadratic effect[4].

It is also informative to inspect the posterior predictive results which are similar to the prior predictive results, except that because we now inspect the posteriors we can use our updated beliefs from after observing the data. If we inspect the posterior predictive plots in Figure 3.2 (bottom panel), we can see that we are not able to perfectly predict the delay in PhD completion using the candidate's age, which also becomes evident by the R^2 of 6%. Moreover, it is not surprising to see that predictions based on our model tend to be more off the mark for cases with longer and shorter delays than with normal delays, whilst our uncertain estimates capture all standard cases. Furthermore, if we compare our prior and posterior predictive distributions (see Figure 3.3), we are less uncertain and more consistent in what we expect *after* observing the data. So, accurate predictions of delay for individual cases may not be possible, but we can predict general trends at group level.

Conclusion

The chapter shows how to properly implement a Bayesian analysis following the steps of the WAMBS checklist. Following this checklist is important for the transparency of research, which is important no matter which estimation paradigm is being implemented. However, it is *even more* important within the Bayesian framework, because there are so many places where bad research practices can be "hidden" within this estimation perspective, especially concerning the prior specification and its impact on the posterior results. Clear reporting and sufficient amounts of detail for reproducing results are important first steps in ensuring that Bayesian results can be trusted and properly interpreted. We therefore recommend including results of the WAMBS checklist as an appendix or as a supplementary file to any Bayesian paper; for an example, see Zweers (2018).

In the end, properly conducting and reporting results is important, but the key is understanding the impact of the prior, especially when sample size is small, since this will ultimately be the element that potentially shifts theories and practices within a field.

Acknowledgement

This work was supported by Grant NWO-VIDI-452-14-006 from the Netherlands organization for scientific research.

Notes

1 Note that the only priors you can tweak in the app are the priors for the intercept and regression coefficients. In Step 7 of the checklist we will return to the specification of the prior for the residuals, σ_ε^2.
2 Historically, Inverse Gamma priors have been used for (residual) variance parameters, due to their conjugate properties that allow for using the Gibbs sampling algorithm. Some alternatives are being discussed in, for example, McNeish (2016). The hyperparameters are, in this example, mildly informative based on the discussion in Van de Schoot, Broere, Perryck, Zondervan-Zwijnenburg, and Van Loey (2015).
3 The relative bias should be interpreted with caution and only in combination with substantive knowledge about the metric of the parameter of interest. For example, with a regression coefficient of .001, a 5% relative deviation level might not be substantively relevant. However, with an intercept parameter of 50, a 1% relative deviation level might already be quite meaningful.
4 Note that testing such results by means of the Bayes Factor is being discussed in Chapters 9 (Klaassen) and 12 (Zondervan-Zwijnenburg & Rijshouwer).

References

Betancourt, M. (2017). A conceptual introduction to Hamiltonian Monte Carlo. *arXiv Preprint arXiv:1701.02434*.

Carpenter, B., Gelman, A., Hoffman, M. D., Lee, D., Goodrich, B., Betancourt, M., & Riddell, A. (2017). Stan: A probabilistic programming language. *Journal of Statistical Software*, 76(1). doi:10.18637/jss.v076.i01.

Depaoli, S., & Van de Schoot, R. (2017). Improving transparency and replication in Bayesian statistics: The WAMBS-Checklist. *Psychological Methods*, 22(2), 240–261. doi:10.1037/met0000065.

Gelman, A., & Rubin, D. B. (1992). Inference from iterative simulation using multiple sequences. *Statistical Science*, 7(4), 457–472. doi:10.1214/ss/1177011136.

Gelman, A., & Shirley, K. (2011). Inference from simulations and monitoring convergence. In S. P. Brooks, A. Gelman, G. L. Jones, and X.-L. Meng (Eds.), *Handbook of Markov Chain Monte Carlo* (pp. 116–162). Boca Raton, FL: Chapman & Hall/CRC Press.

Geweke, J. (1992). Evaluating the accuracy of sampling-based approaches to the calculation of posterior moments. In J. M. Bernardo, A. F. M. Smith, A. P. Dawid, and J. O. Berger (Eds.), *Bayesian Statistics 4* (pp. 169–193). Oxford: Oxford University Press.

Hoffman, M. D., & Gelman, A. (2014). The No-U-turn sampler: Adaptively setting path lengths in Hamiltonian Monte Carlo. *Journal of Machine Learning Research*, 15(1), 1593–1623.

McElreath, R. (2017). Markov chains: Why walk when you can flow? Retrieved from http://elevanth.org/blog/2017/11/28/build-a-better-markov-chain/.

McNeish, D. (2016). Using data-dependent priors to mitigate small sample bias in latent growth models: A discussion and illustration using Mplus. *Journal of Educational and Behavioral Statistics*, 41(1), 27–56. doi:10.3102/1076998615621299.

Merkle, E. C., & Rosseel, Y. (2018). blavaan: Bayesian structural equation models via parameter expansion. *Journal of Statistical Software*, 85(4), 1–30. doi:10.18637/jss.v085.i04.

Merkle, E. C., Rosseel, Y., Garnier-Villarreal, M., Jorgensen, T. D., Hoofs, H., & Van de Schoot, R. (2019). blavaan: Bayesian latent variable analysis, Version 0.3-4. Retrieved from https://CRAN.R-project.org/package=blavaan.

Plummer, M., Stukalov, A., & Denwood, M. (2018). rjags: Bayesian graphical models using MCMC, Version 4-8. Retrieved from https://cran.r-project.org/web/packages/rjags/index.html.

Smid, S. C., McNeish, D., Miočević, M., & Van de Schoot, R. (2019). Bayesian versus frequentist estimation for structural equation models in small sample contexts: A systematic review. *Structural Equation Modeling: A Multidisciplinary Journal.* doi:10.1080/10705511.2019.1577140.

Van de Schoot, R., Broere, J. J., Perryck, K. H., Zondervan-Zwijnenburg, M., & Van Loey, N. E. (2015). Analyzing small data sets using Bayesian estimation: The case of posttraumatic stress symptoms following mechanical ventilation in burn survivors. *European Journal of Psychotraumatology*, *6*(1), 25216. doi:10.3402/ejpt.v6.25216.

Van de Schoot, R., Sijbrandij, M., Depaoli, S., Winter, S. D., Olff, M., & Van Loey, N. E. E. (2018). Bayesian PTSD-trajectory analysis with informed priors based on a systematic literature search and expert elicitation. *Multivariate Behavioral Research*, *53*(2), 267–291. doi:10.1080/00273171.2017.1412293.

Van de Schoot, R., Yerkes, M. A., Mouw, J. M., & Sonneveld, H. (2013). What took them so long? Explaining PhD delays among doctoral candidates. *PLoS One*, *8*(7), e68839. doi:10.1371/journal.pone.0068839.

Van Erp, S., Mulder, J., & Oberski, D. L. (2018). Prior sensitivity analysis in default Bayesian structural equation modeling. *Psychological Methods*, *23*(2), 363–388. doi:10.1037/met0000162.

Zondervan-Zwijnenburg, M. A. J., Peeters, M., Depaoli, S., & Van de Schoot, R. (2017). Where do priors come from? Applying guidelines to construct informative priors in small sample research. *Research in Human Development*, *14*(4), 305–320. doi:10.1080/15427609.2017.1370966.

Zweers, I. (2018). Chapter 5. Similar development in separate educational contexts? Development of social relationships and self-esteem in students with social-emotional and behavioral difficulties in inclusive classrooms and exclusive schools for special education – Supplementary materials. Retrieved from osf.io/yf3mu.

4

THE IMPORTANCE OF COLLABORATION IN BAYESIAN ANALYSES WITH SMALL SAMPLES

Duco Veen

DEPARTMENT OF METHODOLOGY AND STATISTICS, UTRECHT UNIVERSITY, UTRECHT, THE NETHERLANDS

Marthe Egberts

ASSOCIATION OF DUTCH BURN CENTRES, BEVERWIJK, THE NETHERLANDS, DEPARTMENT OF CLINICAL PSYCHOLOGY, UTRECHT UNIVERSITY, UTRECHT, THE NETHERLANDS, DEPARTMENT OF METHODOLOGY AND STATISTICS, UTRECHT UNIVERSITY, UTRECHT, THE NETHERLANDS

Introduction

Complex statistical models, such as Structural Equation Models (SEMs), generally require large sample sizes (Tabachnick, Fidell, & Ullman, 2007; Wang & Wang, 2012). In practice, a large enough sample cannot always be easily obtained. Still, some research questions can only be answered with complex statistical models. Fortunately, solutions exist to overcome estimation issues with small sample sizes for complex models; see Smid, McNeish, Miočević, and Van de Schoot (2019) for a systematic review comparing frequentist and Bayesian approaches. The current chapter addresses one of these solutions, namely Bayesian estimation with informative priors. In the process of Bayesian estimation, the WAMBS checklist (When-to-Worry-and-How-to-Avoid-the-Misuse-of-Bayesian-Statistics; Depaoli & Van de Schoot, 2017) is a helpful tool; see also Chapter 2 (Van de Schoot, Veen, Smeets, Winter, & Depaoli). However, problems may arise in Bayesian analyses with informative priors, and whereas these problems are generally recognized in the field, they are not always described or solved in existing tutorials, statistical handbooks, or example papers. This chapter offers an example of issues arising in the estimation of a Latent Growth Model (LGM) with a distal outcome using Bayesian methods with informative priors and a small data set of young children with burn injuries and their mothers. Moreover, we introduce two additional tools for diagnosing estimation issues: divergent transitions and the effective sample size (ESS) of the posterior parameter samples, available in Stan (Stan Development Team,

2017b) which makes use of an advanced Hamiltonian Monte Carlo (HMC) algorithm called the No-U-Turn-Sampler (NUTS; Hoffman & Gelman, 2014). These diagnostics can be used in addition to the checks described in the WAMBS checklist.

In the following sections, we briefly introduce LGMs and address the role of sample size, followed by an empirical example for which we present an analysis plan. Next, we show the process of adjusting the analysis in response to estimation problems. We show that different solutions can differentially impact the posterior summaries *and* substantive conclusions. This chapter highlights the importance of collaboration between substantive experts and statisticians when an initial analysis plan goes awry.

Latent growth models with small sample sizes

LGMs include repeated measurements of observed variables, and allow researchers to examine change over time in the construct of interest. LGMs can be extended to include distal outcomes and covariates (see Figure 4.1). One of the benefits of specifying an LGM as a SEM, as opposed to a multilevel model as discussed in Chapter 15 (Hox & McNeish), is that growth can be specified as a non-monotonic or even non-linear function. For instance, we can specify an LGM in which part of the growth process is fixed and another part is estimated from the data. In Figure 4.1, two constraints on the relationships between the latent slope and measurement occasions are freed for two waves, thereby estimating $\lambda_{2,2}$ and $\lambda_{2,3}$ from the data. As a result, we allow individuals to differ in the way their manifest variables change from the first to the last measurement.

One drawback of LGMs, however, is that such models generally require large sample sizes. The more restrictions we place on a model, the fewer parameters there are to estimate, and the smaller the required sample size. The restrictions placed should, however, be in line with theory and research questions. Small sample sizes can cause problems such as high bias and low coverage (Hox & Maas, 2001), nonconvergence, or improper solutions such as negative variance estimates (Wang & Wang, 2012, p. 391), and the question is how large should the sample size be to avoid these issues. Several simulation studies using maximum likelihood estimation have provided information on required sample sizes for SEM in general, and LGM specifically. To get an indication of the required sample size, we can use some rather arbitrary rules of thumb. Anderson and Gerbing (1988) recommend $n = 100$–150 for SEM in general. Hertzog, von Oertzen, Ghisletta, and Lindenberger (2008) investigated the power of LGM to detect individual differences in rate of change (i.e., the variance of the latent slope in LGMs). This is relevant for the model in Figure 4.1 because the detection of these differences is needed if the individual rate of change over time (individual parameter estimates for the latent slope) is suitable to be used as a predictor in a regression analysis. In favorable simulation conditions (high Growth Curve Reliability, high correlation between

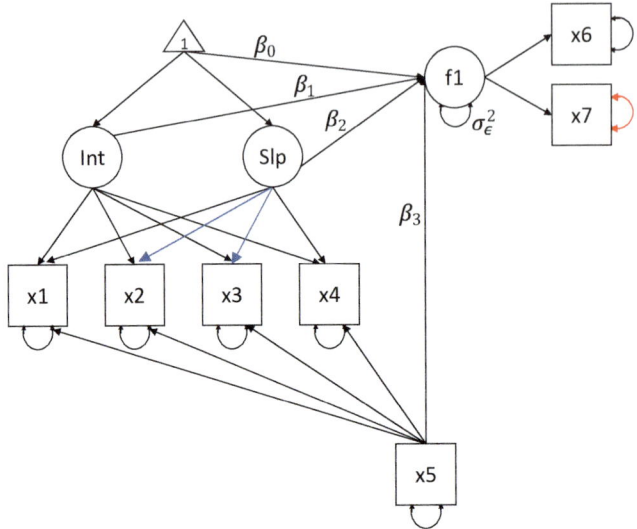

FIGURE 4.1 The LGM as used in the empirical example. The parameters of interest are the intercept of the latent factor $f1$ (β_0), $f1$ regressed on the latent intercept (β_1), the latent slope (β_2) and x5 (β_3) and the residual variance of the latent factor $f1$ (σ_ε^2). The two blue factor loadings indicate freely estimated loadings, $\lambda_{2,2}$ and $\lambda_{2,3}$ (respectively). The red residual variance parameter (θ_{77}) is highlighted throughout the empirical example

intercept and slope, and many measurement occasions), maximum likelihood estimation has sufficient power to detect individual differences in change with $n = 100$. However, in unfavorable conditions even a sample size of 500 did not result in enough power to detect individual differences in change. Additionally, the model in the simulation studies by Hertzog and colleagues contained fewer parameters when compared to the LGM model used in the current chapter, thus suggesting that running the model in this chapter would require even larger sample sizes than those recommended by Hertzog and colleagues.

Bayesian estimation is often suggested as a solution for problems encountered in SEM with small sample sizes because it does not rely on the central limit theorem. A recent review examined the performance of Bayesian estimation in comparison to frequentist estimation methods for SEM in small samples on the basis of previously published simulation studies (Smid, McNeish et al., 2019). It was concluded that Bayesian estimation could be regarded as a valid solution for small sample problems in terms of reducing bias and increasing coverage only when thoughtful priors were specified. In general, naive (i.e., flat or uninformative) priors resulted in high levels of bias. These findings highlight the importance of thoughtfully including prior information when using Bayesian estimation in the context of small samples. Specific simulation studies for LGMs can be found in papers by McNeish (2016a, 2016b); Smid, Depaoli, and Van de Schoot (2019); Van de Schoot, Broere, Perryck, Zondervan-Zwijnenburg, and Van Loey (2015), and Zondervan-Zwijnenburg, Depaoli, Peeters, and Van de Schoot (2019).

In general, it is difficult to label a sample size as small or large, and this can only be done with respect to the complexity of the model. In the remainder of this chapter we use the example of the extensive and quite complex LGM that can be seen in Figure 4.1. We show that with a sample that is small with respect to the complexity of this model, issues arise in the estimation process even with Bayesian estimation with thoughtful priors. Moreover, we provide details on diagnostics, debugging of the analysis, and the search for appropriate solutions. We show the need for both statistical and content expertise to make the most of a complicated situation.

Empirical example: analysis plan

In practice, there are instances in which only small sample data are available; for example, in the case of specific and naturally small or difficult-to-access populations. In these cases, collecting more data is not an option, and simplifying research questions and statistical models is also undesirable because this will not lead to an appropriate answer to the intended research questions. In this section we introduce an empirical example for which only a small data set was available, and at the same time the research question required the complicated model in Figure 4.1.

Research question, model specification, and an overview of data

The empirical example comprises a longitudinal study of child and parental adjustment after a pediatric burn event. Pediatric burn injuries can have long-term consequences for the child's health-related quality of life (HRQL), in terms of physical, psychological, and social functioning. In addition, a pediatric burn injury is a potentially traumatic event for parents, and parents may experience post-traumatic stress symptoms (PTSS; i.e., symptoms of re-experiencing, avoidance, and arousal) as a result. Parents' PTSS could also impact the child's long-term HRQL. It is important to know whether the initial level of parental PTSS after the event or the development of symptoms is a better predictor of long-term child HRQL, since this may provide information about the appropriate timing of potential interventions. Therefore, the research question of interest was how the initial level and the development of mothers' PTSS over time predict the child's long-term HRQL.

In terms of statistical modeling, the research question required an LGM to model PTSS development and a measurement model for the distal outcome; namely, the child's HRQL. The full hypothesized model and the main parameters of interest, i.e., the regression coefficients of the predictors for the child's HRQL, β_0 for the intercept, β_1 for HRQL regressed on the latent intercept, β_2 for HRQL regressed on the latent slope, β_3 for HRQL regressed on the covariate, percentage of Total Body Surface Area (TBSA) burned, and the residual variance σ_ε^2, are displayed in Figure 4.1. Mothers reported on PTSS at four time points (up to 18 months) after the burn injury by filling out the Impact of Event Scale (IES; Horowitz, Wilner, and Alvarez, 1979). The total IES score from each of the four time points was used in the LGM. Eighteen months post-burn, mothers completed the Health Outcomes Burn Questionnaire (HOBQ; Kazis et al., 2002), which consists of 10 subscales. Based on a confirmatory factor analysis, these subscales were divided into three factors, i.e., Development, Behavior, and Concern factors. For illustrative reasons, we only focus on the Behavior factor in the current chapter, which was measured by just two manifest variables. TBSA was used to indicate burn severity; this is the proportion of the body that is affected by second- or third-degree burns and it was used as a covariate. For more detailed information about participant recruitment, procedures, and measurements, see Bakker, Van der Heijden, Van Son, and Van Loey (2013).

Data from only 107 families was available[1]. Even though data were collected in multiple burn centers across the Netherlands and Belgium over a prolonged period of time (namely three years), obtaining this sample size was already a challenge for two main reasons. Firstly, the incidence of pediatric burns is relatively low. Yearly, around 160 children between the ages of 0 and 4 years old require hospitalization in a specialized Dutch burn center (Van Baar et al., 2015). Secondly, the acute hospitalization period in which families were recruited to participate is extremely stressful. Participating in research in this demanding and emotional phase may be perceived as an additional burden by parents.

Still, we aimed to answer a research question that required the complex statistical model displayed in Figure 4.1. Therefore, we used Bayesian estimation with weakly informative priors to overcome the issues of small sample size estimation with ML-estimation, for which the model shown in Figure 4.1 resulted in negative variance estimates.

Specifying and understanding priors

The specification of the priors is one of the essential elements of Bayesian analysis, especially when the sample size is small. Given the complexity of the LGM model relative to the sample size, prior information was incorporated to facilitate the estimation of the model (i.e., step 1 of the WAMBS checklist). In addition to careful consideration of the plausible parameter space (see Chapter 3 by Van de Schoot, Veen, Smeets, Winter, and Depaoli), we used previous results to inform the priors in our current model (Egberts, Van de Schoot, Geenen, & Van Loey, 2017).

The prior for the mean of the latent intercept (α_1) could be regarded as informative with respect to the location specification. The location parameter, or mean of the normally distributed prior $\mathcal{N}(\mu_0, \sigma_0^2)$, was based on the results of a previous study (Egberts et al., 2017, Table 4.1) and set at 26. If priors are based on information from previously published studies, it is important to reflect on the exchangeability of the prior and current study (see Chapter 2 by Miočević, Levy, & Savord). Exchangeability would indicate that

TABLE 4.1 Priors and justification for all priors that are used in the analysis

Parameter	Prior	Justification
group mean of the latent intercept (α_1)	$\mathcal{N}(26, 400)$	Previous article on different cohort (Egberts et al., 2017, Table 1)
group standard deviation of the latent intercept (σ_{Int})	$H\mathcal{N}(0, 400)$	Allows values to cover the entire parameter space for IES
group mean of the latent slope (α_2)	$\mathcal{N}(0, 4)$	Allows values to cover the entire parameter space for IES
group standard deviation of the latent slope (σ_{slope})	$H\mathcal{N}(0, 1)$	Allows values to cover the entire parameter space for IES
x1 – x4 regressed on x5 (β_{ies})	$\mathcal{N}(0, 4)$	Allows values to cover the entire parameter space for IES
group mean relation IES 3 months (x2) regressed on slope ($\mu_{\lambda_{2,2}}$)	$\mathcal{N}(3, 25)$	Centered at 3, which would be the constraint in a linear LGM. Allowed to vary between individuals to allow for between-person differences in the way manifest variables change from the first to the last measurement
group mean relation IES 12 months (x3) regressed on slope ($\mu_{\lambda_{2,3}}$)	$\mathcal{N}(12, 25)$	Centered at 12 which would be the constraint in a linear LGM. Allowed to vary between individuals to allow between-person differences in the way manifest variables change from the first to the last measurement
group standard deviation relation IES 3 months (x2) regressed on slope ($\sigma_{\lambda_{2,2}}$)	$H\mathcal{N}(0, 6.25)$	Allows for large and small between-person differences in the way manifest variables change from the first to the last measurement
group standard deviation relation IES 12 months (x3) regressed on slope ($\sigma_{\lambda_{2,3}}$)	$H\mathcal{N}(0, 6.25)$	Allows for large and small between-person differences in the way manifest variables change from the first to the last measurement
All residual standard deviations x1 – x4 ($\sigma_{\varepsilon ies}$)	$H\mathcal{N}(0, 100)$	Allows values to cover the entire parameter space for the observed variables
Intercepts factor regressions (β_0)	$\mathcal{N}(50, 2500)$	Covers the full factor score parameter space centered at the middle
Factors regressed on Level (β_1)	$\mathcal{N}(0, 4)$	Allows values to cover the entire parameter space for the factor scores
Factors regressed on Shape (β_2)	$\mathcal{N}(0, 2500)$	Allows values to cover the entire parameter space for the factor scores
Factors regressed on TBSA (β_3)	$\mathcal{N}(0, 4)$	Allows values to cover the entire parameter space for the factor scores
Residual standard deviation factors (σ_ε)	$H\mathcal{N}(0, 100)$	Allows values to cover the entire parameter space for the residuals

Note: $\mathcal{N}(.,.)$ is a normal distribution with mean and variance $\mathcal{N}(\mu_0, \sigma_0^2)$, $H\mathcal{N}(\mu_0, \sigma_0^2)$ is a half-normal distribution encompassing only the positive part of the parameter space, $U(.,.)$ is uniform distribution with a lower bound and an upper bound. In Stan code the normal distribution is specified using a mean and standard deviation $\mathcal{N}(\mu_0, \sigma_0)$, not the mean and variance $\mathcal{N}(\mu_0, \sigma_0^2)$; this causes the differences between the code in the data archive and this table.

the samples are drawn from the same population and a higher prior certainty can be used. To evaluate exchangeability, the characteristics of the sample and the data collection procedure were evaluated. Both studies used identical questionnaires and measurement intervals, and the data were collected in exactly the same burn centers. The main difference between the samples was the age of the children (i.e., age range in the current sample: 8 months to 4 years; age range in the previous sample: 8–18 years), and related to that, the age of the mothers also differed (i.e., mean age in the current sample: 32 years; mean age in the previous sample: 42 years). Although generally child age has not been associated with parents' PTSS after medical trauma (e.g., Landolt, Vollrath, Ribi, Gnehm, & Sennhauser, 2003), the two studies are not completely exchangeable as a results of the age difference. Therefore, additional uncertainty about the value of the parameter was specified by selecting a relatively high prior variance (see Table 4.1).

The priors for the regression coefficients are related to the expected scale of their associated parameters. For β_1 a $\mathcal{N}(0, 4)$ prior was specified, thereby allocating the most density mass on the plausible parameter space. Therefore, given the scale of the instruments used, and the parametrization of the factor score model, the latent factor scores can take on values between zero and 100. A regression coefficient of -4 or 4

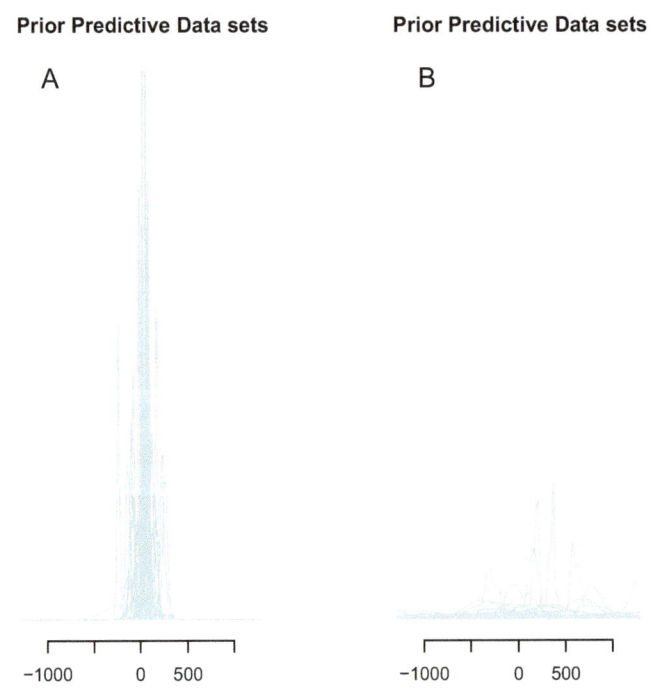

FIGURE 4.2 The effect of changing a single prior in the model specification on the prior predictive distributions of the Latent Factor Scores. The prior for β_1 is changed from weakly informative (panel A; $\mathcal{N}(0, 4)$) to uninformative (panel B; $\mathcal{N}(0, 2500)$)

would be extremely implausible. If our expected value of 26 is accurate for the intercept, this would change our predicted factor score by -104 or 104, respectively. This would constitute a change larger than the range of the construct.

For β_2 in contrast, a $\mathcal{N}(0, 2500)$ prior was specified because small latent slope values, near the prior group mean of the latent slope of zero, should be allowed to have large impacts on the latent factor scores. For instance, a slope value of 0.1 could be associated with a drop of 50 in HRQL, resulting in a coefficient of -500. Figure 4.2 shows what would have happened to the prior predictive distributions for the latent factor scores if a $\mathcal{N}(0, 2500)$ prior was specified for β_1 instead of the $\mathcal{N}(0, 4)$ prior, keeping all other priors constant. The prior predictive densities for the factor scores in panel B of Figure 4.2 place far too much support on parts of the parameter space that are impossible. The factor scores can only take on values between zero and 100 in our model specification. For more information on prior predictive distributions, see Chapter 3.

Empirical example: conducting the analysis

Based on theoretical considerations, we specified the model as shown in Figure 4.1 using the priors as specified in Table 4.1. We used Stan (Carpenter et al., 2017) via RStan (Stan Development Team, 2017a) to estimate the model and we used the advanced version of the HMC algorithm called NUTS. To run the model, we used the following code, which by default ran the model using four chains with 2,000 MCMC iterations of which 1,000 are warmup samples (note that this is similar to burn-in as discussed in earlier chapters):

```
fit_default <- sampling(model, data = list(X = X, I, K, run_estimation = 1), seed =
                         11, show_messages = TRUE)
```

For reproducibility purposes, the Open Science Framework webpage (osf.io/am7pr/) includes all annotated Rstan code and the data.

Upon completion of the estimation, we received the following warnings from Rstan indicating severe issues with the estimation procedure:

```
Warning messages:
1: There were 676 divergent transitions after warmup. Increasing adapt_delta above
0.8 may help. See
http://mc-stan.org/misc/warnings.html#divergent-transitions-after-warmup
2: There were 16 transitions after warmup that exceeded the maximum treedepth.
Increase max_treedepth above 10. See
http://mc-stan.org/misc/warnings.html#maximum-treedepth-exceeded
3: There were 4 chains where the estimated Bayesian Fraction of Missing
Information was low. See
http://mc-stan.org/misc/warnings.html#bfmi-low
4: Examine the pairs() plot to diagnose sampling problems
```

Fortunately, the warning messages also pointed to online resources with more detailed information about the problems. In what follows, we describe two diagnostics to detect issues in the estimation procedure: divergent transitions (this section) and the ESS of the MCMC algorithm (next section).

The most important warning message is about divergent transitions (warning message 1). The appearance of divergent transitions is a strong indicator that the posterior results as shown in column 1 of Table 4.3 *cannot* be trusted (Stan Development Team, 2017b, chapter 14). For detailed, highly technical information on this diagnostic, see Betancourt (2016). Very loosely formulated, the occurrence of many divergent transitions indicates that there is something going wrong in drawing MCMC samples from the posterior. When the estimator moves from one iteration to the next, it does so using a particular step size. The larger steps the estimator can take between iterations, the more effectively it can explore the parameter space of the posterior distribution (compare Figure 4.3A with 4.3B). When a divergent transition occurs, the step size is too large to efficiently explore part of the posterior distribution and the sampler runs into problems when transitioning from one iteration to the next (see Figure 4.3C). The Stan Development Team uses the following analogy to provide some intuition for the problem:

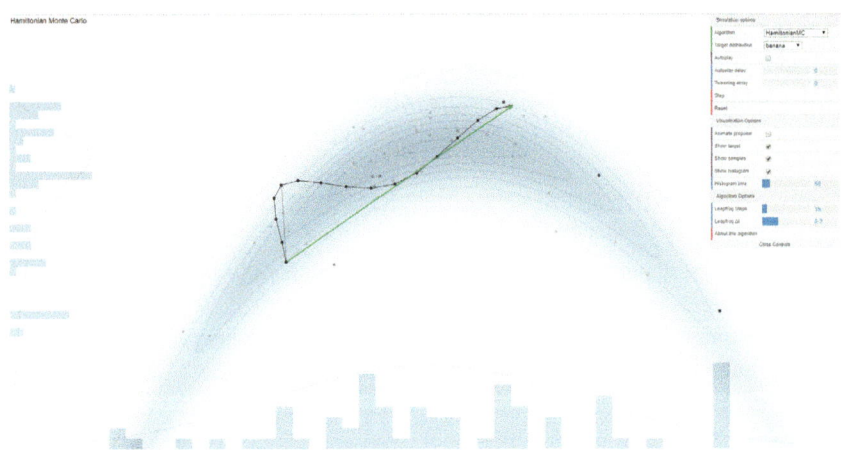

FIGURE 4.3 Effect of decreasing the step size of the HMC on the efficiency of the exploration of the posterior distribution (Panel A and B). The green arrow shows the step between two consecutive iterations. Panel A uses a large step size and swiftly samples from both posterior distributions, one of which is a normal distribution and one of which is a common distributional form for variance parameters. In Panel B, in contrast, the sampler needs more time to sample from both distributions and describe them accurately because the steps between iterations are a lot smaller. Panel C shows an example of a divergent transition, which is indicative of problems with the sampling algorithm. These screenshots come from an application developed by Feng (2016) that provides insight into different Bayesian sampling algorithms and their "behavior" for different shapes of posterior distributions. Copyright © 2016 Chi Feng

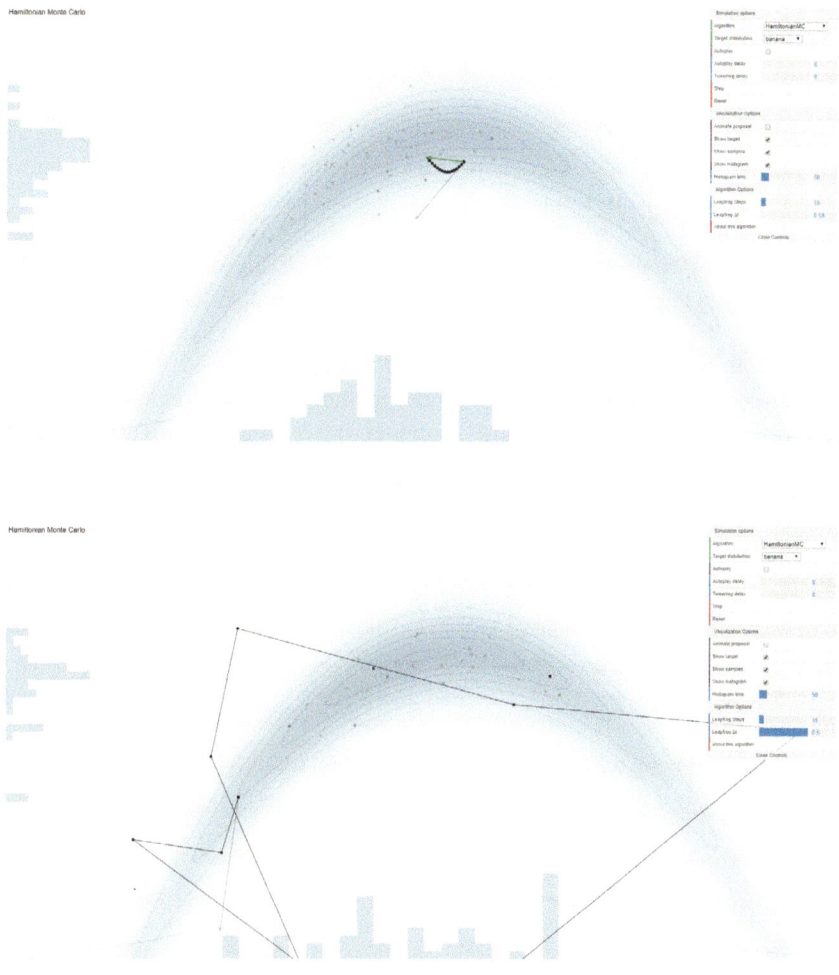

FIGURE 4.3 (Cont.)

For some intuition, imagine walking down a steep mountain. If you take too big of a step you will fall, but if you can take very tiny steps you might be able to make your way down the mountain, albeit very slowly. Similarly, we can tell Stan to take smaller steps around the posterior distribution, which (in some but not all cases) can help avoid these divergences.

(Stan Development Team, 2018)

The posterior results for the parameters of interest (β_0, β_1, β_2, β_3, σ_ε) are shown in Table 4.3, column 1. Note that these results cannot be trusted and should *not* be interpreted because of the many divergent transitions. Divergent transitions can sometimes be resolved by simply taking smaller steps (see next section), which increases computational time.

Debugging

The occurrence of divergent transitions can also be an indication of more serious issues with the model or with a specific parameter. One of the ways to find out which parameter might be problematic is to inspect how efficiently the sampler sampled from the posterior of each parameter. The efficiency of the sampling process can be expressed as the ESS for each parameter, where *sample size* does not refer to the data but to the samples taken from the posterior. In the default setting we saved 1,000 of these samples per chain, so in total we obtained 4,000 MCMC samples for each parameter. However, these MCMC samples are related to each other, which can be expressed by the degree of autocorrelation (point 5 on the WAMBS checklist in Chapter 3). ESS expresses how many independent MCMC samples are equivalent to the autocorrelated MCMC samples that were drawn. If a small ESS for a certain parameter is obtained, there is little information available to construct the posterior distribution of that parameter. This will also manifest itself in the form of autocorrelation (see also Chapter 3) and non-smooth histograms of posteriors. For more details on ESS and how `Rstan` calculates it, see the Stan Reference Manual (Stan Development Team, 2019).

In Table 4.2 we provide the ESS for α_1, β_1, θ_{77} and the factor score of mother and child pair no. 33 (denoted by fs_{33}). Factor score fs_{33} was estimated efficiently

TABLE 4.2 Examples of ESS per parameter for the different model and estimation settings we used. Each column represents a different model, and each row represents a different variable. We report ESS with the corresponding percentage of the total number of iterations that was used to estimate that particular model in brackets

Parameter	Model with default estimation settings	Model with small step size in estimation setting	Alternative I: remove perfect HRQL scores	Alternative II: IG(0.5, 0.5) prior for $_{77}$	Alternative III: replace factor scores with $x7$	Alternative IV: possible increase of variance in latent factor
fs_{33}	2390 (60%)	9843 (123%)*	2219 (55%)	1307 (33%)	–	2485 (62%)
α_1	575 (14%)	1000 (13%)	655 (16%)	145 (4%)	227 (6%)	611 (15%)
β_1	424 (11%)	1966 (25%)	487 (12%)	647 (16%)	58 (1%)	1004 (25%)
θ_{77}	20 (0.5%)	12 (0.2%)	9 (0.2%)	33 (0.8%)	–	46 (1.2%)

* With the highly efficient NUTS sampling algorithm a higher efficiency can be obtained compared to independent MC samples (Stan Development Team, 2019, chapter 15).

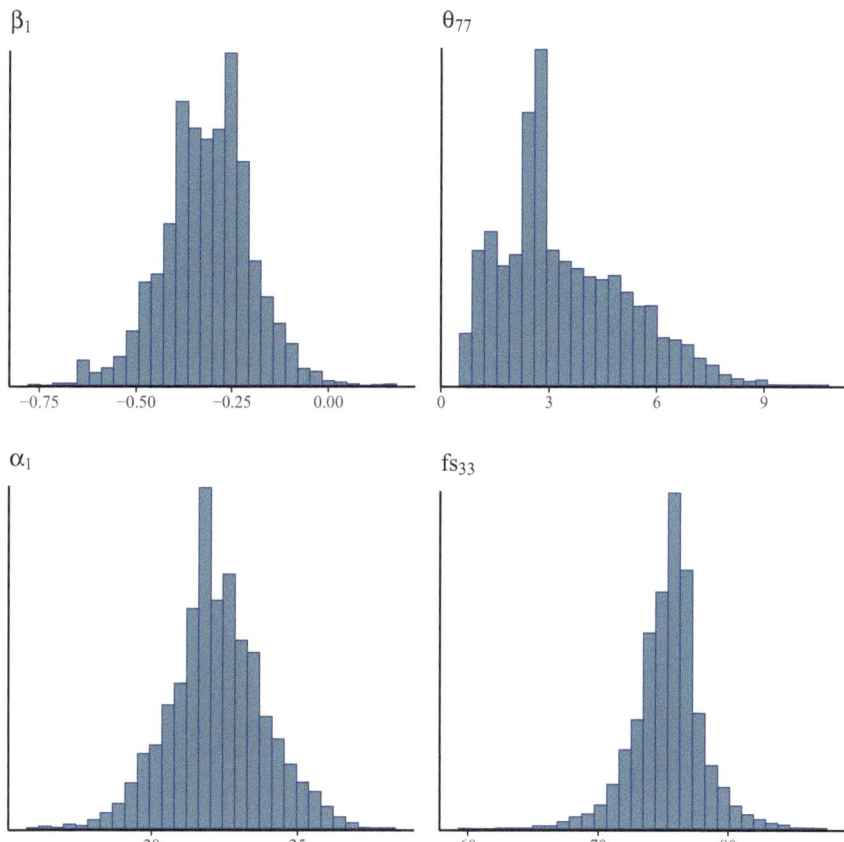

FIGURE 4.4 Histograms of MCMC samples for α_1, β_1, θ_{77} and fs_{33}. θ_{77} has a non-smooth histogram, which indicates low ESS while the smooth histogram for fs_{33} is indicative of higher ESS

and the ESS was 60% of the number of MCMC samples, followed by α_1 (14%) and β_1 (11%). θ_{77}, in contrast, had an ESS of only 0.5% of the number of MCMC samples, indicating an equivalence of only 20 MCMC samples had been used to construct the posterior distribution. There is no clear cut-off value for the ESS, although it is obvious that higher values are better and that 20 is very low. The default diagnostic threshold used in the R package `shinystan` (Gabry, 2018), used for interactive visual and numerical diagnostics, is set to 10%.

The effects of ESS on the histograms of these four parameters can be seen in Figure 4.4, which shows a smooth distribution for fs_{33} but not for θ_{77}. Based on the ESS and the inspection of Figure 4.4, the residual variance parameter θ_{77} was estimated with the lowest efficiency and probably exhibited the most issues in model estimation.

To investigate if there were systematic patterns in the divergences, we plotted the samples of the parameters fs_{33} and θ_{77} against the log posterior (denoted by lp) (see Figure 4.5). lp is, very loosely formulated, an indication of the likelihood of the data given all posterior parameters. lp is sampled for each MCMC iteration as just another parameter. Note that, in contrast to log-likelihoods, lp cannot be used for model comparison. Plots such as those in Figure 4.5 can point us to systematic patterns for the divergent transitions, which would indicate that a particular part of the parameter space is hard to explore. In Figure 4.5A it can be seen that for fs_{33}, which did not exhibit problems in terms of ESS, the divergent transitions are more or less randomly distributed across the posterior parameter space. Also, the traceplot and histogram for fs_{33} would pass the WAMBS checklist on initial inspection. There is one hotspot around the value of -1700 for the lp where a cluster of divergent transitions occurs. This is also visible in the traceplot, where it can be seen that one of the chains is stuck and fails to efficiently explore the

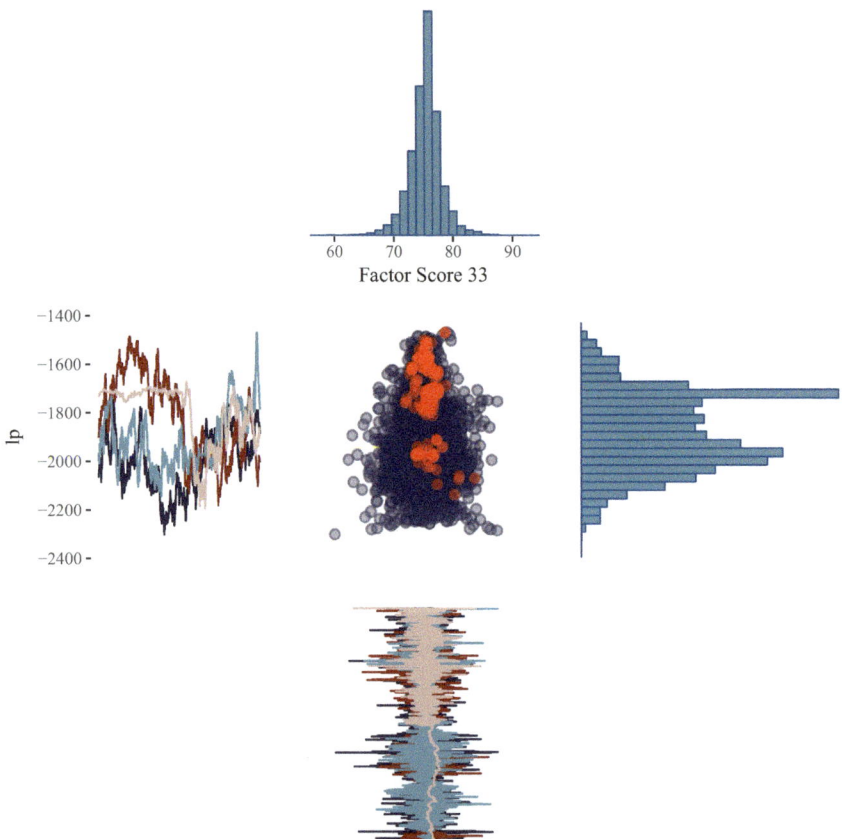

FIGURE 4.5 Plot of the posterior samples of lp (y-axis) against fs_{33} (x-axis, panel A) and θ_{77} (x-axis, panel B) with divergent transitions marked by red dots. Additionally, the histograms and trace plots of the corresponding parameters have been placed on the margins

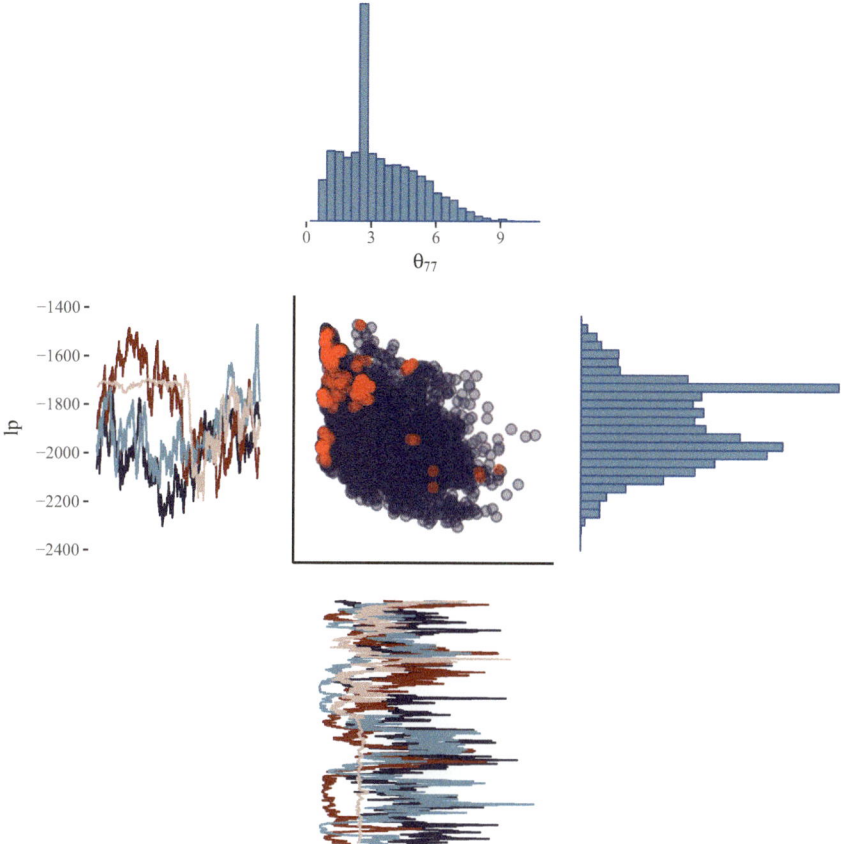

FIGURE 4.5 (Cont.)

parameter space shown as an almost horizontal line for many iterations. On closer inspection, a similar behavior in one of the chains could be seen for fs_{33} as well.

In Figure 4.5B it can be seen that for θ_{77}, which exhibited problems in terms of ESS, the divergent transitions occur mainly in a very specific part of the posterior parameter space, i.e., many divergent transitions occur close to zero. This also shows up in the traceplot, where for several iterations the sampler could not move away from zero. This indicates that our sampling algorithm ran into problems when exploring the possibility that θ_{77} might be near zero. Note that a similar issue arises in one chain around the value of 2.5 for many iterations, resulting in a hotspot which corresponds to the deviant chain for *lp*. Perhaps an additional parameter could be found which explains the issues concerning this systematic pattern of divergent transitions. For now, we continued with a focus on θ_{77}.

The first solution, also offered in the warning message provided by Stan, was to force Stan to use a smaller step size by increasing the *adapt_delta* setting of the estimator. We also dealt with the second warning by increasing *max_treedepth*, although this is related to efficiency and not an indication of model error and validity issues. To make sure we could still explore the entire posterior parameter space, we extended the number of iterations post warmup to 2,000 for each chain (iter - warmup in the code below). We used the following R code:

```
fit_small_step <- sampling(model,
                    data=list(X = X, I, K, run_estimation = 1),
                    control=list(adapt_delta = .995,
                                max_treedepth = 16),
                    warmup = 3000, iter = 5000, seed = 11235813)
```

We inspected the ESS for the same parameters again, which can be seen in Table 4.2. The problems seem to occur for the θ_{77} parameter again, and it has

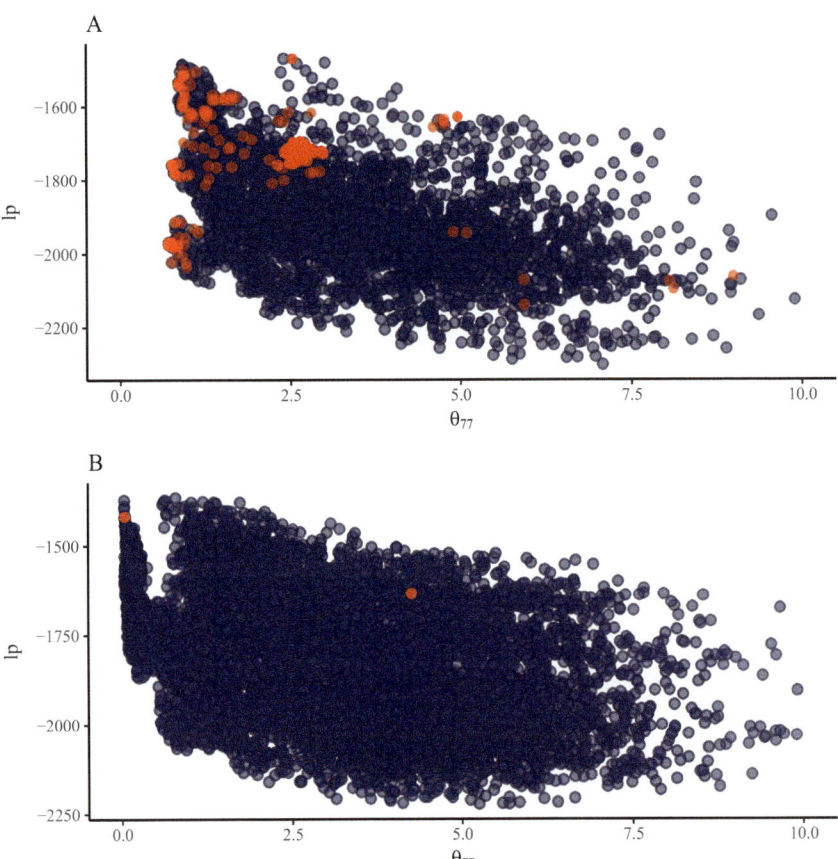

FIGURE 4.6 Plots of the posterior samples of *lp* against θ_{77} for the default estimation settings (panel A) and the estimation settings that have been forced to take smaller step sizes (panel B). Divergent transitions are indicated by red dots

even decreased in efficiency. We compared the posterior for θ_{77} and *lp* between the default estimation settings and the estimation settings forcing a smaller step size in Figure 4.6. The smaller step sizes have decreased the number of divergent transitions to almost zero. Also, they enabled more exploration of posterior parameter values near zero. However, the posterior distribution still showed signs of problematic exploration given the strange pattern of MCMC samples close to 0.5 (see step 6 of the WAMBS checklist; do posterior estimates make substantive sense?). Apparently, the solution offered by the Rstan warning message to decrease the step size, which often solves the issue of obtaining divergent transitions, failed to provide an efficient result in this case. Thus, the posterior estimates in Table 4.3, column 2 still cannot be trusted. In the next section, we briefly explore different solutions that might help us to obtain trustworthy results.

Moving forward: alternative models

At this stage in the analysis process we continue to face difficulties with obtaining trustworthy posterior estimates due to divergent transitions. After exploring a smaller step size in the previous section, there are multiple options that can be considered and these can be based on statistical arguments, substantive theoretical arguments or, ideally, on both. Some statistical options can be sought in terms of the reparameterization of the model (Gelman, 2004); that is, the reformulation of the same model in an alternative form, for instance by using non-centered parametrizations in hierarchical models, see Betancourt and Girolami (2015). This needs to be done carefully and with consideration of the effects on prior implications and posterior estimates. The optimal course of action will differ from one situation to another, and we show five arbitrary ways of moving forward, but all require adjustments to the original analysis plan. We considered the following options:

1. Subgroup removal: We removed 32 cases that scored perfectly, i.e., a score of 100, on the manifest variable $x7$. This would potentially solve issues with the residual variance of $x7$ (θ_{77}).
2. Changing one of the priors: We specified a different prior on θ_{77}, namely, an Inverse Gamma ($IG(0.5, 0.5)$) instead of a Half-Normal ($H\mathcal{N}(0, 100)$) (see Van de Schoot et al., 2015). The IG prior forced the posterior distribution away from zero. If θ_{77} was zero, this implies that $x7$ is a perfect indicator of the latent variable. Since a perfect indicator is unlikely, we specified a prior that excludes this possibility.
3. Changing the distal outcome: We replaced the latent distal outcome with the manifest variable $x7$. θ_{77} estimates contained values of zero, which would indicate that $x7$ is a good or perfect indicator and could serve as a proxy for the latent variable. Replacing the latent factor with a single manifest indicator reduces the complexity of the model.

TABLE 4.3 Results for the parameters of interest in the different models that we estimated. The mean parameter values are reported with the 95% credibility intervals in brackets

	Model with default estimation settings	Model with small step size in estimation setting	Alternative I: remove perfect HRQL scores	Alternative II: IG(0.5, 0.5) prior on θ_{77}	Alternative III: replace factor scores with x^{7*}	Alternative IV: possible increase of variance in latent factor
β_0	66.28 [39.58, 83.68]	66.83 [38.89, 84.12]	65.56 [48.78, 75.83]	62.10 [30.95, 83.52]	69.76 [39.04, 93.51]	64.46 [47.21, 78.71]
β_1	-0.32 [-0.55, -0.10]	-0.31 [-0.53, -0.09]	-0.23 [-0.44, -0.01]	-0.32 [-0.53, -0.10]	-0.40 [-0.67, -0.11]	-0.22 [-0.51, 0.10]
β_2	-31.87 [-74.80, -7.63]	-31.46 [-76.41, -7.42]	-19.39 [-44.93, -7.47]	-39.16 [-92.18, -7.81]	-47.06 [-96.94, -12.19]	-35.66 [-64.16, -15.30]
β_3	-0.61 [-0.92, -0.31]	-0.62 [-0.93, -0.31]	-0.40 [-0.67, -0.14]	-0.61 [-0.93, -0.30]	-0.78 [-1.16, -0.41]	-0.53 [-1.02, -0.06]
ε	8.36 [3.77, 10.88]	7.93 [2.92, 10.77]	4.76 [0.54, 8.29]	7.40 [1.98, 10.87]	10.06 [3.73, 13.74]	6.63 [2.07, 10.63]
Divergent transitions present	YES	YES	YES	YES	YES	NO
To what extent do we need to adjust analytic strategy? **	Not at all	Not at all	Substantially; we generalize to a different (known) population	Negligible; theory behind research question remains the same	Substantially; data-driven change of model (replacing measurement model with a single manifest variable)	Substantially; we generalize to a different (unknown) population

* note that this changes the model in a way that makes Figure an inaccurate representation.
** Assessed by the authors: DV for statistical input, and ME as the content specialist on this research area.

4. A possible increase of variance in the distal latent factor score: we removed cases that exhibited little variation between the scores on x6 and x7.

We ran the model using these four adjustments (see osf.io/am7pr/ for details). Table 4.3 presents the posterior results of these additional analyses and an assessment of the extent to which the alternatives required adjustments to the original research question. The first three alternative solutions still contained divergent transitions, and consequently the results could not be trusted. The fourth alternative solution did not result in divergent transitions. The ESS of the fourth alternative solution was still low, both in terms of the percentage of iterations and in absolute value (see Table 4.2). Although the low ESS in terms of percentage may not be resolved, the absolute ESS can be raised by increasing the total number of iterations. Even though we could draw conclusions using results from the fourth alternative solution, the rather arbitrary removal of cases changed the original research question. We investigated, and thus generalized to, a different population compared to the original analysis plan. Using an alternative model or a subset of the data could provide a solution to estimation issues. However, this could impact our substantive conclusions; for example, see β_1 in Table 4.3, for which the 95% credibility interval in the fourth alternative contained zero, in contrast to credibility intervals for this parameter obtained using other alternative solutions. As substantive conclusions can be impacted by the choices we make, the transparency of the research process is crucial.

Conclusion

Bayesian estimation with (weakly) informative priors is suggested as a solution to deal with small sample size issues. The current chapter illustrated the process of conducting Bayesian estimation with (weakly) informative priors along with the potential problems that can arise. The WAMBS checklist was a helpful tool in this process, and we propose supplementing the checklist steps with an inspection of the effective number of samples taken using MCMC. As we have shown, a low ESS can point toward specific parameters to investigate, which is especially useful for complex models with many parameters, as investigating each parameter individually would be time-consuming. We recommend using advanced statistical software (such as `Stan`) because the implemented algorithms (e.g., HMC or NUTS) can have a positive impact on the ESS, and estimates of ESS are readily available. Moreover, the use of advanced algorithms such as HMC or NUTS provides additional diagnostic information about the estimation in the form of divergent transitions, which can be used in addition to the WAMBS checklist.

The empirical example showed that even Bayesian estimation with informative priors has limits in terms of its performance for complex models with small sample sizes. Thus, using a Bayesian analysis should not be considered a "quick fix". Careful consideration of the analysis steps and the intermediate results is imperative. Different solutions can differentially impact the posterior parameter estimates and thereby the substantive conclusions, and there is a need for constant interaction and collaboration between applied researchers, who formulate the research questions, and the statisticians, who possess the statistical and methodological knowledge.

Acknowledgements

Both authors were supported by the Netherlands Organization for Scientific Research (grant number NWO-VIDI-452-14-006). This work was a result of the collaborative efforts of our project team, including Dr. Nancy van Loey and Prof. Dr. Rens van de Schoot. The synthetic data used in the empirical example were based on a study funded by the Dutch Burns Foundation (Grant No. 07.107). We thank all participating parents and the research team in the burn centers in the Netherlands and Belgium.

Note

1 The data used in the current chapter are synthetic data based on the covariance matrix of the original data, in order to avoid interference with substantive papers still in preparation at the time of writing the current chapter. The syn function from the synthpop R package was used to generate the synthetic data (Nowok, Raab, and Dibben (2016).

References

Anderson, J. C., & Gerbing, D. W. (1988). Structural equation modeling in practice: A review and recommended two-step approach. *Psychological Bulletin*, *103*(3), 411.

Bakker, A., Van der Heijden, P. G. M., Van Son, M. J. M., & Van Loey, N. E. E. (2013). Course of traumatic stress reactions in couples after a burn event to their young child. *Health Psychology*, *32*(10), 1076–1083.

Betancourt, M. (2016). Diagnosing suboptimal cotangent disintegrations in Hamiltonian Monte Carlo. *arXiv Preprint arXiv:1604.00695*.

Betancourt, M., & Girolami, M. (2015). Hamiltonian Monte Carlo for hierarchical models. *Current Trends in Bayesian Methodology with Applications*, *79*, 30.

Carpenter, B., Gelman, A., Hoffman, M. D., Lee, D., Goodrich, B., Betancourt, M., Riddell, A. (2017). Stan: A probabilistic programming language. *Journal of Statistical Software*, *76*(1). doi:10.18637/jss.v076.i01.

Depaoli, S., & Van de Schoot, R. (2017). Improving transparency and replication in Bayesian statistics: The WAMBS-Checklist. *Psychological Methods*, *22*(2), 240–261. doi:10.1037/met0000065.

Egberts, M. R., Van de Schoot, R., Geenen, R., & Van Loey, N. E. (2017). Parents' post-traumatic stress after burns in their school-aged child: A prospective study. *Health Psychology*, *36*(5), 419.

Feng, C. (2016). The Markov-chain Monte Carlo interactive gallery. Retrieved from https://chi-feng.github.io/mcmc-demo/.

Gabry, J. (2018). shinystan: Interactive visual and numerical diagnostics and posterior analysis for Bayesian models. Retrieved from https://CRAN.R-project.org/package=shinystan.

Gelman, A. (2004). Parameterization and Bayesian modeling. *Journal of the American Statistical Association*, *99*(466), 537–545.

Hertzog, C., von Oertzen, T., Ghisletta, P., & Lindenberger, U. (2008). Evaluating the power of latent growth curve models to detect individual differences in change. *Structural Equation Modeling: A Multidisciplinary Journal*, *15*(4), 541–563.

Hoffman, M. D., & Gelman, A. (2014). The No-U-turn sampler: Adaptively setting path lengths in Hamiltonian Monte Carlo. *Journal of Machine Learning Research*, *15*(1), 1593–1623.

Horowitz, M., Wilner, N., & Alvarez, W. (1979). Impact of Event Scale: A measure of subjective stress. *Psychosomatic Medicine*, *41*(3), 209–218.

Hox, J. J., & Maas, C. J. M. (2001). The accuracy of multilevel structural equation modeling with pseudobalanced groups and small samples. *Structural Equation Modeling: A Multidisciplinary Journal*, *8*(2), 157–174. doi:10.1207/S15328007SEM0802_1.

Kazis, L. E., Liang, M. H., Lee, A., Ren, X. S., Phillips, C. B., Hinson, M. I., Goodwin, C. W. (2002). The development, validation, and testing of a health outcomes burn questionnaire for infants and children 5 years of age and younger: American Burn Association/Shriners Hospitals for Children. *Journal of Burn Care & Rehabilitation*, *23*(3), 196–207.

Landolt, M. A., Vollrath, M., Ribi, K., Gnehm, H. E., & Sennhauser, F. H. (2003). Incidence and associations of parental and child posttraumatic stress symptoms in pediatric patients. *Journal of Child Psychology and Psychiatry*, *44*(8), 1199–1207.

McNeish, D. (2016a). On using Bayesian methods to address small sample problems. *Structural Equation Modeling: A Multidisciplinary Journal*, *23*(5), 750–773. doi:10.1080/10705511.2016.1186549.

McNeish, D. M. (2016b). Using data-dependent priors to mitigate small sample bias in latent growth models: A discussion and illustration using M plus. *Journal of Educational and Behavioral Statistics*, *41*(1), 27–56.

Nowok, B., Raab, G. M., & Dibben, C. (2016). synthpop: Bespoke creation of synthetic data in R. *J Stat Softw*, *74*(11), 1–26.

Smid, S. C., Depaoli, S., & Van de Schoot, R. (2019). Predicting a distal outcome variable from a latent growth model: ML versus Bayesian estimation. *Structural Equation Modeling*. doi: 10.1080/10705511.2019.1604140

Smid, S. C., McNeish, D., Miočević, M., & Van de Schoot, R. (2019). Bayesian versus frequentist estimation for structural equation models in small sample contexts: A systematic review. *Structural Equation Modeling: A Multidisciplinary Journal*, 1–31. doi:10.1080/10705511.2019.1577140

Stan Development Team. (2017a). RStan: The R interface to Stan, R package version 2.16.2. Retrieved from http://mc-stan.org.

Stan Development Team. (2017b). The Stan Core Library, Version 2.16.0. Retrieved from http://mc-stan.org.

Stan Development Team. (2018). Brief guide to Stan's warnings. Retrieved from https://mc-stan.org/misc/warnings.html#divergent-transitions-after-warmup.

Stan Development Team. (2019). Stan Reference Manual. Retrieved from https://mc-stan.org/docs/2_19/reference-manual/.

Tabachnick, B. G., Fidell, L. S., & Ullman, J. B. (2007). *Using multivariate statistics* (Vol. 5). Boston, MA: Pearson.

Van Baar, M., Dokter, J., Vloemans, A., Beerthuizen, G., Middelkoop, E., & Werkgroep Nederlandse Brandwonden Registratie R3 (2015). Epidemiologie. In *Handboek Brandwondenzorg*. Retrieved from http://handboek.brandwondenzorg.nl/deel_0/ii-epidemiologie.

Van de Schoot, R., Broere, J. J., Perryck, K. H., Zondervan-Zwijnenburg, M., & Van Loey, N. E. (2015). Analyzing small data sets using Bayesian estimation: The case of posttraumatic stress symptoms following mechanical ventilation in burn survivors. *European Journal of Psychotraumatology*, *6*(1), 25216. doi:10.3402/ejpt.v6.25216.

Wang, J., & Wang, X. (2012). *Structural equation modeling: Applications using Mplus*. Chichester: John Wiley & Sons.

Zondervan-Zwijnenburg, M. A. J., Depaoli, S., Peeters, M., & Van de Schoot, R. (2019). Pushing the limits: The performance of ML and Bayesian estimation with small and unbalanced samples in a latent growth model. *Methodology*. doi:https://doi.org/10.1027/1614-2241/a000162

5

A TUTORIAL ON BAYESIAN PENALIZED REGRESSION WITH SHRINKAGE PRIORS FOR SMALL SAMPLE SIZES

Sara van Erp

DEPARTMENT OF METHODOLOGY AND STATISTICS, TILBURG UNIVERSITY, TILBURG, THE NETHERLANDS

Introduction

In the current "Age of Big Data", more and more data is being collected and analyzed. Personal tracking devices allow data to be continuously collected, websites often track online behavior of their users, and large-scale research projects combine data from various sources to obtain a complete picture. These efforts result in large data sets with hundreds or thousands of variables. However, such data sets pose problems in terms of small sample sizes relative to the number of variables. As an example, consider the prediction of the number of murders in a community based on 125 predictors (Redmond & Baveja, 2002). We might use a simple linear regression model to determine the effects of each of the predictors. In order to fit such a model, we would need at least 125 observations, i.e., communities in this case. Now suppose we have collected data on 126 communities. We would be able to fit our linear regression model, but we would be overfitting our model to that specific sample and our results would not generalize well to a different sample from the population (McNeish, 2015). This problem would be exacerbated if we wanted to fit a more complex model including, for example, interactions between the predictors.

Penalization methods offer a solution to this problem. Regular ordinary least squares regression minimizes the sum of squared residuals to find the estimates for regression coefficients. Penalized regression adds a penalty term to this minimization problem. The goal of this penalty term is to shrink small coefficients towards zero, while simultaneously leaving large coefficients large. By doing so, penalization methods aim to avoid overfitting such that the obtained results are generalizable to a different data set from the same population. Popular penalized regression methods include the ridge, lasso, and elastic net penalties. An illustration of the classical lasso penalty is provided in the left column of Figure 5.1. The contours of the sum of squared residuals for two regression coefficients, β_1 and β_2 are shown as black

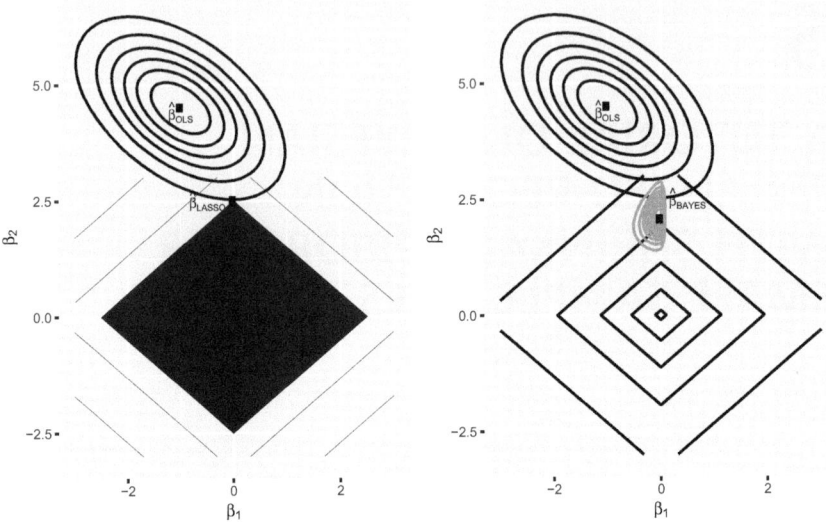

FIGURE 5.1 Contour plots illustrating classical and Bayesian penalization

elliptical lines. The classical ordinary least squares solution, $\hat{\beta}_{OLS}$, is the minimum of the sum of squared residuals which lies in the center of the contour lines. The solid black diamond represents the constraint region for the classical lasso penalty function. The lasso solution, $\hat{\beta}_{LASSO}$, is the minimum of the sum of squared residuals plus the lasso penalty term. Graphically, this solution corresponds to the point where the sum of squared residuals contour meets the constraint region of the lasso. It is clear that the lasso solution shrinks both coefficients, with β_1 becoming exactly zero in this example. This illustrates the main advantage of the classical lasso penalty, namely that it can perform automatic variable selection due to its ability to shrink small coefficients to exactly zero. By shrinking the coefficients, penalized regression will lead to an increase in bias but at the same time avoids overfitting (i.e., the bias-variance tradeoff). A comprehensive overview of classical penalized regression can be found in Hastie, Tibshirani, and Wainwright (2015).

The focus of this chapter is on Bayesian penalization, because of several advantages it has over the classical framework. Aside from the usual advantages in terms of automatic uncertainty estimates and intuitive Bayesian interpretations of quantities such as credibility intervals, the Bayesian approach offers three advantages specific to the context of penalization.

Advantage 1: natural penalization through the prior distribution

First, penalization can be incorporated naturally in a Bayesian framework through the prior distribution; see also Chapters 1–4 (Miočević, Levy, & Savord; Miočević, Levy, & Van de Schoot; Van de Schoot, Veen, Smeets, Winter, & Depaoli; Veen & Egberts). Specifically, we can choose the prior distribution in such a way that it will shrink small effects towards zero, while keeping substantial effects large. By doing so, the prior performs similarly to the penalty term in classical penalized regression. There are prior distributions that, combined with a specific posterior estimate, lead to exactly the same solution as classical penalization methods. For example, specifying double-exponential prior distributions for the regression coefficients will result in posterior modes that are the same as the classical lasso estimates (Park & Casella, 2008). These Bayesian analogues of classical penalization methods have been shown to perform similarly to and in some cases better than the classical penalization methods (Kyung, Gill, Ghosh, & Casella, 2010; Li & Lin, 2010).

Advantage 2: simultaneous estimation of the penalty parameter

The second advantage of Bayesian penalization lies in the fact that the penalty parameter can be estimated with other model parameters in a single step. The penalty parameter arises in the penalty function of classical penalization methods and determines the amount of shrinkage towards zero. Large values of the penalty parameter lead to more shrinkage towards zero and a penalty parameter equal to 0 will result in no shrinkage at all. Generally, the penalty parameter is determined based on cross-validation, but in Bayesian penalization it is simply a parameter in the prior distribution which can be given its own prior distribution.

Advantage 3: flexibility in types of penalties

The final advantage of Bayesian penalization is that it offers flexibility in terms of the type of penalties that can be considered. Classical penalization methods rely on optimization techniques to find the minimum of the penalized regression function. It is therefore easiest to consider penalty functions that are convex, meaning that they will result in one minimum. Bayesian penalized regression, on the other hand, employs Markov Chain Monte Carlo (MCMC) sampling, which allows a more straightforward implementation of penalties that are not convex.

The right column of Figure 5.1 illustrates Bayesian penalization using the double-exponential prior on the regression coefficients. The elliptical contour lines represent the sum of squared residuals, or the likelihood, centered around the classical ordinary least squares estimate $\hat{\beta}_{OLS}$. The diamond-shaped contour lines represent the double-exponential prior, which is similar to the classical lasso constraint region in the left side Figure. The main difference between classical and Bayesian penalization is the fact that Bayesian penalization results in a full posterior distribution while classical penalization results only in a point estimate. The contour of the posterior distribution is shown in grey and is clearly a compromise between the prior and the likelihood. The posterior mode estimate, $\hat{\beta}_{BAYES}$, is included and corresponds to the classical lasso solution. This double-exponential or lasso prior distribution is just one of many shrinkage priors available. In this chapter, I will summarize the most popular shrinkage priors and illustrate their use in a linear regression model using the flexible software program Stan (Carpenter et al., 2017); see also Chapters 3 (Van de Schoot et al.) and 4 (Veen & Egberts).

Running example: communities and crime

Throughout this chapter we will use a linear regression model to attempt to predict the number of murders in US communities (Redmond & Baveja, 2002). All code for running this example is available online at the Open Science Framework (osf.io/am7pr/). The data set is obtained from the University of California, Irvine machine learning repository (Dua & Graff, 2019) and includes 125 possible predictors (four are non-predictive and 18 are potential outcomes to predict) of various types of crimes for 2,215 communities. We will focus on the number of murders per 100,000 residents. The predictors include characteristics of the community as well as law enforcement characteristics. Dummy variables are created for the two nominal predictors in the data set, resulting in a total of 172 predictors. All continuous predictors are standardized to have a mean of zero and a variance of one. This is generally recommended in penalized regression to avoid the results depending on the scales of the predictors (Hastie et al., 2015). The implementation of the methods in the bayesreg package also requires the predictors to be on the same scale.[1]

Software

There are three different R packages that can be used for Bayesian penalized regression with Stan: rstanarm (Stan Development Team, 2016), brms (Bürkner, 2017), and bayesreg. Rstanarm and brms both allow the user to specify multilevel generalized linear models with formula syntax in the same way as classical multilevel generalized linear models are specified in the (g)lm(er) functions in R. Both packages support various shrinkage priors. The bayesreg package is more restricted since it currently only supports linear regression models. Contrary to rstanarm and brms, the bayesreg package is specifically designed to perform Bayesian penalized regression and has all the shrinkage priors implemented that will be discussed in the next section. We will therefore use the bayesreg package to illustrate the shrinkage priors in this chapter, although we will note which of the shrinkage priors are available in rstanarm and brms. All three packages return a Stan fit object that can be further processed and several package-specific post-estimation functions.

To fit the Bayesian penalized linear regression model with bayesreg, the package needs to be installed first following the instructions available here: https://github.com/sara-vanerp/bayesreg. Currently, missing data is not supported in bayesreg. However, it is possible to first impute the missing data using a package such as mice (Van Buuren & Groothuis-Oudshoorn,

2011) and then fit the model on each of the imputed data sets. The posterior draws for each fitted model can subsequently be combined to obtain the results. For our example, we will simply remove the observations with missingness and focus on the 343 communities with complete data. After installation, the package can be loaded into R and the model can be fit as follows:

```
library(bayesreg)
fit <- stan_reg_lm(X = X, y = y, N_train = 172, prior = "lasso")
```

The required arguments for this function are: a numeric predictor matrix X, a numeric matrix of outcomes Y, the sample size of 172 is used to estimate the model, and the prior choice. The remaining observations in the data are used to estimate the prediction error of the model.

Shrinkage priors

The goal of a shrinkage prior is to shrink small coefficients towards zero, while keeping large coefficients large. This behavior can be obtained through various types of shrinkage priors, although most shrinkage priors share some general characteristics to ensure this behavior. Specifically, shrinkage priors have a peak at zero to shrink small coefficients. Most shrinkage priors have heavy tails, which allow large coefficients to escape the shrinkage. In this section, we will discuss various shrinkage priors that are popular in the literature. The shrinkage priors are classified into two types: (1) classical counterparts, i.e., shrinkage priors that have been developed as equivalents to classical penalty functions; and (2) Bayesian origin, i.e., shrinkage priors that come from the Bayesian literature and

TABLE 5.1 Overview of the shrinkage priors

Class	Prior	Implemented in	References
Classical counterparts	Ridge	bayesreg, brms, rstanarm	(Hsiang, 1975)
	Lasso	bayesreg, brms, rstanarm	(Park & Casella, 2008)
	Elastic net	bayesreg	(Li & Lin, 2010)
Bayesian origin	Student's t	bayesreg, brms, rstanarm	(Griffin & Brown, 2005; Meuwissen, Hayes, & Goddard, 2001)
	Spike-and-slab	bayesreg	(George & McCulloch, 1993; Mitchell & Beauchamp, 1988)
	Hyperlasso	bayesreg	(Griffin & Brown, 2011)
	Horseshoe	bayesreg, brms, rstanarm	(Carvalho, Polson, & Scott, 2010; Piironen & Vehtari, 2017)
	Regularized horseshoe	bayesreg, brms, rstanarm	(Piironen et al., 2017)

do not have a clear classical counterpart. Table 5.1 provides an overview of the shrinkage priors in each class with references and the R packages in which each prior is implemented.

Classical counterparts

Figure 5.2 shows the densities (left) and survival functions (right) for the shrinkage priors corresponding to classical penalty functions. The survival function is equal to 1 minus the cumulative distribution function and is the probability that the parameter has a value greater than the values on the x-axis. For example, at $x = 0$, the survival function equals .5 for all shrinkage priors because each prior is symmetric around zero and thus the probability mass on positive values equals .5. The survival function is insightful to illustrate the tail behavior of the priors: the slower the survival function goes to zero, the heavier the tails. The Bayesian equivalent of the ridge penalty is a normal prior distribution centered around zero. The classical lasso penalty corresponds to a double-exponential prior distribution around zero. It can be seen from Figure 5.2 that the lasso prior is more peaked and has heavier tails compared to the ridge prior. The lasso prior will therefore exert more shrinkage towards zero for small coefficients, but less shrinkage for large coefficients. The classical elastic net penalty is a combination of the ridge and lasso penalties, which becomes apparent from Figure 5.2: its peak and tail lie in between those of the ridge and lasso priors.

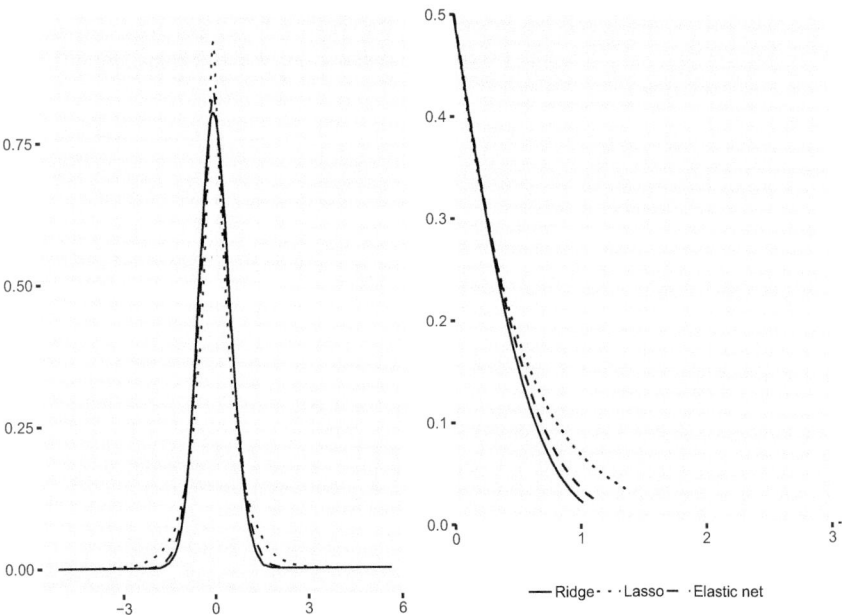

FIGURE 5.2 Density plot and survival function for the shrinkage priors with a classical counterpart

The exact form of the shrinkage priors depends on the values of the hyperparameters in the priors. For the ridge and lasso priors, the only hyperparameter is the scale which influences how spread out the prior will be. In bayesreg, these scales are equal to $\frac{\sigma_\varepsilon}{\ell}$, where σ_ε is the standard deviation of the errors. Especially for the lasso prior, including the error standard deviation in the prior is important to avoid multimodal posteriors (Park & Casella, 2008). The ℓ parameter has a similar role to the penalty parameter in classical penalized regression. Larger values for ℓ result in a smaller prior variance and thus more shrinkage towards zero. The elastic net prior requires specification of two penalty parameters: ℓ_1 which determines the influence of the lasso, and ℓ_2 which determines the influence of the ridge. Thus, setting ℓ_1 to 0 results in the ridge prior and setting ℓ_2 to zero results in the lasso prior. In bayesreg, the ℓ parameter is given a standard half-Cauchy prior distribution, so that its value is automatically determined by the data. However, other options to determine ℓ are possible, such as empirical Bayes methods or cross-validation.

Bayesian origin

Figure 5.3 presents the densities (left) and survival functions (right) for the shrinkage priors with a Bayesian origin. Student's t-distribution is similar to a normal distribution but has heavier tails. As a result, Student's t prior is more adept at leaving substantial coefficients large compared to the ridge prior. However, Student's t prior is not as peaked around zero compared to the other shrinkage priors with a Bayesian origin. The more peaked the distribution, the more shrinkage towards zero for small coefficients. The hyperlasso prior is more peaked around zero. The hyperlasso can be seen as an extension of the lasso, but with heavier tails to avoid too much shrinkage of large coefficients. The hyperlasso is a so-called global-local shrinkage prior, with a global shrinkage parameter that simultaneously shrinks all coefficients towards zero and local shrinkage parameters for each regression coefficient that allow large coefficients to escape the global shrinkage. The horseshoe prior is another global-local shrinkage prior that is very popular in the Bayesian literature. It has an asymptote at zero and heavy tails, which make the horseshoe very adept at shrinking small coefficients heavily towards zero but leaving the large coefficients large. In practice, however, it might be necessary to have some shrinkage of large coefficients. For example, some parameters might be weakly identified, meaning that there is not enough information in the data to estimate them. In this case, the heavy tails of the horseshoe prior can lead to an unstable MCMC sampler. The regularized horseshoe prior has been proposed to solve this issue. Its density is not included in Figure 5.3 since it is very similar to that of the horseshoe. Specifically, small coefficients will be shrunken in the same way as with the horseshoe prior. The main difference is that the regularized horseshoe induces some slight shrinkage on large coefficients as well. Finally, we have the spike-and-slab prior, which is a mixture of two distributions: a peaked

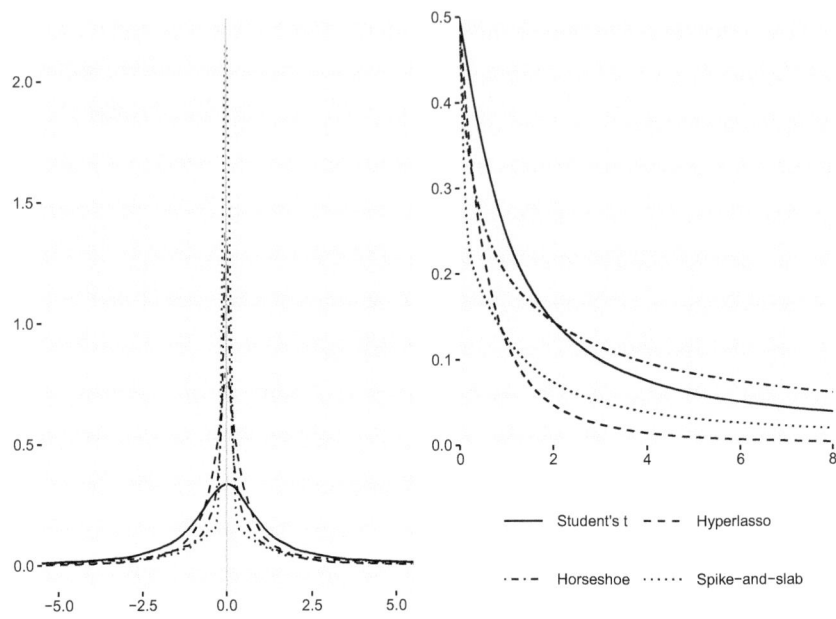

FIGURE 5.3 Density plot and survival function for the shrinkage priors with a Bayesian origin

distribution around zero for the small coefficients (the spike), and a vague distribution for the large coefficients (the slab). The bayesreg implementation of the spike-and-slab prior has a normal spike with a very small variance of .001, which is very peaked around zero, and a Cauchy slab, which has heavy tails. This can also be seen from Figure 5.3.

The hyperparameters that need to be specified for each of the shrinkage priors with a Bayesian origin in bayesreg vary. For the Student's t and horseshoe priors, no hyperparameters need to be specified since all parameters are given a prior distribution in the program. For the hyperlasso, the degrees of freedom need to be specified with smaller degrees of freedom resulting in a heavier-tailed prior. The default value in bayesreg is .5, but similarly to the horseshoe prior, this might not shrink weakly identified parameters enough so it might be necessary to specify a higher value for the degrees of freedom. The regularized horseshoe prior has the most flexibility in terms of tuning. First, for the global shrinkage parameter (which determines the general shrinkage for all coefficients simultaneously) a scale (scale_global) and degrees of freedom (global_df) parameter need to be specified. The scale influences how wide the peak is and defaults to 1. A smaller scale leads to more overall shrinkage of all coefficients. If prior information regarding the number of relevant predictors is available, it is better to determine the global scale based on this information. This can be done by setting the p0 argument equal to the a priori assumed number of relevant predictors. The global degrees of freedom parameter determines the tail behavior and defaults to 1, with larger values leading to lighter tails. For the local shrinkage parameters (which allow truly large coefficients to escape the global shrinkage), only the degrees of freedom (`local_df`) need to be specified, with 1 as default and larger values resulting in lighter tails. Finally, the regularized horseshoe differs from the horseshoe prior by asserting some shrinkage on large coefficients. This shrinkage is determined by a t-distribution with some scale (`slab_scale`) and degrees of freedom (`slab_df`). Both default to 1. Finally, for the spike-and-slab prior, a decision needs to be made on the prior for the mixing probabilities. The mixing probabilities influence whether a coefficient falls in the spike or the slab of the prior, and thus whether the coefficient will be shrunken heavily towards zero (in case of the spike) or not (in case of the slab). The first option in `bayesreg` is a Bernoulli prior on the mixing probabilities, in which each coefficient will be assigned to either the spike or the slab, with probability .5. The second option is a uniform prior, which is more flexible since the prior on each coefficient will be a mixture of the spike and the slab, where the influence of the spike and the slab is weighted by the mixing probabilities.

Practical considerations

So far, we have discussed various shrinkage priors. However, in order to apply these shrinkage priors, there are some practical issues to consider. These issues include: (1) how to choose a shrinkage prior; and (2) how to select variables based on the results.

Choice of the shrinkage prior

The type of prior information encoded in shrinkage priors is the same: some of the values for the coefficients are so small, they should be shrunken towards zero, and only substantial coefficients should remain large. However, the priors vary in the way this information is translated in practice. First, depending on the prior used and the hyperparameters chosen, the amount of shrinkage towards zero for small coefficients varies. In general, the more peaked the prior is around zero, the heavier the shrinkage for small coefficients. Second, the amount of shrinkage for large coefficients varies across priors and hyperparameters. This is mainly influenced by the heaviness of the tails. For example, compared to the lasso prior, the ridge prior has lighter tails and will therefore shrink large coefficients more towards zero than the lasso prior (given that the scale is the same in both priors). The first step in choosing a specific shrinkage prior and its hyperparameters is therefore to understand its behavior. This can be easily done by sampling draws from various priors and hyperparameter settings and comparing the density plots. To this end, the code for creating Figures 5.2 and

5.3 is made available online at osf.io/am7pr/ and can be adapted to compare various hyperparameter settings.

In general, the goal of Bayesian penalization is to avoid overfitting. To evaluate this property, we can split the data in a training and test set. We estimate the model on the training set and then use the resulting estimates for the regression coefficients to compute the responses in the test set. The prediction mean squared error (PMSE) summarizes the prediction error by taking the mean of the squared differences between computed and true responses in the test set. In bayesreg, the function pmse_lm computes the PMSE. In general, when the number of predictors is smaller than the sample size, most shrinkage priors discussed in this chapter will lead to similar prediction errors. The shrinkage priors vary more in terms of prediction errors when the number of predictors exceeds the sample size. There is some evidence that global-local shrinkage priors such as the (regularized) horseshoe and hyperlasso perform best in this situation (Van Erp, Oberski, & Mulder, 2019), but more research in this area is required. One option to choose a shrinkage prior for the application at hand is to fit the model using various shrinkage priors and then use the PMSE to guide the choice for the prior. When reporting the results, it is important to state that this strategy was used and which other shrinkage priors (including their hyperparameters) were considered.

There are two other important criteria to consider when choosing a shrinkage prior: (1) computation time, and (2) desired complexity of the resulting model. First, the computation time can vary greatly between the shrinkage priors. In general, if a shrinkage prior becomes more complex, the computation time increases, especially when adaptation of the Hamiltonian Monte Carlo sampler settings is needed. Second, since the shrinkage priors vary in the amount of shrinkage they perform, the eventual number of excluded predictors can vary across shrinkage priors. Thus, if a very sparse solution is desired, a very peaked shrinkage prior should be chosen. Note that the number of excluded predictors depends heavily on the criterium that is used to select predictors, which will be discussed in the next subsection.

To continue with the communities-and-crime example, let us compare several shrinkage priors according to the criteria mentioned above. Recall that we have a total of 172 predictors (including recoded dummy variables) and observations from 343 communities. Half of the observations (172) are used as a training set and the remaining 171 observations are used to test the model. Three different shrinkage priors are compared: the lasso, the hyperlasso, and the spike-and-slab prior with Bernoulli mixing probabilities. We can fit, for example, the spike-and-slab prior as follows:

```
fit.ssp <- stan_reg_lm(X = X, y = y, N_train =172, prior = "mixture", hyperprior_mix
= "Bernoulli", iter = 2000, chains = 4, seed = 27022019)
```

The spike-and-slab prior takes longest with 367 seconds and results in 3,851 transitions after warmup that exceeded the maximum treedepth. Therefore, we need to increase the max_treedepth setting of the sampler above 10, which will lead to an increased computation time. In general, the spike-and-slab prior has a large computation time and we might decide to not choose this prior based on time considerations.

The computation time is lowest for the hyperlasso (20 seconds), followed by the lasso (29 seconds). The PMSEs for the lasso and hyperlasso do not differ much (55.4 and 55.2, respectively). Note there are no clear cutoffs out there when a difference in PMSE is substantial or not, so it comes down to personal interpretation.

Variable selection

One of the main goals of penalized regression is to automatically select relevant predictors. Classical penalization methods such as the lasso are able to shrink small coefficients exactly to zero, thereby performing automatic variable selection. Bayesian penalization methods, on the other hand, do not perform automatic variable selection and thus a criterion is needed to select relevant predictors. Different criteria exist. One option is to simply include those predictors for which the posterior estimate exceeds a certain cut-off value, such as .1. However, it has been shown that this arbitrary choice of cut-off value leads to high false inclusion rates (Van Erp et al., 2019). A second option is to include a predictor when the credibility interval for that coefficient does not cover zero. In this approach, a choice needs to be made regarding the posterior probability to include in the credibility interval. The optimal credibility interval in terms of correct and false inclusion rates varies across priors and types of data sets. An overview of optimal credibility intervals for various simulated data sets can be found in Van Erp et al. (2019), and I use this overview to determine the credibility interval to use for the communities-and-crime example. Since we have 172 predictors and 172 observations in the training set, we select the optimal credibility intervals corresponding to condition 6, in which the ratio of predictors to observations is most equal to our example, leading to 30% intervals for both priors. We can then use the following function in bayesreg to select the variables:

```
select_lm(fit, X = X, prob = 0.3)
```

In this case, the priors select almost the same number of variables, 50 for the lasso and 47 for the hyperlasso. It appears that the shrinkage priors perform very similarly in this application, both in terms of prediction error and in terms of variable selection. To check this graphically, we can plot the posterior estimates and credibility intervals for the priors. Here, we will use the 30% credibility intervals, to immediately see which predictors are included in the model:

```
fitlist <- list(fit.lasso, fit.hyperlasso)
names(fitlist) <- c("lasso", "hyperlasso")
plots <- plot_est(fitlist, est = "mean", CI = 0.30, npar = 50, pred.nms = colnames(X))
```

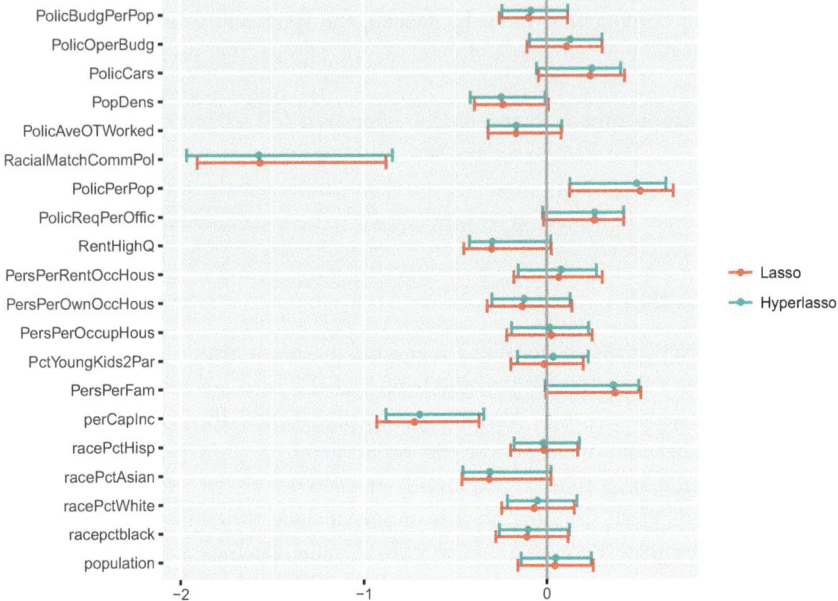

FIGURE 5.4 Comparison of posterior mean estimates and 30% credibility intervals obtained with the lasso and hyperlasso priors for a selection of predictors

The function returns a list of plots such as the one presented in Figure 5.4. Indeed, we see no substantial differences between the results of the lasso and hyperlasso. Of the predictors shown in Figure 5.4, both shrinkage priors select the racial match between community and police force, the number of police officers, and the per capita income as predictors for the number of murders in the community.

One issue with the credibility interval criterion for variable selection is its dependency on the posterior probability included in the interval, which differs across shrinkage priors and data characteristics. Moreover, credibility intervals only consider the marginal posteriors per regression coefficient separately. This might not be optimal for shrinkage priors that shrink parameters jointly (e.g., the global-local shrinkage parameters), in which case the joint credibility interval might perform differently than the marginal intervals (Piironen et al., 2017; Van der Pas, Szabo, & Van der Vaart, 2017). An alternative that does take into account the joint posterior distribution is projection predictive variable selection which is implemented in the `projpred` package (Piironen, Paasiniemi, & Vehtari, 2018).

Acknowledgement

This chapter was supported by the Netherlands Organization for Scientific Research through a Research Talent Grant (406-15-264).

Note

1 Throughout this chapter, we use the bayesreg package available from https://github.com/sara-vanerp/bayesreg. Note that there is also a bayesreg package available on CRAN (Makalic & Schmidt, 2016) which has implemented several of the shrinkage priors in linear and logistic regression models. However, contrary to the bayesreg package used in this chapter, by Van Erp, the bayesreg package on CRAN, by Makalic and Schmidt, only has a subset of the shrinkage priors implemented that are discussed in this chapter.

References

Bürkner, P.-C. (2017). Brms: An R package for Bayesian multilevel models using stan. *Journal of Statistical Software*, *80*(1), 1–28. doi:10.18637/jss.v080.i01.

Carpenter, B., Gelman, A., Hoffman, M. D., Lee, D., Goodrich, B., Betancourt, M., Riddell, A. (2017). Stan: A probabilistic programming language. *Journal of Statistical Software*, *76*(1). doi:10.18637/jss.v076.i01.

Carvalho, C. M., Polson, N. G., & Scott, J. G. (2010). The horseshoe estimator for sparse signals. *Biometrika*, *97*(2), 465–480.

Dua, D., & Graff, C. (2019). *UCI machine learning repository* [http://archive.ics.uci.edu/ml]. https://archive.ics.uci.edu/ml/datasets/Communities+and+Crime+Unnormalized.

George, E. I., & McCulloch, R. E. (1993). Variable selection via Gibbs sampling. *Journal of the American Statistical Association*, *88*(423), 881.

Griffin, J. E., & Brown, P. J. (2005). Alternative prior distributions for variable selection with very many more variables than observations. University of Warwick. Centre for Research in Statistical Methodology. https://warwick.ac.uk/fac/sci/statistics/crism/research/paper05-10.

Griffin, J. E., & Brown, P. J. (2011). Bayesian hyper-lassos with non-convex penalization. *Australian & New Zealand Journal of Statistics*, *53*(4), 423–442.

Hastie, T., Tibshirani, R. J., & Wainwright, M. (2015). *Statistical learning with sparsity*. New York, NY: Chapman & Hall/CRC Press.

Hsiang, T. C. (1975). A Bayesian view on ridge regression. *The Statistician*, *24*(4), 267.

Kyung, M., Gill, J., Ghosh, M., & Casella, G. (2010). Penalized regression, standard errors, and Bayesian lassos. *Bayesian Analysis*, *5*(2), 369–411. doi:10.1214/10-ba607.

Li, Q., & Lin, N. (2010). The Bayesian elastic net. *Bayesian Analysis*, *5*(1), 151–170. doi:10.1214/10-ba506.

Makalic, E., & Schmidt, D. F. (2016). High-dimensional Bayesian regularised regression with the bayesReg package. *arXiv Preprint arXiv:1611.06649*.

McNeish, D. (2015). Using lasso for predictor selection and to assuage overfitting: A method long overlooked in behavioral sciences. *Multivariate Behavioral Research*, *50*(5), 471–484. doi:10.1080/00273171.2015.1036965.

Meuwissen, T. H., Hayes, B. J., & Goddard, M. E. (2001). Prediction of total genetic value using genome-wide dense marker maps. *Genetics*, *157*(4), 1819–1829.

Mitchell, T. J., & Beauchamp, J. J. (1988). Bayesian variable selection in linear regression. *Journal of the American Statistical Association*, *83*(404), 1023–1032.

Park, T., & Casella, G. (2008). The Bayesian lasso. *Journal of the American Statistical Association*, *103*(482), 681–686. doi:10.1198/016214508000000337.

Piironen, J., Betancourt, M., Simpson, D., & Vehtari, A. (2017). Contributed comment on article by Van der Pas, Szabo, and Van der Vaart. *Bayesian Analysis*, *12*(4), 1264–1266.

Piironen, J., Paasiniemi, M., & Vehtari, A. (2018). *Projpred: projection predictive feature selection*. R package version 1.1.0.

Piironen, J., & Vehtari, A. (2017). Sparsity information and regularization in the horseshoe and other shrinkage priors. *Electronic Journal of Statistics*, *11*(2), 5018–5051.

Redmond, M., & Baveja, A. (2002). A data-driven software tool for enabling cooperative information sharing among police departments. *European Journal of Operational Research*, *141*(3), 660–678. doi:10.1016/s0377-2217(01)00264-8.

Team, S. D. (2016). *Rstanarm: Bayesian applied regression modeling via stan*. R package version 2.13.1.

Van Buuren, S., & Groothuis-Oudshoorn, K. (2011). Mice: Multivariate imputation by chained equations in R. *Journal of Statistical Software*, *45*(3), 1–67.

Van der Pas, S., Szabo, B., & Van der Vaart, A. (2017). Uncertainty quantification for the horseshoe (with discussion). *Bayesian Anal.*, *12*(4), 1221–1274. doi:10.1214/17-BA1065.

Van Erp, S., Oberski, D. L., & Mulder, J. (2019). Shrinkage priors for Bayesian penalized regression. *Journal of Mathematical Psychology*, *89*, 31–50. doi:10.1016/j.jmp.2018.12.004.

# PART II
n = 1

6

ONE BY ONE

The design and analysis of replicated randomized single-case experiments

Patrick Onghena

FACULTY OF PSYCHOLOGY AND EDUCATIONAL SCIENCES, CENTRE FOR METHODOLOGY OF EDUCATIONAL RESEARCH, KU LEUVEN, BELGIUM

Introduction

A solution to the problem of small sample sizes for the design and analysis of empirical research can be found in at least two ways. The first, most common, way is by examining the behavior of large-sample inferential techniques if sample size becomes smaller and smaller, and by determining the sample size at which these techniques break down; see, for example, Chapter 17 (Smid & Rosseel). The guiding question is: "How low can you go?" A second, radically different, way is to intensively study a single participant (see also Chapter 7; Maric & Van der Werff) and to use replication logic or meta-analysis to arrive at the small sample. The present chapter takes the latter perspective. Because usually large numbers of repeated measurements for each participant are recommended, this perspective paradoxically offers a "large n" solution to the problem of small sample sizes.

Besides the repeated measurements, another part of the small sample size solution presented in this chapter lies in the addition of classical experimental design elements that can support the inference: randomization, blocking, and replication (Fisher, 1926). The result will be a "single-case experiment". In the first section of this chapter, this kind of experiment will be introduced, and in the subsequent sections some design and analysis options will be added.

The single-case experiment

A single-case experiment is defined as an experiment in which one unit is observed repeatedly during a certain period of time under different levels of at least one manipulated variable (Barlow, Nock, & Hersen, 2009). This definition is important to make the distinction between single-case experiments and other types of single-case research (e.g., qualitative case studies or observational time-series research).

Furthermore, this definition clarifies that randomization and replication are not intrinsic parts of a single-case experiment. Randomization and replication are considered in this chapter as additional tools that may substantially increase the internal and external validity, and hence the credibility, of single-case experimental research.

Example

Randy is taking sleeping pills for his sleeping problems but lately he has also started to experience disturbingly severe dizziness in the morning. He contacts his physician with this complaint and together they wonder whether the dizziness is caused by the sleeping pills. They decide to set up a two-week experiment in which Randy will register the severity of his dizziness daily on a seven-point scale, while taking the sleeping pills on some days and while replacing them with placebo pills on other days.

They contact a pharmacist, who prepares a strip with 14 identical capsules; seven of them contain the active sleeping medication and seven contain powdered sucrose. The capsules are unlabelled and randomly ordered to make sure that neither Randy nor the physician will know which pills are taken on which days, to rule out expectancy effects and confirmation bias. So together they set up a randomized placebo-controlled double-blind clinical trial on a single participant. After two weeks, Randy returns to his physician and shows his results. These can be found in Figure 6.1.

Without knowing the exact sequence in which the active medication and the placebo have been administered, these results only show the general distribution of the complaints during the two-week period. This is the point where the pharmacist is contacted again to disclose the randomization sequence. The sequence happens to be

E   C   E   C   C   E   C   E   E   C   C   E   E   C

with *E* for *Experimental treatment* (sleeping pill) and *C* for *Control treatment* (placebo pill). If Figure 6.1 is transformed by connecting the dots for each experimental condition, Figure 6.2 is obtained.

Figure 6.2 shows that, by eyeballing, taking the sleeping pills is associated with higher severity ratings than taking the placebo pills. However, this is not always the case: the full line and the dotted line intersect. For example, on Day 10, a morning after taking a placebo pill, the complaints are more severe than on Day 9, a morning after taking the active sleeping medication. Now the patient and the physician may want to interpret and summarize these results even further. They may want to quantify the effect (using a measure of effect size) or they may want to know whether the effect is statistically significant

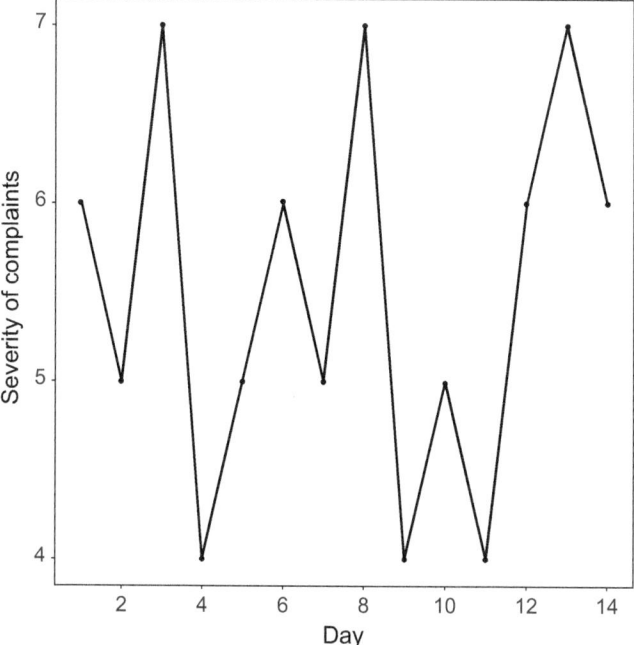

FIGURE 6.1 Example data for two weeks' daily registrations of the severity of dizziness on a seven-point scale by a single participant

(using inferential techniques). Ultimately, they have to decide on a course of action: continue or discontinue the sleeping pills, or eventually conducting some more follow-up experiments. These data and their analysis will be revisited in the Analysis section of this chapter.

Design of single-case experiments

Single-case experimental designs have been classified in many different ways, using divergent terminology (see, for example, Barlow et al., 2009). This section features one possible classification that is based on the two additional design elements: randomization and replication. Replicated single-case experiments represent one of the small sample size solutions that is central to this book.

The randomized experimental approach

In single-case experiments, *randomization* refers to the random assignment of measurement occasions to treatments. Random assignment of measurement occasions to treatments provides statistical control over both known and unknown variables that are time related (e.g., "history", "maturation"; Shadish,

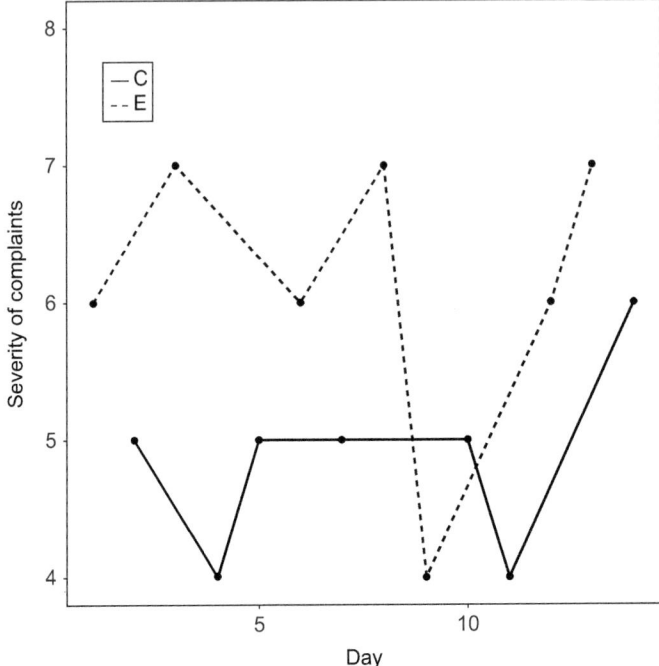

FIGURE 6.2 Example data of Figure 6.1 but distinguishing between the days when taking a sleeping pill (E for *Experimental treatment*) and days taking a placebo pill (C for *Control treatment*)

Cook, & Campbell, 2002). In addition, this random assignment is the basis for a statistical test, mentioned later in this chapter: the randomization test.

The specific random assignment procedure is intimately linked to the design of the experiment. Two broad design categories can be distinguished: alternation designs and phase designs. Alternation designs have rapid alternation of levels of the manipulated variable, just as in the Randy example. Their design characteristic is that each level of the manipulated variable can be implemented at each measurement occasion. Phase designs have consecutive measurement occasions under the same level of the manipulated variable. Their design characteristic is that the measurement occasions are divided in phases, and that the number of phases is preplanned and limited.

Alteration designs

The random assignment procedure in alternation designs is most straightforward and comparable to the random assignment procedure in group comparison designs. Because each level of the manipulated variable can be implemented at each measurement occasion, it is like tossing a coin to determine the level at each measurement occasion. A Completely Randomized Design (CRD) is obtained by randomly selecting a sequence of levels, given a prespecified total number of measurement occasions, number of levels, and number of measurement occasions for each level. To take the Randy example: there are 14 measurement occasions, two levels, and seven measurement occasions for each level. Therefore, the random assignment procedure consists of randomly selecting one sequence out of $\binom{14}{7} = 3432$ possibilities.

A CRD is rarely used in practice because it includes possibilities in which the levels are all grouped together. In the Randy example, this means that

C C C C C C C E E E E E E E

would be one of the possible designs to work with. In order to avoid such sequences, researchers use other designs, such as the Randomized Block Design (RBD). In an RBD, blocks of levels are constructed and random assignment only occurs within blocks. In the Randy example, this could mean that blocks of C E pairs are constructed and that it is randomly determined for each pair whether the order is "C E" or "E C". The obtained sequence mentioned before can be symbolized as

[EC]   [EC]   [CE]   [CE]   [EC]   [CE]   [EC]

with the square brackets indicating that random ordering only occurred within the brackets. The random assignment procedure for an RBD would consist of randomly selecting one sequence out of $2^7 = 128$ possibilities.

One could, however, argue that an RBD is overly restrictive regarding the number of permissible sequences. For example, there is no obvious reason why a sequence like

E E C E C C E C E E C C E C

should be avoided, although it is impossible given the RBD specification. A workable compromise between a CRD and an RBD is to use the specifications of the CRD but to limit the number of consecutive measurement occasions for the same level. In the Randy example, this could mean that there are 14 measurement occasions, two levels, and seven measurement occasions for each level, and that the maximum number of consecutive measurement occasions for the same level is specified at two (to avoid phases of three consecutive measurement occasions for the same level). This random assignment procedure implies that 518 possibilities of the original 3,432 CRD possibilities are permissible, which is more than four times the number of RBD possibilities. The logic of this design is most similar to what Barlow et al. (2009) called an Alternating Treatments Design (ATD).

Phase designs

The random assignment procedure in phase designs is less obvious and has no corresponding group comparison design analogue. Because the measurement occasions are divided in phases and the number of phases is preplanned and limited, it is not possible to randomly determine the level at each measurement occasion. For example, phase designs are denoted as AB designs (two levels of the manipulated variable, two phases), ABA designs (two levels of the manipulated variable, three phases, with the third phase called a "reversal" or "withdrawal" phase), ABAB designs (two levels of the manipulated variable, four phases), ABACABA designs (three levels of the manipulated variable, seven phases), and so on. Phase designs need phases, so once a certain level of the manipulated variable is started, several measurement occasions for that level should follow.

The one component of phase designs that can be randomly determined is the moment of the first measurement occasion after a phase transition. Figure 6.3 shows

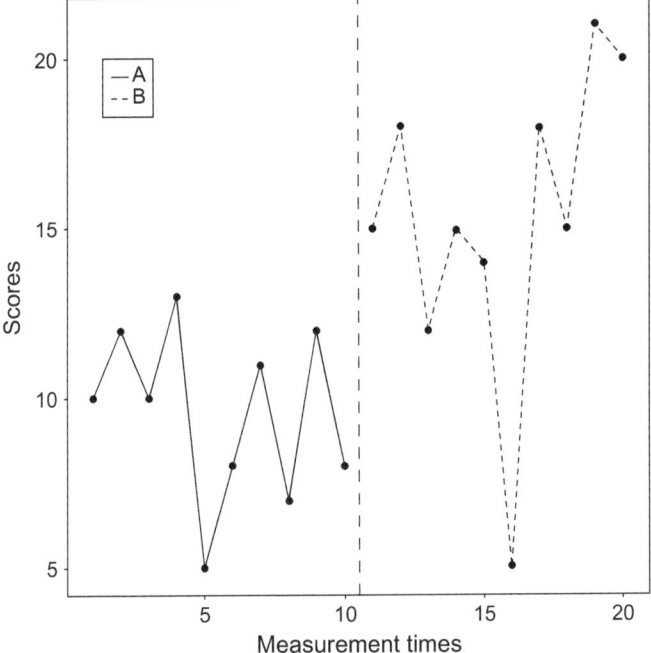

FIGURE 6.3 Hypothetical data for a single-case experiment using an AB design with 20 measurement occasions: 10 in the baseline phase (A) and 10 in the treatment phase (B)

hypothetical results for an AB design. There are 20 measurement occasions, 10 for level A and 10 for level B. The first measurement occasion after the (only) phase transition is the 11th. This moment might have been randomly determined. For example, given 20 measurement occasions and at least three measurement occasions in each phase, this results in 15 possibilities going from

A A A B B B B B B B B B B B B B B B B B

to

A A A A A A A A A A A A A A A A A B B B

Random assignment in such an AB design involves randomly selecting one of the 15 possibilities out of this list. A similar procedure can be followed in ABA and ABAB designs, and other phase designs, with the list of possibilities for each of these designs generated by combining the possible moments for two or more phase transitions.

Phase logic can be combined with alternation logic if the order of the phases is allowed to be determined randomly. For example, if the previous specifications can be extended to include designs with a B phase before an A phase, then the previous 15 possibilities are combined with another 15 possibilities going from

B B B A A A A A A A A A A A A A A A A A

to

B B B B B B B B B B B B B B B B B A A A

The combination of phase logic and alternation logic results in even more combination possibilities for ABA designs, ABAB designs, ABACABA designs, and so on.

The replicated experimental approach

Replication is essential for many research endeavors, and replicability may even be considered as a demarcation criterion between science and non-science (Open Science Collaboration, 2015). In single-case research, replicability pertains to the results at the single-case level, and two basic procedures have been part of single-case research since its earliest inception (Barlow et al., 2009): direct replication and systematic replication. Direct replication is the repetition of the same experiment by the same researcher; systematic replication is the repetition of the experiment with one or more variations as compared to the original experiment (e.g., another setting, another outcome variable, another treatment). From a design perspective, the distinction between sequential and simultaneous replications is crucial (Onghena & Edgington, 2005).

Sequential replication designs

The most common way to include replication in the design is by performing single-case experiments one by one. For example, single-case experiments in a hospital might be performed with consecutive patients. The results of the earlier experiments in the series can be used as prior information to optimize the later single-case experiments. This does not mean that in such a sequential replication design, the next experiment is only started if the previous one is completely finished; it just means that the timing is not preplanned and that the replications do not necessarily overlap in time.

Simultaneous replication designs

A special category of single-case designs is derived if the replications are preplanned and simultaneous. In a so-called "multiple-baseline across-participants design", several AB phase designs are conducted at the same time, and the B phases are started at different "staggered" moments. For example, Figure 6.4 shows the results of a four-week multiple-baseline design across three children for evaluating the effect of a behavioral intervention on the general distress level of the children as assessed daily by the staff at a daycare center. The intervention is started after the first week for the first child, after the second week for the second child, and after the third week for the third child. If there is a functional relation between the intervention and the distress, then the distress is expected to decrease after the intervention is implemented for the target child, but not for other children. In order to check for this differential effect, the results of all children are monitored simultaneously. If there would be a more general external cause of the decrease in distress, then all children would be affected (e.g., by a change in policy at the daycare center). Hence in multiple-baseline across-participants designs both within-AB and between-AB comparisons are possible and important. Simultaneous replication designs, in contrast to sequential replication designs, have the advantage that the confounding effects of "history" (external events) can be controlled by the between-series comparisons (Onghena & Edgington, 2005).

Classical multiple-baseline designs, with AB phase designs as building blocks, have also been proposed across behaviors (within one participant) and across settings (within one participant), but simultaneous replication designs can be constructed with other phase and alternation designs as well.

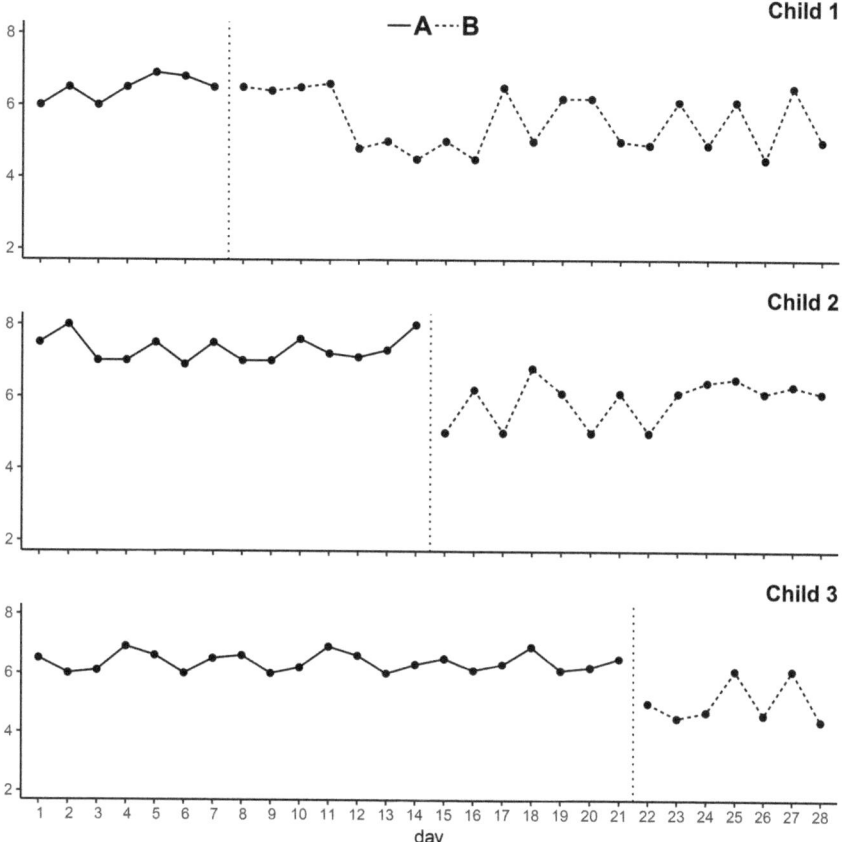

FIGURE 6.4 Hypothetical data for a single-case experiment using a four-week multiple-baseline design across three children for evaluating the effect of a behavioral intervention on the general distress level of the children as assessed daily by the staff at a daycare center

Analysis of single-case experiments

Several authors have contended that there is controversy regarding the analysis of data collected in single-case experiments and that these controversies should be resolved before making recommendations (see, for example, Kratochwill et al., 2010), but this is not the point of departure in the present section. Controversies in data analysis are intrinsic to making sense of data and to scientific inference in general, and single-case research is no exception (see, for example, discussions on Bayesian versus frequentist statistics, Neyman–Pearson versus Fisher approaches, and parametric versus nonparametric techniques; Silberzahn et al., 2018). Our point of departure is that all techniques that have been proposed for general data analysis can, in one way or another, be modified to suit single-case data analysis, taking into account the defining characteristics of single-case data (for an elaboration of this perspective, see Onghena, Michiels, Jamshidi, Moeyaert, & Van Den Noortgate, 2018).

Without going into the details of all possible data-analytical techniques, it is important to highlight three different dichotomies that have to be taken into account when analyzing (single-case) data. These dichotomies are sometimes muddled up in applications or discussions and lead to dispensable controversy. The first dichotomy is descriptive versus inferential use of statistics. The other two dichotomies fall within the realm of inferential statistics: model- versus design-based inference on the one hand, and unilevel versus multilevel inference on the other hand.

Descriptive versus inferential statistics

Statistics can be used for description and statistics can be used for inference (Moore & Notz, 2017). *Descriptive use* refers to summarizing the observations at hand and *inferential use* refers to making statements (inferences) about unobserved quantities or patterns. In the latter case it is important to be explicit about the kind of inferences one wants to make: population inferences, causal inferences, or inferences to future observations.

If description is the only purpose, then tables, graphs, and descriptive measures suffice. Visual inspection and analysis, which is the most common and popular technique for analyzing single-case data, falls within this category. Visual analysis involves a time-series plot of the results and a systematic interpretation of six data aspects that should be evident in the plot: the level of the measurements within and between phases, possible trends, the variability within and between phases, the immediacy of the effect after the introduction of the treatment, the overlap of the measurements in different phases, and the consistency of data patterns across similar phases (Kratochwill et al., 2010). In addition, each of these data aspects may be quantified using a descriptive measure or an effect size statistic (Tanious, De, Michiels, Van Den Noortgate, & Onghena, 2019).

Model- versus design-based inference

If statistics are used for inferential purposes, then one of the most basic distinctions is the distinction between model- and design-based inference (Koch & Gillings, 1984). In model-based inference, a statistical model is fitted to the observed data and the parameters and their uncertainty are estimated from the data. In design-based inference, the data are analyzed in accordance with the way the data were collected; the only stochastic element entering the calculations refers to the sampling scheme or the assignment procedure. Although in practice both model and design information might be integrated and combined, the results of model-based inference and design-based inference in their purest forms do not necessarily coincide (Gregoire, 1998). A prototypical example of model-based inference for a single-case experiment is time-series analysis (Tarlow & Brossart, 2018). A prototypical example of design-based inference for a single-case experiment is a randomization test and a confidence interval based on randomization test inversion (Michiels, Heyvaert, Meulders, & Onghena, 2017).

Unilevel versus multilevel inference

In replication designs, more than one level of inference is involved: the repeated measurements are nested within participants, and the participants can be conceptualized as a random sample from a target population (Moeyaert, Ferron, Beretvas, & Van Den Noortgate, 2014; Onghena et al., 2018). In this setting, multilevel inference can be conceptualized as a meta-analytical model (Van Den Noortgate & Onghena, 2003) or can be the result of using combination methods following a design-based approach (Levin, Ferron, & Gafurov, 2018; Tyrell, Corey, Feldman, & Silverman, 2013). Figure 6.5 shows the fourfold classification that arises by crossing the two inferential dichotomies, together with the prototypical examples.

An example of unilevel design-based inference

Unilevel design-based inference will be used for the Randy example and the data in Figures 6.1 and 6.2. This approach was selected because it is appealing for a properly designed experiment with a limited number of repeated measurements, and because it is relatively easy to explain and to understand. Furthermore, the approach stays close to the data and the data description, and makes minimal statistical assumptions, which is most compatible with the behavior analytical perspective from which the single-case experimental design tradition grew (Jacobs, 2019).

Take the data in Figure 6.2. In the Rubin model for causal inference, the causal effect is defined by E − C at a given measurement occasion and the Average Causal Effect is obtained by averaging over all measurement occasions (Holland, 1986). The fundamental problem of causal inference is that on a given

	Model-based	**Design-based**
Unilevel	Time series models	Randomization-based inference
Multilevel	Meta-analytical models	Combination methods

FIGURE 6.5 Classification of data-analytic strategies for (replicated) single-case experiments

measurement occasion only one observation (for one of the treatment levels) can be made; the observation for the other treatment level (the counterfactual) is missing. For example, on Day 1, there is an observation for E, but there is no observation for C. On Day 2, it is the other way around, and so on. The observed data were:

E	C	E	C	C	E	C	E	E	C	C	E	E	C
6	5	7	4	5	6	5	7	4	5	4	6	7	6

but the counterfactual is missing:

C	E	C	E	E	C	E	C	C	E	E	C	C	E
?	?	?	?	?	?	?	?	?	?	?	?	?	?

The design-based solution to the fundamental problem of causal inference is to examine what happens if there was no relation between x and y whatsoever (i.e., null hypothesis reasoning). In that case, the missing data are known. If the null hypothesis were true, then exactly the same series of data would be observed irrespective of the treatment level to which that occasion was assigned.

This null hypothesis reasoning can now be used to evaluate whether the observed data are extreme or unexpected in any way, given that the null hypothesis is true. A first step is to summarize the data in a test statistic. Suppose Randy and the physician agreed to take the absolute difference in means as their primary outcome (absolute difference because they were not sure about the direction of the effect). For the observed data, this test statistic amounts to $| 6.1428 - 4.8571 | = 1.2857$ on the seven-point scale. The second step is to calculate this test statistic for all random assignments that could have been chosen. This calculation makes sense, because if the null hypothesis were true, then the data are a fixed time series of numbers whatever random assignment was selected.

Suppose an RBD was used, then a total of 128 test statistic values are calculated (with the observed value as one of them). These 128 values form the reference distribution in which the observed value is located. A dot plot representation of the reference distribution for the difference in means between T and C is shown in Figure 6.6. The calculations needed to construct this reference distribution are tedious, but fortunately user-friendly software is available (see Bulté & Onghena, 2008, 2009, 2013; De, Michiels, Vlaeyen, & Onghena, 2017).

A third step is to calculate the probability to arrive at a test statistic value that is equal to or even more extreme than the observed value if the null hypothesis were true. This is the p-value of the randomization test. Figure 6.6 shows that the observed value of 1.2857 is in the right tail. Actually, there are four positive values equal to 1.2857 and one even larger, and there are four negative values

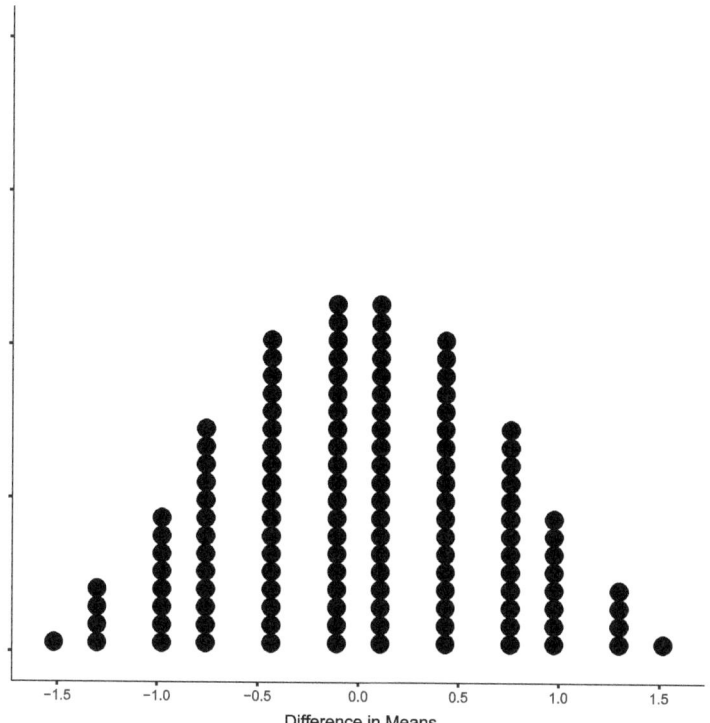

FIGURE 6.6 Dot plot of the randomization distribution for the difference in means between the E- and the C-scores in Figure 6.2 if an RBD was used

equal to −1.2857 and one even smaller. Therefore, the *p*-value is 10/128 = .0781. If a traditional 5% significance level were used, this result would be labeled as "not statistically significant".

However, as was mentioned before, in design-based inference the data are analyzed in accordance with the way the data were collected. If the data were collected using a CRD, then the randomization test *p*-value would have been 154/3432 = .0449. If the data were collected using a more prudent ATD with a maximum of two consecutive measurement occasions for the same level, then the randomization test *p*-value would have been 24/518 = .0463.

One caveat is that *p*-values should always be interpreted cautiously. For a randomized single-case experiment, such as in this example, neither random sampling nor a population of participants is involved. Hence classical population inference is out of the question. The only inference that is possible is *causal inference* for the particular participant involved in the study. Furthermore, this causal inference is probabilistic and tentative. There is no 100% certainty that the sleeping pills are responsible for the increase in dizziness, and the results of this experiment cannot guarantee that a reduction of the medication in the future will have the same beneficial effect as in the actual experiment.

Conclusion

In this chapter, a small sample size solution was provided by turning the problem upside down. Instead of looking at the population of participants from which only a small number of participants can be sampled, the starting point can be an intensive study of a single participant that can be repeated in other participants. In this perspective, a single participant is considered as the population and repeated measurements constitute the sample from that population. If there is more than one participant, then the results for the other participants are considered replications. In addition, the chapter demonstrated how randomized single-case experiments can be designed and analyzed. The resulting inference is about establishing a functional relation between a manipulated variable and an outcome variable for a single participant, which can be accomplished by using counterfactual reasoning, as illustrated with an example.

References

Barlow, D. H., Nock, M. K., & Hersen, M. (2009). *Single case experimental designs: Strategies for studying behavior for change* (3rd ed.). Boston, MA: Pearson/Allyn and Bacon.

Bulté, I., & Onghena, P. (2008). An R package for single-case randomization tests. *Behavior Research Methods*, *40*(2), 467–478. doi:10.3758/BRM.40.2.467.

Bulté, I., & Onghena, P. (2009). Randomization tests for multiple baseline designs: An extension of the SCRT-R package. *Behavior Research Methods*, *41*(2), 477–485. doi:10.3758/BRM.41.2.477.

Bulté, I., & Onghena, P. (2013). The single-case data analysis package: Analysing single-case experiments with R software. *Journal of Modern Applied Statistical Methods*, *12* (2), 450–478.

De, T. K., Michiels, B., Vlaeyen, J. W. S., & Onghena, P. (2017). One by one: A Shiny web-app for the design and analysis of single-case experiments. Poster presented at the useR! annual conference, Brussels, Belgium. www.user2017.brussels/uploads/Tamal-Kumar-De_170623_103005.pdf.

Fisher, R. A. (1926). The arrangement of field experiments. *Journal of the Ministry of Agriculture of Great Britain*, *33*, 503–513.

Gregoire, T. G. (1998). Design-based and model-based inference in survey sampling: Appreciating the difference. *Canadian Journal of Forest Research*, *28*(10), 1429–1447.

Holland, P. W. (1986). Statistics and causal inference. *Journal of the American Statistical Association*, *81*(396), 945–960. doi:10.1080/01621459.1986.10478354.

Jacobs, K. W. (2019). Replicability and randomization test logic in behavior analysis. *Journal of the Experimental Analysis of Behavior*, *111*(2), 329–341. doi:10.1002/jeab.501.

Koch, G. G., & Gillings, D. B. (1984). Inference, design based vs. model based. In N. L. Johnson and S. Kotz (Eds.), *Encyclopedia of statistical sciences* (Vol. 4, pp. 84–88). New York, NY: Wiley.

Kratochwill, T. R., Hitchcock, J. R., Horner, R. H., Levin, J. R., Odom, S. L., Rindskopf, D. M., & Shadish, W. R. (2010). Single-case design technical documentation. What Works Clearinghouse. https://files.eric.ed.gov/fulltext/ED510743.pdf.

Levin, J. R., Ferron, J. M., & Gafurov, B. S. (2018). Comparison of randomization-test procedures for single-case multiple-baseline designs. *Developmental Neurorehabilitation*, *21* (5), 290–311. doi:10.1080/17518423.2016.1197708.

Maric, M., & Van der Werff, V. (2020). Single-case experimental designs in clinical intervention research. In R. van de Schoot and M. Miočević (Eds.), *Small sample size solutions: A guide for applied researchers and practitioners*. Abingdon: Taylor & Francis.

Michiels, B., Heyvaert, M., Meulders, A., & Onghena, P. (2017). Confidence intervals for single-case effect size measures based on randomization test inversion. *Behavior Research Methods*, *49*(1), 363–381. doi:10.3758/s13428-016-0714-4.

Moeyaert, M., Ferron, J. M., Beretvas, S., & Van Den Noortgate, W. (2014). From a single-level analysis to a multilevel analysis of single-subject experimental data. *Journal of School Psychology*, *52*(2), 191–211. doi:10.1016/j.jsp.2013.11.003.

Moore, D. S., & Notz, W. I. (2017). *Statistics: Concepts and controversies* (9th ed.). New York, NY: W. H. Freeman.

Onghena, P., & Edgington, E. S. (2005). Customization of pain treatments: Single-case design and analysis. *Clinical Journal of Pain*, *21*(1), 56–68. doi:10.1097/00002508-200501000-00007.

Onghena, P., Michiels, B., Jamshidi, L., Moeyaert, M., & Van Den Noortgate, W. (2018). One by one: Accumulating evidence by using meta-analytical procedures for single-case experiments. *Brain Impairment*, *19*(1), 33–58. doi:10.1017/BrImp.2017.25.

Open Science Collaboration. (2015). Estimating the reproducibility of psychological science. *Science*, *349*(6251), aac4716. 10.1126/science.aac4716.

Shadish, W. R., Cook, T. D., & Campbell, D. T. (2002). *Experimental and quasi-experimental designs for generalized causal inference*. Boston, MA: Houghton Mifflin.

Silberzahn, R., Uhlmann, E. L., Martin, D. P., Anselmi, P., Aust, F., Awtrey, E., ... Nosek, B. A. (2018). Many analysts, one data set: Making transparent how variations in analytic choices affect results. *Advances in Methods and Practices in Psychological Science*, *1* (3), 337–356. doi:10.1177/2515245917747646.

Smid, S. C., & Rosseel, Y. (2020). SEM with small samples: Two-step modeling and factor score regression versus Bayesian estimation with informative priors. In R. van de Schoot and M. Miočević (Eds.), *Small sample size solutions: A how to guide for applied researchers and practitioners*. Abingdon: Taylor & Francis.

Tanious, R., De, T. K., Michiels, B., Van Den Noortgate, W., & Onghena, P. (2019). Assessing consistency in single-case ABAB phase designs. *Behavior Modification*. doi:10.1177/0145445519837726.

Tarlow, K. R., & Brossart, D. F. (2018). A comprehensive method of single-case data analysis: Interrupted Time-Series Simulation (ITSSIM). *School Psychology Quarterly*, *33*(4), 590–603. doi:10.1037/spq0000273.

Tyrell, P. N., Corey, P. N., Feldman, B. M., & Silverman, E. D. (2013). Increased statistical power with combined independent randomization tests used with multiple-baseline design. *Journal of Clinical Epidemiology*, *66*(6), 691–694. doi:10.1016/j.jclinepi.2012.11.006.

Van Den Noortgate, W., & Onghena, P. (2003). Hierarchical linear models for the quantitative integration of effect sizes in single-case research. *Behavior Research Methods, Instruments & Computers*, *35*(1), 1–10. doi:10.3758/BF03195492.

7
SINGLE-CASE EXPERIMENTAL DESIGNS IN CLINICAL INTERVENTION RESEARCH

Marija Maric

DEPARTMENT OF DEVELOPMENTAL PSYCHOLOGY, UNIVERSITY OF AMSTERDAM, AMSTERDAM, THE NETHERLANDS

Vera van der Werff

DEPARTMENT OF DEVELOPMENTAL PSYCHOLOGY, UNIVERSITY OF AMSTERDAM, AMSTERDAM, THE NETHERLANDS

Introduction

Testing effects of clinical interventions has been an exciting and demanding endeavor for many psychology researchers for over seven decades. Most researches use Randomized Controlled Trial (RCT) designs to answer questions about the efficacy of their interventions, and the underlying mechanisms; see also Chapter 10 (Kavelaars). In RCTs, participants are randomized to either an active intervention under investigation or to a wait-list and/or alternative intervention condition, and the mean effects on a certain construct (e.g., depression symptoms) are compared across conditions. Because of their experimental character and great applicability, RCTs are seen as the gold standard for intervention research (Versluis, Maric, & Peute, 2014). At the same time, several challenges have been identified related to the conduct of RCTs (i.e., time- and cost-intensiveness) and dissemination of results (i.e., do the results generalize to participants met in usual clinical practice (Cartwright & Munro, 2010). In the past two decades one other design has received increasing attention, namely single-case experimental design (SCED); see also Chapter 6 (Onghena).

SCEDs have been recognized as a valuable alternative for RCTs or as a necessary initial step (Gaynor & Harris, 2008; Maric, Wiers, & Prins, 2012; Norell-Clarke, Nyander, & Jansson-Fröjmark, 2011). SCEDs can be utilized in populations high in heterogeneity or specific comorbidity, when collecting large data would be unfeasible within the time limits of a research project. A SCED could also be conducted as a first step in testing effects of innovative interventions prior to doing this in RCTs. In that way, the two designs can complement each other. An example of this strategy is illustrated in Jarrett and Ollendick's (2012) study in which an innovative therapy protocol has been tested in eight young clients with comorbid attention deficit hyperactivity disorder (ADHD) and anxiety disorders. Therapy protocol involved elements of individual cognitive behavioral therapy (CBT) for anxiety and parent training for ADHD. As we know almost nothing about which treatment could be used to tackle this type of comorbidity (Maric, 2018), this study can be seen as an important first step generating initial information about the effectiveness of this new therapy form, after which clinical researchers could have a go and test it in a large group study. Finally, and importantly, the value of SCEDs lays in the fact that these designs also form a great opportunity to stimulate collaboration between research and practice, unifying questions that emerge from clinical practice and research methodology to test these questions on a single-client level (Borckardt et al., 2008; Maric, 2018).

The goal of the current chapter is to define the most important characteristics of SCEDs in the context of clinical intervention research and provide a client case example. We conclude with an outline of the current challenges in the use of SCEDs in clinical intervention research.

Single-case experimental designs: definition and most important features

A SCED evaluates treatment effects on a case-by-case basis. The participant receives several assessments before, during, and after treatment. In contrast to an RCT, there is no comparison between groups. A SCED is a within-subject design in which participants are compared with themselves. For example, the treatment phase (the so-called B phase) is compared to the time period before the treatment, in which the client did not receive any treatment: the so-called baseline (A phase). In this way, a participant forms its own "control group" (Smith, 2012). To form a good control, the participant gets multiple assessments in the different phases. Even though it seems like there is just one participant serving the complete study, there are many data points observed and nested in this one individual. Also, although the term "single-case" suggests that a SCED concerns the analysis of just one participant, it can also be more than that. For example, meta-analysis methods are increasingly implemented nowadays based on multiple SCED studies (Manolov, Guilera, & Sierra, 2014; Onghena, Michiels, Jamshidi, Moeyaert, & Van Den Noortgate, 2018). SCEDs can be used to provide answers to the questions related to intervention effectiveness; examples include: "Does mindfulness work better than doing nothing?" or "Does cognitive therapy work better than behavioral therapy?" Also, mechanisms underlying intervention effects could be tested: "Do anxiety symptoms change before ADHD symptoms change during an intervention or vice versa?" or

"Does combined child and parent training work via changes in child or parent behavior?"

These types of questions could be tested using different types of SCEDs. An informative overview of different designs can be found in Tate et al. (2016) and Barlow, Nock, and Hersen (2009). Whenever possible and especially in experimental research it is preferable to have a SCED with at least two phases (the previously mentioned AB design) or three phases, an ABC design with baseline period A followed by, for example, two different intervention periods or one intervention period and a follow-up phase (B and C).

One of the strongest experimental SCEDs is the multiple-baseline single-case design in which different participants are randomized to different lengths of the baseline period (e.g., each three clients to the lengths of three, four, and five weeks). With multiple-baseline SCED it is therefore possible to account for the passage of time or maturity effects. An example of such a multiple-baseline SCED can be found in the previously mentioned study of Jarrett and Ollendick (2012). Eight children with comorbid anxiety disorders and ADHD were randomized over three different baseline periods (two, three, or four weeks), and were subsequently treated with a combination of CBT and parent training over a period of 10 weeks. Greater improvements were found in the treatment phase as compared to the baseline phase for both anxiety and ADHD symptoms.

Extensive pre-, between-phases, post-, and follow-up assessments of the core participants' symptoms or treatment goals could be measured during a single-case study. Frequent observations during all phases of a SCED study are an important characteristic of SCED research and are a necessary requirement for most single-case data-analysis techniques. Therefore, it is useful to have shorter assessments of participants' complaints and/or therapy goals that can be implemented on a weekly, daily, and/or hourly base. If the SCED group of participants is a rather homogeneous one (e.g., clients mainly with sleeping problems in the absence of comorbidity) then, for example, one subscale from extensive assessments taken at pre-treatment can be used and administered on a weekly basis to all participants. But if a SCED study group is a rather heterogeneous one in its types of problems, then an elegant solution is to personalize assessments and administer them regularly over time. The researchers could then make a selection of a few items from pre-treatment assessments on which the participant scores are the least adaptive and administer these regularly. In this, the so-called "idiosyncratic approach", each participant provides ratings on his or her own set of items (Weisz et al., 2011).

Currently, many innovative data-analysis approaches are utilized to understand the single-case data. Because visual inspection of data (i.e., graphs) is susceptible to bias (for a review, see Brossart, Parker, Olson, & Mahadevan, 2006), researchers mostly use one or more types of quantitative data-analysis techniques in their studies. Examples include mixed-model analysis with which estimated endpoints and rates of change in symptoms between two phases can be compared (Maric, De Haan, Hogendoorn, Wolters, & Huizenga, 2015), ipsative z-score (Gaynor & Harris, 2008), and cross-lagged correlations (Joos, Onghena, & Pieters, 1996) to investigate mechanisms underlying an intervention, and Reliable Change Index (Jacobson & Truax, 1991) to calculate pre- to post-intervention clinically reliable changes in participants' symptoms. Two of these methods are illustrated in a case example that follows. A more complete overview of currently available data-analysis techniques can be found in Heyvaert and Onghena (2014) and Manolov and Moeyaert (2017).

Clinical case example

A fictional single-case study described here was concerned with the efficacy of CBT in a 17-year-old girl dealing with social and generalized anxiety disorder. The main research question was whether exposure therapy (the A phase) is sufficient in decreasing anxiety complaints in this girl, or whether cognitive therapy (the B phase) would have additional effects over and above exposure. Additionally, we were interested in the mechanisms underlying the treatment efficacy, i.e., how CBT works for this girl. To answer this question, change in negative cognitions (potential working mechanism) was studied in relation to changes in anxiety (outcome measure).

Each A and B phase (see Figure 7.1) consisted of five weekly sessions of either exposure or cognitive therapy. Weekly assessments of anxious symptoms were conducted (Hogendoorn et al., 2013), and the data is presented in panel A (Figure 7.1). As different types of anxiety disorders can be characterized by different types of cognitions, negative cognitions are measured with weekly idiosyncratic assessment (personalized questionnaire) using five items from the Children's Automatic Thought Scale-Negative (CATS-N; Hogendoorn et al., 2010) that was administered at pre-treatment. This data is presented in panel B (Figure 7.1).

To answer the first research question (Does cognitive therapy have an additional effect over and above exposure therapy?), a mixed-models analysis in R version 3.6.0 (R Core Team, 2013) was used, using the nlme package (Pinheiro, Bates, DebRoy, Sarkar, & Team, 2013); see the Open Science Framework for the data and syntax used (osf.io/am7pr/). Full details of the data can be found in Maric et al. (2015). As noted on page 232, "The model is described by the following function:"

$$y_i = \beta_{intercept} + \beta_1 * phase_i + \beta_2 * time\ in\ phase_i + \beta_3 * phase_i * time\ in\ phase_i + \varepsilon_i \qquad (7.1)$$

In Equation 7.1, y_i denotes the outcome variable score at time point i, $phase_i$ denotes the phase in which time point i is contained (coded as 0 for baseline and 1 for treatment), and $time\_in\_phase_i$ denotes time points within each phase. The term ε_i denotes the residual at time point i. The parameter $\beta_{intercept}$ is interpreted as the baseline intercept, β_1 as the treatment–baseline difference in

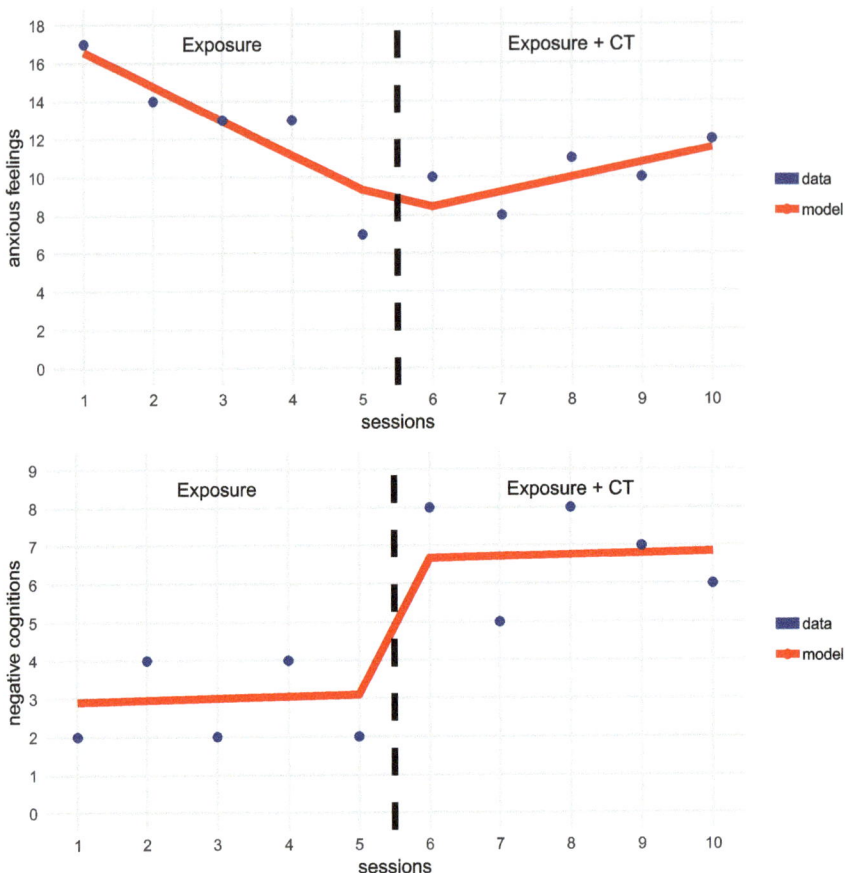

FIGURE 7.1 Panel A: self-reported anxiety feelings of the participant. Panel B: self-reported negative cognitions of the participant

intercepts, β_2 as the baseline slope, and β_3 as the treatment–baseline difference in slopes. Consequently, intercept differences between phases can be directly assessed by testing whether β_1 differs significantly from 0; analogously, slope differences can be assessed by testing β_3. Note that these parameter estimates can also be interpreted as an effect size (Cumming, 2014).

Four parameters are estimated:

- $\beta_{intercept}$ = baseline intercept, scores of symptoms at the end of the A phase, after five observations;
- β_1 = phase, difference in scores between end of the B phase (10th observation) and end of the A phase (5th observation);
- β_2 = time in phase, rate of change in scores in th A phase;
- β_3 = time in phase * phase, difference in rate of change in scores between the B phase and A phase.

The results are displayed in Table 7.1 and indicate a significant change in anxiety feelings and negative cognitions in the A phase. There are significant lower anxiety symptoms at the end of the A phase in comparison to the end of the B phase. Anxiety symptoms decrease at a higher rate during the A phase than during the B phase. Similarly, significantly lower levels of negative cognitions are found during the A phase than during the B phase. There are no significant differences in the rate of change in negative cognitions between the phases. The results show no additional effects of cognitive therapy over and above exposure; the results even show increases in anxiety and negative cognitions during the B phase, which could be explained in different ways (e.g., the client becomes more aware of negative cognitions during the cognitive therapy phase).

To answer the second research question (Are changes in negative cognitions an important mechanism underlying the effects of CBT?) we analyzed weekly data (10 observation points, both the A and B phases, Figure 7.2) using cross-lagged correlations. This analysis gives us information about the *lags* – the measure of association between the two time series (in our case negative cognitions and anxiety data) – and about the temporality of changes and direction of correlations between these two symptoms. The current analysis contains a commonly used test with a standard number of five *lags* (Borckardt et al., 2008) and the relationship between the two variables (negative cognitions and anxiety) is studied forwards and backwards over time to trace whether cognitions change before anxiety changes or vice versa.

The results are presented in Table 7.2 and there are two significant correlations on *lags* + 1 and + 2 showing that change in anxiety precedes change in negative cognitions. The correlations are both negative: an increase in

TABLE 7.1 Treatment efficacy results using mixed models

	Estimate	SE	p	95% confidence interval	
				Lower bound	Upper bound
Anxious feelings					
Intercept (b_0)	9.32	.53	<.001	8.02	10.62
Phase (b_1)	2.21	.73	.023	0.42	3.99
Time_in_phase (b_2)	1.82	.23	<.001	1.25	2.38
Time_in_phase * phase (b_3)	-2.59	.30	<.001	-3.34	-1.85
Negative cognitions					
Intercept (b_0)	3.09	.39	<.001	2.13	4.04
Phase (b_1)	3.75	.54	<.001	2.43	5.07
Time_in_phase (b_2)	-0.05	.17	.799	-0.47	0.37
Time_in_phase * phase (b_3)	0.00	.22	.992	-0.55	0.55

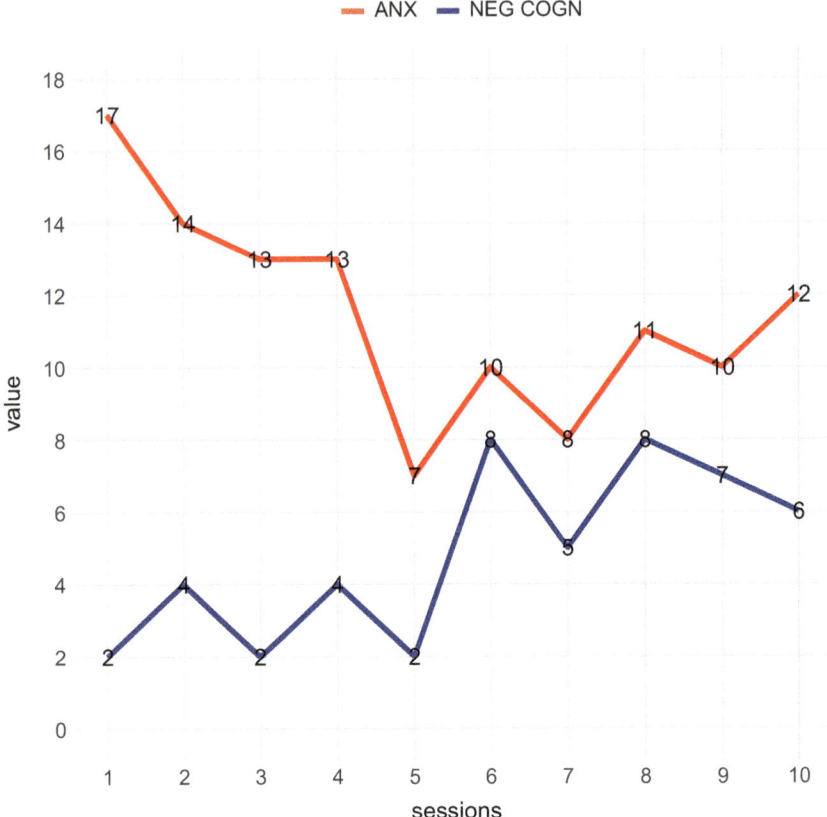

FIGURE 7.2 Negative cognitions and anxiety feelings (raw data)

anxiety is related to a decrease in negative cognitions, or a decrease in anxiety is related to an increase in negative cognitions. Lag -4 shows a significant positive correlation, which means that change in negative cognitions precedes change in anxiety. The correlation is positive: the decline in negative cognitions precedes a decline in anxiety, or an increase in negative cognitions precedes an increase in anxiety. The expectation based on existing theory (Stallard, 2009) that decreases in negative cognitions are related to decreases in anxiety symptoms is only partially confirmed for this participant, because the main results show increases in anxiety being related to decreases in negative cognitions. However, single-case results may not always be in line with existing theories based on large group studies, and especially in the case of working mechanisms, it is possible that CBT effects can be explained by many different individual mechanisms.

TABLE 7.2 Cross-lagged correlations between negative cognitions and anxiety feelings across 10 treatment sessions

Lag	r	p
− 05	+ .13	.283
− 04	+ .47*	.032
− 03	+ .05	.404
− 02	+ .28	.170
− 01	− .31	.188
0	− .31	.224
+ 01	− .72**	.007
+ 02	−. 48*	.047
+ 03	−. 44	.050
+ 04	−. 22	.207
+ 05	+ .33	.073

Note. *Negative lag* means that the change in negative cognitions preceded a change in anxiety feelings; *positive lag* means that the change in anxiety feelings preceded a change in negative cognitions.
* $p < 0.05$
** $p < 0.01$

Conclusion

SCEDs are making their comeback as a powerful method to test intervention effects on a level of a single participant. A quick Web of Science search for single-case studies in clinical psychology and psychiatry indeed shows 107 records published between 2019–2009 as opposed to 36 records published between 1999–2009. Cost-effectiveness, the possibility of investigating innovative interventions and individual mechanisms of change, and the potential of SCEDs to improve the quality of mental health care are benefits associated with this type of research design. Although current SCED methods are very useful in testing intervention effects, several challenges remain that, it is our hope, will be addressed in the time to come. First, it is currently unknown how many individual SCED studies are necessary for inclusion in an intervention study to be able to conclude that an intervention is effective. Guidelines of the Task Force of the American Psychological Association (1995) suggest that an intervention is considered as *well-established* if a series of at least nine SCED studies demonstrate efficacy. However, we do not have recent, quantitative, research-underpinned idea or guidelines about the minimal number of SCEDs to be included in a research study. Second, to be able to use SCED data analyses, frequent observations of changes in participants' symptoms are required. Third, and related to the previous point, especially in some clinical research projects it is not always feasible to have a (very long) baseline period. This is why single-case design involving only the "treatment phase" is included in international guidelines (Tate et al., 2016), albeit not as a design that can be used to draw strong causal inferences. Current data-analysis methods require at least two phases being compared to each other. However, because of the practical constraints in clinical research, we should work on the possibilities of analyzing single-case data in which only one phase (i.e., treatment) is present. Finally, cross-lagged correlations as described in this chapter are currently used to investigate mechanisms underlying treatment effects in SCED research, although with this method we can only investigate correlations of two variables over time. The question remains whether statistical mediation techniques used in large group studies could be used for single-case research. Despite these challenges, SCEDs can currently readily be used as a method to test intervention effects.

References

American Psychological Association. (1995). Training in and dissemination of empirically-validated psychological treatments: Report and recommendations. Division of Clinical Psychology, Task Force on Promotion and Dissemination of Psychological Procedures. *Clinical Psychologist, 48*(1), 3–23.

Barlow, D. H., Nock, M. K., & Hersen, M. (2009). *Single case experimental designs: Strategies for studying behavior for change* (3rd ed.). Boston, MA: Pearson/Allyn and Bacon.

Borckardt, J. J., Nash, M. R., Murphy, M. D., Moore, M., Shaw, D., & O'Neil, P. (2008). Clinical practice as natural laboratory for psychotherapy research: A guide to case-based time-series analysis. *American Psychologist, 63*(2), 77–95.

Brossart, D. F., Parker, R. I., Olson, E. A., & Mahadevan, L. (2006). The relationship between visual analysis and five statistical analyses in a simple AB single-case research design. *Behavior Modification, 30*(5), 531–563.

Cartwright, N., & Munro, E. (2010). The limitations of randomized controlled trials in predicting effectiveness. *Journal of Evaluation in Clinical Practice, 16*(2), 260–266.

Cumming, G. (2014). The new statistics: Why and how. *Psychological Science, 25*(1), 7–29. doi:10.1177/0956797613504966.

Gaynor, S. T., & Harris, A. (2008). Single-participant assessment of treatment mediators: Strategy description and examples from a behavioral activation intervention for depressed adolescents. *Behavior Modification, 32*(3), 372–402.

Heyvaert, M., & Onghena, P. (2014). Analysis of single-case data: Randomisation tests for measures of effect size. *Neuropsychological Rehabilitation, 24*(3–4), 507–527.

Hogendoorn, S. M., De Haan, E., Wolters, L. H., Vervoort, L., Prins, P. J. M., De Bourgraaf, A., Goodman, W. K. (2013). The Anxiety Severity Interview for Children and Adolescents: An individualized repeated measure of anxiety severity. *Clinical Psychology, 21*(6), 525–535.

Hogendoorn, S. M., Wolters, L. H., Vervoort, L., Prins, P. J. M., Boer, F., Kooij, E., & De Haan, E. (2010). Measuring negative and positive thoughts in children: An adaptation of the Children's Automatic Thoughts Scale (CATS). *Cognitive Therapy and Research, 34*(5), 467–478.

Jacobson, N. S., & Truax, P. (1991). Clinical significance: A statistical approach to defining meaningful change in psychotherapy research. *Journal of Consulting Clinical Psychology, 59* (1), 12–19.

Jarrett, M. A., & Ollendick, T. H. (2012). Treatment of comorbid attention-deficit/hyperactivity disorder and anxiety in children: A multiple baseline design analysis. *Journal of Consulting Clinical Psychology, 80*(2), 239–244.

Joos, S., Onghena, P., & Pieters, G. (1996). Het effect van een interventie nagaan: Een illustratieve casus met toepassing van tijdreeksenanalyse en randomiseringstoetsen. *Gedragstherapie, 29*, 93–109.

Manolov, R., Guilera, G., & Sierra, V. (2014). Weighting strategies in the meta-analysis of single-case studies. *Behavior Research Methods, 46*(4), 1152–1166.

Manolov, R., & Moeyaert, M. (2017). How can single-case data be analyzed? Software resources, tutorial, and reflections on analysis. *Behavior Modification, 41*(2), 179–228.

Maric, M. (2018). Single-Case Experimental Designs in CBT. *Special Issue Gedragstherapie, 2*, 158–170.

Maric, M., De Haan, E., Hogendoorn, S. M., Wolters, L. H., & Huizenga, H. M. (2015). Evaluating statistical and clinical significance of intervention effects in single-case experimental designs: An SPSS method to analyze univariate data. *Behavior Therapy, 46*(2), 230–241.

Maric, M., Wiers, R. W., & Prins, P. J. (2012). Ten ways to improve the use of statistical mediation analysis in the practice of child and adolescent treatment research. *Clinical Child and Family Psychology Review, 15*(3), 177–191.

Norell-Clarke, A., Nyander, E., & Jansson-Fröjmark, M. (2011). Sleepless in Sweden: A single subject study of effects of cognitive therapy for insomnia on three adolescents. *Behavioural and Cognitive Psychotherapy, 39*(3), 367–374.

Onghena, P., Michiels, B., Jamshidi, L., Moeyaert, M., & Van Den Noortgate, W. (2018). One by one: Accumulating evidence by using meta-analytical procedures for single-case experiments. *Brain Impairment, 19*(1), 33–58. doi:10.1017/BrImp.2017.25.

Pinheiro, J., Bates, D., DebRoy, S., Sarkar, D., & Team, R. C. (2013). nlme: Linear and nonlinear mixed effects models. *R Package Version, 3*(1), 111.

R Core Team (2013). R: A language and environment for statistical computing. Vienna: R Foundation for Statistical Computing. Retrieved from www.R-project.org/.

Smith, J. D. (2012). Single-case experimental designs: A systematic review of published research and current standards. *Psychological Methods, 17*(4), 510–550.

Stallard, P. (2009). *Anxiety: Cognitive behaviour therapy with children and young people.* London: Bruner-Routledge.

Tate, R. L., Perdices, M., Rosenkoetter, U., Shadish, W., Vohra, S., Barlow, D. H., McDonald, S. (2016). The single-case reporting guideline in behavioural interventions (SCRIBE) 2016 statement. *Physical Therapy, 96*(7), e1-e10.

Versluis, A., Maric, M., & Peute, L. (2014). N= 1 studies in onderzoek en praktijk:(Hoe) heeft de behandeling gewerkt? *De Psycholoog, 49*(3), 10–20.

Weisz, J. R., Chorpita, B. F., Frye, A., Ng, M. Y., Lau, N., Bearman, S. K., Hoagwood, K. E. (2011). Youth top problems: Using idiographic, consumer-guided assessment to identify treatment needs and to track change during psychotherapy. *Journal of Consulting Clinical Psychology, 79*(3), 369–380.

8

HOW TO IMPROVE THE ESTIMATION OF A SPECIFIC EXAMINEE'S ($n = 1$) MATH ABILITY WHEN TEST DATA ARE LIMITED

Kimberley Lek
DEPARTMENT OF METHODOLOGY AND STATISTICS, UTRECHT UNIVERSITY, UTRECHT, THE NETHERLANDS

Ingrid Arts
DEPARTMENT OF METHODOLOGY AND STATISTICS, UTRECHT UNIVERSITY, UTRECHT, THE NETHERLANDS

Introduction

In practice, (test) data for a specific examinee can be limited. A teacher or psychologist might be interested, for instance, in estimating the math ability of a specific examinee, but the scope of the math test the examinee completed is limited. Or, the teacher or psychologist might be interested in the question of how reliable the examinee's score is on the test (i.e., the error variance), but the examinee did not answer enough items or tests to accurately estimate this reliability. In such cases, it can be beneficial to supplement the information from the single examinee with other information sources. This chapter explores two such sources. The first is the rich but often ignored source of teacher knowledge. The second is the possibility of using test results of more or less 'similar' examinees (e.g., examinees with the same or comparable test scores). This chapter discusses how teacher knowledge and test results of 'similar' examinees can be used to improve the estimation of an examinee's math ability.

Estimating math ability

Imagine that we are interested in the math skills of a specific examinee, 'David'. In order to get an idea of David's math ability, we let him complete a certain math test. Afterwards, we attempt to estimate two things: T_i, i.e., David's 'true' math ability; and $\sigma^2_{T_i}$, the error variance of $\widehat{T}_i$ (the estimate of T_i). The latter tells us something about the test's suitability to estimate David's ability. We could base our estimate of T_i and $\sigma^2_{T_i}$ on David's single test take[1]. By doing so, we might, however, run into two problems. First, the estimate of $\sigma^2_{T_i}$ is quite unstable after only one (or a few) test(s). By 'unstable' we mean that if we could re-test David over and over again, brainwashing him after every test, the estimate of $\sigma^2_{T_i}$ based on each of these tests would vary considerably. Second, because of time constraints, the scope of any math test will be necessarily limited. Therefore, our notion of David's math ability might be too limited if we base our estimate too strictly on $\widehat{T}_i$. These different problems boil down to the same underlying problem: we might not have enough information to satisfactorily estimate T_i and $\sigma^2_{T_i}$.

One way of solving the above problems is to turn to other sources of information. In order to estimate T_i, we could, for instance, ask David's (math) teacher for information. Having observed David in class for a long period of time, his teacher has unique knowledge about how David responds to math questions, whether he is able to come up with suitable strategies to find solutions to math problems, et cetera. This makes the teacher a very rich – but often ignored – source of information. Regarding the estimate of $\sigma^2_{T_i}$, we could not only rely on David's test results but also on the test results of 'similar' other examinees. 'Similar' could, for instance, mean that these other examinees have the same or a comparable test score as David. Assuming that $\sigma^2_{T_i}$ is comparable for David and the other selected examinees, we can reach a more stable estimate of $\sigma^2_{T_i}$.

This chapter discusses in greater detail how teacher knowledge and the test results of other examinees can be used to, respectively, improve the estimate of T_i and $\sigma^2_{T_i}$. Regarding the former, we show how teacher knowledge can be elicited such that it can be used as an additional information source in assessing David's math ability. This is followed by a demonstration of an app for primary school teachers developed specifically for this purpose. Regarding the latter, we will explain how a suitable number of 'other examinees' can be selected. We will explain how to create a balanced selection of other examinees in order to reach a stable estimate of $\sigma^2_{T_i}$ while keeping in mind that the number should not be so large that this estimate becomes 'meaningless' for David. Note that we use 'David' as an example, but the techniques explained in this chapter can be used for any (educational) test and with any examinee.

Teacher knowledge

When T_i is difficult to estimate based on test data, we could turn to the teacher. An advantage is that teachers have a broad view of the ability of their pupils, resulting from class observations, projects, answers to the teacher's questions, et cetera. Other than information from 'similar' examinees (see next section), the teacher provides a source of information that is focused on the *specific* pupil, such as David. In order to incorporate the teacher's knowledge in our estimate of T_i, we can make use of the Bayesian toolbox (see Chapter 1, Miočević, Levy, and Van de Schoot; as well as Kaplan & Depaoli, 2013; Kruschke, 2014;

Van de Schoot et al., 2014). The idea of Bayesian statistics is simple: we incorporate the teacher's knowledge in a prior distribution. This is a distribution containing all information that we have collected prior to the (test) data collection. We then update this prior knowledge with the (test) data to obtain a posterior distribution, which is a compromise of teacher knowledge and test data (see Figure 8.1).

The difficulty with this approach is the translation of expert (in this example, the teacher) knowledge into a prior distribution. This 'translation' is called *expert elicitation* (see O'Hagan et al., 2006) and several so-called expert elicitation tools have been developed (see, for instance, Veen, Stoel, Zondervan-Zwijnenburg, & Van de Schoot, 2017; Zondervan-Zwijnenburg, Van de Schoot-Hubeek, Lek, Hoijtink, & Van de Schoot, 2017). We developed an online elicitation instrument specifically tailored to primary school teachers (see Lek & Van de Schoot, 2018b). With the help of this elicitation instrument, teachers translate their knowledge about the pupils into a prior in a structured, easy, and non-technical way. In the remainder of this section, we discuss the elicitation instrument in detail, using screenshots from the online app. The Dutch version of the app can be found here: utrecht-university.shinyapps.io/oordeelsvormingPO/, and the English translation of this app can be found here: utrecht-university.shinyapps.io/teacherjudgment/. The annotated R code and potential newer version can be found on the OSF (osf.io/8uk9z/).

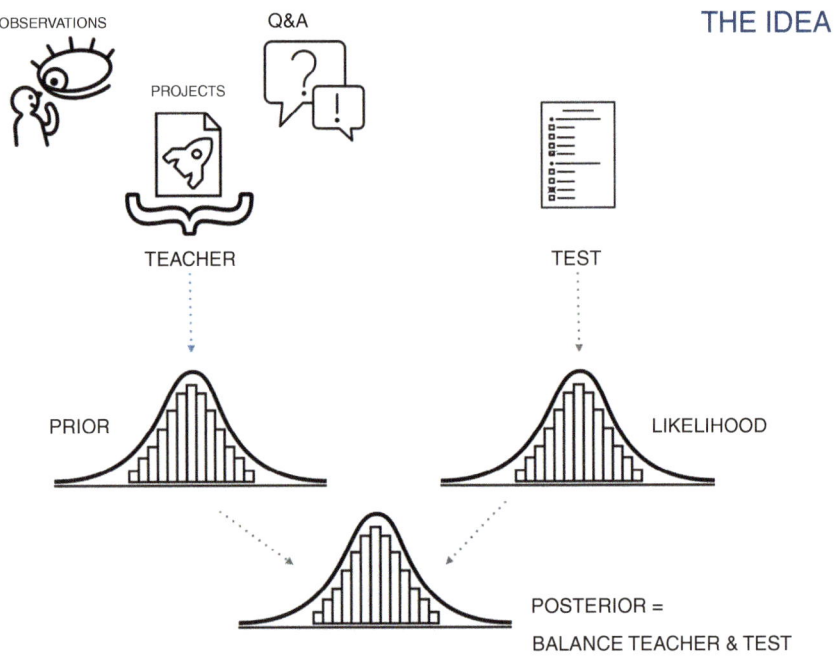

FIGURE 8.1 The idea of incorporating teacher knowledge in the estimate of math ability

Steps of the expert elicitation instrument

The elicitation app consists of eight tabs: 'Home', 'Groups' (Dutch: *Groepjes*), 'Student codes', 'Positioning' (Dutch: *Positioneren*), 'Class overview' (Dutch: *Klasoverzicht*), 'Download', 'Upload' and 'Compare with test results' (Dutch: *Vergelijken met toetsresultaat*). Each tab must be completed to proceed to the next one (although it is possible to return to a previous tab and adjust data). The app is built using R (R Core Team, 2013) and the `Shiny` package (Chang, Cheng, Allaire, Xie, & McPherson, 2017). Note that, like other Shiny apps, our app does not yet allow for the possibility of interrupting the process and continuing at a later time: all tabs (until the Download tab) must be completed in one session. Also, when left unused for too long, the app will time out and the user has to reload the app and start from the beginning.

Home

The app starts with an explanation of its purpose and a schematic overview of the different steps. The overview shows that the first steps (until 'Download') must be completed *before* the teacher administers the test, whereas the last steps (starting from 'Upload') should be taken *after* the test results are known.

Defining groups

In the second step, the teacher must divide the class into different groups, each containing students with comparable math levels (see Figure 8.2). The goal of this step is to ease the positioning step later; instead of positioning all pupils at once, teachers can do it for each group of similar pupils separately. There is a maximum of five groups. Each pupil that takes the test is assigned to a single group. The teacher can select a label for each group. If the groups are not labeled, they will simply be called Group 1, 2, 3, 4, and 5. To ensure anonymity, a code is assigned to each student in a group, consisting of a letter and one or two digits.

Our hypothetical pupil 'David' is also placed in a group. Based on his math ability, the teacher places him in Group 1.

Student codes

The teacher can download either a Word or HTML file with codes for all pupils in their class (see Figure 8.3). The teacher can, for every student in each group, enter the student's name next to the code. In order to comply with privacy laws, teachers should keep this file confidential. Teachers need this file again in the next step and when the test results for the students are known, so it is important not to lose or misplace this file.

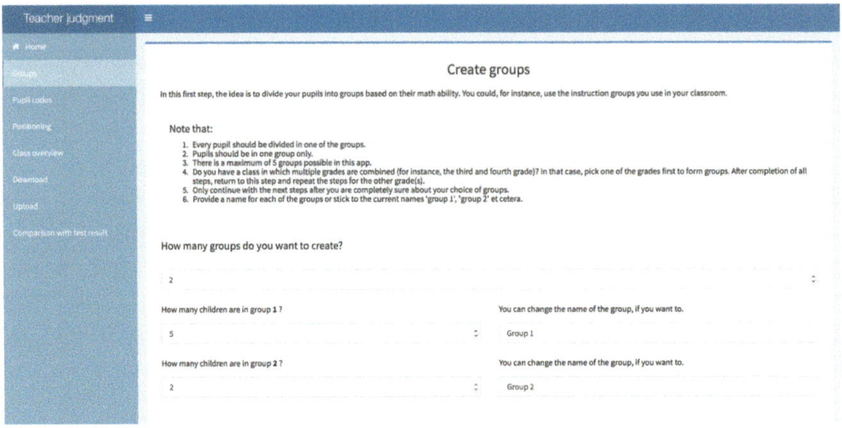

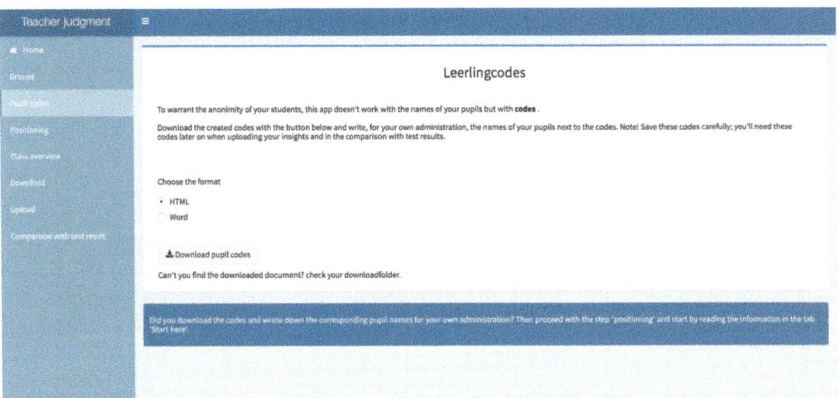

FIGURE 8.2 Grouping of pupils

FIGURE 8.3 Downloading pupil codes

Positioning

In the positioning step, teachers are presented with five 'puppets', each of which represents 20% of the general student population. Drawing from all the information they have about a specific pupil, the teachers are asked to position their pupils with respect to these puppets. If David were a relatively poor student compared to other pupils his age, his teacher might, for instance, position him at the first or second puppet. Then, the teacher is presented with the opportunity to further refine this placement for increasing degrees of certainty with more puppets in subsequent screens; respectively 10, 25, and 50 puppets. In this way, the positioning of the pupil – potentially – becomes more and more precise. Eventually, the number of puppets and the positioning of the pupil(s) using these puppets is translated into a statistical prior distribution (for technical details, see Lek & Van de Schoot, 2018b).

In the app, the positioning is done as follows. First, the teacher selects a group by clicking on the tab with the group name (see Figure 8.4A). For every student in the group (coded, so the teacher should keep the file they created in the previous tab close at hand), the teacher first positions the student in the range of the five puppets (see Figure 8.4A). This is similar to asking whether the teacher thinks the student belongs to the 0–20% range of all, say, Dutch students, to the 21–40% range, the 41–60% range, and so on. If the teacher knows (some of) his/her students well enough, she or he can further refine the five-point scale by clicking the 'Yes' option in the blue bar at the bottom of the screen. This is illustrated in Figure 8.4B. The teacher can then proceed to position the pupil on a 10-point (10-puppet) scale (does this student perform in the 0–10% range, in the 11–20% range, and so on; see Figure 8.5B). This can be refined even further, if the teacher is sufficiently confident in his or her assessment, to a 25-point scale (see Figure 8.5C) and a 50-point scale (see Figure 8.5D), by assigning the student to a puppet on the scale and clicking the 'Yes' option in the blue bar on the

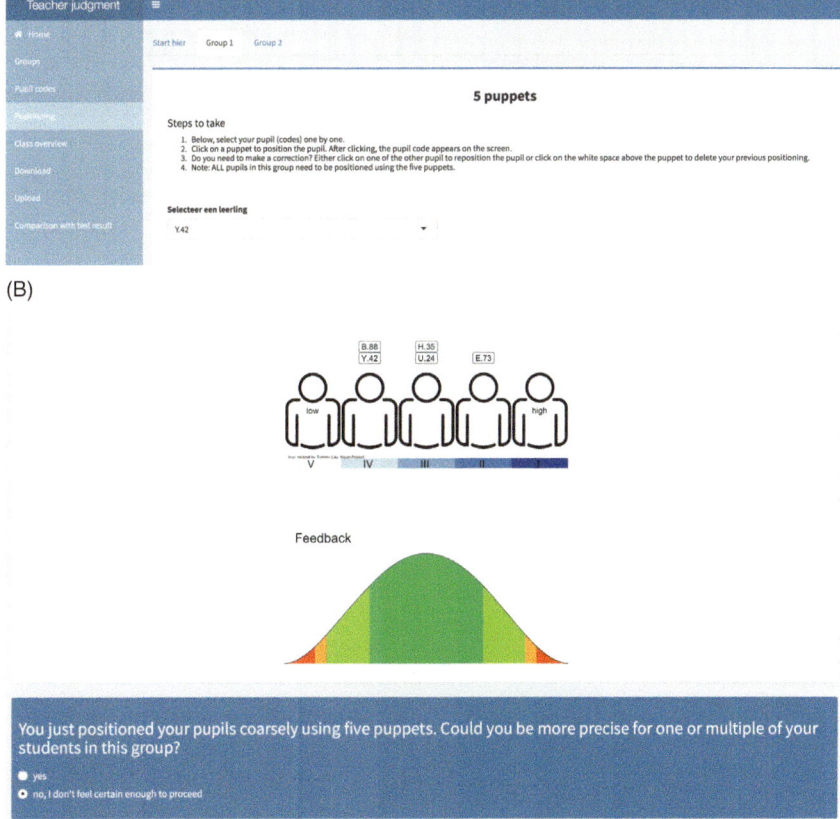

FIGURE 8.4 Overview of the positioning part: positioning is done per tab for each of the groups (A); when the teacher is certain enough, he or she can proceed to more puppets (B)

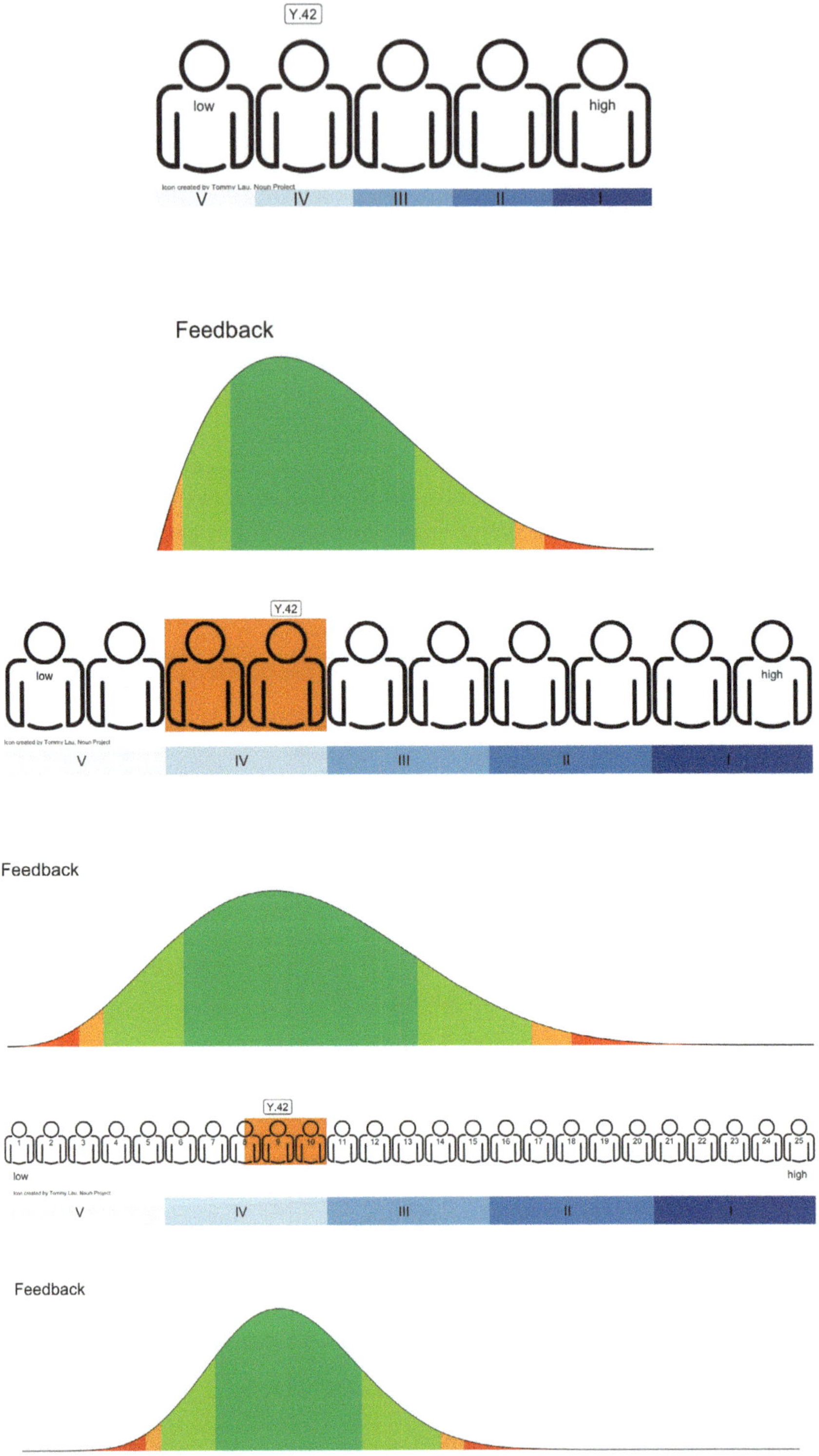

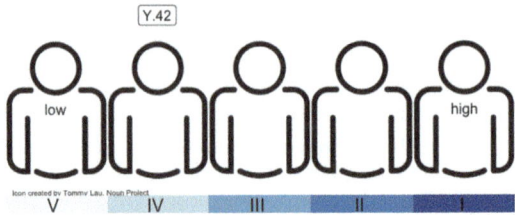

FIGURE 8.5 Positioning using different numbers of puppets, with five, 10, 25, and 50 puppets

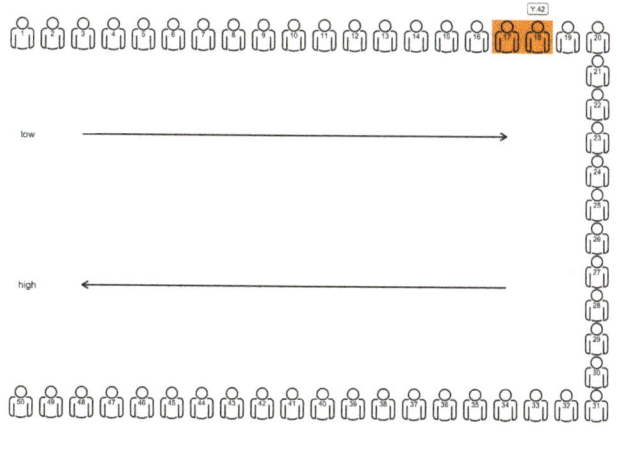

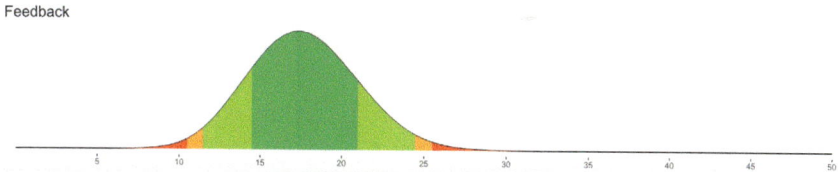

FIGURE 8.5 (Cont.)

bottom of the screen. Note that in practice few teachers use the 50-point scale, probably because the precise positioning of students in such detail is difficult (see Lek & Van de Schoot, 2018b).

As can be seen in Figures 8.4 and 8.5, the teacher sees the resulting prior distribution as 'feedback'. For instance, she or he can see that this distribution gets increasingly peaked the more puppets are used for positioning. The coloring helps the teacher to interpret the prior. The darkest green color shows, for instance, the 68% credible interval of the prior. Clicking the 'Start here' button – see left corner, Figure 8.4A – yields an explanation of how the prior distribution and the coloring can be interpreted.

The teacher can choose to either fine-tune the positioning of a single group before moving on to the next one, or to work down from positioning all groups first on the five-point scale before moving on to the 10-point scale. The downside of the latter method is that the user has to scroll back to the top to change to a different group, and then has to scroll down again to the correct the positioning scale.

David is assigned code 'Y.42'. The teacher knows David fairly well and recognizes that his math abilities are somewhat below average. David is therefore represented by puppet 18 out of 50.

Class overview

By clicking the 'Create overview' button, the positioning of all students in the class is visualized by a colored bar (see Figure 8.6A). The width of this colored bar depends on the precision indicated previously by the teacher (i.e., whether the teacher used a scale of five, 10, 25, or 50 puppets). Specifically, the x-axis shows the possible positions from 1 to 50. Whenever the teacher used a scale smaller than 50 puppets for positioning the student, the colored bar spreads over more than one position. In Figure 8.6A, for instance, the students 'B.88', 'E.73', 'U.24', and 'H.35' from 'Group 1' and the student 'M.39' from 'Group 2' received a position on the five-point (five-puppet) scale (puppets 2, 4, 3, 3, and 5 out of five, respectively), whereas student 'Y.42' (David) received a position on the whole 50-point (50-puppet) scale (puppet 18 out of 50) and student 'Z.18' received a position on the 25-puppet scale. Note that each specified group (in this example, two groups) is represented with a different color.

The app presents an overview per group below the class overview with absolute positioning (see Figure 8.6B). This overview presents the corresponding

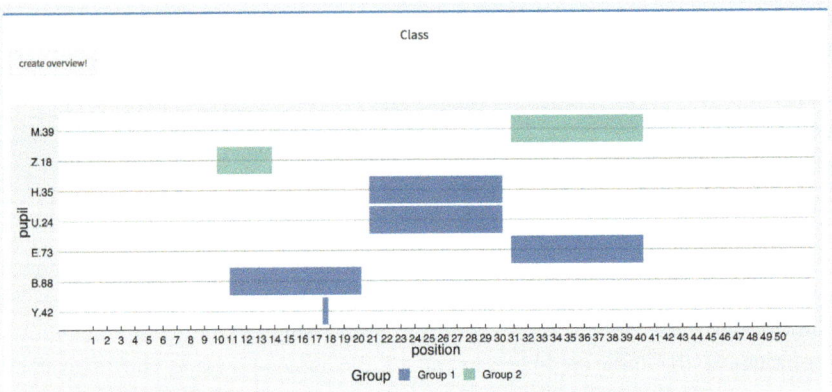

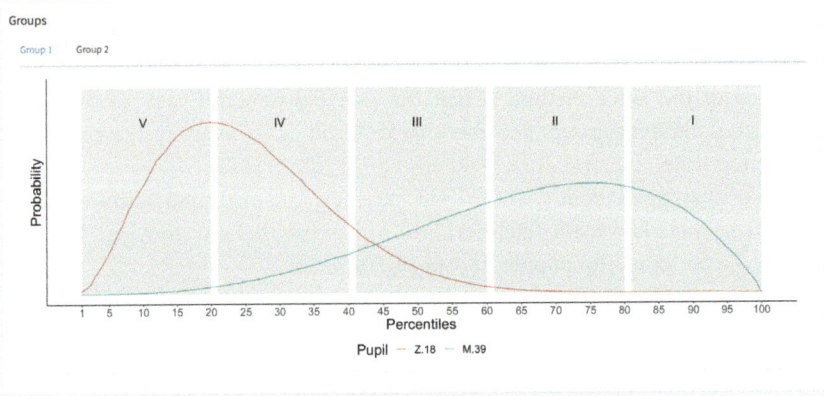

FIGURE 8.6 Class overview (A) and group overview (B)

beta distributions with the percentiles on the x-axis and the probability on the y-axis. Every student is represented by a different colored line. The lines are slightly jittered to avoid complete overlap of distributions for students with equal positioning.

Download

The teacher can now download a .csv file with his or her student positioning by clicking the 'Download' button. The app should not be closed before the download is completed. Teachers should not make any adjustments to the downloaded file.

Upload

Once the results of the test are known, teachers can upload the .csv file they had downloaded in the previous tab (see Figure 8.7). This file contains the positioning of the students. Uploading this file makes it possible to compare the positioning of the students with the test results in the next tab.

Compare with test results

For each student, the teacher can enter the percentile score on the test (see the upper part of Figure 8.8). For most tests, these percentile scores are provided in the manual that comes with the test. In the resulting figure – see Figure 8.8 – this percentile score is represented by a black, dashed line. In the same figure, the teacher's positioning of the specific student is represented by the corresponding beta distribution. The location of the dashed black line compared to the distribution of the teachers' estimate shows the degree to which the teacher's expectations match the test results, and vice versa.

David's performance on the test slightly exceeded his teacher's expectation, although the test result is still within the dark green area of the teacher's beta distribution (corresponding to the teacher's 68% credible interval).

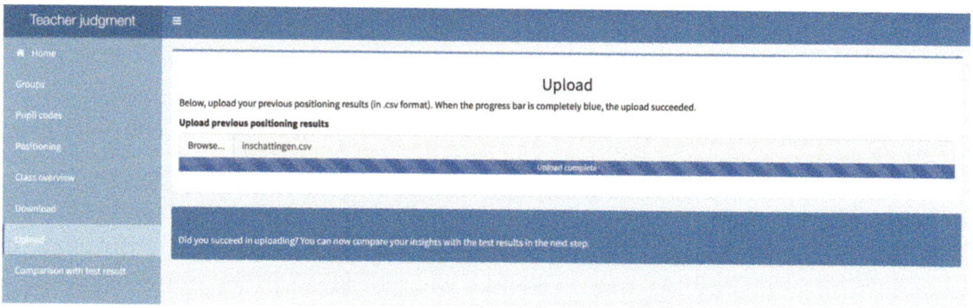

FIGURE 8.7 Uploading the results

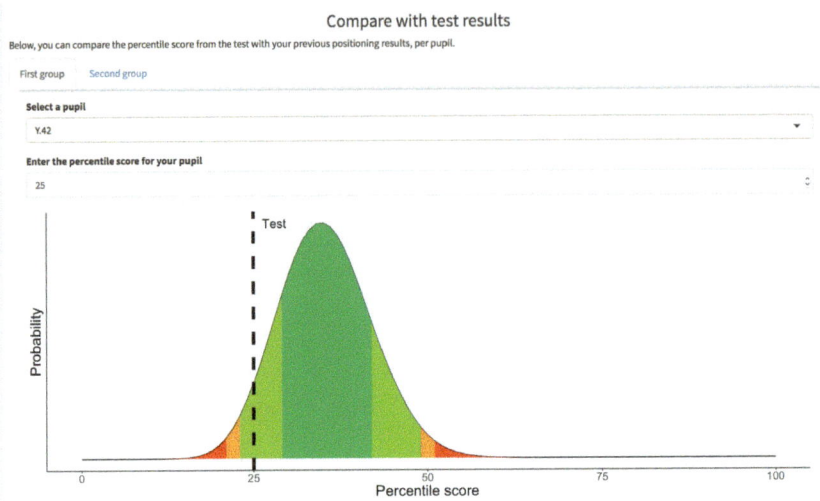

FIGURE 8.8 A comparison with test result(s)

Other ('similar') examinees

The error variance $\sigma^2_{T_i}$ for David indicates how David's test score may fluctuate from test to test if we were able to test him over and over again. A large error variance, for instance, indicates that we should be careful with interpreting the obtained test score, since this test score may differ notably from David's potential next test score. Just as with the ability T_i, the error variance $\sigma^2_{T_i}$ is generally unknown and should therefore be estimated. Usually, the square root of the error variance is estimated, which is called the 'standard error of measurement', here abbreviated as SEm.

There are multiple options to estimate the SEm. The most popular option within the Classical Test Theory is to base the SEm-estimate on the test results of all pupils in the test's norm population. This results in a single SEm-estimate for all pupils who take the test. In this chapter (and in Lek & Van de Schoot, 2018a) we call this SEm-estimate the 'single SEm' or 'classical SEm'. Another option is to base the SEm-estimate for a particular pupil on the test results of all pupils who have the same test score as this pupil. In this way, multiple SEm-estimates are obtained; one for each possible test score. In this chapter (and in Lek & Van de Schoot, 2018a) we call this SEm-estimate the 'conditional SEm', since the SEm-estimate is estimated conditionally on the obtained test score. Finally, it is also possible to base the SEm-estimate solely on the test results of a specific examinee, such as David (Hu et al., 2016). We call this SEm-estimate the 'person-specific SEm', since a SEm-estimate is obtained for each examinee individually. What distinguishes the three SEm-estimates is thus the number of test results that are used in the estimation of the SEm and thus the number of unique SEm-estimates. At one extreme, we use all available information (i.e., the test results of all norm-population examinees) to estimate a single SEm. At the other extreme, we use only information from specific examinees to estimate their corresponding SEms for all examinees individually.

The advantage of using information from many other (similar or not so similar) examinees is that the resulting SEm-estimate is relatively stable. By 'stable' we mean that if we tested David (or any other examinee) again, the SEm-estimate would be unlikely to change. On the other hand, when the number of completed test items or tests is small, the limitation of David's test result(s) could lead to a very unstable SEm-estimate. The disadvantage, however, is that the resulting SEm-estimate might not be representative of the 'true' error variance in the case of David (or any other examinee).

Indeed, the more test information we use from other examinees, the more assumptions we are making about the SEm. When using the person-specific SEm, for example, we allow a unique error variance for each individual. We thus anticipate the situation in which not every examinee is tested as accurately as the next. Examinees differ in, for instance, concentration, test anxiety, and mother tongue, making it highly unlikely that the ability of these diverse examinees is measured equally well (Lek, Van de Schoot-Hubeek, Kroesbergen, & Van de Schoot, 2017).

When using the conditional SEm, on the other hand, we assume that all examinees with the same test score also have the same SEm. This assumption is based on the notion that a test measures the ability of children/examinees more precisely (i.e., with less error) when their ability matches the difficulty of the test items. Using test score as a proxy for ability, the conditional SEm allows the SEm-estimate to differ for examinees with different ability levels, but not between examinees with the same ability level.

Finally, when using the single or classical SEm, we need to assume that every examinee is tested with an equal measurement error variance (see Molenaar, 2004; Sijtsma, 2009). When the assumption of (conditional) equal measurement

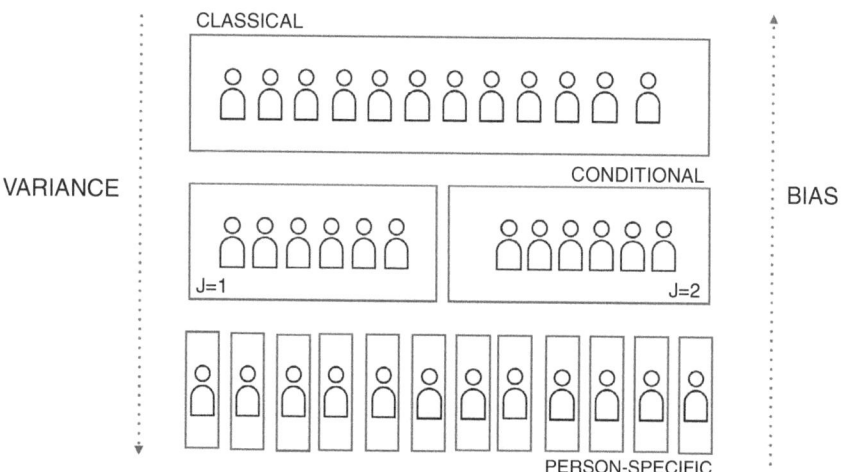

FIGURE 8.9 Bias-variance trade-off, single-, conditional, and person-specific SEm

error variance is not met, the classical and conditional SEms lead to biased SEm-estimates. When choosing between the classical (single), conditional, and person-specific SEm, we therefore need to balance 'variance' (the stability of the resulting SEm-estimate) and bias (the assumptions we need to make). This is called the bias–variance trade-off, illustrated in Figure 8.9. Ideally, we want to use the person-specific SEm to limit the number of assumptions we need to make to prevent a biased estimate of SEm for David. However, if test data from David are limited, we might want to base ourselves on test results from other examinees as well, to prevent a 'wrong' SEm-estimate due to instability. In Lek & Van de Schoot, 2018a), we discuss how one can choose wisely for one of the SEm-estimate options in specific test situations using the bias–variance trade-off.

Conclusion

Sometimes, our (test) data are too limited to accurately estimate, for instance, the math ability of a single examinee. In this chapter, we demonstrated how test information from a single examinee can be supplemented with other information sources to solve this limited-data problem. We first showed how information from the examinee's teacher can be used to obtain a more accurate estimate of a specific examinee's math ability (T_i) by using Bayesian statistics. The option to use teacher knowledge is especially interesting when the scope of the test is (too) limited for the ability one wants to measure. We then discussed how test results from other (similar or not so similar) examinees can be used to obtain a more stable estimate of the error variance of the estimate $\widehat{T}_i$. Together, these two examples show that test information from a single examinee can be enriched by other information sources. In the case of the error variance, we often do this by default. Conventionally, test results from all norm population examinees are used to estimate the SEm, the square root of the error variance. This chapter, however, shows that we should be aware of the restrictive assumptions that are made when opting for this 'single' or 'classical' SEm. We should think carefully whether test results from a smaller group of examinees would suffice. While being a rich source of information, teacher knowledge is often neglected. This chapter demonstrates how teacher knowledge can be elicited with the help of a purposely developed app. Teacher knowledge can thus be used to obtain a more accurate estimate of T_i.

Acknowledgment

This work was supported by an NWO-talent (Dutch Research Council) grant (406-15-062). Icons in the figures of this chapter are created by Annette Spithoven (distribution). Headsofbirds (large eye), (Piece of paper with rocket) Wouter Buning, Iconsphere (Text balloons), Sam Smith (Bracket), ABDO (test), Tommy Lau and Elizabeth Lopez (puppets in respectively Figure 8.4/8.5 and Figure 8.9) from the noun project (thenounproject.com).

Note

1 Usually, David's obtained score is used as estimate of T_i; Hu et al. (2016) show how $\sigma^2 T_i$ can be estimated based on a single test take.

References

Chang, W., Cheng, J., Allaire, J. J., Xie, Y., & McPherson, J. (2017). *Shiny: Web application framework for R. R package version 1.0.5*. Retrieved from https://CRAN.R-project.org/package=shiny.

Hu, Y., Nesselroade, J. R., Erbacher, M. K., Boker, S. M., Burt, S. A., Keel, P. K., ... Klump, K. (2016). Test reliability at the individual level. *Structural Equation Modeling: A Multidisciplinary Journal, 23*(4), 532–543. doi:10.1080/10705511.2016.1148605.

Kaplan, D., & Depaoli, S. (2013). Bayesian statistical methods. In T. D. Little (Ed.), *Oxford handbook of quantitative methods* (pp. 407–437). Oxford: Oxford University Press.

Kruschke, J. K. (2014). *Doing Bayesian data analysis: A tutorial with R, JAGS, and stan* (2nd ed.). Boston, MA: Academic Press.

Lek, K., & Van de Schoot, R. (2018a). A comparison of the single, conditional and person-specific standard error of measurement: What do they measure and when to use them? *Frontiers in Applied Mathematics and Statistics, 4,* 1–27. doi:10.3389/fams.2018.00040.

Lek, K., & Van de Schoot, R. (2018b). Development and evaluation of a digital expert elicitation method aimed at fostering elementary school teachers' diagnostic competence. *Frontiers in Education, 3,* 1–14. doi:10.3389/feduc.2018.00082.

Lek, K., Van de Schoot-Hubeek, W., Kroesbergen, E. H., & Van de Schoot, R. (2017). Hoe zat het ook alweer? Het betrouwbaarheidsinterval in intelligentietests. *De Psycholoog, 1*(1), 10–24.

Molenaar, P. C. M. (2004). A manifesto on psychology as idiographic science: Bringing the person back into scientific psychology, this time forever. *Measurement Interdisciplinary Research and Perspectives, 2*(4), 201–218. doi:10.1207/s15366359mea0204_1.

O'Hagan, A., Buck, C. E., Daneshkhah, J. R., Eiser, R., Garthwaite, P. H., Jenkinson, D. J., ... Rakow, T. (2006). *Uncertain judgements: Eliciting experts' probabilities*. Chichester: Wiley.

R Core Team (2013). R: A language and environment for statistical computing. Vienna: R Foundation for Statistical Computing. Retrieved from www.R-project.org/.

Sijtsma, K. (2009). On the use, the misuse, and the very limited usefulness of Cronbach's alpha. *Psychometrika, 74*(1), 107–120. doi:10.1007/s11336-008-9101-0.

Van de Schoot, R., Kaplan, D., Denissen, J., Asendorpf, J. B., Neyer, F. J., & Van Aken, M. A. (2014). A gentle introduction to Bayesian analysis: Applications to developmental research. *Child Development, 85*(3), 842–860.

Veen, D., Stoel, D., Zondervan-Zwijnenburg, M., & Van de Schoot, R. (2017). Proposal for a five-step method to elicit expert judgment. *Frontiers in Psychology, 8,* 2110.

Zondervan-Zwijnenburg, M., Van de Schoot-Hubeek, W., Lek, K., Hoijtink, H., & Van de Schoot, R. (2017). Application and evaluation of an expert judgment elicitation procedure for correlations. *Frontiers in Psychology, 8,* 90.

9

COMBINING EVIDENCE OVER MULTIPLE INDIVIDUAL ANALYSES

Fayette Klaassen

DEPARTMENT OF METHODOLOGY AND STATISTICS, UTRECHT UNIVERSITY, UTRECHT, THE NETHERLANDS

Introduction

Hypothesis testing is omnipresent in behavioral and biomedical research, and usually concerns testing for population effects. For example, is there a difference between groups *on average*? This chapter presents a Bayesian method to evaluate hypotheses for each person in a sample and aggregate this result to answer the question whether a hypothesis holds for *everyone* in the sample, rather than on average. Using an empirical data set, the methodology is illustrated step by step: from formulating the research question and hypotheses to modelling the data and drawing conclusions. This chapter is structured as follows. First, informative hypotheses and Bayes factors are introduced and explained. Next, a data set and corresponding set of hypotheses is introduced that can be used for the question 'Does everyone have the same best informative hypothesis?' The section 'Individual Bayes factors' describes how individual Bayes factors can be interpreted. The section 'Aggregating Bayes factors' explains how these individual Bayes factors can be combined. Throughout these sections, the methods are applied to the example data set and hypotheses. Finally, the conclusions and limitations are discussed.

Informative hypotheses and Bayes factors

Analysis of variance (ANOVA) and regression models are frequently used in behavioral and biomedical research. For example, consider a psychology researcher interested in the effect of interference on a memory task. The researcher plans an experiment where participants are presented with a word to memorize, followed by a mask, and then asked to recall the word. The mask is a random sequence of letters (*non-word*), a word that differs by one letter from the target word (*similar word*), or a random word (*different word*). The outcome variable is reaction time. The researcher intends to test the null hypothesis $H_0 : \mu_{non-word} = \mu_{different\ word} = \mu_{similar\ word}$ that the mean reaction times in the three conditions are equal to one another against the unconstrained alternative H_{alt} : not H_0, which states the expectation that at least one of the condition mean reaction times is not equal to the other conditions.

Analyzing the data by means of null hypothesis significance testing on the group mean response times implies the research question is whether the theory that all condition means are equal (i.e., there is no difference in accuracy between the different conditions) can be rejected. The actual research question might deviate from this assumption in two ways. First, the researcher might not be interested in rejecting the null hypothesis, but in finding evidence for a specific theory (Klugkist, Van Wesel, & Bullens, 2011; Van de Schoot, Hoijtink, & Romeijn, 2011). Specific expectations can be tested via one-sided or post hoc testing in some cases (Silvapulle & Sen, 2004). Alternatively, these expectations can be evaluated directly by formulating informative or order-constrained hypotheses, see Hoijtink (2012) or Chapter 11 (Vanbrabant & Rosseel). Second, the researcher might not be interested in whether the *average* response time is equal across conditions, but whether the score for *each person* is equal across groups.

If researchers have specific expectations, they can formulate so-called informative hypotheses (Hoijtink, 2012; Klugkist, Laudy, & Hoijtink, 2005). Combinations of order and equality constraints can be placed on the parameters to express an informed expectation. For example, $H_1 : \mu_{similar\ word} > \mu_{different\ word} > \mu_{non-word}$ describes the expectation that the mean reaction time in the similar word condition is larger than the mean reaction time in the different word condition, which in turn is larger than the average response time in the non-word condition. Another informative hypothesis is $H_2 : \mu_{similar\ word} > \{\mu_{different\ word}, \mu_{non-word}\}$, which describes the expectation that the average reaction time in the similar word condition is larger than both other conditions, with no expected ordering between those average reaction times. Hypotheses with order constraints ('<' and '>') are also referred to as *order constrained* hypotheses. Such informative hypotheses can be compared to each other by means of an F-bar test (Silvapulle & Sen, 2004; Vanbrabant & Rosseel, 2020; Vanbrabant, Van de Schoot, & Rosseel, 2015) or with Bayes factors (Hoijtink, 2012; Klugkist et al., 2005), which are used for the method in this chapter. Bayes factors are defined in Bayes' theorem, which describes how knowledge about the relative belief in hypotheses can be updated with evidence in data:

$$\frac{P(H_1)}{P(H_2)} \times \frac{P(data|H_1)}{P(data|H_2)} = \frac{P(H_1|data)}{P(H_2|data)} \quad (9.1)$$

Equation 9.1 shows how the prior odds $P(H_1)/P(H_2)$, the ratio of the prior probability of H_1 and H_2 can be updated with the Bayes factor $P(data|H_1)/P(data|H_2)$, the relative evidence in the data for H_1 and H_2 into the posterior odds $P(H_1|data)/P(H_2|data)$, the relative probabilities of the hypotheses, given the data. A Bayes factor then quantifies the relative evidence in the data for two hypotheses (Kass & Raftery, 1995). Thus, $BF_{12} = 10$ means that H_1 is supported 10 times more by the data than H_2. Alternatively, $BF_{12} = .5$ means that H_1 is .5 times as much supported by the data than H_2, or in other words, H_2 is $1/.5 = 2$ times more supported than H_1. In addition to compare the evidence for a pair of hypotheses, the Bayes factor can be used to find which hypothesis from a set is most supported by the data. The computation of Bayes factors used in this chapter relies on vast literature on the topic. This will not be discussed in detail here, but the interested reader is referred to Kass and Raftery (1995). The computation of Bayes factors for informative hypotheses with inequality constraints is described in Hoijtink (2012), Klugkist et al. (2005), Klugkist, Laudy and Hoijtink (2010), and Mulder, Hoijtink and Klugkist (2010).

Common statistical analyses, like ANOVA and regression, test for the presence of group-level effects. If $F_{12} = 10$, we have 10 times more support that the mean reaction times are ordered as in H_1 compared to the ordering in H_2. However, if an effect is detected at the group level this does not imply that the effect is true for each individual (Hamaker, 2012). For example, it might be that for part of the population H_1 reflects the true average reaction times well, but that for another part of the population there is no effect of condition (H_0). At the group level, the conditions appear to have an effect, but this is not true for every individual. A researcher might not be interested in the *average* differences between groups, but in the *individual* effects (Haaf & Rouder, 2017; Molenaar, 2004). The data can also be used to analyze hypotheses on a case-by-case level by computing a *BF* for each individual. If a researcher is interested in answering the question whether an informative hypothesis holds for everyone in a sample, he needs to be able to synthesize the *BFs* from single-case analyses into an aggregate *BF*.

Data, model and hypotheses

This section introduces the Time Estimation data set that is used as an example throughout this chapter. Annotated R code to reproduce the results can be found on the Open Science Framework (osf.io/am7pr/). The individual-level model and hypotheses considered for this data set are presented. The first paragraph introduces the model at the individual level. The next paragraphs introduce the informative hypotheses considered for the parameters in this model. The difference between individual and average hypotheses is discussed.

The Time Estimation data set is presented in Van der Ham, Klaassen, Van Schie and Cuperus (2019). This data set consists of the results of a within-subject experiment where 29 participants were each exposed to movie clips in two conditions. In each condition, participants watched 10 movie clips of 7–90 seconds and rated the *emotional valence* and *arousal* on a nine-point Likert scale they experienced after each clip, and estimated the *duration* of the clip. The content of the movies was chosen such that the set contained a range of levels of arousal and emotional valence (e.g., starving lion, coconut shells; Van der Ham et al. (2019). Of the 20 movie clips in total, 10 were presented in the *Virtual Reality* (VR) condition, where participants wore a VR headset, and 10 clips were presented in a *real life* (RL) scenario in the cinema. The main interest of this experiment is the effect of *condition*, *valence* and *arousal* on the *relative time estimation*. That is, the interest is in the extent to which the mode of watching a clip, its perceived valence and arousal affect how much duration estimates deviate relative to the true duration.

Individual-level model

Testing whether a hypothesis holds for all individuals requires data to be collected for multiple individuals and have multiple measurements for each person to estimate the individual parameters. The example data illustrated in the previous section has a nested structure. That is, the available measurements are nested within individuals. For each person $i = 1, \ldots, n$ a complete data set of 20 measurements is available. Since the interest of the research is to measure the effect of *valence*, *arousal* and *condition* on the *relative time estimation*, the data are modelled using the following regression model:

$$\text{RelTimeEst}^i_m = \beta^i_{intercept} + \beta^i_{condition} \text{Condition}^i_m + \beta^i_{valence} \text{Valence}^i_m \\ + \beta^i_{arousal} \text{Arousal}^i_m + \varepsilon^i_m \qquad (9.2)$$

where the relative time estimation (RelTimeEst) of person i to movie $m = 1, \ldots, M$ is predicted based on the Condition that movie was presented in (VR = 0, RL = 1), the rated Valence and the rated Arousal of the movie clip. By modelling the data for each individual in a separate regression model we can make predictions at the individual level.

Hypotheses

Hypotheses can be formed for the parameters of any individual model. A researcher could be interested in testing the null hypothesis

$$H^i_0 : \beta^i_{condition} = \beta^i_{valence} = \beta^i_{arousal} = 0 \qquad (9.3)$$

Note that H^i_0 is the null hypothesis for person i, meaning that $n = 29$ null hypotheses can be formulated. The superscript differentiates H^i_0 from the average null hypothesis

$$H_0 : \beta_{condition} = \beta_{valence} = \beta_{arousal} = 0 \qquad (9.4)$$

that hypothesizes the *average* effect of condition, valence and arousal to be all zero.

TABLE 9.1 Hypotheses considered for the Time Estimation data. The left column presents the population hypotheses considered in the original paper by Van der Ham et al. (2019). The right column presents the equivalence of these hypotheses in subject-specific hypotheses, considered in the current chapter

Population hypotheses	Individual hypotheses
$H_1 : \beta_{condition} = 0, \beta_{valence} > 0, \beta_{arousal} > 0$	$H_1^i : \beta_{condition}^i = 0, \beta_{valence}^i > 0, \beta_{arousal}^i > 0$
$H_2 : \beta_{condition} > 0, \beta_{valence} > 0, \beta_{arousal} > 0$	$H_2^i : \beta_{condition}^i > 0, \beta_{valence}^i > 0, \beta_{arousal}^i > 0$
H_{1c} : not H_1	H_{1c}^i : not H_1^i

A researcher could be interested in whether *for all participants* H_0^i is a good hypothesis. This can be represented in the following so-called For-all hypothesis:

$$H_{(\cdot)}^{\forall i} : H_{(\cdot)}^1 \& \ldots \& H_{(\cdot)}^i \& \ldots \& H_{(\cdot)}^I \tag{9.5}$$

where the superscript $\forall i$ means that for all $i = 1, \ldots, n$, the subscript$(\cdot)$ indicates a common hypothesis number such that the For-all hypothesis $H_{(\cdot)}^{\forall i}$ expresses the expectation that $H_{(\cdot)}^i$ holds for *all* individuals i.

Van der Ham et al. (2019) were not interested in testing the null hypothesis as shown in Equation 9.4. Rather, they had formulated three informative hypotheses about the population regression coefficients. These hypotheses are presented in the left column of Table 9.1. H_1 specifies the expectation that that there is no effect of condition, while valence and arousal have a positive effect on relative time estimation, while H_2 describes the expectation that all regression coefficients are positive. Finally, H_{1c} is the complement of H_1 and specifies the expectation that at least one of the regression coefficients for arousal and valence is not positive or that the effect of condition is different from zero. The equivalent of these average hypotheses was considered at the individual level. These individual hypotheses are presented in the right column of Table 9.1. The only difference with the population level hypotheses is that the hypotheses now concern individual regression coefficients rather than population regression coefficients.

Summing up, this chapter considers evaluating the same hypothesis at the individual level over a group of individuals, to evaluate whether a theory holds for everyone. These hypotheses can take the form of informative hypotheses that are translated expectations from theories, rather than a standard null or alternative hypothesis.

Individual Bayes factors

Bayesian statistics is well suited to compare multiple hypotheses, whether they are null hypotheses, unconstrained or informative, like those introduced in the previous section. A Bayes factor quantifies the relative evidence in the data for two hypotheses (Kass & Raftery, 1995). More specifically, a Bayes factor is the rate with which the prior beliefs are updated into posterior beliefs, as shown in Equation 9.1. That is, prior to data collection, a researcher already has knowledge about the probability of two hypotheses that can be quantified to express their relative probability. For example, if the researcher expects both hypotheses to be equally probable before observing the data, the prior ratio is .5/.5. The prior ratio is updated with data and the resulting Bayes factor then quantifies how the data influenced this prior knowledge, summing up an updated ratio. Bayes factors are mostly used to evaluate hypotheses on population effects (i.e., there are no differences in the average reaction times between the conditions). In this chapter, the interest is in describing the relative evidence for two hypotheses for a specific individual. For this purpose, the *BF* can be computed per subject. The section 'Aggregating Bayes factors' demonstrates how this individual-level evidence can be synthesized.

To analyze individual hypotheses presented in Table 9.1 using *BF*s, two steps need to be executed. First, the hypotheses need to be evaluated separately, which is described in this section. In the next section it is demonstrated how the individual Bayes factors can be aggregated. For binomial data (e.g., number of successful trials per condition), a stand-alone Shiny application is also available to evaluate and aggregate individual-level hypotheses (Klaassen, Zedelius, Veling, Aarts & Hoijtink, 2018).

Analysis

The R (R Core Team, 2013) package bain, developed by Gu, Mulder and Hoijtink (2017), was used to evaluate informative hypotheses for each person. All code presented in this chapter is also available on the Open Science Framework (https://osf.io/am7pr/). To read the data into R the following code can be used:

```
#install bain
install.packages("bain")
#load bain
library(bain)
```

Next, the data can be loaded with:

```
#read data from the online repository
data <- read.table(file = "https://raw.githubusercontent.com/fayette
klaassen/gpbf/master/data.txt", header = TRUE)
# determine the number of unique ppnrs = the number of cases
N <- length(unique(data$ppnr))
```

Next, a Bayes factor has to be computed for each person, for the hypotheses in Table 9.1. The code below first creates an empty list to store the results of each person in. Inspecting the names() of the data tells us how the variables are stored in R, so that these names can be used in later functions. A random seed is set to make the results replicable. Next, a loop over all subjects is created, such that the data of that subject is selected. The function `bain` requires the estimates of the linear model as input. These are obtained by running the linear regression model `lm()`, where TimePerception is predicted by Condition, Valence and Arousal. Finally, the function `bain` is executed, where the estimates of the linear model for person i are used to evaluate the hypotheses provided. The hypotheses can be entered in quotation marks, separating hypotheses by a semicolon. The names of the variables that were inspected earlier can be used to refer to the relevant regression coefficients.

```
# create an empty list to store results
results <- vector("list", length = N)
names(data)

## [1] "ppnr"      "TimePerception" "Valence"    "Arousal"
## [5] "Condition"

set.seed(7561) # seed to create replicable results

for(i in 1:N) {# loop over N individuals
    data_i <- data[data$ppnr == i,] #subset data for ppnr == i

    fit_i <- lm(formula = TimePerception ~ Condition + Valence + Arousal,
                data = data_i) #execute linear model

# save the results of bain analysis.
results[[i]] <- bain(fit_i, "Condition=0 & Valence>0 & Arousal>0;
                      Condition>0 & Valence>0 & Arousal>0")
    }
```

Results

To obtain the final results, the code below can be executed. First, looking at the names of the `bain` output for the first person tells us there is an object named fit and a `BFmatrix` resulting from the analysis. The column labeled 'BF' (the seventh column) of the fit object contains the Bayes factors of each hypothesis, H_1^i and H_2^i in Table 9.1, against their complement (H_{1c}^i and H_{2c}^i). The `BFmatrix` contains the Bayes factors comparing H_1^i to H_2^i and vice versa. The first row and second column contain the BF_{12}^i.

```
names(results[[1]]) # view the names of the bain output for first person ([[1]]).

##  [1] "fit"                       "BFmatrix"
##  [3] "b"                         "prior"
##  [5] "posterior"                 "call"
##  [7] "model"                     "hypotheses"
##  [9] "independent_restrictions"  "estimates"
## [11] "n"
```

```
# view the output of fit and bfmatrix
results[[1]]$fit

##         Fit_eq    Com_eq        Fit_in     Com_in         Fit         Com
## H1    0.691829  1.627527  0.091389727  0.2382186  0.063226065  0.3877072
## H2    1.000000  1.000000  0.003370348  0.1499276  0.003370348  0.1499276
## Hu          NA        NA           NA         NA           NA         NA
##                   BF        PMPa        PMPb
## H1    0.16307685    0.878852  0.13755298
## H2    0.01917411    0.121148  0.01896141
## Hu            NA          NA  0.84348561

results[[1]]$BFmatrix

##              H1         H2
## H1    1.0000000   7.254363
## H2    0.1378481   1.000000
```

To collect the relevant results for all subjects, the following code can be used. First, an output table is created, with two columns and n rows. Next, a loop over all persons saves the relevant Bayes factors in this output matrix.

```
output <- matrix(0, nrow = N, ncol = 2) # create output table with
N rows and 4 columns
colnames(output) <- c("BF1c", "BF12") # name the columns of the
output

for(i in 1:N){ # loop over persons
  BFtab <- results[[i]]$fit # obtain the fit table of person i
  # compute relevant bfs
  BF1c <- results[[i]]$fit[1,7]
  BF12 <- results[[i]]$BFmatrix[1,2]
  # save the 4 bfs in the i-th row of the output matrix
  output[i,] <- c(BF1c,BF12)
}

output # view the final output
```

The individual Bayes factors are presented in Table 9.2. The table shows that H_1^i is preferred over H_{1c}^i for 16 out of 29 subjects, and preferred over H_2^i for 22 out of 29 subjects. The next step is to synthesize this evidence into an aggregated BF for $H_{(\cdot)}^{\forall i}$.

Aggregating Bayes factors

Independent Bayes factors can be aggregated into a combined Bayes factor by taking their product (Klaassen et al., 2018). The interpretation of this product is the evidence that H_1 is preferred over H_2 for persons $1, \ldots, n$, where n is the number of individuals. This again shows that the individuals are evaluated separately: their evidence is combined but kept intact at the individual level. The scale of this product

TABLE 9.2 Bayes factors comparing H_1^i to H_{1c}^i and to H_2^i for all $i = 1, \ldots, 29$ subjects in the Time Estimation data set. Values above 1 indicate a preference for H_1^i, and values below 1 indicate a preference for H_{1c}^i and H_2^i, respectively

i	BF_{1c}^i	BF_{12}^i
1	0.16	7.25
2	0.96	1.74
3	2.77	1.77
4	0.17	6.97
5	<0.01	<0.01
6	3.25	2.83
7	1.52	2.64
8	8.10	1.57
9	5.48	0.96
10	0.70	9.55
11	0.03	0.01
12	3.66	1.79
13	0.05	8.24
14	0.27	1.02
15	3.71	2.98
16	3.02	3.40
17	0.09	0.20
18	5.39	3.33
19	0.34	4.35
20	1.08	3.36
21	0.08	0.06
22	2.37	1.04
23	1.30	2.43
24	2.50	0.27
25	0.37	6.16
26	2.30	1.87
27	0.80	0.50
28	2.18	2.22
29	1.49	3.12

depends on the number of observations included and is therefore difficult to compare from study to study. To make the output comparable over studies, we can take the geometric mean of the product of Bayes factors, the gPBF. This is the equivalent to an average, but then for products rather than a sum. The gPBF is the average relative evidence for two hypotheses in an individual. We can evaluate how many of the individual Bayes factors describe evidence in favor of the same hypothesis as the gPBF. This is called the Evidence Rate (ER). The ER is used to evaluate to what extent individuals indeed come from the same population. If the ER is 1, all individuals show evidence for the preferred hypothesis by the gPBF. If the ER is (near) 0, almost no individuals show evidence for the preferred hypothesis by the gPBF. Another measure that can be used to evaluate the geometric mean and the individual Bayes factors is the Stability Rate (SR). This is the proportion of individual Bayes factors that expresses evidence for the same hypothesis as the gPBF, but with stronger evidence. This quantifies the (in)balance of individual Bayes factors. If it is .5, the gPBF is affected equally by larger a smaller Bayes factors, while if it is close to 1, most cases express evidence stronger than the mean itself, and only a few cases with relatively weak or reverse evidence diminish the effect. If the SR is close to 0, this indicates that the gPBF is determined by a few strong cases, with most other cases expressing weaker evidence or reverse evidence. Together, these three measures (gPBF, ER and SR) provide information about how uniform the population can be expected to be with regard to the considered hypotheses, and what the expected relative evidence is for a next person.

In what follows it is explained how the evidence of multiple individual Bayes factors can be aggregated to answer the question 'Does everyone?' The results of the example analysis are presented and interpreted.

Analysis

The individual Bayes factors can then be aggregated using a function available on the Open Science Framework (https://osf.io/am7pr/). The function requires as input a matrix with n rows and K columns, where n represents the total of individuals and K the number of Bayes factors for which the aggregate conclusion is of interest. The output of the individual analyses created in the previous section fulfills this requirement and can be used in the function. The output of the function is a list that contains: a table containing the gPBF for all Bayes factors considered; the individual Bayes factors used as input; and the sample size n.

```
gpout <- gPBF(output)
gpout
```

The function can be applied to any collection of individual Bayes factors. If you use your own software to compute Bayes factors at the individual level, and create a matrix of n rows and K columns, the function gPBF() can be applied. This function computes the geometric product over all n individuals for each of the m comparisons of interest (for example, $m = 3$, with BF_{12} BF_{1c} and BF_{21}). The ER is computed as the proportion of individual BF_s that support the same hypothesis as the gPBF, and the SR is computed as the proportion of individual BF_s that express stronger evidence than the gPBF.

Results

Table 9.3 presents the gPBF, the ER and the SR for the Time Estimation data.

TABLE 9.3 Geometric mean of the product of individual Bayes factors (gPBF), Evidence Rate (ER) and Stability Rate (SR) for the comparison of the For-all hypotheses $H_1^{\forall i}$ versus $H_{1c}^{\forall i}$ and $H_2^{\forall i}$

	$BF_{1c}^{\forall i}$	$BF_{12}^{\forall i}$
gPBF	0.649	1.130
ER	0.448	0.759
SR	0.345	0.690

The results show that based on the gPBF there is no clear evidence that H_1^i is preferred over H_{1c}^i or H_2^i for everyone, or vice versa. Specifically, Table 9.3 shows that $gPBF_{1c} = .649$, indicating that the average individual evidence is 1.54 times stronger in favor of H_{1c}^i compared to H_1^i. The ER for $BF_{1c}^{\forall i}$ shows that the proportion of individual Bayes factors preferring H_{1c}^i is .448, quantifying the earlier observation that 44.8% of individual Bayes factors prefer H_{1c}^i over H_1^i. The SR of .345 indicates that there are relatively few cases expressing stronger evidence in favor of H_1^i than the gPBF. Together with the weak evidence, this indicates that the hypotheses do not describe the subjects well as a group together. Neither the informative hypothesis nor its complement can predict the group of subjects adequately. For the comparison H_1^i to H_2^i we find that the gPBF is 1.130, not indicating a clear preference for either hypothesis. The ER of .759 tells us that most subjects express support for H_1^i, and the SR of .690 indicates that the gPBF is influenced somewhat by strong evidence for H_2^i by some subjects. Indeed, Table 9.2 shows that subjects 5, 11 and 21 express relatively strong evidence for H_1^i (a factor of 16.67 or higher). The results indicate that the hypotheses considered are not likely to hold for all subjects. Moreover, it seems possible that while H_1^i might be a better description than H_2^i for some subjects, it clearly does not apply to all individuals.

In the group-level analysis an average preference for H_1 over both H_{1c} and H_2 was found (Van der Ham et al., 2019). These analyses cannot be compared thoughtlessly. After all, in the group-level model, individual effects are shrunk to the average effect and dependent on another. However, we do get some insight that on average H_1 seems to be a good model, while it appears from the individual analysis to not hold for all individuals. Future research could develop new theories that might indeed describe all individuals, or try to explain the separation in effects found in the individual analysis. Perhaps an unmeasured variable explains why for some individuals H_1^i is preferred over H_2^i and for others not.

Conclusion and limitations

This chapter has demonstrated how one can evaluate whether a hypothesis is supported *for all individuals*. To answer such question, the geometric Bayes factor was introduced, which synthesizes the evidence from multiple individuals. The goal of this chapter is twofold. First, it invites researchers to rethink their own research questions and hypotheses. What is the goal of an experiment? Is it to show average effects, or demonstrate the iniquitousness of a theory? If an effect, theory or model holds on average in a population, this is no proof of the existence of such an effect in any individual specifically. Second, if indeed a researcher is interested in investigating whether a hypothesis is supported by everyone, this chapter presents the steps required to analyze this question and how to draw conclusions. The methodology is easy to use and apply to users already familiar with Bayesian (order-constrained) hypothesis testing.

The data required for the proposed methodology can also be analyzed with multilevel models. Multiple measurements are required for each person in each condition to be able to draw inference about individual effects. In a multilevel model this data can be modelled, for example, by including random effects that account for the dependency between individual subjects, in order to generalize to a population effect. By constraining the individual effects to be normally distributed around the average effect, a phenomenon called *shrinking* occurs: the individual effects are being pulled towards the mean; see Chapter 5 (Van Erp). A multilevel model can be used to test the variance of individual effects, but not to evaluate whether a hypothesis applies to each individual separately. The methodology in this chapter answers a different question, namely whether the evidence at the individual level is homogeneous over a sample of individuals.

It is important to keep in mind that the consistency of a Bayes factor depends on sample size. For the methodology presented in this chapter, that implies that the number of subjects and measures per condition are both important. The number of subjects affects the stability of the ER and SR (Klaassen et al., 2018), while the number of replications affects the consistency of the individual Bayes factors.

Another important consideration is the number of hypotheses to consider in a comparison. The more hypotheses are considered in a set, the more difficult it is to find one clear best hypothesis.

References

Gu, X., Mulder, J., & Hoijtink, H. (2017). Approximated adjusted fractional Bayes factors: A general method for testing informative hypotheses. *British Journal of Mathematical and Statistical Psychology*, 71(2), 229–261. doi:10.1111/bmsp.12110.

Haaf, J. M., & Rouder, J. N. (2017). Developing constraint in Bayesian mixed models. *Psychological Methods*, 22(4), 779–798. doi:10.1037/met0000156.

Hamaker, E. L. (2012). Why researchers should think "within-person": A paradigmatic rationale. In M. R. Mehl and S. Conner (Eds.), *Handbook of research methods for studying daily life* (pp. 43–61). New York, NY: Guilford.

Hoijtink, H. (2012). *Informative hypotheses: Theory and practice for behavioral and social scientists*. Boca Ranton, FL: Taylor & Francis.

Kass, R. E., & Raftery, A. E. (1995). Bayes factors. *Journal of the American Statistical Association*, 90(430), 773–795. doi:10.1080/01621459.1995.10476572.

Klaassen, F., Zedelius, C., Veling, H., Aarts, H., & Hoijtink, H. (2018). All for one or some for all? Evaluating informative hypotheses for multiple N=1 studies. *Behavior Research Methods*, *50*(6), 2276–2291. doi:10.3758/s13428-017-0992-5.

Klugkist, I., Laudy, O., & Hoijtink, H. (2005). Inequality constrained analysis of variance: A Bayesian approach. *Psychological Methods*, *10*(4), 477–493. doi:0.1037/1082-989X.10.4.477.

Klugkist, I., Laudy, O., & Hoijtink, H. (2010). Bayesian evaluation of inequality and equality constrained hypotheses for contingency tables. *Psychological Methods*, *15*(3), 281–299. doi:10.1037/a0020137.

Klugkist, I., Van Wesel, F., & Bullens, J. (2011). Do we know what we test and do we test what we want to know? *International Journal of Behavioral Development*, *35*(6), 550–560. doi:10.1177/0165025411425873.

Molenaar, P. C. M. (2004). A manifesto on psychology as idiographic science: Bringing the person back into scientific psychology, this time forever. *Measurement Interdisciplinary Research and Perspectives*, *2*(4), 201–218. doi:10.1207/s15366359mea0204_1.

Mulder, J., Hoijtink, H., & Klugkist, I. (2010). Equality and inequality constrained multivariate linear models: Objective model selection using constrained posterior priors. *Journal of Statistical Planning and Inference*, *140*(4), 887–906. doi:10.1016/j.jspi.2009.09.022.

R Core Team. (2013). R: A language and environment for statistical computing. Vienna: R Foundation for Statistical Computing. Retrieved from www.R-project.org/.

Silvapulle, M. J., & Sen, P. K. (2004). *Constrained statistical inference: Order, inequality and shape constraints*. London: Wiley.

Van de Schoot, R., Hoijtink, H., & Romeijn, J. W. (2011). Moving beyond traditional null hypothesis testing: Evaluating expectations directly. *Frontiers in Psychology*, *2*, 24. doi:10.3389/fpsyg.2011.00024.

Van der Ham, I. J. M., Klaassen, F., Van Schie, K., & Cuperus, A. (2019). Elapsed time estimates in virtual reality and the physical world: The role of arousal and emotional valence. *Computers in Human Behavior*, *94*, 77–81. doi:10.1016/j.chb.2019.01.005.

Vanbrabant, L., Van de Schoot, R., & Rosseel, Y. (2015). Constrained statistical inference: Sample-size tables for ANOVA and regression. *Frontiers in Psychology*, *5*, 1–8.

10

GOING MULTIVARIATE IN CLINICAL TRIAL STUDIES

A Bayesian framework for multiple binary outcomes

Xynthia Kavelaars

DEPARTMENT OF METHODOLOGY AND STATISTICS, TILBURG UNIVERSITY, TILBURG, THE NETHERLANDS

Introduction

Clinical trials often compare a new treatment to standard care or a placebo. If the collected data provide sufficient evidence that the new treatment is better than the control treatment, the new treatment is declared superior. Since these superiority decisions ultimately contribute to a decision about treatment adoption, proper error control is crucial to ensure that better treatments are indeed selected. Key to regulating decision errors is collecting sufficient information: A quantity that is often expressed in terms of a minimum number of participants, or required sample size.

Recruiting sufficiently large samples can be challenging, however. This is especially true in an era in which medicine is increasingly personalized (Hamburg & Collins, 2010; Ng, Murray, Levy, & Venter, 2009). *Personalization of medicine* refers to the targeting of treatments at specific patient and/or disease characteristics under the assumption that patients with different (disease) characteristics respond differently to treatments (Goldberger & Buxton, 2013). Since personalization limits the target population of the treatment, inclusion and exclusion criteria for trials become more stringent and the eligible number of participants decreases. This inherently decreases the sample size of studies conducted with the same resources. Consequences of small samples may be substantial: Trials may be left underpowered and decisions about superiority might remain inconclusive.

The problem associated with small sample sizes due to stringent inclusion criteria is illustrated by the CAR-B study (Schimmel, Verhaak, Hanssens, Gehring, & Sitskoorn, 2018). CAR-B aims to improve treatment for cancer patients with 11–20 metastatic brain tumors (i.e. tumors that originate from another site in the body and have spread to the brain). These patients have a life expectancy of one or two months and are currently treated with whole-brain radiation therapy. However, whole-brain radiation has adverse side effects: The treatment damages brain tissue and results in severe cognitive impairment. Local radiation of the individual tumors (stereotactic surgery) is a promising alternative that spares healthy tissue and prevents cognitive decline without increasing mortality. The protective effect on cognition has been demonstrated in a related population of patients with fewer brain tumors (Chang et al., 2009; Yamamoto et al., 2014). However, investigating whether local radiation reduces side effects in the current target population is difficult: Clinicians are reluctant to prescribe the alternative treatment and not all referred patients are eligible for participation, leaving the researchers unable to recruit the required sample.

To improve decision-making with limited samples, studies such as CAR-B might combine information from multiple outcomes. The current chapter introduces a Bayesian decision-making framework to combine two binary outcomes. Since superiority with two outcomes can be defined in multiple ways, several criteria to evaluate treatments are discussed in the "Decision rules" section. Evaluation of these decision rules requires a statistical analysis procedure that combines the outcomes. The "Data analysis" section outlines such a multivariate approach for Bayesian analysis of binary outcomes. The proposed decision-making strategy is illustrated in the "Computation in practice" section, which introduces an online app to analyze real data (for an online version go to https://utrecht-university.shinyapps.io/multiple_binary_outcomes/ – for the annotated R code go to https://osf.io/am7pr/ – and for potential newer versions go to https://github.com/XynthiaKavelaars). Since trials with limited access to participants aim for the smallest sample possible, the chapter continues with "Sample size considerations" to explain how interim analyses during the trial may improve efficiency compared to traditional sample size estimation before running the trial. The "Concluding remarks" section highlights some extensions of the framework. Throughout the chapter, the comparison of local and whole-brain radiation in the CAR-B study serves as an example with cognitive functioning and quality of life as the outcomes under consideration.

Decision rules

A key element of decision-making is the decision rule: A procedure to decide whether a treatment is considered superior. When dealing with two outcomes, superiority can be defined in several ways (Food and Drug Administration, 2017), such as a favorable effect on:

1. The most important outcome ("Single-outcome rule")
2. Both outcomes ("All rule")
3. Any of the outcomes ("Any rule")
4. The sum of outcomes ("Compensatory rule")

Each of these decision rules weighs the effects of the two outcomes differently. The *Single-outcome rule* evaluates the data from one outcome and ignores the other outcome in the decision procedure. In the CAR-B study, local radiation would be the treatment of preference if it impairs cognitive functioning less than whole-brain radiation, irrespective of the effects on quality of life. The *All rule* evaluates both outcomes, and requires favorable effects on each of them. Compared to whole-brain radiation, more patients should maintain both cognitive functioning *and* quality of life after local radiation. The *Any rule* requires a beneficial effect on at least one outcome and ignores any result on the other outcome. Local radiation would be considered superior if fewer patients experience cognitive side effects, a lower quality of life, or both. The *Compensatory rule* also requires at least one favorable treatment effect, but the compensatory mechanism poses a restriction on the second outcome. The new treatment may perform better, similarly, or even worse than the control treatment on this outcome, but the rule takes the size of the treatment differences into account to weigh beneficial and adverse effects. A net advantage on the sum of outcomes is required, such that several outcome combinations would result in a preference for local radiation. Superiority is concluded as long as favorable effects on cognitive functioning outweigh unfavorable effects on quality of life or vice versa.

The aforementioned decision rules ultimately lead to a conclusion about the treatment *difference*: The new treatment is considered superior if the difference between the new and the control treatment is larger than zero according to the decision rule of interest. For each of the decision rules, the corresponding superiority region is plotted in Figure 10.1. These superiority regions graphically represent how the treatment differences on both individual outcomes should be related to result in superiority: If the probability that the treatment difference falls in the marked area is sufficiently large, the treatment would be declared superior.

Selecting a decision rule

The choice for a decision rule should be guided by the researcher's standard for superiority. To illustrate this, consider the following situations (see Figure 10.2 for a graphical representation):

1. Local radiation performs better on cognitive functioning as well as quality of life
2. Local radiation performs better on cognitive functioning and similarly on quality of life
3. Local radiation performs much better on cognitive functioning and slightly worse on quality of life
4. Local radiation performs slightly better on cognitive functioning and much worse on quality of life

If outcomes are equally important, most researchers would either (a) set a high standard and consider local radiation superior if both outcomes demonstrate an advantage (situation 1), or (b) balance outcomes and consider local radiation superior if advantages outweigh disadvantages (situations 1–3). Situation 4 is

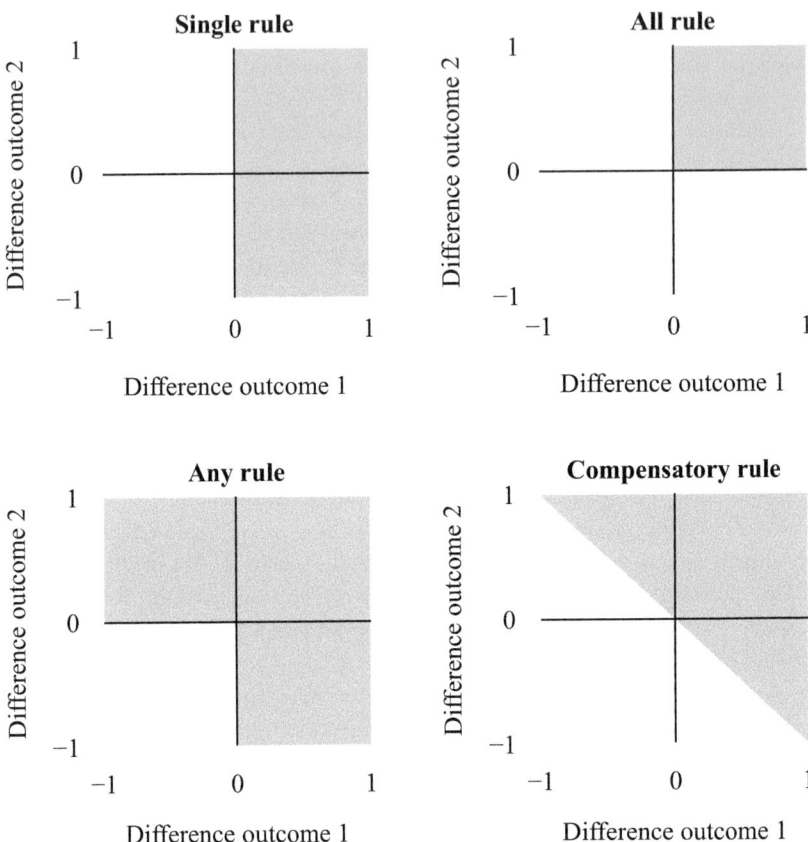

FIGURE 10.1 Superiority regions (shaded areas) for different decision rules

unlikely to result in a preference for local radiation, unless cognitive functioning is much more important than quality of life.

While the All rule applies to the high standard and differentiates situation 1 (superior) from situations 2–4 (not superior), the Compensatory rule balances results and distinguishes situations 1–3 (superior) from situation 4 (not superior). The Single and Any rules do not meet these standards and would conclude that local radiation performs better in all situations, including the fourth. These rules should be used only when unfavorable effects can safely be ignored in the presence of a specific (Single rule) or any (Any rule) favorable effect.

Data analysis

To evaluate the decision rules discussed in the previous section, treatment comparison requires a procedure to quantify evidence in favor of the new treatment. The current section introduces the elements of a Bayesian approach to analyze data from two binary outcomes: likelihood, prior, and posterior distributions.

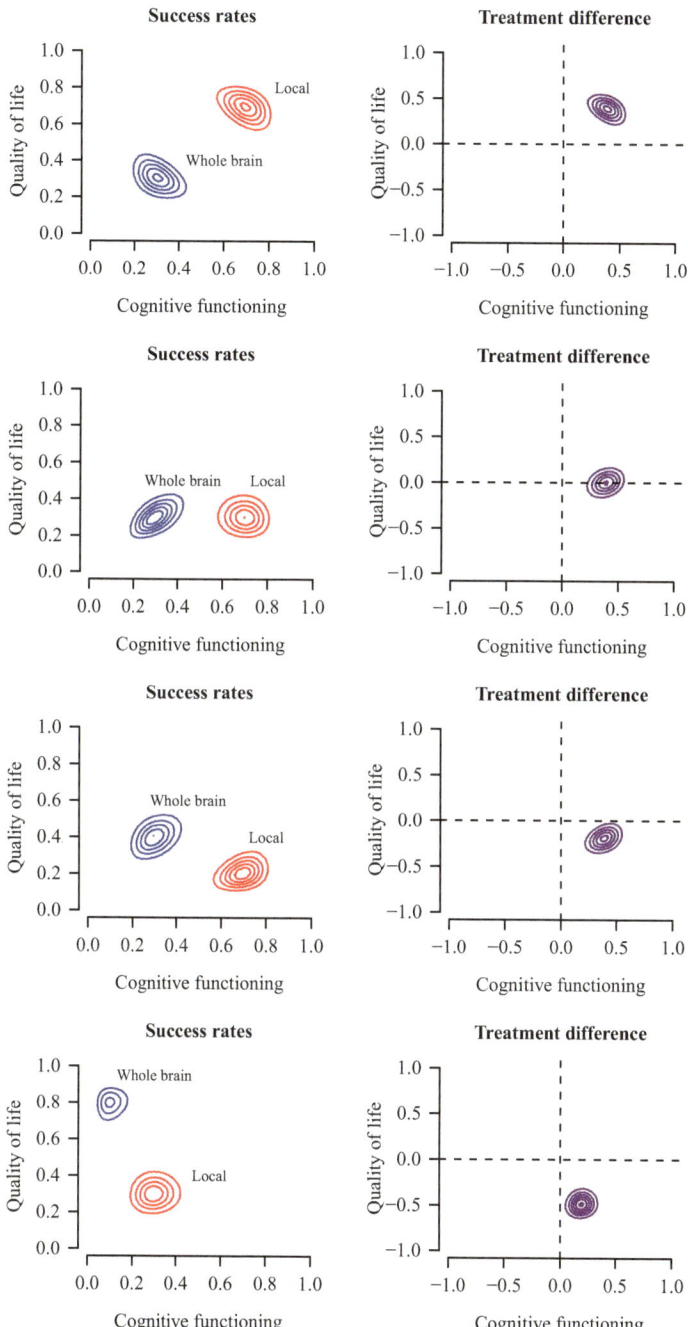

FIGURE 10.2 Example posterior distributions (left panels) and distributions of the treatment difference (right panels) for four different potential treatment differences (local radiation–whole-brain radiation) in the CAR-B study

Description of the data and specification of the likelihood

Binary data have two values, traditionally labeled as 1 for success and 0 for failure. In general, *success* refers to improvement or absence of decline, and *failure* indicates the opposite: decline or absence of improvement respectively. Considering two outcomes together results in two binary responses per participant that can take four different combinations (see Table 10.1). The patient can have successes on both outcomes (x_{11}^{obs}); a success on one outcome, but not on the other (x_{10}^{obs} or x_{01}^{obs}); or failures on both outcomes (x_{00}^{obs}). The total number of successes on a particular outcome equals the sum of simultaneous and separate successes on that outcome, such that $x_1^{obs} = x_{11}^{obs} + x_{10}^{obs}$, etc.

The multivariate likelihood of the outcomes is based on the four response frequencies. These four response frequencies reflect (a) the individual success rates, and (b) the relation between outcomes. The latter serves as an additional source of information that may contribute to more efficient decision-making (Food and Drug Administration, 2010).

Specification of prior information

Prior information represents prior beliefs about success rates of individual treatments as well as the difference between treatments. These prior beliefs can, for example, incorporate information from comparable studies into the current one. Prior beliefs about two binary outcomes are quantified by four prior frequencies, expressed as $x_{11}^{prior}, x_{10}^{prior}, x_{01}^{prior}$, and x_{00}^{prior} (Olkin & Trikalinos, 2015). Each of these individual prior frequencies incorporates information about one of the response frequencies in the data ($x_{11}^{obs}, x_{10}^{obs}, x_{01}^{obs}$ and x_{00}^{obs}). Conveniently, one can think of these prior observations as an extra dataset, where the total number of observations in this prior dataset reflects the strength of the prior beliefs. Strong prior beliefs are translated to many prior observations, whereas weak prior beliefs can be expressed through small numbers of prior observations. An uninformative prior specification for the analysis of two binary outcomes would be a half observation for each response combination, such that the total number of prior observations equals two (Berger, Bernardo, & Sun, 2015). This specification is also called *Jeffrey's prior* and conveys virtually no

TABLE 10.1 Response combinations for two binary outcomes

	Outcome 2		
Outcome 1	Success	Failure	Total
Success	x_{11}	x_{10}	x_1
Failure	x_{01}	x_{00}	$n - x_1$
Total	x_2	$n - x_2$	n

information about the success rates of individual outcomes or the correlation between outcomes. If both treatments have this specification, no prior information about the treatment difference is provided either.

The posterior distribution

The posterior distribution reflects prior beliefs after they have been updated with the data and indicate the posterior success rates of individual outcomes in relation to each other; see also Chapters 1–3 (Miočević, Levy, & Van de Schoot; Miočević, Levy, & Savord; Van de Schoot, Veen, Smeets, Winter, & Depaoli). The posterior response frequencies equal the sum of prior and observed frequencies, such that $x_{11}^{post} = x_{11}^{prior} + x_{11}^{obs}$, etc. Examples of posterior distributions for treatment effects with two outcomes are graphically presented in Figure 10.2.

Comparison of the two posterior distributions allows for decision-making about treatment superiority, by quantifying evidence for a relevant treatment difference as a posterior probability. This posterior probability depends on the definition of superiority as defined via the decision rule and allows for two decisions. If the posterior probability exceeds a pre-specified threshold (often .95 or .99 in clinical trials; Food and Drug Administration, 2010), evidence is strong enough to consider the treatment superior. If the posterior probability is lower than the threshold, there is not sufficient evidence to conclude superiority.

Computation in practice

The online supplement offers a Shiny app to analyze real data using the framework proposed in the previous sections. If the researcher enters the prior $(x_{11}^{prior}, x_{10}^{prior}, x_{01}^{prior}, x_{00}^{prior})$ and observed $(x_{11}^{obs}, x_{10}^{obs}, x_{01}^{obs}, x_{00}^{obs})$ response frequencies for two treatments, the application:

a. Computes the posterior probability of a treatment difference given the introduced decision rules
b. Plots the posterior treatment distributions
c. Plots the posterior distribution of the treatment difference
d. Computes the prior, observed and posterior correlations between outcomes

The Shiny app including user guide can be found at https://utrecht-university.shinyapps.io/multiple_binary_outcomes/ (for the annotated R code and potential newer versions go to https://github.com/XynthiaKavelaars).

The method and app are illustrated with artificial data from two treatment distributions with two negatively correlated binary outcome variables ($n = 100$ cases per treatment). The true success probabilities of the experimental and control treatments were .60 and .40 on both outcomes respectively, such that the experimental treatment performs better on both individual outcomes. The data were used to quantify evidence in favor of the experimental treatment according to the different decision rules (Single, Any, All, Compensatory). The observed response frequencies were entered in the four upper-left cells under "Experimental treatment" and "Control treatment" in the *Data* tab (see Figure 10.3). The app subsequently computed the total observed successes and failures in the margins as well as the observed correlations.

Without any prior knowledge about the treatments or treatment differences, Jeffrey's prior served as a prior distribution, such that each response category was assigned a half observation. After entering the prior frequencies in the *Prior* tab, the app provided the successes and failures per outcome and the prior correlation between outcomes (Figure 10.4).

The *Treatment distributions* tab showed the posterior treatment distributions and posterior correlations of both treatments (Figure 10.5).

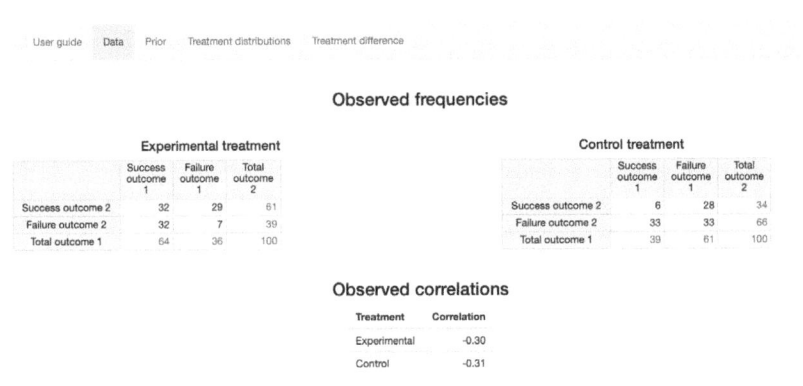

FIGURE 10.3 Screenshot of *Data* tab

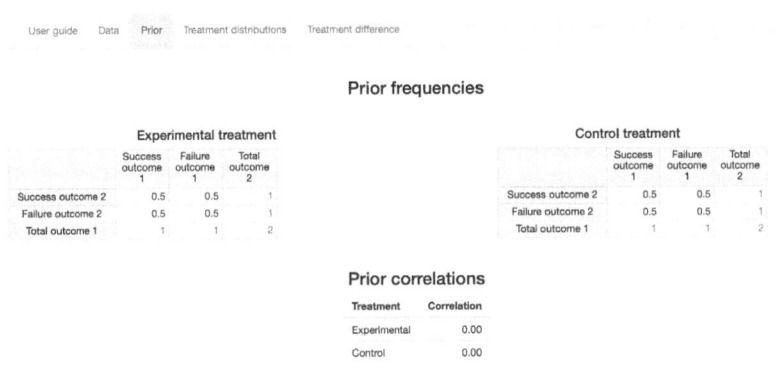

FIGURE 10.4 Screenshot of *Prior* tab

Going multivariate in clinical trial studies **147**

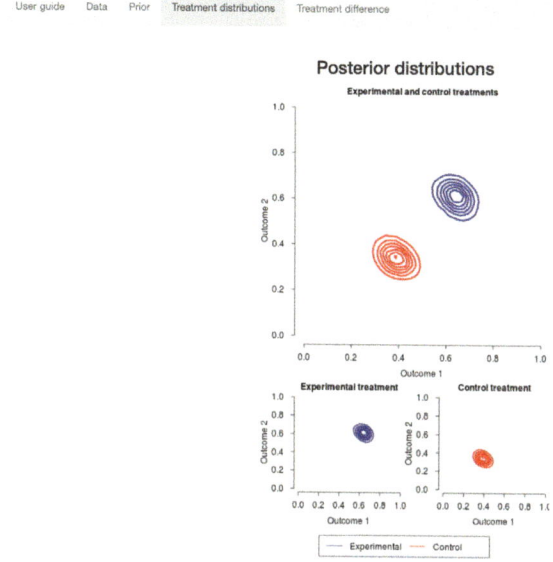

FIGURE 10.5 Screenshot of *Treatment distributions* tab

The *Treatment difference* tab (Figure 10.6) presented the distribution of the posterior treatment difference and the evidence in favor of the experimental treatment according to the proposed decision rules.

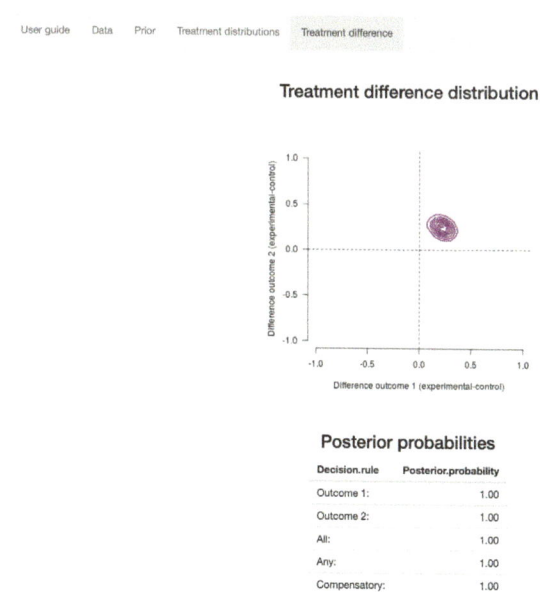

FIGURE 10.6 Screenshot of *Treatment difference* tab

Sample size considerations

When the availability of participants is limited, a highly relevant question is how much data are minimally needed to make a sufficiently powerful decision. Since the sample size traditionally determines when to stop data collection, researchers often estimate the required number of participants before running the trial. Efficient a priori sample size estimation is difficult due to uncertainty about one or multiple treatment differences, regardless of the number of outcomes, since treatment differences are unknown in advance and need to be estimated. However, small inaccuracies in their estimation may have important consequences. Overestimating a treatment difference results in too small a sample to make a powerful decision, while (limited) underestimation needlessly extends the trial.

In trials with multiple outcomes, the required sample size also depends on the decision rule as illustrated in Figure 10.7. The figure shows how evidence in favor of the decision rule under consideration changes for the example data from the "Computation in practice" section, while increasing the sample size in steps of one observation per group. Although the posterior probabilities of all decision rules ultimately approach one and conclude superiority as the data accumulate, different decision rules require different numbers of observations to arrive at that conclusion. With the data presented in Figure 10.7, the Any rule

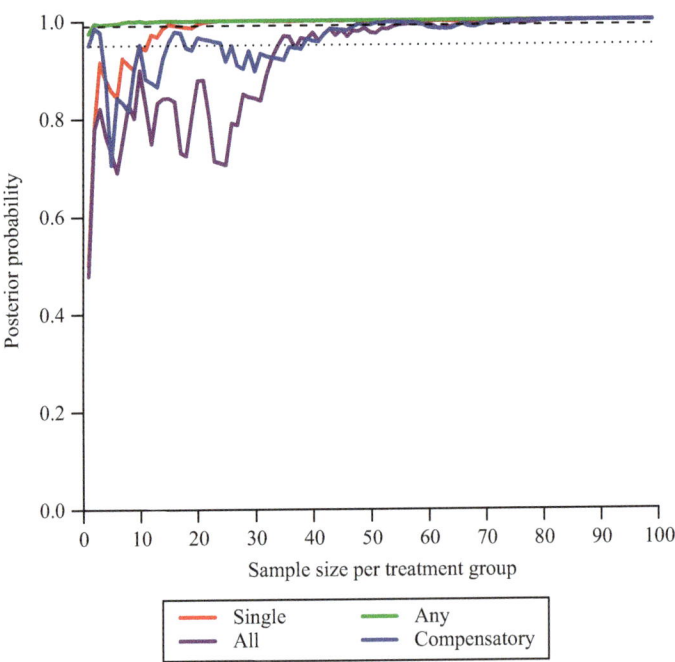

FIGURE 10.7 Example of evidence collection as data accumulate for different decision rules and two different decision criteria (dots = .95; dashes = .99)

requires fewest observations to cross decision thresholds, followed by the Compensatory and Single outcome rules. The All rule requires the largest sample.

The relative efficiency of decision rules displayed in Figure 10.7 is specific to the particular scenario, since different relations between outcomes require different sample sizes to evaluate a specific decision rule (Food and Drug Administration, 2010). To provide an idea of the influence of the correlation between the outcomes, posterior treatment distributions for three correlation structures are displayed in Figure 10.8. This influence affects the proportion of overlap between the distribution of the posterior treatment difference and the superiority region of a decision rule, such that evidence in favor of the new treatment (i.e. posterior probability) as well as the required sample size to reach the decision threshold differ.

Figure 10.9 illustrates how the amount of evidence for each decision rule depends on the correlation when treatment differences are identical. The Single rule is not sensitive to the correlation: The proportion of the difference distribution that overlaps with the superiority region is similar for each correlation structure. The required sample size to conclude superiority will be the same. The All rule has a (slightly) larger proportion of overlap between the distribution of the difference and the superiority region when the correlation is positive. Compared to negatively correlated outcomes, the same amount of evidence can thus be obtained with a smaller sample. The Any and Compensatory rules demonstrate the relationship between the correlation structure and sample size more clearly. The distribution of the treatment difference falls completely in the superiority region when outcomes are negatively correlated (implying a posterior probability of one), while uncorrelated or positively correlated data result in a part of the distribution outside the superiority region (i.e. a posterior probability below one). The sample size will be smallest with negatively correlated outcomes.

In summary, several sources of uncertainty complicate a priori sample size estimation in trials with multiple outcomes: Treatment differences on individual outcomes, the correlation between outcomes, and the decision rule influence the required number of observations. The difficulty of accurately estimating the sample size interferes with the potential efficiency gain of multiple outcomes, such that a priori sample size estimation may be inadequate with small samples and multiple outcomes (Rauch & Kieser, 2015).

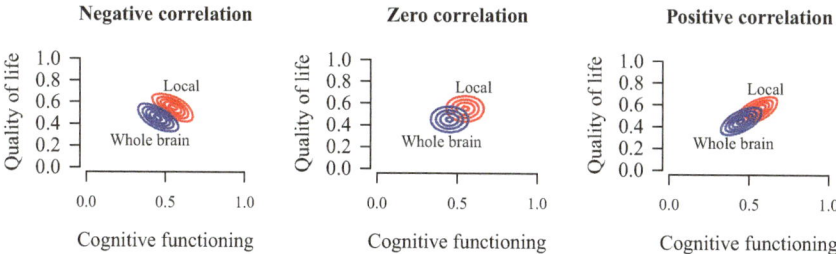

FIGURE 10.8 The influence of the correlation between outcomes on posterior treatment distributions

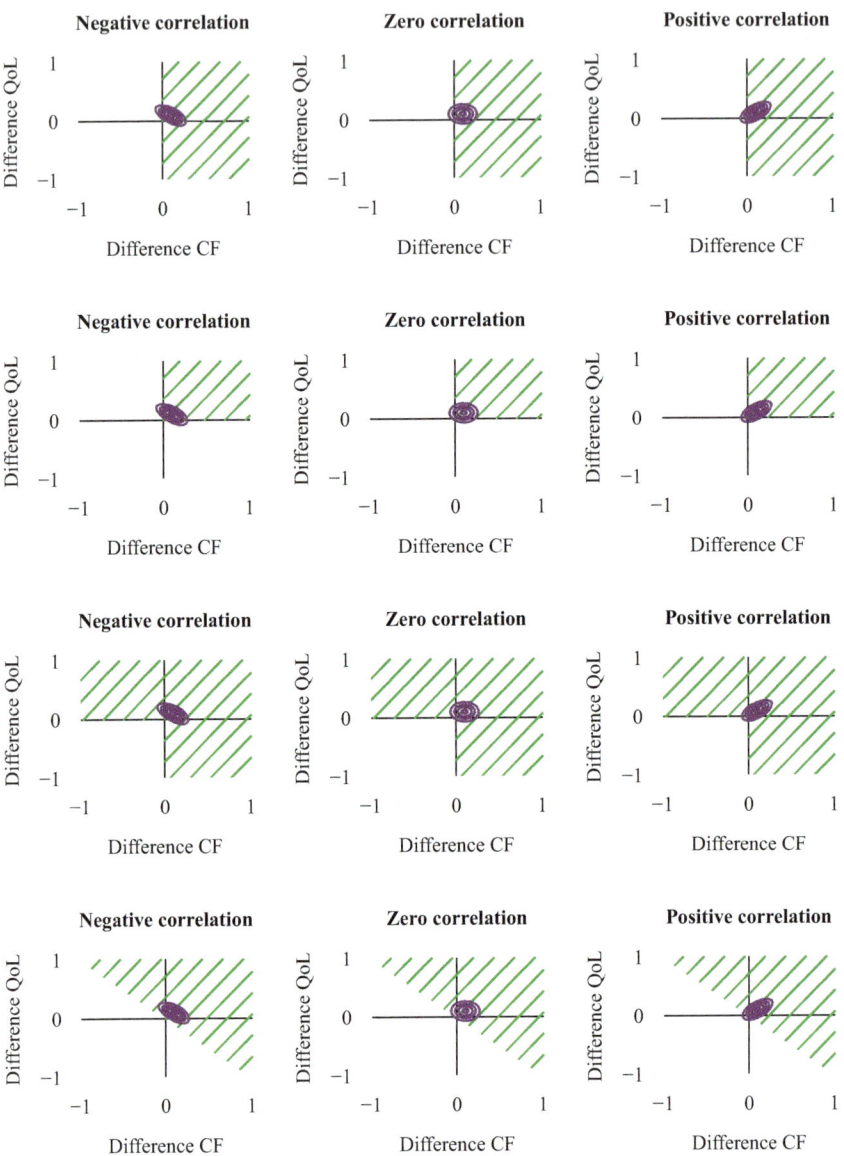

FIGURE 10.9 The influence of the correlation on the evidence for various decision rules. A larger proportion of overlap between the distribution of the treatment difference and the superiority region (shaded area) indicates more evidence. CF = cognitive functioning; QoL = Quality of Life

Adaptive trial design

To reduce the impact of unknown information on the efficiency of trials the sample size can be estimated while running the trial, using a method called *adaptive stopping* (Berry, Carlin, Lee, & Muller, 2010). Adaptive stopping performs one or multiple interim analyses and stops the trial as soon as evidence is conclusive, such that efficiency is optimized. Compared to a priori sample size estimation, adaptive stopping may result in early trial termination if the treatment difference is larger than expected (i.e. underestimated). If the treatment difference appears smaller than anticipated (i.e. overestimated) and evidence remains inconclusive, the trial may be extended beyond the planned sample size. Adaptive stopping thus forms a flexible alternative that embraces the uncertainties of the traditional a priori estimated sample size (Bauer, Bretz, Dragalin, König, & Wassmer, 2016; Thorlund, Haggstrom, Park, & Mills, 2018).

Although interim analyses form an attractive approach to improve efficiency, adaptive trials must be designed carefully (Food and Drug Administration, 2010; Sanborn & Hills, 2014). The final decision about superiority potentially requires several interim decisions to evaluate whether evidence is strong enough to draw a conclusion. Without properly adjusting the design to repeated decision-making, the risk of falsely concluding superiority (i.e. Type I error) over all decisions is larger than anticipated, as shown in Figure 10.10 (Sanborn & Hills, 2014). To keep the Type I error risk over *all* decisions acceptable, the Type I error rate for *individual* decisions must be adjusted (Jennison & Turnbull, 1999). A 5% Type I error risk over multiple decisions consequentially results in individual decisions that have a Type I error risk below 5%. The size of the adjustment depends on the number of interim decisions: More decisions require a larger adjustment of the Type I error rate for individual decisions (see Figure 10.10).

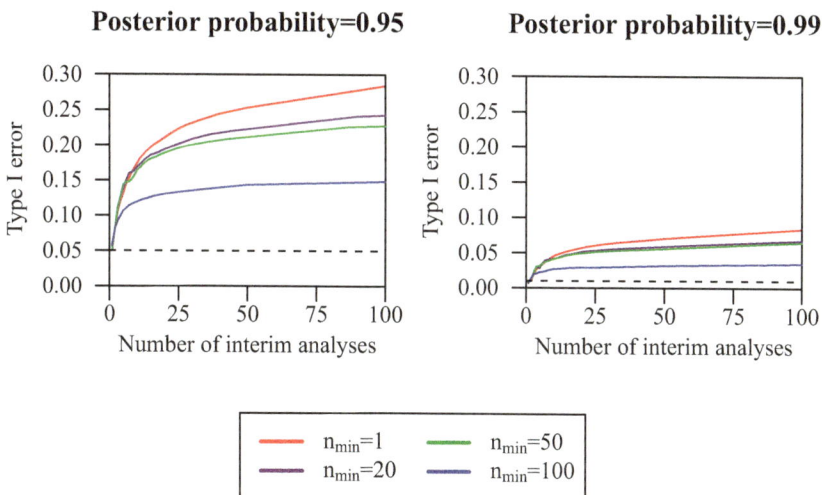

FIGURE 10.10 The empirical Type I error probability as a function of the number of interim analyses for different n_{min} when the decision threshold is not corrected for the number of interim analyses. Dashed lines indicate the desired thresholds of $\alpha = .05$ (posterior probability = .95) and $\alpha = .01$ (posterior probability = .99)

A key element in Type I error control is the decision threshold: the lower limit for the posterior probability to conclude superiority. The decision threshold equals $1-\alpha$, where α is the maximum Type I error probability (Marsman & Wagenmakers, 2017). A 5% risk of an incorrect superiority decision ($\alpha = .05$) results in a minimal posterior probability of .95. A very high threshold might be attractive to minimize Type I errors, but does not contribute to efficient decision-making: A larger sample size is required to regulate the chance to detect a true treatment difference (i.e. to protect power). The decision threshold thus relates the Type I error and required sample size via the number of interim analyses (Shi & Yin, 2019). Limiting the number of decisions is key to efficiently designing an adaptive trial (Jennison & Turnbull, 1999). To this end, the Food and Drug Administration (2010) recommends balancing the number of interim analyses with decision error rates, by carefully choosing three design parameters:

1. The sample size to look at the data for the first time (n_{min})
2. The number of added participants if the previous analysis did not provide sufficient evidence (interim group size)
3. The sample size to stop the trial if evidence is not strong enough to conclude superiority (n_{max})

The sample size at the first interim analysis (n_{min}) should not be too small for two reasons. First, a small interim sample size could detect unrealistically large treatment effects only and needlessly increases the number of interim analyses. Second, very small samples increase the probability of falsely concluding superiority (Schönbrodt, Wagenmakers, Zehetleitner, & Perugini, 2017). As shown in Figure 10.7, the posterior probability is unstable with few observations and becomes more stable as the number of observations increases. Single observations can be influential in small samples, and this influence diminishes as the sample size increases. A larger n_{min} automatically reduces the number of interim analyses as well as the Type I errors and requires a smaller correction of the decision threshold, as illustrated in Figure 10.10. However, a too large n_{min} limits efficiency: Superiority may have been concluded with a smaller sample and potential participant recruitment is needlessly extended.

If the first interim analysis did not result in conclusive evidence, the sample size can be increased in several steps. The interim group size of added participants should be chosen with the inconclusive results of the previous analysis in mind, such that the new sample provides a reasonable chance of detecting a treatment difference given the earlier lack of evidence. The number of observations between interim analyses may be the same throughout the trial, or can differ per interim analysis if that would benefit the trial's efficiency. It should be chosen carefully, however, since too small and too large group sizes both reduce efficiency (Jennison & Turnbull, 1999). A too small group size needlessly increases the number of interim analyses, while a too large group size reduces the flexibility to terminate the trial as soon as the decision criterion has been met.

Ideally, the sample size to terminate the trial if the data do *not* provide sufficient evidence for superiority (n_{max}) equals the sample size that is required to detect the smallest treatment effect of clinical interest (Food and Drug Administration, 2010). In practice, n_{max} will often be limited by the maximum number of available participants and may be smaller than optimal, which has the same consequence as a too small (a priori estimated) sample size: A limited n_{max} restricts the power to detect small treatment differences.

Concluding remarks

The current chapter presented a Bayesian framework for decision-making with multiple outcomes and illustrated how decisions with two outcomes may help a small sample, when (a) using a decision rule that combines information from two outcomes efficiently, and (b) designing a trial adaptively. Without giving all the mathematical details, I have tried to provide a clear intuition to the approach and software to carry out the analysis.

The proposed approach has several extensions that may accommodate more realistic decisions. First, more than two outcomes can be included, such that researchers might weigh treatment differences on three or more relevant aspects. Increasing the number of outcomes may further improve efficiency, but more outcomes also increase the complexity of the data analysis.

Second, although equal importance of outcomes was assumed throughout the chapter, unequal importance of outcomes could be incorporated. The Compensatory rule in particular could be adapted easily to, for example, include survival into a decision; an outcome that is in many cases more important than cognitive side effects. However, user-friendly software packages for more outcomes remain to be developed.

Third, the applicability of adaptive designs can be strongly improved with clear guidelines on the concrete choice of design parameters. Optimal design of interim analyses is necessary to do justice to the potential flexibility of adaptive trials.

Acknowledgement

This work was supported by a NWO (Dutch Research Council) research talent grant (no. 406.18.505). I thank Maurits Kaptein and Joris Mulder (both Tilburg University, The Netherlands), and the reviewers for sharing their insights and providing comments that greatly improved the manuscript.

References

Bauer, P., Bretz, F., Dragalin, V., König, F., & Wassmer, G. (2016). Twenty-five years of confirmatory adaptive designs: Opportunities and pitfalls. *Statistics in Medicine, 35*(3), 325–347.

Berger, J. O., Bernardo, J. M., & Sun, D. (2015). Overall objective priors. *Bayesian Analysis, 10*(1), 189–221.

Berry, S. M., Carlin, B. P., Lee, J. J., & Muller, P. (2010). *Bayesian adaptive methods for clinical trials*. Boca Raton, FL: Chapman & Hall/CRC Press.

Chang, E. L., Wefel, J. S., Hess, K. R., Allen, P. K., Lang, F. F., Kornguth, D. G., Meyers, C. A. (2009). Neurocognition in patients with brain metastases treated with radiosurgery or radiosurgery plus whole-brain irradiation: A randomised controlled trial. *Lancet Oncology*, *10*(11), 1037–1044.

Food and Drug Administration. (2010). Guidance for industry: Adaptive design clinical trials for drugs and biologics. Center for Drug Evaluation and Research, US Food and Drug Administration, Silver Spring, MD. https://wayback.archive-it.org/7993/20170403220223/https://www.fda.gov/ucm/groups/fdagov-public/@fdagov-drugs-gen/documents/document/ucm201790.pdf.

Food and Drug Administration. (2017). Multiple endpoints in clinical trials guidance for industry. Center for Biologics Evaluation and Research (CBER). www.fda.gov/regulatory-information/search-fda-guidance-documents/multiple-endpoints-clinical-trials-guidance-industry. www.fda.gov/media/102657/download.

Goldberger, J. J., & Buxton, A. E. (2013). Personalized medicine vs guideline-based medicine. *JAMA*, *309*(24), 2559–2560.

Hamburg, M. A., & Collins, F. S. (2010). The path to personalized medicine. *New England Journal of Medicine*, *363*(4), 301–304.

Jennison, C., & Turnbull, B. W. (1999). *Group sequential methods with applications to clinical trials*. New York, NY: Chapman & Hall/CRC Press.

Marsman, M., & Wagenmakers, E.-J. (2017). Three insights from a Bayesian interpretation of the one-sided P value. *Educational and Psychological Measurement*, *77*(3), 529–539.

Ng, P. C., Murray, S. S., Levy, S., & Venter, J. C. (2009). An agenda for personalized medicine. *Nature*, *461*(7265), 724–726.

Olkin, I., & Trikalinos, T. A. (2015). Constructions for a bivariate beta distribution. *Statistics & Probability Letters*, *96*, 54–60.

Rauch, G., & Kieser, M. (2015). Adaptive designs for clinical trials with multiple endpoints. *Clinical Investigation*, *5*(5), 433–435.

Sanborn, A. N., & Hills, T. T. (2014). The frequentist implications of optional stopping on Bayesian hypothesis tests. *Psychonomic Bulletin & Review*, *21*(2), 283–300.

Schimmel, W. C. M., Verhaak, E., Hanssens, P. E. J., Gehring, K., & Sitskoorn, M. M. (2018). A randomised trial to compare cognitive outcome after gamma knife radiosurgery versus whole brain radiation therapy in patients with multiple brain metastases: Research protocol CAR-study B. *BMC Cancer*, *18*(1), 218.

Schönbrodt, F. D., Wagenmakers, E.-J., Zehetleitner, M., & Perugini, M. (2017). Sequential hypothesis testing with Bayes factors: Efficiently testing mean differences. *Psychological Methods*, *22*(2), 322.

Shi, H., & Yin, G. (2019). Control of Type I error rates in Bayesian sequential designs. *Bayesian Analysis*, *14*(2), 399–425.

Thorlund, K., Haggstrom, J., Park, J. J. H., & Mills, E. J. (2018). Key design considerations for adaptive clinical trials: A primer for clinicians. *BMJ*, *360*, k698.

Yamamoto, M., Serizawa, T., Shuto, T., Akabane, A., Higuchi, Y., Kawagishi, J., Tsuchiya, K. (2014). Stereotactic radiosurgery for patients with multiple brain metastases (JLGK0901): A multi-institutional prospective observational study. *Lancet Oncology*, *15*(4), 387–395.

PART III
Complex hypotheses and models

11

AN INTRODUCTION TO RESTRIKTOR
Evaluating informative hypotheses for linear models

Leonard Vanbrabant
DEPARTMENT OF DATA ANALYSIS, GHENT UNIVERSITY, GHENT, BELGIUM

Yves Rosseel
DEPARTMENT OF DATA ANALYSIS, GHENT UNIVERSITY, GHENT, BELGIUM

Introduction

In this chapter we introduce the R package `restriktor` that enables easy application of evaluating informative hypotheses. In many psychological fields, researchers have specific expectations about the relation between the means of different groups or between (standardized) regression coefficients. For example, in experimental psychology, it is often tested whether the mean reaction time *increases* or *decreases* for different treatment groups (see, for example, Kofler et al., 2013). In clinical trials, it is often tested whether a particular treatment is *better* or *worse* than other treatments (see, for example, Roberts, Roberts, Jones, & Bisson, 2015). In observational studies, researchers often have clear ideas about whether the direction of the effects is *positive* or *negative* (see, for example, Richardson, Abraham, & Bond, 2012), indicated by symbols like "<" and ">". Testing such specific expectations directly is known under various names, such as *one-sided testing*, *order-constrained hypothesis testing*, *constrained statistical inference*, and *informative hypothesis testing*. For the remainder of this chapter, we will refer to this kind of analysis as informative hypothesis testing (IHT; Hoijtink, 2012).

Many applied researchers are already familiar with IHT in the context of the classical one-sided *t*-test, where one mean is restricted to be greater or smaller than a fixed value (e.g., $\mu_1 > 0$) or another mean (e.g., $\mu_1 > \mu_2$). The method of constraining parameters readily extends to the AN(C)OVA and multiple regression (e.g., linear, logistic, Poisson) setting where more than one constraint can be imposed on the (adjusted) means or regression coefficients (Silvapulle & Sen, 2005). IHT has several benefits compared to classical null-hypothesis significance testing (e.g., $H_0 : \mu_1 = \mu_2 = \mu_3 = \mu_4$ against H_{alt}: not all four means are equal). First, testing specific expectations directly does not require multiple significance tests (Hoijtink, 2012; Klugkist, Van Wesel, & Bullens, 2011; Van de Schoot et al., 2011). In this way, we avoid an inflated Type I error rate or a decrease in power that results from corrections of the significance level α. Second, to avoid multiple testing issues with ordered means, an ANOVA is often combined with contrasts to directly test the specific pattern. However, contrast tests are not the same as informative hypothesis tests (Baayen, Klugkist, & Mechsner, 2012). Third, incorporating order constraints in the analysis will result in substantially more power (e.g., Bartholomew, 1961a, 1961b; Kuiper & Hoijtink, 2010; Perlman, 1969; Robertson, Wright, & Dykstra, 1988; Vanbrabant, Van de Schoot, & Rosseel, 2015; Van de Schoot & Strohmeier, 2011). Vanbrabant et al. (2015) showed that using ordered means and multiple one-sided regression coefficients yields adequate power with 50% of the sample size required by ANOVA and regression (respectively).

Evaluating an informative hypothesis requires two hypothesis tests, which are in the statistical literature often called *hypothesis test Type A* and *hypothesis test Type B*. Under the null hypothesis test of hypothesis test Type A, only the parameters (e.g., means or regression coefficients) that are involved in the order-constrained hypothesis are constrained to be equal (e.g., $H_{A0} : \mu_1 = \mu_2 = \mu_3 = \mu_4$) and it is tested against the order-constrained hypothesis (e.g., $H_{A1} : \mu_1 < \mu_2 < \mu_3 < \mu_4$). For hypothesis test Type B, the null hypothesis states that all restrictions hold in the population (e.g., $H_{B0} : \mu_1 < \mu_2 < \mu_3 < \mu_4$) and it is tested against the hypothesis where no constraints are imposed on the parameters (e.g., H_{B1}: at least one restriction is violated), although some equality constraints (if present) may be preserved under the alternative unconstrained hypothesis. Rejecting the null hypothesis would mean that at least one order constraint is violated. To find evidence in favor of an order-constrained hypothesis, a combination of hypothesis test Type B and hypothesis test Type A (in this order) is used. The rationale is that if hypothesis test Type B is not significant, we do not reject the null hypothesis that all restrictions hold in the population. However, hypothesis test Type B cannot make a distinction between inequality and equality constraints. Therefore, if hypothesis test Type B is not significant, the next step is to evaluate hypothesis test Type A. If we reject H_{A0} we can conclude that at least one inequality constraint is strictly true. Then, if we combine the evidence of hypothesis test Type B and hypothesis Type A, we can say that we have found indirect evidence in favor of (or against) the order-constrained hypothesis.

In the remainder of this chapter, we demonstrate for four examples how to evaluate informative hypotheses using `restriktor`. For each example, we show (1) how to set up the constraint syntax, (2) how to test the informative hypothesis, and (3) how to interpret the results. In the first example, we impose order constraints on the means of a one-way ANOVA model. In the second example, we impose order constraints on the means of an ANOVA model, where we test whether the effect size is at least small according to guidelines for Cohen's d. In the third example, we impose order constraints on the standardized regression coefficients of a linear model. In the fourth example, we impose order constraints on newly defined parameters; that is, on three covariate-conditional effects of gender on the outcome variable. To ensure the reproducibility of chapter results, the data sets for each of the examples are available in the restriktor package. More information about how to import your own data into R can be found online at www.restriktor.ugent.be/tutorial/importdata.html. Before we continue with the examples, we first explain how to get started. The annotated R code described below can also be found on the Open Science Framework (osf.io/am7pr/).

Getting started

Installing restriktor

To install restriktor, open R, and type:

```
install.packages("restriktor")
```

If the restriktor package is installed, the package needs to be loaded into R. This can be done by typing:

```
library(restriktor)
```

If the package is loaded, the following startup message should be displayed (note that the version number 0.2–15 changes in future releases):

```
## This is restriktor 0.2-15
## restriktor is BETA software! Please report any bugs.
```

A more detailed description about how to get started with restriktor can be found online at restriktor.org/gettingstarted.html.

The constraint syntax

The easiest way in restriktor to construct the constraint syntax for factors is to use the factor-level names (e.g., A, B, C), preceded by the factor name (e.g., Group). For covariates, we can refer simply by their name. Order constraints are defined via inequality constraints (<, or >) or by equality constraints (==). The constraint syntax is enclosed within single quotes. For example, for a simple order-constrained hypothesis with three means (i.e., $H: \mu_1 < \mu_2 < \mu_3$), the constraint syntax might look as follows:

```
myConstraints <-' GroupA < GroupB
                  GroupB < GroupC '
```

More information about the constraint syntax can be found online at restriktor.org/tutorial/syntax.html.

Testing the informative hypothesis

In restriktor, the iht() function is used for IHT. The minimal requirements for this function are a constraint syntax and a fitted unconstrained model. In an unconstrained model no (in)equality constraints are imposed on the means or regression coefficients. Currently, iht() can deal with unconstrained models of class lm (standard linear model/ANOVA), mlm (multivariate linear model), rlm (robust linear model) and glm (generalized linear model). By default, the function uses the F-bar test statistic (Kudô, 1963; Wolak, 1987). The F-bar statistic is an adapted version of the classical F statistic and can deal with order constraints. More information about all available options can be found online at restriktor.org/tutorial/contest.html.

Estimation of the restricted estimates and inference

Instead of testing the informative hypothesis, the (restricted) regression coefficients/means might be of interest. In this case, the restriktor() function can be used. The first argument to restriktor() is the fitted unconstrained linear model. The second argument is the constraint syntax. The output shows the restricted estimates and the corresponding standard errors, t-test statistics, two-sided p-values, and the multiple R^2. The output also provides information about the type of computed standard errors. By default, conventional standard errors are computed but heteroskedastic robust standard errors are also available. Again, more information about all available options can be found online at restriktor.org/tutorial/restriktor.html.

Example 1: Ordered-constrained means of a one-way ANOVA model

In this example, we use the "anger management" data set. These data denote a person's decrease in aggression level between week 1 (intake) and week 8 (end of training) for four different treatment groups of anger management training, namely (1) no training, (2) physical training, (3) behavioral therapy, and (4) a combination of physical exercise and behavioral therapy. The purpose of the study was to test the assumption that the exercises would be associated with a reduction in the mean aggression levels. In particular, the hypothesis of interest was $H_1 : \mu_{\text{No}} < \{\mu_{\text{Physical}} = \mu_{\text{Behavioral}}\} < \mu_{\text{Both}}$. This hypothesis states that the decrease in aggression levels is smallest for the "no training" group, larger for the "physical training" and "behavioral therapy" group, with no preference for either method, and largest in the "combination of physical exercise and behavioral therapy" group (Hoijtink, 2012, pp. 5–6).

In practice, hypothesis H_1 is usually evaluated with an ANOVA, where the null hypothesis $H_0 : \mu_{\text{No}} = \mu_{\text{Physical}} = \mu_{\text{Behavioral}} = \mu_{\text{Both}}$ is tested against the unconstrained hypothesis H_{unc}: not all four means are equal. The results from the global F-test revealed that the four means are not equal ($F_{(4,36)} = 18.62$, $p < .001$). At this point, we do not know anything about the ordering of the means. Therefore, the next step would be to use pairwise comparisons with corrections for multiple testing (e.g., Bonferroni, Tukey, and FDR). The results with FDR (False Discovery Rate) adjusted p-values showed three significant ($p \leq .05$) mean differences (MD), namely between the "Behavioral-No" exercises ($MD = 3.3$, $p = .001$), the "Behavioral-Physical" exercises ($MD = 2.3$, $p = .018$) and the "Both-Physical" exercises ($MD = 3.3$, $p = .001$). A graphical representation of the means is shown in Figure 11.1. Based on the results of the global F test and the pairwise comparisons, it would not be an easy task to derive an unequivocal conclusion about hypothesis H_1.

In what follows, we show all steps and the restriktor syntax to evaluate the informative hypothesis H_1 directly.

Step 1: Set up the constraint syntax

In R, categorical predictors are represented by "factors". For example, the "Group" variable has four factor levels: "No", "Physical", "Behavioral", and "Both". In addition, the factor levels are presented in alphabetical order and it may therefore be convenient to re-order the levels. This can be done in R by typing:

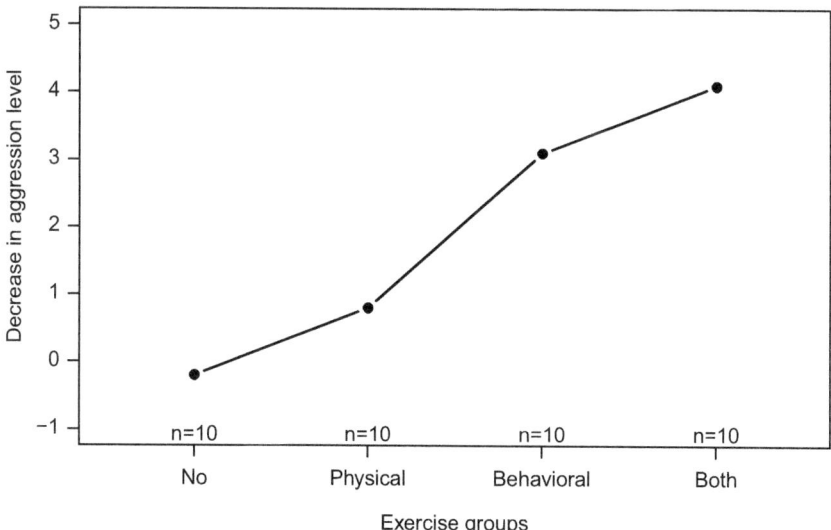

FIGURE 11.1 Means plot: reduction of aggression levels after eight weeks of anger management training

```
AngerManagement$Group <- factor(AngerManagement$Group,
                                levels = c("No", "Physical",
                                           "Behavioral",
                                           "Both"))
```

Next, the constraint syntax for hypothesis H_1 might look as follows:

```
myConstraints1 <- ' GroupNo         < GroupPhysical
                   GroupPhysical   == GroupBehavioral
                   GroupBehavioral  < GroupBoth '
```

Step 2: Test the informative hypothesis

Since an ANOVA model is a special case of the multiple regression model, we can use the linear model for our ANOVA example. Then, we can fit the unconstrained linear model as follows:

```
fit_ANOVA <- lm(Anger ~ -1 + Group, data = AngerManagement)
```

The tilde ~ is the regression operator. On the left-hand side of the operator we have the response variable Anger and on the right-hand side we have the factor Group. We removed the intercept (-1) from the model so that the estimates reflect the group means. Next, we can test the informative hypothesis using the iht() function. This is done as follows:

```
iht(fit_ANOVA, myConstraints1)
```

The first argument to iht() is the fitted unconstrained linear model. The second argument is the constraint syntax. By default, the function prints an overview of all available hypothesis tests. The results are shown below. Some parts are removed due to its length.

```
Restriktor: restricted hypothesis tests (36 residual degrees of freedom):

Multiple R-squared reduced from 0.674 to 0.608

Constraint matrix:
   GroupNo  GroupPhysical  GroupBehavioral  GroupBoth  op  rhs  active
1:    0           1              -1             0      ==   0    yes
2:   -1           1               0             0      >=   0    no
3:    0           0              -1             1      >=   0    no

Overview of all available hypothesis tests:

Global test: H0: all parameters are restricted to be equal (==)
         vs. HA: at least one inequality restriction is strictly true (>)
    Test statistic: 25.4061,  p-value: <0.0001
```

```
Type A test: H0: all restrictions are equalities (==)
      vs. HA: at least one inequality restriction is strictly true (>)
    Test statistic: 25.4061,  p-value: <0.0001

Type B test: H0: all restrictions hold in the population
      vs. HA: at least one restriction is violated
    Test statistic: 7.2687,  p-value: 0.04518
```

At the top of the output the constraint matrix is shown. This matrix is constructed internally based on the text-based constraint syntax but could have been constructed manually. The constraint matrix is comparable to the contrast matrix but treated differently in the constraint framework. The "active" column indicates if a constraint is violated or not. If no constraints are active, this would mean that all constraints are in line with the data. In the remainder, an overview of the available hypothesis tests is given. Information about how to obtain a more detailed output for each hypothesis test can be found in the help file or online at restriktor.org/tutorial/contest.html.

Step 3: Interpret the results

To evaluate the informative hypothesis H_1, we first conduct hypothesis test Type B. Not rejecting this hypothesis test would mean that the order constraints are in line with the data. The results from hypothesis test Type B, however, show that hypothesis H_1 is rejected in favor of the best-fitting (i.e., unconstrained) hypothesis ($\bar{F}^B_{(0,1,2;36)} = 7.27$, $p = .045$)[1]. In other words, the constraints are not supported by the data and we conclude that the informative hypothesis H_1 does not hold.

Estimation of the restricted estimates and inference

Instead of testing the informative hypothesis H_1, the restricted means might be of interest. The restricted means can be computed as follows:

```
restr_ANOVA <- restriktor(fit_ANOVA, constraints = myConstraints1)
```

By default, the print() function prints a brief overview of the restricted means:

```
print(restr_ANOVA)

Call:
conLM.lm(object = fit_ANOVA, constraints = myConstraints1)

restriktor (0.1-80.711): restricted linear model:

Coefficients:
    GroupNo  GroupPhysical  GroupBehavioral  GroupBoth
     -0.20          1.95             1.95        4.10
```

We can clearly see that the `GroupPhysical` and the `GroupBehavioral` means are constrained to be equal. If desired, a more extensive output can be requested using the `summary()` function:

```
summary(restr_ANOVA)

Call:
conLM.lm(object = fit_ANOVA, constraints = myConstraints1)

Restriktor: restricted linear model:

Residuals:
   Min     1Q  Median      3Q     Max
-3.100 -1.275  -0.025   1.200   5.050

Coefficients:
                Estimate Std. Error t value Pr(>|t|)
GroupNo         -0.20000    0.65233  -0.3066 0.7609210
GroupPhysical    1.95000    0.46127   4.2275 0.0001544 ***
GroupBehavioral  1.95000    0.46127   4.2275 0.0001544 ***
GroupBoth        4.10000    0.65233   6.2851 2.895e-07 ***
---
Signif. codes:  0 '***' 0.001 '**' 0.01 '*' 0.05 '.' 0.1 ' ' 1

Residual standard error: 2.0629 on 36 degrees of freedom
Standard errors: standard
Multiple R-squared reduced from 0.674 to 0.608

Generalized Order-Restricted Information Criterion:
  Loglik  Penalty    Goric
-84.1621   2.8918 174.1079
```

The output shows the restricted group means and the corresponding (standard) standard errors, t-test statistics and two-sided p-values. The multiple $R^2 = .674$ refers to the unconstrained model and the $R^2 = .608$ refers to the order-constrained model. The reduction in R^2 provides additional evidence that at least one order constraint is violated. Both R^2s are equal only if all constraints are in line with the data. The last part of the output provides information for model selection using the generalized order-restricted information criterion (GORIC), which is a modification of the Akaike information criterion. More information and an example can be found online at restriktor.org/tutorial/example6.html.

Example 2: Ordered-constrained means with effect sizes

The p-value is not a measure for the size of an effect (Nickerson, 2000). Therefore, in an AN(C)OVA the question should be whether the differences between the group means are relevant. To answer this question, the popular effect-size measure Cohen's d (Cohen, 1988) can be used, and is given by: $d = (\mu_{max} - \mu_{min})/\sigma_{pooled}$, where μ_{max} is the largest and μ_{min} is the smallest of the m means, and σ_{pooled} is the pooled standard deviation within the populations. According to Cohen, values of 0.2, 0.5, and 0.8 indicate a small, medium, and large effect, respectively.

In this example, we use the Zelazo, Zelazo, and Kolb (1972) data set, which is available in restriktor. The data consist of ages in months at which a child starts to walk for four treatment groups. For simplicity we only consider three treatment groups. The excluded group is the "Control" group. The first treatment group ("Active") received a special walking exercise for 12 minutes per day beginning at the age of one week old and lasting seven weeks. The second group ("Passive") received daily exercises but not the special walking exercises. The third group ("No") were checked weekly for progress (the other two groups got daily exercises) but they did not receive any special exercises. The purpose of the study was to test the claim that the walking exercises are associated with a reduction in the mean age at which children start to walk.

If we ignore the effect sizes, the informative hypothesis can be formulated as: $H_2 : \mu_{Active} < \mu_{Passive} < \mu_{No}$. The results from hypothesis test Type B ($\bar{F}^B_{(0,1,2;14)} = 0$, $p = 0$) and hypothesis test Type A ($\bar{F}^A_{(0,1,2;14)} = 5.978$, $p = .028$) provide evidence in favor of the informative hypothesis. However, for practical relevance of the treatments, the mean differences between the groups should at least indicate a small effect. To answer this question, we reformulate hypothesis H_2 such that the effect sizes are included. The pooled within group standard deviation equals 1.516:

$$H_2^d = \begin{array}{l} \frac{(\mu_{Passive} - \mu_{Active})}{1.516} > 0.2 \\ \frac{(\mu_{No} - \mu_{Passive})}{1.516} > 0.2. \end{array}$$

This hypothesis states that we expect at least 0.2 * 1.516 standard deviations between the means, which indicates a small effect size. Next, we show how to evaluate this informative hypothesis.

Step 1: Set up the constraint syntax

Again, we use the factor-level names preceded by the factor name to construct the constraint syntax. The effect sizes can be easily computed within the constraint syntax using the arithmetic operator /:

```
myConstraints2 <- ' (GroupPassive - GroupActive ) / 1.516 > 0.2
                   (GroupNo      - GroupPassive) / 1.516 > 0.2 '
```

Step 2: Test the informative hypothesis

Since we excluded the "Control" group, we need to take a subset of the original data. The subset() function in R is an easy way to select observations. This is done in R by typing:

```
subData <- subset(ZelazoKolb1972, subset = Group != "Control")
```

Then, the unconstrained linear model can be fit as follows:

```
fit_ANOVAd <- lm(Age ~ -1 + Group, data = subData)
```

Next, we test the informative hypothesis using the fitted unconstrained model `fit_ANOVAd` and the constraint syntax `myConstraints2`:

```
iht(fit_ANOVAd, constraints = myConstraints2)
```

Step 3: Interpret the results

The results from hypothesis test Type B ($\bar{F}^{B}_{(0,1,2;14)} = 0$, $p = 1$) and hypothesis test Type A ($\bar{F}^{A}_{(0,1,2;14)} = 3.19$, $p = .089$) show that if we include a small effect size in the informative hypothesis, the initial significant results become irrelevant. This clearly demonstrates the importance of including effect sizes in the hypothesis.

Example 3: Order-constrained (standardized) linear regression coefficients

In this example, we show how order constraints can be imposed on the standardized regression coefficients, denoted by β^Z, of a linear model. We use the "exam" data set, which is available in restriktor. The model relates students' "exam scores" ("Scores") to the "averaged point score" ("APS"), the amount of "study hours" ("Hours"), and "anxiety score" ("Anxiety"). It is hypothesized that "APS" is the strongest predictor, followed by "study hours" and "anxiety scores", respectively. In symbols, this informative hypothesis can be written as $H_3: \beta^Z_{APS} > \beta^Z_{Hours} > \beta^Z_{Anxiety}$. Since the hypothesis is in terms of which predictor is stronger, we should be aware that each predictor has its own scale. To avoid spurious conclusions, the predictor variables should be standardized first[2]. This can be done in R by typing:

```
Exam$Hours_Z   <- (Exam$Hours   - mean(Exam$Hours))   / sd(Exam$Hours)
Exam$Anxiety_Z <- (Exam$Anxiety - mean(Exam$Anxiety)) / sd(Exam$Anxiety)
Exam$APS_Z     <- (Exam$APS     - mean(Exam$APS))     / sd(Exam$APS)
```

Step 1: Set up the constraint syntax

Then, the constraint syntax corresponding H_3 might look as follows:

```
myConstraints3 <- ' APS_Z  > Hours_Z
                   Hours_Z > Anxiety_Z '
```

Step 2: Test the informative hypothesis

Next, we fit the unconstrained linear model. The response variable is "Scores" and the predictor variables are the three centered covariates:

```
fit_exam <- lm(Scores ~ APS_Z + Hours_Z + Anxiety_Z,
data = Exam)
```

The informative hypothesis H_3 can be evaluated using the unconstrained model `fit_exam` and the constraint syntax `myConstraints3`:

```
iht(fit_exam, constraints = myConstraints3)
```

Step 3: Interpret the results

The results from hypothesis test Type B show that the order-constrained hypothesis is not rejected in favor of the unconstrained hypothesis ($\bar{F}^B_{(0,1,2;16)} = 0$, $p = 1$). The results from hypothesis test Type A show that the null hypothesis is rejected in favor of the order-constrained hypothesis ($\bar{F}^A_{(0,1,2;16)} = 12.38$, $p = .003$). Thus, we have found strong evidence in favor of the informative hypothesis H_3.

Example 4: Testing order constraints on newly defined parameters

Here, we show how order constraints can be imposed between newly defined parameters, e.g., simple slopes. The original data are based on two cohort studies of children from 0 to 4 and 8 to 18 years old with burns, and their parents (e.g., Bakker, Van der Heijden, Van Son, & Van Loey, 2013; Egberts et al., 2016). Since the original data are not publicly accessible, we simulated data based on the original model parameters. This simulated data set is available in restriktor. For illustrative reasons we focus only on the data provided by the mother. For the current illustration we included five predictor variables in the data set: a child's gender (0 = boys, 1 = girls), age, the estimated percentage of the total body surface area affected by second or third degree burns ("TBSA"), and parental guilt and anger feelings in relation to the burn event. The model relates post-traumatic stress symptoms (PTSS) to the five predictor variables and can be written as a linear function:

$$\text{PTSS}_i \sim \beta_{intercept} + \beta_1 \text{gender}_i + \beta_2 \text{age}_i + \beta_3 \text{guilt}_i + \beta_4 \text{anger}_i + \beta_5 \text{TBSA}_i$$
$$+ \beta_6(\text{gender}_i * \text{guilt}_i) + \beta_7(\text{gender}_i * \text{anger}_i) + \beta_8(\text{gender}_i * \text{TBSA}_i) + \varepsilon_i,$$

where $\beta_{intercept}$ is the intercept, β_1 to β_5 are the regression coefficients for the main effects, and β_6 to β_8 are the regression coefficients for the interaction effects.

We hypothesized that the mean difference in PTSS between mothers of girls and mothers of boys would increase for simultaneously higher levels of guilt, anger, and TBSA. To test this informative hypothesis, we selected three different settings for guilt, anger, and TBSA, namely small, medium, and large. For illustrative reasons, for the small level we chose the values 0, 0, 1 for guilt, anger, and TBSA respectively. For the medium level we chose the variable means, which are 2.02, 2.06, and 8.35, respectively, and for the large level we chose 4, 4, and 20, respectively. Then, the resulting three effects (small, medium, large) can be calculated respectively as follows:

$$\text{smallEffect} = \beta_1 + \beta_6 0 + \beta_7 0 + \beta_8 1$$

$$\text{mediumEffect} = \beta_1 + \beta_6 2.02 + \beta_7 2.06 + \beta_8 8.35$$

$$\text{largeEffect} = \beta_1 + \beta_6 4 + \beta_7 4 + \beta_8 20.$$

Note that each effect reflects a mean difference between boys and girls. Then, the informative hypothesis can be expressed as:

$$H_4 : \text{smallEffect} < \text{mediumEffect} < \text{largeEffect}.$$

Step 1: Set up the constraints syntax

A convenient feature of the `restriktor` constraint syntax is the option to define new parameters, which take on values that are an arbitrary function of the original model parameters. This can be done using the `:=` operator. In this way, we can compute the desired effects and impose order constraints among these effects. Then, the constraint syntax might look as follows:

```
myConstraints4 <- 'smallEffect  := gender + 0*gender.guilt +
                                   0*gender.anger +
                                   1*gender.TBSA

                   mediumEffect := gender + 2.02*gender.guilt +
                                   2.06*gender.anger +
                                   8.35*gender.TBSA

                   largeEffect  := gender + 4*gender.guilt +
                                   4*gender.anger +
                                   20*gender.TBSA

                   smallEffect  < mediumEffect
                   mediumEffect < largeEffect'
```

It is important to note that variable/factor names of the interaction effects in objects of class `lm`, `rlm`, `glm`, and `mlm` contain a semi-colon (`:`) between the variable names (e.g., gender:guilt). To use these parameters in the constraint syntax, the semi-colon must be replaced by a dot (.) (e.g., gender.guilt).

Step 2: Test the informative hypothesis

Based on outlier diagnostics[3] we identified 13 outliers (approximately 4.7% of the data). Therefore, we use robust methods. The unconstrained robust linear model using MM estimation (Yohai, 1987) can be fitted as follows:

```
library(MASS)
fit_rburns <- rlm(PTSS ~ gender*guilt + gender*anger +
                  gender*TBSA + age,
                  data = Burns, method = "MM")
```

On the right-hand side of the regression operator (~) we included the three interaction effects using the * operator. The main effects are automatically included. Note that the interaction operator * is not an arithmetic operator as used in the constraint syntax. Then, the informative hypothesis can be evaluated as follows:

```
iht(fit_rburns, constraints = myConstraints4)
```

Step 3: Interpret the results

The results from hypothesis test Type B ($\bar{F}^B_{MM(0,1,2;269)} = 0$, $p = 1$) show that the order-constrained hypothesis is not rejected in favor of the unconstrained hypothesis. The results from hypothesis test Type A show that the null hypothesis is rejected in favor of the order-constrained hypothesis ($\bar{F}^A_{MM(0,1,2;269)} = 5.35$, $p = .044$). Hence, we can conclude that the data provide enough evidence that the gender effect increases for higher levels of guilt, anger, and TBSA.

The non-robust results from hypothesis test Type A would have led to a different conclusion, namely that the null hypothesis would not have been rejected in favor of the order-constrained hypothesis ($\bar{F}^A_{(0,1,2;269)} = 3.65$, $p = .107$). This clearly demonstrates that ignoring outliers may result in misleading conclusions.

Conclusion

IHT has been shown to have major benefits compared to classical null-hypothesis testing. Unfortunately, applied researchers have been unable to use these methods because user-friendly freeware and a clear tutorial were not available. Therefore, in this chapter we introduced the user-friendly R package restriktor for evaluating (robust) informative hypotheses. The procedure was illustrated using four examples. For each example, we showed how to set up the constraint syntax, how to evaluate the informative hypothesis and how to interpret the results. All results were obtained by the default settings of the software package `restriktor`. If desired, they can readily be adjusted.

We only discussed frequentist methods for evaluating informative hypotheses. Of course, examples 1–4 could have been evaluated in the Bayesian framework; see Chapter 12 (Zondervan-Zwijnenburg & Rijshouwer; see also Berger & Mortera, 1999; Gu, Mulder, Deković, & Hoijtink, 2014; Hoijtink, 2012; Klugkist, Laudy, & Hoijtink, 2005; Mulder, Hoijtink, & Klugkist, 2010) but we believe that the frequentist methods are a welcome addition to the applied user's toolbox and may help convince applied users unfamiliar with Bayesian statistics to include order constraints in their hypothesis. In addition, robust IHT as discussed in this chapter does not seem to exist in the Bayesian framework (yet).

It must be noted that the `restriktor` package is not finished yet, but it is already very useful for most users. The package is actively maintained, and new options are being added. We advise the reader to monitor the restriktor website (restriktor.org) for updates.

Notes

1. The null distribution is a mixture of F distributions mixed over the degrees of freedom. Therefore, in this example, the p-value $Pr(\overline{F} \geq \overline{F}_{obs})$ approximately equals $w_0 Pr(F_{0,36} \geq \overline{F}_{obs}) + w_1 Pr(F_{1,36} \geq \overline{F}_{obs}/1) + w_2 Pr(F_{2,36} \geq \overline{F}_{obs}/2)$, where $Pr(F_{0,36} \geq \overline{F}_{obs})$ equals 0 by definition. Hence the notation $\overline{F}_{(0,1,2;36)}$. w is the level probability, the probability that the order-constrained maximum likelihood estimates have j levels (under the null-hypothesis), where m = the number of inactive order constraints; and the w_m sum to 1.
2. Standardized regression coefficients can be obtained by standardizing all the predictor variables before including them in the model. For example: $Z(APS_i) = (APS_i - mean(APS))/sd(APS)$, where sd is the standard deviation.
3. The outliers were identified with robust Mahalanobis distances larger than the 99.5% quantile of a χ^2_8 distribution.

References

Baayen, C., Klugkist, I., & Mechsner, F. (2012). A test of order-constrained hypotheses for circular data with applications to human movement science. *Journal of Motor Behavior*, *44*(5), 351–363.

Bakker, A., Van der Heijden, P. G. M., Van Son, M. J. M., & Van Loey, N. E. E. (2013). Course of traumatic stress reactions in couples after a burn event to their young child. *Health Psychology*, *32*(10), 1076–1083.

Bartholomew, D. J. (1961a). Ordered tests in the analysis of variance. *Biometrika*, *48*(3/4), 325–332.

Bartholomew, D. J. (1961b). A test of homogeneity of means under restricted alternatives. *Journal of the Royal Statistical Society. Series B (Methodological)*, *23*(2), 239–281.

Berger, J. O., & Mortera, J. (1999). Default Bayes factors for non-nested hypothesis testing. *Journal of the American Statistical Association*, *94*(446), 542–554.

Cohen, J. (1988). *Statistical power analysis for the behavioral sciences* (2nd ed.). Hillsdale, NJ: Erlbaum.

Egberts, M. R., Van de Schoot, R., Boekelaar, A., Hendrickx, H., Geenen, R., & Van Loey, N. E. E. (2016). Child and adolescent internalizing and externalizing problems 12 months postburn: The potential role of preburn functioning, parental posttraumatic stress, and informant bias. *European Child & Adolescent Psychiatry*, *25*(7), 791–803.

Gu, X., Mulder, J., Deković, M., & Hoijtink, H. (2014). Bayesian evaluation of inequality constrained hypotheses. *Psychological Methods*, *19*(4), 511–527.

Hoijtink, H. (2012). *Informative hypotheses: Theory and practice for behavioral and social scientists*. Boca Raton, FL: Taylor & Francis.

Klugkist, I., Laudy, O., & Hoijtink, H. (2005). Inequality constrained analysis of variance: A Bayesian approach. *Psychological Methods*, *10*(4), 477–493. doi:10.1037/1082-989X.10.4.477.

Klugkist, I., Van Wesel, F., & Bullens, J. (2011). Do we know what we test and do we test what we want to know? *International Journal of Behavioral Development*, *35*(6), 550–560. doi:10.1177/0165025411425873.

Kofler, M. J., Rapport, M. D., Sarver, D. E., Raiker, J. S., Orban, S. A., Friedman, L. M., & Kolomeyer, E. G. (2013). Reaction time variability in ADHD: A meta-analytic review of 319 studies. *Clinical Psychology Review*, *33*(6), 795–811.

Kudô, A. (1963). A multivariate analogue of the one-sided test. *Biometrika*, *50*(3/4), 403–418.

Kuiper, R. M., & Hoijtink, H. (2010). Comparisons of means using exploratory and confirmatory approaches. *Psychological Methods*, *15*(1), 69–86.

Mulder, J., Hoijtink, H., & Klugkist, I. (2010). Equality and inequality constrained multivariate linear models: Objective model selection using constrained posterior priors. *Journal of Statistical Planning and Inference*, *140*(4), 887–906. doi:10.1016/j.jspi.2009.09.022.

Nickerson, R. S. (2000). Null hypothesis significance testing: A review of an old and continuing controversy. *Psychological Methods*, *5*(2), 241–301.

Perlman, M. D. (1969). One-sided testing problems in multivariate analysis. *Annals of Mathematical Statistics*, *40*(2), 549–567.

Richardson, M., Abraham, C., & Bond, R. (2012). Psychological correlates of university students' academic performance: A systematic review and meta-analysis. *Psychological Bulletin*, *138*(2), 353–387.

Roberts, N. P., Roberts, P. A., Jones, N., & Bisson, J. I. (2015). Psychological interventions for post-traumatic stress disorder and comorbid substance use disorder: A systematic review and meta-analysis. *Clinical Psychology Review*, *38*, 25–38.

Robertson, T., Wright, F. T., & Dykstra, R. L. (1988). *Order restricted statistical inference*. New York, NY: John Wiley.

Silvapulle, M. J., & Sen, P. K. (2005). *Constrained statistical inference: Order, inequality, and shape constraints*. Hoboken, NJ: John Wiley & Sons.

Wolak, F. (1987). An exact test for multiple inequality and equality constraints in the linear regression model. *J. Am. Stat. Assoc.*, *82*, 782–793.

Van de Schoot, R., Hoijtink, H., Mulder, J., Van Aken, M. A. G., Orobio de Castro, B., Meeus, W., & Romeijn, J. W. (2011). Evaluating expectations about negative emotional states of aggressive boys using Bayesian model selection. *Developmental Psychology*, *47*(1), 203–212.

Van de Schoot, R., & Strohmeier, D. (2011). Testing informative hypotheses in SEM increases power: An illustration contrasting classical hypothesis testing with a parametric bootstrap approach. *International Journal of Behavioral Development*, *35*(2), 180–190.

Vanbrabant, L., Van de Schoot, R., & Rosseel, Y. (2015). Constrained statistical inference: Sample-size tables for ANOVA and regression. *Frontiers in Psychology*, *5*, 1–8.

Yohai, V. J. (1987). High breakdown-point and high efficiency robust estimates for regression. *Annals of Statistics*, *15*(2), 642–656.

Zelazo, P. R., Zelazo, N. A., & Kolb, S. (1972). "Walking" in the newborn. *Science*, *176* (4032), 314–315.

12
TESTING REPLICATION WITH SMALL SAMPLES
Applications to ANOVA

Mariëlle Zondervan-Zwijnenburg
DEPARTMENT OF METHODOLOGY AND STATISTICS, UTRECHT UNIVERSITY, UTRECHT, THE NETHERLANDS

Dominique Rijshouwer
DEPARTMENT OF PSYCHOLOGY, UTRECHT, THE NETHERLANDS

Introduction

Concerns about the replicability of studies were expressed as early as in 1979 by Robert Rosenthal, who believed that future insights would solve this problem. However, the field of psychological science is still struggling to establish replicability, as was clearly shown with the Reproducibility Project: Psychology (RPP; Open Science Collaboration, 2015). Increased awareness of the noisiness of results obtained using small samples is an important step towards improving this situation (Lindsay, 2015). Results obtained with smaller samples are less likely to be replicated than those obtained with larger samples (Cohen, 1962).

One of the difficulties in replicating small sample research is that small samples are particularly sensitive to "researcher degrees of freedom": decisions that researchers make in the design and analysis of the data (Simmons, Nelson, & Simonsohn, 2011). For example, researchers decide to combine categories, exclude scores, add comparisons, add covariates, or transform measures. Unfortunately, modifications are more common if results do not support the hypothesis. For example, the impact of an extreme score will more often be detected and adjusted if it causes a non-significant result as compared to a significant result. With small samples, these decisions can easily affect the significance of results, leading to inflated false-positive rates (Simmons et al., 2011).

Another issue is publication bias: studies with statistically significant results are published more often than studies with non-significant results. Small sample studies are often underpowered, leading to non-significant results and hence a reduced chance to be published. On the other hand, small studies that do find significant effects appear impressive and are more likely to be published.

Thus, researcher degrees of freedom and publication bias can lead to overestimation of effects and an inflated false-positive rate in the literature (Simmons et al., 2011). Small sample findings therefore can easily be spurious, meaning that their replication is of great importance.

Different replication research questions require different methods. Here, we distinguish four main research questions that can be investigated if a new study is conducted to replicate an original study:

1. Is the new effect size similar to the original effect size?
2. Is the new effect size different from the original effect size?
3. Are the new findings different from the original findings?
4. What is the effect size in the population?

Note that questions 1 and 2 differ in where the burden of proof lies. Question 1 looks to *provide support* for the equality of effect sizes, whereas question 2 is aimed at *falsifying* the claim of equality of effect sizes in favor of a conclusion that the effect size was not replicated.

For all four replication research questions we recommend statistical methods and apply them to an empirical example. Note that Anderson and Maxwell (2016) also documented replication research questions and associated methods, although not specifically for small samples. In the current chapter, we adopt several suggestions from Anderson and Maxwell (2016) and add more recent methods. R-code (R Core Team, 2017) for reproducing all chapter results is provided as Supplementary Material available on the Open Science Framework (https://osf.io/am7pr/). We demonstrate the four replication research methods for the replication of Henderson, De Liver, and Gollwitzer (2008) by Lane and Gazerian (2016). First, we introduce the original study by Henderson et al. and its replication by Lane and Gazerian. This is followed by a discussion of the four replication research questions and their associated methods.

Example: original study and its replication

Henderson et al. (2008) conducted a series of experiments showing that people who planned the implementation of a chosen goal (i.e., people with an "implemental mind-set") have stronger attitudes, even towards topics unrelated to their actions. Experiment 5 is the one that was replicated by Lane and Gazerian (2016). It is designed to demonstrate that a focus on information that supports the previously made decision is the reason that attitude strength increases with an implemental mind-set. The experiment included three conditions with 46 participants in total. The first condition was a neutral condition in which participants described things they did on a typical day. The second condition was an implemental one-sided focus condition. Participants in this condition chose a romantic topic to write about and wrote down three reasons for that choice. The third condition was the implemental two-sided focus condition in which participants made their choice and wrote down three reasons for and three reasons against this choice. Afterwards, participants in all conditions answered three questions rating their attitude ambivalence with respect to the issue of making public a list with names of convicted sex offenders (e.g., "I have strong mixed emotions both for and against making the list of convicted sex offenders available to the general public rather than just the police").

The descriptive statistics of the data from the experiment by Henderson et al. (2008) are provided in Table 12.1. The effect of the conditions on attitude ambivalence was significant, using an alpha value of .05, as Henderson et al. report: $F(2, 43) = 3.36$, $p = .044$, $\eta^2 = .13$, $\omega^2 = .09$, $r = .26$. We have added the effect size ω^2, because it is less biased than effect size η^2 for small samples (Okada, 2013). Furthermore, we also computed the effect size r as used in the RPP as an additional effect size measure (see Appendix 3 of the RRP available at osf.io/z7aux). Assuming that all predictors (i.e., the dummy condition variables) contributed equally to the explained variance, r^2 is the explained variance per predictor, and r is the correlation coefficient per predictor. If the conditions did not contribute equally, r^2 and r are the average explained variance or correlation coefficient per condition.

Post hoc comparisons revealed that the implemental mind-set, one-sided group demonstrated significantly lower amounts of ambivalence compared to the implemental mind-set, two-sided, group: $t(28) = 2.45$, $p = .021$, Cohen's $d = .93$, Hedges' $g = .50$. For the t-test we added Hedges' g to correct for an upward bias that Cohen's d shows with small samples. Hedges' g is obtained by multiplying Cohen's d by the correction factor $(1 - \frac{3}{4df-1})$ (Hedges, 1981). The mean of the neutral mind-set group was in the middle, but it was not significantly higher or lower than the means of other conditions (see descriptive statistics in Table 12.1). Henderson et al. (2008) write: "Critically, the findings showed that it was the evaluatively one-sided analysis of information, rather than simply the act of deciding itself, that fostered a spillover of decreased ambivalence" (pp. 406–407).

Lane and Gazerian (2016) replicated the experiment with 70 participants, but found no significant effect of condition on ambivalence: $F(2, 67) = 1.70$, $p = .191$,

TABLE 12.1 Descriptive statistics for confirmatory information processing from the original study: Henderson et al. (2008), and the new study: Lane and Gazerian (2016)

	Neutral		One-sided implemental		Two-sided implemental	
	n	μ (SD)	n	μ (SD)	n	μ (SD)
Original	16	1.23 (1.64)	15	0.16 (1.85)	15	1.82 (1.86)
New	24	-0.38 (1.44)	23	-0.14 (1.66)	23	0.39 (1.25)

$\eta^2 = .05$, $\omega^2 = .02$, $r = .16$ (see also the descriptive statistics in Table 12.1). The post hoc difference test between the one-sided and two-sided implemental mind-set groups was not significant either: $t(44) = 1.24$, $p = .222$, Cohen's $d = .36$, Hedges' $g = .25$. Based on the lack of significance in the new study, Lane and Gazerian conclude that the effect may not replicate.

Four replication methods

Evaluating the significance (and direction) of the effect in the new study and using it as a measure for replication, as was a main method of Lane and Gazerian, is called "vote-counting". Vote-counting, however, does not take into account the magnitude of the differences between effect sizes (Simonsohn, 2015), it is not a statistical test of replication (Anderson & Maxwell, 2016; Verhagen & Wagenmakers, 2014), and it leads to misleading conclusions in underpowered replication studies (Simonsohn, 2015). Thus, vote-counting is a poor method to assess replication. In the following, we discuss four alternative replication research questions and methods.

Question 1: Is the new effect size similar to the original effect size?

A frequentist approach to this replication research question is the equivalence test (e.g., Walker & Nowacki, 2011). This test requires the researcher to specify a region of equivalence for the difference between the original and new effect size. If the confidence interval of the difference between effects falls entirely within this region, the effect sizes are considered equivalent. However, it is difficult to set a region of equivalence that is reasonably limited while at the same time the confidence interval for the difference between effects has a chance to entirely fit within the interval. Therefore, we do not elaborate on the equivalence test and focus instead on Bayesian approaches.

To evaluate whether the new effect size is similar to the original effect size, we can compute a Bayes factor (BF; Jeffreys, 1961); see also Chapter 9 (Klaassen). A BF expresses the shift in belief, relative to our prior belief, after observing the data for two competing hypotheses. A BF of 1 is undecided. BFs smaller than 1 indicate preference for the null hypothesis, whereas BFs larger than 1 favor the alternative hypothesis. The two competing hypotheses in the BF can be operationalized in many ways, but in the replication setting, one of the evaluated hypotheses is often the null effect (i.e., the effect size is zero). To evaluate the current research question, a proper alternative hypothesis is that the effect in the new study is similar to the effect in the original study (Harms, 2018a; Ly, Etz, Marsman, & Wagenmakers, 2018; Verhagen & Wagenmakers, 2014). In this case, the BF evaluates whether the new study is closer to a null effect, or closer to the original effect, where the original effect forms the prior distribution in the BF for the new effect. Verhagen and Wagenmakers (2014) developed this BF for the t-test. Harms (2018a) extended the Replication BF to the ANOVA F-test and developed the `ReplicationBF` R package to compute it based on the sample sizes and test statistics of the original and new study. For the ANOVA by Henderson et al. (2008) replicated by Lane and Gazerian (2016), we obtain a Replication BF of 0.42^1, which means that the evidence for the null hypothesis of no effect is 2.40 (i.e., 1/0.42) times stronger than the evidence for the alternative hypothesis that the effect is similar to that in the original study. See Figure 12.1 for a visualization by the `ReplicationBF` package. The R package also includes the Replication BF for *t*-tests as proposed by Verhagen and Wagenmakers (2014). For the post hoc *t*-test we find a Replication BF of .72, which is again in favor of a null effect. Thus, the Replication BF does not support replication of the omnibus ANOVA effect, nor does it support the replication of the post hoc result that the one-sided mind-set group scores lower on ambivalence than the two-sided mind-set group.

Ly et al. (2018) provided a simple calculation to obtain the Replication BF by Verhagen and Wagenmakers (2014) for all models for which a BF can be obtained: Evidence Updating (EU) Replication

$$\text{BF} = \frac{\text{BF combined data}}{\text{BF original data}} \quad (12.1)$$

This calculation (12.1) assumes, however, that the data are exchangeable (see Chapter 2 for a discussion on exchangeability; Miočević, Levy, & Savord). If the original and new study are not based on the same population, the combined data may demonstrate artificially inflated variances due to different means and standard deviations. To minimize the impact of non-exchangeable datasets, Ly et al. (2018) suggest transforming the data. Here, the grand mean

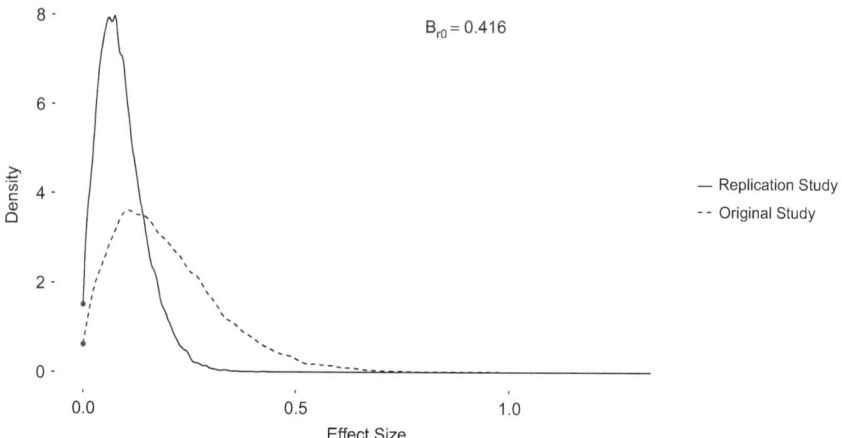

FIGURE 12.1 The Replication BF by Harms (2018a). The original study is the prior for the effect size and the replication study is the posterior based on that prior and the new study. The ratio of the two distributions at 0 on the x-axis is the Replication BF

in Henderson et al. (2008) is actually 1.03 points higher than the grand mean in Lane and Gazerian (2016). To address this issue, we converted the responses to Z-scores.

To compute the BFs for the combined and original datasets, we can use the point-and-click software JASP (JASP Team, 2018) or the BayesFactor package (Morey & Rouder, 2018) in R. For both software packages, the BF for the combined data is 1.50, and the BF for the original data is 1.59. Hence, the EU Replication BF = 1.50/1.59 = .94, which favors the ANOVA null hypothesis that the effect is zero. For the post hoc analysis with the alternative hypothesis that the one-sided mind-set group scores lower than the two-sided mind-set group, the BF for the combined data is 6.66 (see Figure 12.2 for the accompanying JASP plot) and the BF for the original data is 5.81. Hence, the EU Replication BF = 6.66/5.81 = 1.15 for the replication of the original effect. Thus, the EU Replication BF is ambiguous about the replication of the omnibus ANOVA effect (i.e., BF = .94), nor does it provide strong support for the replication of the post hoc result.

Note that the BFs according to the method presented in Ly et al. (2018) are higher than those calculated by the ReplicationBF package by Harms (2018b), even though both are extensions of Verhagen and Wagenmakers (2014). Harms (2018a) and Ly et al. (2018) discuss several differences between both approaches: (1)

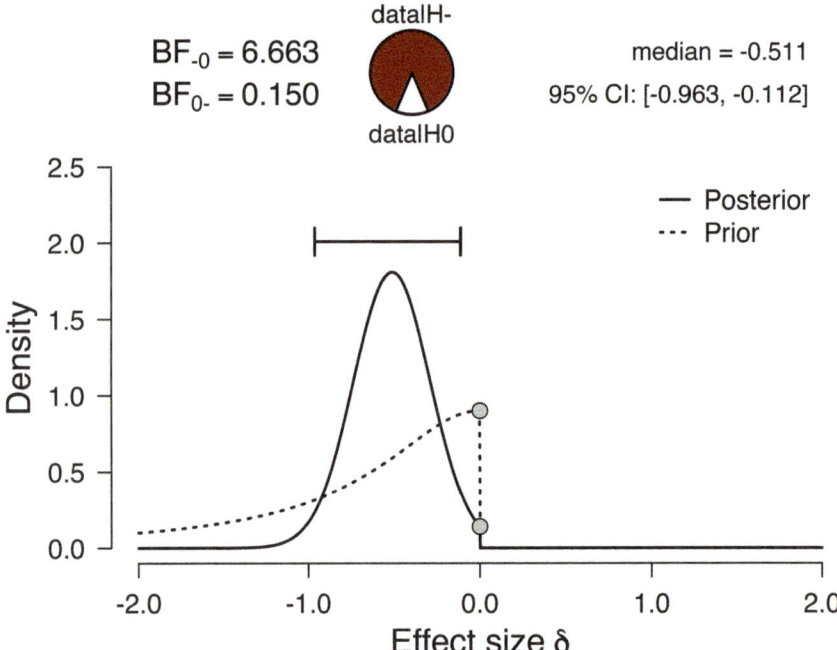

FIGURE 12.2 BF with default prior settings in the combined data for the one-sided t-test. The ratio of the two distributions at 0 on the x-axis is the BF

both methods use different priors (i.e., uniform in `ReplicationBF` R package, Cauchy in `JASP` and the `BayesFactor` R package), (2) the EU Replication BF assumes exchangeability to compute the BF for the combined data, and (3) for ANOVA models the BF computed in the `ReplicationBF` package is based on the sample size and test statistics, whereas `JASP` and the `BayesFactor` package use a more elaborate model that involves the full dataset(s). `JASP` currently also has a Summary Statistics module for *t*-tests, regression analyses, and analyses of frequencies. Whenever possible, we recommend applying both methods to obtain a more robust evaluation of replication.

Question 2: Is the new effect size different from the original effect size?

To test whether the new effect size is different from the effect size in the original study, we would preferably compute a confidence interval for the difference in effect sizes. The literature does not provide such an interval for η^2 or ω^2. However, with an iterative procedure based on descriptive statistics we can obtain separate confidence intervals for ω^2 in the original and new study (Steiger, 2004). Let us denote the original study with subscript *original*, and the new study with subscript *new*. For the original study $\omega^2_{original} = .09$, 95% CI [.00, .30] (see Supplementary Materials for all calculations). For the new study $\omega^2_{new} = .02$, 95% CI [.00, .22]. With these confidence intervals, we can calculate a confidence interval for the difference between both effect sizes, $\Delta\omega^2$, by applying the modified asymmetric method introduced by Zou (2007) for correlations and squared correlations. This method takes into account that some effect sizes have asymmetric distributions or cannot take on negative values (such as ω^2). $\Delta\omega^2 = .07$, 95% CI [-.15, .29]. Since zero is in the confidence interval of the difference between the effect sizes, we do not reject the hypothesis that the effect sizes are equal, and thus we retain the hypothesis that the new effect replicates the original one.

For the post hoc difference between the one-sided and two-sided implemental conditions we can compute the 95% confidence interval for standardized mean differences (i.e., Cohen's $d_{original} = .93$ and Cohen's $d_{new} = .36$) as given in Bonett (2009) and included in the Supplementary Materials. The difference between Cohen's *d* for both studies is .57, 95% CI [-0.96, 2.10]. Since zero lies in the confidence interval, we do not reject replication of the original effect size.

Alternatively, Patil, Peng, and Leek (2016) describe how non-replication of an effect size can be tested with a prediction interval. A 95% prediction interval aims to include the (effect size) estimate in the next study for 95% of the replications. Patil and colleagues (see Supplementary Materials) apply this method on *r* as calculated in the RPP. Following their methods, we find that the prediction interval for $r_{original} = .26$ ranges from -.12 to .57. The estimate for the new study, $r_{new} = .16$, lies within the interval of estimates that are expected given replication (i.e., -0.12 to 0.57). Hence, we do not reject replication of the original effect size. Note that Patil et al. apply their method on *r*, which is considered problematic when *r* is based on more than two groups (see, for example, Appendix 3 at osf.io/z7aux). The post hoc *t*-test value of $r_{original}$ is .42 with a prediction interval ranging from -0.03 to 0.73. For the new study, $r_{new} = .18$. Again, the correlation estimate for the new study lies within the prediction interval, and we do not reject the hypothesis that the original effect has been replicated.

The confidence intervals for the difference between effect sizes and the prediction intervals in this example can be considered to be quite wide. If the study results are uncertain (i.e., based on small samples), the associated confidence and prediction intervals will less often reject replication of the original effect size. However, especially with small studies, a failure to reject replication does not necessarily imply replication, but rather a lack of power, which suggests that the above methods may be inadequate for small samples.

Question 3: Are the new findings different from the original findings?

In contrast to the first two replication research questions which concerned effect sizes, the current question concerns study findings in general. The prior predictive *p*-value can be used to answer this question (Box, 1980; Zondervan-Zwijnenburg, Van de Schoot, & Hoijtink, 2019). The calculation of the prior predictive *p*-value starts with the simulation of datasets from the predictive distribution (with the sample size used in the new study) that are to be expected, given the original results. Subsequently, the new observed data from the replication attempt are compared to the predicted data with respect to relevant findings as summarized in H_{RF}. This hypothesis includes the relevant findings of the original study in an informative hypothesis (Hoijtink, 2012) and can include the ordering of parameters (e.g., $\mu_1 > \mu_2$), the sign of parameters (e.g., $\mu_1 > 0, \mu_2 < 0$), or the exact value of parameters (e.g., $\mu_1 = 3, \mu_2 = -2$). Any combination of constraints is possible. The deviation from the hypothesis for each of the predicted datasets and for the new dataset is expressed in the statistic that we call $\bar{F}$. Lower $\bar{F}$ values indicate a better fit with the relevant features specified in H_{RF}. With $\alpha = .05$, replication of the study findings is rejected if the misfit with H_{RF} in the new study is equal to or higher than in the extreme 5% of the predicted data. All computations can be conducted in an online interactive application presented at osf.io/6h8x3 or with the `ANOVAreplication` R package (Zondervan-Zwijnenburg, 2018). The online application (utrecht-university.shinyapps.io/anovareplication) and R package can take either raw data or summary statistics and sample sizes as input.

The results and conclusion of Henderson et al. (2008) lead to the following: $H_{RF} : \mu_{\text{One-sided implemental}} < (\mu_{\text{Two-sided implemental}}, \mu_{\text{Neutral}})$; Cohen's $d_{\text{One-sided implemental, Two-sided implemental}} > .8$.

If we run the test, we find that the prior predictive *p*-value = .130. Hence, we do not reject replication of the original study findings. Figure 12.3 shows the statistic $\bar{F}$ for each of the predicted datasets and the replication by Lane and

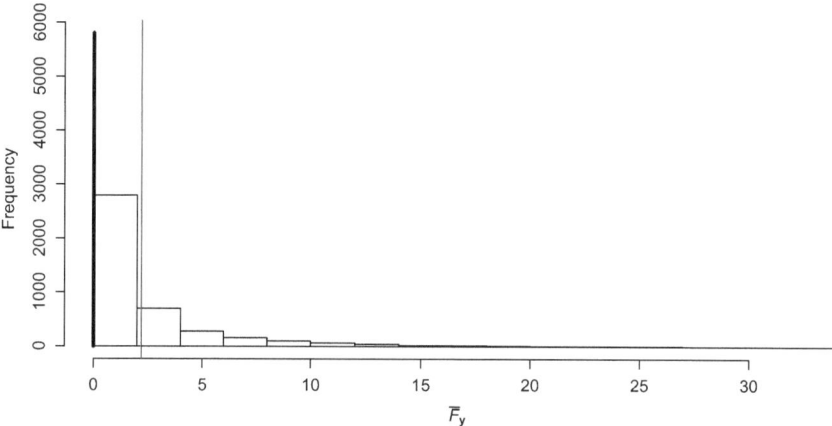

FIGURE 12.3 Prior predictive p-value. The histogram concerns $\bar{F}$ scores for each of the 10,000 predicted datasets with respect to the replication hypothesis. The thick black line represents the 5,805 predicted datasets that had an $\bar{F}$-score of exactly 0 and were perfectly in line with the replication hypothesis. The red line indicates the $\bar{F}$-score of 2.20 for the new study. The $\bar{F}$ score for the new data is positioned in the extreme 13.0% of the predicted data (prior predictive p = .130)

Gazerian (2016). Note that we do not have to run a post hoc analysis with this method, because the conclusion for the post hoc contrast was incorporated in H_{RF} with "Cohen's $d_{\text{One–sided implemental, Two–sided implemental}} > .8$". For the prior predictive p-value, an original study with large standard errors (e.g., due to a small sample) leads to a wide variety of predicted datasets, thus making it hard to reject replication of the original study conclusions. With the ANOVAreplication R package we can calculate the power to reject replication when all means would be equal in the new study. Here, the statistical power was only .66, which means that the probability that we do not reject replication incorrectly (i.e., a Type II error) is 1-.66=.34. When we calculate the required sample size to obtain sufficient power, we find that a sample size of 41 per group would be required to reject replication of H_{RF} in a sample with equal group means.

Question 4: What is the effect size in the population?

At the end of the day, most researchers are concerned with the effect in the population. To determine the population effect based on an original and new study, numerous meta-analytic procedures have been proposed. For close replications, the fixed-effect meta-analysis can be used, which assumes that there is one underlying population from which both studies are random samples. Consequently, there is only one underlying true effect size. However, the standard fixed-effect meta-analysis does not take publication bias into account. As a result, standard fixed-effect meta-analyses overestimate effect sizes.

The frequentist hybrid meta-analysis (Van Aert & Van Assen, 2017b), and the Bayesian snapshot hybrid method (Van Aert & Van Assen, 2017a) are two meta-analytic methods developed for situations with a single replication effort that take into account the significance of the original study (which could be caused by publication bias). Both methods are part of the puniform R package (Van Aert, 2018) and available as online interactive applications. The required input are descriptive statistics and effect sizes. The frequentist hybrid meta-analysis results in a corrected meta-analytic effect size and its associated confidence interval and p-value. The output also includes the results of a standard fixed-effect meta-analysis for comparison. The Bayesian snapshot hybrid method quantifies the relative support, given the original and replication study, for four effect size categories: zero, small, medium, and large. Currently, both methods can be used for correlations and t-tests. However, the correlation for the original ANOVA as computed by the RPP cannot be used for the meta-analytic methods, because its standard error cannot be computed for more than two groups.

For the post hoc t-test results of Henderson et al. (2008) and Lane and Gazerian (2016), the bias-corrected Hedges' g is .37, 95% CI [-0.48, 0.94], $p = .232$. Thus, we cannot reject the hypothesis that the effect in the population is zero. The standard (uncorrected) fixed-effect meta-analytic estimate was .60, 95% CI [0.12,1.07], $p = .014$. Whereas the fixed-effect meta-analytic effect sizes was significant at $\alpha = .05$, the hybrid meta-analysis effect size is lower and has a wider 95% confidence interval. The snapshot hybrid method with equal prior probabilities for the four effect size categories indicated that a small effect size received the highest support (37.8%), followed by no effect size (30.2%), a medium effect size (25.5%), and a large effect size (6.6%).

Besides meta-analyses that take significance of the original study into account, we can also calculate the BF for an effect versus no effect, based on the scaled combined data using JASP. The BF in favor of an ANOVA effect is 1.50. The BF in favor of a post hoc t-test effect is 6.66. Hence, the evidence in the combined data is positive with respect to the existence of an effect. Note that this combined analysis does not correct for publication bias and assumes exchangeability. Alternatively, Etz and Vandekerckhove (2016) developed a BF for t-tests, univariate F-tests (i.e., for up to two groups), and univariate regression analyses that takes into account publication bias, but unfortunately this BF has only been developed for the MATLAB software package, which is not commonly used in the social sciences and will not be described further.

Discussion

In this chapter, we presented replication research questions and associated statistical techniques. In the example we used, the replication BFs pointed mostly towards a null effect instead of a replication of the original effect; the confidence intervals around the difference between effect sizes indicated that the difference between the original and new study may be zero, but that they had low power;

the prior predictive *p*-value demonstrated non-replication of the original study conclusions; and meta-analyses indicated that the population effect is small, anecdotal, or not significantly different from zero.

We also discussed how the different methods perform with small samples. BFs and the Bayesian snapshot meta-analysis have the advantage over null-hypothesis significance testing (NHST) methods (e.g., confidence intervals and the prior predictive *p*-value) that they cannot be underpowered. The evidence by the BF may not be overwhelming, but at least it indicates the relative plausibility of one hypothesis over the other after observing the data. With additional data and Bayesian updating methods (see also Chapter 9), the evidence can become more convincing. NHST methods, on the other hand, often result in non-significant findings with small samples, and it remains unclear whether the (non)replication effect was absent, or whether the analysis was underpowered.

An advantage of the prior predictive *p*-value is that it allows the user to test the replication of the original study findings summarized in H_{RF}. This hypothesis can include multiple parameters, and it can convey information on their size and ordering. In the ANOVA setting, the effect size (e.g., η^2) does not provide information about the direction of the effect. Hence, it is useful to evaluate relevant features that can cover the ordering of group means.

The preferred method to test replication depends on the replication research question at hand. Furthermore, given a replication research question, it can be insightful to apply multiple methods to test replication (Harms, 2018a). Testing replication yields more meaningful results with larger sample sizes, and this holds for all methods described in this chapter. Testing replication of small sample research is challenging, but since small samples are more susceptible to researcher degrees of freedom, it is of utmost importance to critically evaluate small sample results with replication studies.

Author note

The first author is funded through the Consortium Individual Development by a Gravitation program grant of the Dutch Ministry of Education, Culture and Science, and the Netherlands Organization for Scientific Research (grant number 024.001.003).

Note

1 We report BF up to two decimal places, but use all available information for calculations.

References

Anderson, S. F., & Maxwell, S. E. (2016). There's more than one way to conduct a replication study: Beyond statistical significance. *Psychological Methods*, *21*(1), 1–12. doi:10.1037/met0000051.

Bonett, D. G. (2009). Meta-analytic interval estimation for standardized and unstandardized mean differences. *Psychological Methods*, *14*(3), 225–238. doi:10.1037/a0016619.

Box, G. E. P. (1980). Sampling and Bayes' inference in scientific modelling and robustness. *Journal of the Royal Statistical Society. Series A (general)*, *143*(4), 383–430. doi:10.2307/2982063.

Cohen, J. (1962). The statistical power of abnormal-social psychological research: A review. *Journal of Abnormal Social Psychology*, *65*(3), 145–153. doi:10.1037/h0045186.

Etz, A., & Vandekerckhove, J. (2016). A Bayesian perspective on the reproducibility project: Psychology. *PLoS One*, *11*(2), e0149794. doi:10.1371/journal.pone.0149794.

Harms, C. (2018a). A Bayes factor for replications of ANOVA results. *American Statistician*. doi:10.1080/00031305.2018.1518787.

Harms, C. (2018b). ReplicationBF: Calculating replication Bayes factors for different scenarios. Retrieved from https://github.com/neurotroph/ReplicationBF.

Hedges, L. V. (1981). Distribution theory for Glass's estimator of effect size and related estimators. *Journal of Educational Statistics*, *6*(2), 107–128. doi:10.3102/10769986006002107.

Henderson, M. D., De Liver, Y., & Gollwitzer, P. M. (2008). The effects of an implemental mind-set on attitude strength. *Journal of Personality and Social Psychology*, *94*(3), 396–411. doi:10.1037/0022-3514.94.3.396.

Hoijtink, H. (2012). *Informative hypotheses: Theory and practice for behavioral and social scientists*. Boca Raton, FL: Taylor & Francis.

JASP Team. (2018). JASP Version 0.9.1.

Jeffreys, H. (1961). *Theory of probability* (3rd ed.). Oxford: Oxford University Press.

Lane, K. A., & Gazerian, D. (2016). Replication of Henderson, De Liver, & Gollwitzer (2008, JPSP, Expt. 5). osf.io/79dey.

Lindsay, D. S. (2015). Replication in psychological science. *Psychological Science*, *26*(12), 1827–1832. doi:10.1177/0956797615616374.

Ly, A., Etz, A., Marsman, M., & Wagenmakers, E.-J. (2018). Replication Bayes factors from evidence updating. *Behavior Research Methods*, 1–11. doi:10.3758/s13428-018-1092-x.

Morey, R. D., & Rouder, J. N. (2018). BayesFactor: Computation of Bayes factors for common designs [R package version 0.9.12-4.2]. Retrieved from https://CRAN.R-project.org/package=BayesFactor.

Okada, K. (2013). Is omega squared less biased? A comparison of three major effect size indices in one-way ANOVA. *Behaviormetrika*, *40*(2), 129–147. doi:10.2333/bhmk.40.129.

Open Science Collaboration. (2015). Estimating the reproducibility of psychological science. *Science*, *349*(6251), aac4716. 10.1126/science.aac4716.

Patil, P., Peng, R. D., & Leek, J. T. (2016). What should researchers expect when they replicate studies? A statistical view of replicability in psychological science. *Perspectives on Psychological Science*, *11*(4), 539–544. doi:10.1177/1745691616646366.

R Core Team. (2017). R: A language and environment for statistical computing. Vienna: R Foundation for Statistical Computing.

Rosenthal, R. (1979). The file drawer problem and tolerance for null results. *Psychological Bulletin*, *86*(3), 638–641. doi:10.1037/0033-2909.86.3.638.

Simmons, J. P., Nelson, L. D., & Simonsohn, U. (2011). False-positive psychology: Undisclosed flexibility in data collection and analysis allows presenting anything as significant. *Psychological Science*, *22*(11), 1359–1366. doi:10.1177/0956797611417632.

Simonsohn, U. (2015). Small telescopes: Detectability and the evaluation of replication results. *Psychological Science*, *26*(5), 559–569. doi:10.1177/0956797614567341.

Steiger, J. H. (2004). Beyond the F test: Effect size confidence intervals and tests of close fit in the analysis of variance and contrast analysis. *Psychological Methods, 9*(2), 164–182. doi:10.1037/1082-989X.9.2.164.

Van Aert, R. C. (2018). Puniform: Meta-analysis methods correcting for publication bias [R package version 0.1.0]. Retrieved from https://CRAN.R-project.org/package=puniform.

Van Aert, R. C., & Van Assen, M. A. (2017a). Bayesian evaluation of effect size after replicating an original study. *PLoS One, 12*(4), e0175302. doi:10.1371/journal.pone.0175302.

Van Aert, R. C., & Van Assen, M. A. (2017b). Examining reproducibility in psychology: A hybrid method for combining a statistically significant original study and a replication. *Behavior Research Methods, 50*(4), 1515–1539. doi:10.3758/s13428-017-0967-6.

Verhagen, J., & Wagenmakers, E.-J. (2014). Bayesian tests to quantify the result of a replication attempt. *Journal of Experimental Psychology: General, 143*(4), 1457–1475. doi:10.1037/a0036731.

Walker, E., & Nowacki, A. S. (2011). Understanding equivalence and noninferiority testing. *Journal of General Internal Medicine, 26*, 192–196. doi:10.1007/s11606-010-1513-8.

Zondervan-Zwijnenburg, M. A. J. (2018). ANOVAreplication: Test ANOVA replications by means of the prior predictive p-value. Retrieved from https://CRAN.R-project.org/package=ANOVAreplication.

Zondervan-Zwijnenburg, M. A. J., Van de Schoot, R., & Hoijtink, H. (2019). Testing ANOVA replications by means of the prior predictive p-value. doi:10.31234/osf.io/6myqh.

Zou, G. Y. (2007). Toward using confidence intervals to compare correlations. *Psychological Methods, 12*(4), 399–413. doi:10.1037/1082-989X.12.4.399.

13

SMALL SAMPLE META-ANALYSES
Exploring heterogeneity using MetaForest

Caspar J. van Lissa
DEPARTMENT OF METHODOLOGY AND STATISTICS, UTRECHT UNIVERSITY, UTRECHT, THE NETHERLANDS

Introduction

Meta-analysis is the act of statistically summarizing the findings of several studies on a single topic (Borenstein, Hedges, Higgins, & Rothstein, 2009). Some consider meta-analyses to be the golden standard of scientific evidence (Crocetti, 2016). This reputation is not entirely deserved, however, as meta-analysis comes with its own pitfalls. One of these is that meta-analyses often present a small sample problem. The fact that each of the studies included in the meta-analysis is based on a larger sample of participants does not mean that the problem of small sample sizes is any less relevant than in primary research. Particularly in the social sciences, the number of studies on any topic is typically low, because conducting research is cost- and time-intensive. In an investigation of 705 psychological meta-analyses, the median number of studies was 12 (Van Erp, Verhagen, Grasman, & Wagenmakers, 2017), and in 14 meta-analyses from education science, the median number of studies was 44 (De Jonge & Jak, 2018). Small sample sizes thus appear to be the rule, rather than the exception.

The issue of small sample sizes is compounded by a related challenge: Between-studies heterogeneity (Higgins & Thompson, 2002). Differences between the studies can introduce heterogeneity in the effect sizes found. These two problems are related, because small samples have limited statistical power to adequately account for sources of between-studies heterogeneity. In this chapter, I discuss how the related problems of small sample sizes and between-studies heterogeneity can be overcome using MetaForest: A machine-learning-based approach to identify relevant moderators in meta-analysis (Van Lissa, 2017). After presenting the general principles underlying this technique, I provide a tutorial example for conducting a small sample meta-analysis, using the R package `metaforest` (Van Lissa, 2018).

Models for meta-analysis

Classic meta-analysis can be conceptualized as a weighted average of study effect sizes, where studies with a larger sample accrue greater weight. The simplest statistical model used to assign these weights is the so-called fixed-effect model (Hedges & Vevea, 1998). The fixed-effect model does not account for between-studies heterogeneity. This model assumes that all studies tap into one true effect size (T), and that any differences between observed effect sizes are due to sampling error. This assumption is probably valid when the included studies are very close replications.

In most cases, however, this assumption is too restrictive, and we assume that some between-studies heterogeneity exists. If we can assume that the heterogeneity is "random", or normally distributed, we can use a random-effects model, which assumes that each study taps into an underlying (normal) distribution of true effect sizes (Hedges & Vevea, 1998). The random-effects model estimates the mean and standard deviation of this distribution. This model is the appropriate choice if the studies are similar (e.g., replications from different labs), but some small unknown random differences might have crept in. In the random-effects model, the weight accorded to each effect size is no longer purely based on its sample size – it is also based on the estimated between-studies heterogeneity. In the hypothetical case that the between-studies heterogeneity is estimated to be zero, the weights are the same as in the fixed-effect model. When heterogeneity is larger, however, the study weights are adjusted to be more equal, because each study now conveys some information about a different area of the underlying distribution of effect sizes. If the between-studies heterogeneity would be huge, all studies would be weighted equally.

Between-studies heterogeneity

A common application of meta-analysis in the social sciences is to summarize a diverse body of literature on a specific topic. The literature typically covers similar research questions, investigated in different laboratories, using different methods, instruments, and samples (Maxwell, Lau, & Howard, 2015). The assumption of the random-effects model, that there is one underlying normal distribution of true effect sizes, likely breaks down in such cases (Hedges & Vevea, 1998), because these between-studies differences might introduce heterogeneity in the effect sizes.

Researchers can account for between-studies differences by coding them as *moderator variables*, and controlling for their influence using meta-regression (Higgins & Thompson, 2004). Similar to classic regression, meta-regression posits that the outcome – in this case, the effect size of a study – is a function of the value of the moderators for that study. Both the fixed-effects and random-effects model can be extended to meta-regression. The advantage of coding between-studies differences as moderators, rather than using them as exclusion criteria, is that all studies can be included, as long as any differences are controlled for using meta-regression.

Too many moderators

Like any regression-based technique, meta-regression requires relatively many cases per parameter (Guolo & Varin, 2017). But in heterogeneous fields of research, there are often many potential moderators. We typically do not know beforehand which moderators will affect the effect size found. If we just include all moderators in a meta-regression, we risk overfitting the data (Higgins & Thompson, 2004). *Overfitting* means that the model fits the observed data very well, but does not generalize to new data, or the population (Hastie, Tibshirani, & Friedman, 2009). This is because it captures noise in the data, not just genuine effects. The more moderators are included, the more prone a model becomes to overfitting.

The problem of small samples is compounded by the existence of between-studies differences that could potentially influence the effect size of a study. The more potential moderators, the larger the sample that would be required to adequately account for their influence. Moreover, these two problems tend to go hand in hand. When there is a small body of literature on a given topic, it tends to be comprised of idiosyncratic studies.

How to deal with moderators?

Based on my experience as a statistical consultant, I have found that the question of how to deal with moderators is one of the most common challenges researchers face when conducting a meta-analysis. One common approach appears to be to diligently code moderators, but then omit them from the analysis. Most data sets I have requested from authors of published meta-analyses contained more moderators than discussed in the paper. In one extreme case, a meta-analysis of 180 studies reported a single moderator, whereas the raw data set contained over 190 moderators – more variables than studies. Of course, the problem of having many potentially relevant moderators is not resolved by failing to report them. They will introduce between-studies heterogeneity regardless. It is unlikely that this selective reporting is ill-intentioned, as I have found most authors of meta-analyses to be very willing to share their data. A more likely explanation is that authors lack concrete guidelines on how to whittle down the list of potential moderators to a manageable number.

A second common practice appears to be to preselect moderators using univariate meta-regressions, and to retain those whose *p*-value falls below a certain threshold. This is problematic, as (1) the *p*-value is not a measure of variable importance, (2) repeated tests inflate the risk of false positive results, and (3) coefficients in the model are interdependent, and omitting one moderator can influence the effect of others. Another approach is to run a model including all moderators, and then eliminate non-significant ones. This is problematic for all but the second aforementioned reasons. Additionally, when the number of moderators is relatively large compared to the number of studies included, the risk of overfitting increases.

A method for exploratory moderator selection

What is needed is a technique that can explore between-studies heterogeneity and perform variable selection, identifying relevant moderators from a larger set of candidates, without succumbing to overfitting. The recently developed Meta-Forest algorithm meets these requirements (Van Lissa, 2017). MetaForest is an adaptation of the random forest algorithm (Breiman, 2001; Strobl, Malley, & Tutz, 2009) for meta-analysis. Random forests are a powerful machine learning algorithm for regression problems, with several advantages over linear regression. First, random forests are robust to overfitting. Second, they are non-parametric, and can inherently capture non-linear relationships between the moderator and effect size, or even complex, higher-order interactions between moderators. Third, they perform variable selection, identifying which moderators contribute most strongly to the effect size found.

Understanding random forests

The *random forest* algorithm combines many *tree models* (Hastie et al., 2009). A tree model can be conceptualized as a decision tree, or a flowchart: Starting with the full data set, the model splits the data into two groups. The splitting decision is based on the moderator variables; the model finds a moderator variable, and the value on that variable, along which to split the data set. It chooses the moderator and value that result in the most homogenous post-split groups possible. This process is repeated for each post-split group; over and over again, until a stopping criterion is reached. Usually, the algorithm is stopped when the post-split groups contain a minimum number of cases.

One advantage of regression trees is that it does not matter if the number of moderators is large relative to the sample size, or even exceeds it. Second, trees are non-parametric; they do not assume normally distributed residuals or linearity, and intrinsically capture non-linear effects and interactions. These are substantial advantages when performing meta-analysis on a heterogeneous body of literature. Single regression trees also have a limitation, however, which is that they are extremely prone to overfitting. They will simply capture all patterns in the data, both genuine effects and random noise (Hastie et al., 2009).

Random forests overcome this limitation of single regression trees. First, many different bootstrap samples are drawn (e.g., 1,000). Then, a single tree is grown on each bootstrap sample. To ensure that each tree learns something unique from the data, only a small random selection of moderators is made available to choose from at each splitting point. Finally, the predictions of all tree models are averaged. This renders random forests robust to overfitting:

Because each tree captures some of the true patterns in the data, and overfits some random noise that is only present in its bootstrap sample, overfitting cancels out on aggregate. Random forests also make better predictions: Where single trees predict a fixed value for each "group" they identify in the data, random forests average the predictions of many trees, which leads to smoother prediction curves.

An earlier chapter pointed out that bootstrapped confidence intervals for hypothesis testing are not valid as a small sample technique (see also Chapter 18 by Hox). As samples get smaller, their representativeness of the population decreases. Consequently, bootstrap resampling will be less likely to yield an accurate approximation of the sampling distribution. The purpose of bootstrapping in random forests is different from hypothesis testing, however: It aims to ensure that every tree model explores some unique aspects of the *data at hand*. Thus, concerns regarding bootstrapped hypothesis tests are not directly relevant here.

Meta-analytic random forests

To render random forests suitable for meta-analysis, a weighting scheme is applied to the bootstrap sampling, which means that more precise studies exert greater influence in the model building stage (Van Lissa, 2017). These weights can be uniform (each study has equal probability of being selected into the bootstrap sample), fixed-effects-based (studies with smaller sampling variance have a larger probability of being selected), or random-effects-based (studies with smaller sampling variance have a larger probability of being selected, but this advantage is diminished as the amount of between-studies heterogeneity increases). Internally, `MetaForest` relies on the ranger R package; a fast implementation of the random forests in C++ (Wright & Ziegler, 2015).

Tuning parameters

Like many machine learning algorithms, random forests have several "tuning parameters": Settings that might influence the results of the analysis, and whose optimal values must be determined empirically. The first is the number of candidate variables considered at each split of each tree. The second is the minimum number of cases that must remain in a post-split group within each tree. The third is unique to MetaForest; namely, the type of weights (uniform, fixed-, or random-effects). The optimal values for these tuning parameters are commonly determined using cross-validation (Hastie et al., 2009). Cross-validation means splitting the data set many times; for example, into 10 equal parts. Then, predictions are made for each of the parts of the data, using a model estimated on all of the other parts. This process is conducted for all possible combinations of tuning parameters. The values of tuning parameters that result in the lowest cross-validated prediction error are used for the final model. For cross-validation, `MetaForest` relies on the well-known machine learning R package caret (Kuhn, 2008).

Understanding the output

The output of a MetaForest analysis is somewhat different from what researchers schooled in the general linear model might be familiar with. Three parts of the output, in particular, warrant further clarification.

Predictive performance

Just like regression, random forests offer a measure of explained variance similar to R^2. Whereas R^2 refers to the variance explained in the data *used to estimate the model*, random forests provide an estimate of how much variance the model would explain in a *new data set* (Hastie et al., 2009). This distinction between "retrodictive" and "predictive" performance is important: The retrodictive R^2 increases with every moderator added to the model, even when the model is overfit. However, such an overfit model would make terrible predictions for new data.

Random forests provides an estimate of predictive performance, called R^2_{oob} (Breiman, 2001). The subscript *oob* stands for "out-of-bag" and refers to the way this estimate is obtained: By predicting each case in the data set from those trees that were trained on bootstrap samples *not* containing that case. A second estimate of predictive R^2, R^2_{cv}, is obtained during cross-validation (*cv*), by predicting cases not used to estimate the model. Predictive R^2 becomes negative when a model is overfit, because the model makes worse predictions than the mean for new data. A negative R^2_{oob} or R^2_{cv} can thus be interpreted as a sign of overfitting. Positive values estimate how well the model will predict the effect sizes of new studies.

Variable importance

The second relevant type of output are variable importance metrics, which quantify the relative importance of each moderator in predicting the effect size. These metrics are analogous in function to the (absolute) standardized regression coefficients (β^z) in regression: They reflect the strength of each moderator's relationship with the outcome on a common metric. However, whereas betas reflect linear, univariate, partial relationships, MetaForest's variable importance metrics reflect each moderator's contribution to the predictive power of the final model across all linear-, non-linear-, and interaction effects. Variable importance is estimated by randomly permuting, or shuffling, the values of a moderator, thereby annulling any relationship that moderator had with the outcome, and then observing how much the predictive performance of the final model drops. If performance drops a lot, the moderator must have been important. Variable importance can be negative when a moderator is weakly associated with the outcome, and random shuffling coincidentally strengthens the relationship. Such moderators can be dropped from the model. In the R package `metaforest`, variable importance can be plotted using the `VarImpPlot()` function.

Effects of moderators

Random forests are not a black box: Partial dependence plots can be used to visualize the shape of the marginal relationship of each moderator to the effect size, averaging over all values of the other moderators. Researchers commonly inspect only univariate marginal dependence plots. Exploring all possible higher-order interactions swiftly becomes unmanageable; with just 10 moderators, the number of bivariate interactions is 45, and the number of trivariate interactions is 120. In order to plot bivariate interactions with a specific moderator of theoretical relevance, you can use the `PartialDependence()` function in conjunction with the moderator argument.

Accounting for dependent data

Studies often report multiple effect sizes; for example, because several relevant outcomes have been measured. In traditional meta-analysis, one might account for this dependency in the data by using a multilevel analysis (Van Den Noortgate, López-López, Marín-Martínez, & Sánchez-Meca, 2015). With random forests, dependent data leads to an under-estimation of the aforementioned out-of-bag error, which is used to calculate R^2_{oob} and variable importance (Janitza, Celik, & Boulesteix, 2016). If the model has been estimated based on some effect sizes from one study, it will likely have an advantage at predicting other effect sizes from the same study. Thus, the out-of-bag error will be misleadingly small, and hence, the R^2_{oob} will be positively biased. In MetaForest, this problem is overcome by using clustered bootstrap sampling, as proposed by Janitza et al. (2016).

Suitability for small samples

MetaForest has been evaluated in simulation studies, in terms of its predictive performance, power, and ability to identify relevant versus irrelevant moderators (Van Lissa, 2017). The full syntax of these simulations is available at osf.io/khjgb/. To determine practical guidelines for the usage of MetaForest with small samples, it is instructive to examine under what conditions a model estimated using MetaForest predicts new data with greater accuracy than the mean at least 80% of the time. The simulation studies indicated that MetaForest met this criterion in most cases with as few as 20 included studies, except when the effect size of moderators was small (data were simulated based on a linear model, with an effect size of .2), and residual heterogeneity was very large (as compared to values commonly reported in psychological meta-analyses; Van Erp et al. (2017). This suggests that MetaForest is suitable as a small sample solution.

In applied research, the true effect size and residual heterogeneity are unknown. So how do you determine whether MetaForest has detected any reliable effects of moderators? One possibility is to adapt the published syntax of these simulation studies to conduct a custom-made power analysis. Second, with a larger data set, one could set aside part of the data, a "test set". One could then estimate the model on the remaining part of the data, the "training set", and compute a predictive R^2 on the test set; R^2_{test}. With small samples, however, this approach is problematic, because what little data there is should go into the main analysis. Consequently, the most feasible small sample solution might be to examine the R^2_{oob} or R^2_{cv}, as alternatives to the R^2_{test}.

Feature pre-selection

One pitfall with random forests is that they can overfit if a data set contains many *irrelevant* predictors; moderators unrelated to the outcome. Recall that at every split of each tree, a random subset of moderators is made available to choose from. If there are many "noise" predictors, the model will occasionally be forced to select among only irrelevant predictors. This risk is increased when the sample is small, and there are relatively many predictors relative to cases. Thus, it might be desirable to eliminate some noise variables. As mentioned before, noise variables can be identified by their negative variable importance. However, in a small model with many noise variables, these variable importance metrics can vary substantially when re-running the analysis, due to Monte Carlo error introduced by the random aspects of the analysis – Bootstrap sampling, and the random subset of variables considered at each split. Consequently, it can be useful to replicate the analysis, visualize the distribution of variable importance metrics, and filter out variables that have a (mostly) negative variable importance across replications. This is accomplished by using the `preselect()` function, which can implement a simple replication of the analysis, or a bootstrapped replication, or a recursive selection algorithm.

Using MetaForest for small samples

To illustrate how to use MetaForest to identify relevant moderators in a small sample meta-analysis, I will re-analyze the published work of Fukkink and Lont (2007), who have graciously shared their data. The authors examined the effectiveness of training on the competency of childcare providers. The sample is small, consisting of 78 effect sizes derived from 17 unique samples. Exploratory moderator analysis was an explicit goal of the original work: "The first explorative question concerns the study characteristics that are associated with experimental results." Data for this tutorial are included in the `metaforest` package.

```r
# Install metaforest. This needs to be done only once.
install.packages("metaforest")
# Load the metaforest package
library(metaforest)
# Assign the fukkink_lont data to an object called "data"
data <- fukkink_lont
# Set a seed for the random number generator,
# so analyses can be replicated exactly.
set.seed(62)
```

For any random forest model, it is important to check whether the model converges. Convergence is indicated by stabilization of the cumulative mean squared out-of-bag prediction error (MSE_{oob}), as a function of the number of trees in the model. We run the analysis once with a very high number of trees, and pick a smaller number of trees, at which the model is also seen to have converged, to speed up computationally heavy steps, such as replication and model tuning. We re-examine convergence for the final model.

```r
# Run model with many trees to check convergence
check_conv <- MetaForest(yi~.,
                         data = data,
                         study = "id_exp",
                         whichweights = "random",
                         num.trees = 20000)
# Plot convergence trajectory
plot(check_conv)
```

This model has converged with approximately 10,000 trees (Figure 13.1). We now apply moderator pre-selection with this number of trees, using the preselect() function. The "recursive" pre-selection algorithm conducts one MetaForest analysis, drops the moderator with the most negative variable importance, and then re-runs the analysis, until all remaining variables have positive importance. This recursive algorithm is replicated 100-fold. Using preselect_vars(), we retain only those moderators for which a 50% percentile interval of the variable importance metrics does not include zero (variable importance is counted as zero when a moderator is not included in the final step of the recursive algorithm). The results of this preselection can be plotted using plot () (see Figure 13.2).

```r
# Model with 10000 trees for replication
mf_rep <- MetaForest(yi~.,
                     data = data,
                     study = "id_exp",
                     whichweights = "random",
                     num.trees = 10000)
# Recursive preselection
preselected <- preselect(mf_rep,
                         replications = 100,
                         algorithm = "recursive")
# Plot results
plot(preselected)
```

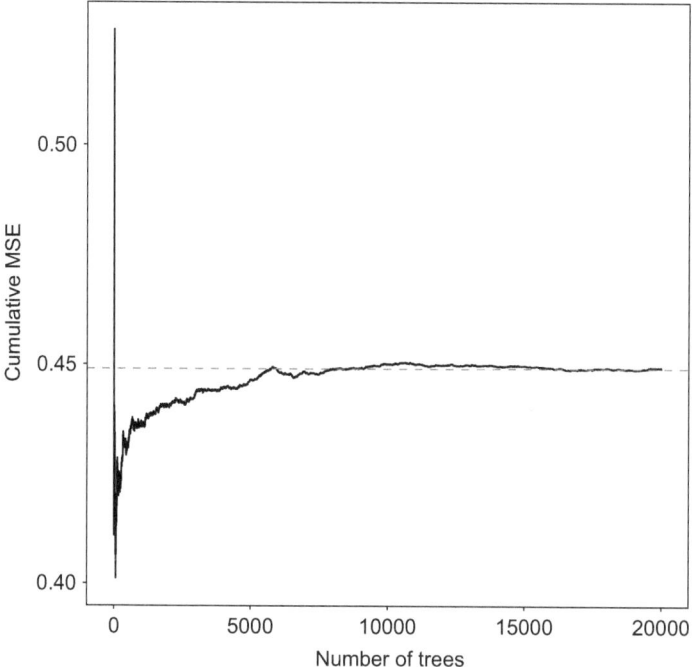

FIGURE 13.1 Convergence plot

```
# Retain moderators with positive variable importance in more than
# 50% of replications
retain_mods <- preselect_vars(preselected, cutoff = .5)
```

Next, we tune the model using the R package caret, which offers a uniform workflow for any machine learning task. The function ModelInfo_mf() tells caret how to tune a MetaForest analysis. As tuning parameters, we consider all three types of weights (uniform, fixed-, and random-effects), the number of candidate variables at each split from 2–6, and a minimum node size from 2–6. We select the model with smallest root mean squared prediction error (RMSE) as the final model, based on 10-fold clustered cross-validation. Clustered cross-validation means that effect sizes from the same study are always included in the same fold, to account for the dependency in the data. Note that the number of folds cannot exceed the number of clusters in the data. Moreover, if the number of clusters is very small, one might have to resort to specifying the same number of folds as clusters. Model tuning is computationally intensive and might take a long time.

```
# Load caret
library(caret)
# Set up 10-fold clustered CV
grouped_cv <- trainControl(method = "cv",
                           index = groupKFold(data$id_exp, k = 10))
```

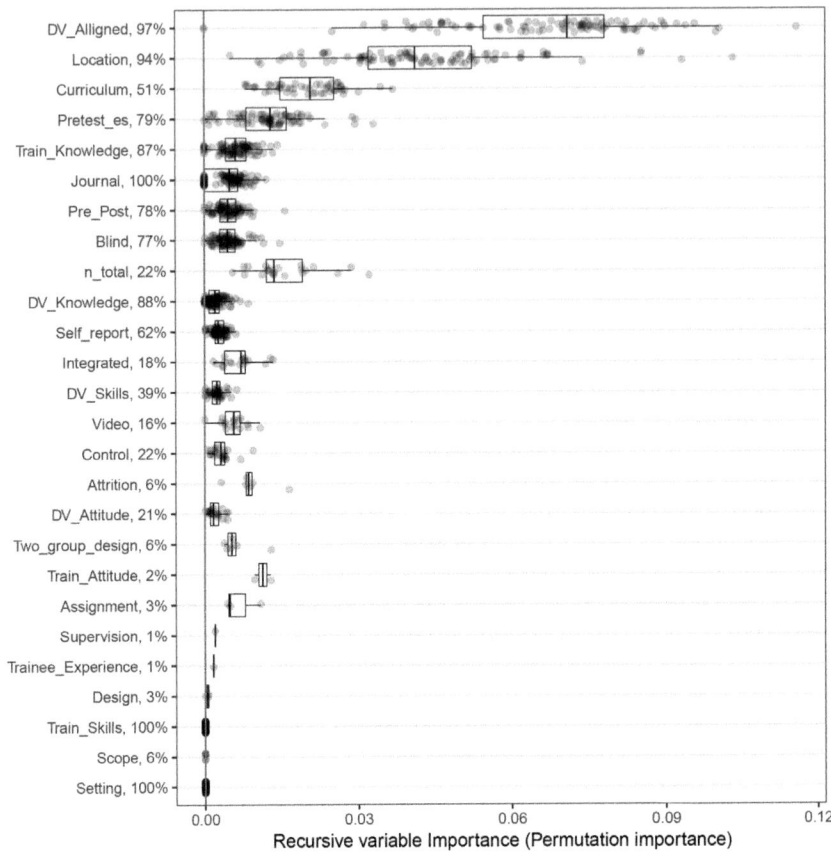

FIGURE 13.2 Replicated variable importance for moderator pre-selection

```
# Set up a tuning grid
tuning_grid <- expand.grid(whichweights = c("random", "fixed", "unif"),
                           mtry = 2:6,
                           min.node.size = 2:6)

# X should contain only retained moderators, clustering variable, and vi
X <- data[, c("id_exp", "vi", retain_mods)]

# Train the model
mf_cv <- train(y = data$yi,
               x = X,
               study = "id_exp", # Name of the clustering variable
               method = ModelInfo_mf(),
               trControl = grouped_cv,
               tuneGrid = tuning_grid,
               num.trees = 10000)
# Extract R^2_cvVan Lissa,
r2_cv <- mf_cv$results$Rsquared[which.min(mf_cv$results$RMSE)]
```

Based on the root mean squared error, the best combination of tuning parameters were uniform weights, with four candidate variables per split, and a minimum of two cases per terminal node. The object returned by train already contains the final model, estimated with the best combination of tuning parameters.

```
# Extract final model
final <- mf_cv$finalModel
# Extract R^2_oob from the final model
r2_oob <- final$forest$r.squared
# Plot convergence
plot(final)
```

We can conclude that the model has converged (Figure 13.3), and has a positive estimate of explained variance in new data, $R^2_{oob} = 0.13$, $R^2_{cv} = 0.48$. Now, we proceed to interpreting the moderator effects, by examining variable importance (Figure 13.4), and partial dependence plots (Figure 13.5).

```
# Plot variable importance
VarImpPlot(final)
# Sort the variable names by importance
ordered_vars <- names(final$forest$variable.importance)[
    order(final$forest$variable.importance, decreasing = TRUE)]
```

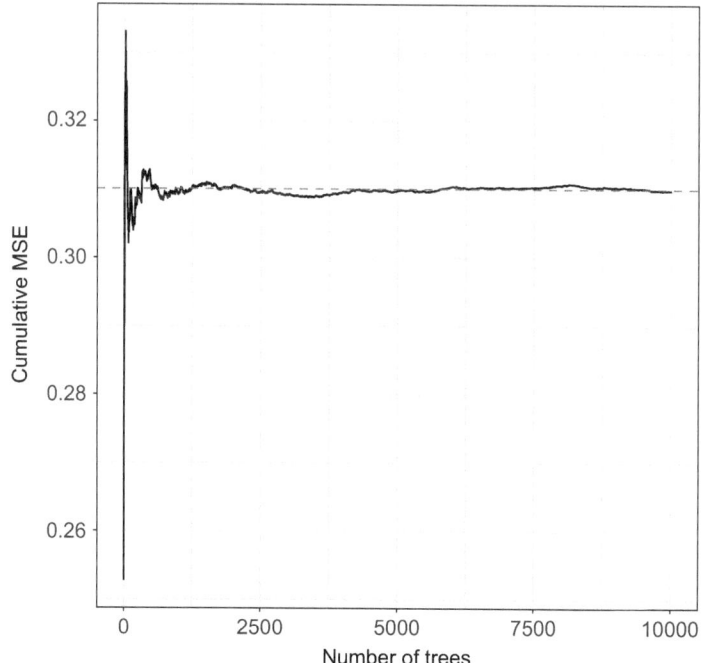

FIGURE 13.3 Convergence plot for final model

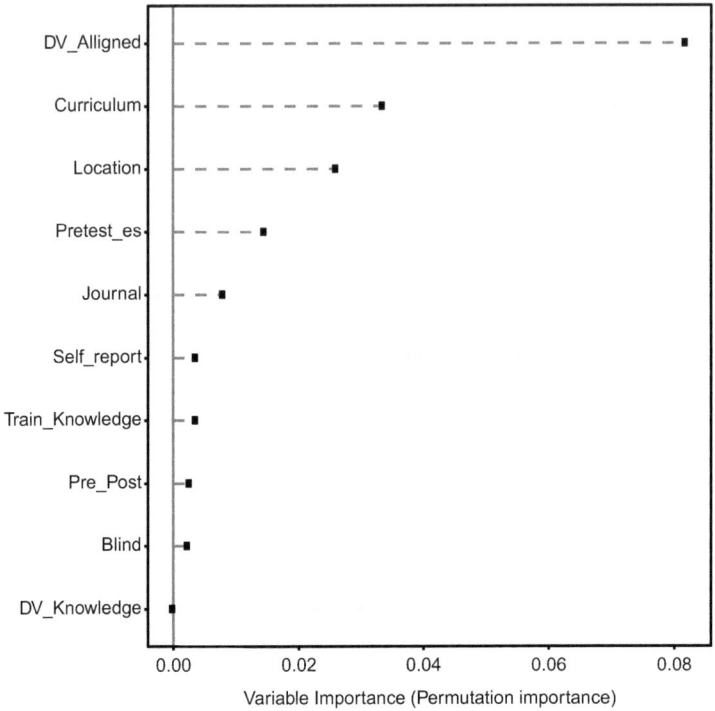

FIGURE 13.4 Variable importance plot

```
# Plot partial dependence
PartialDependence(final, vars = ordered_vars,
                  rawdata = TRUE, pi = .95)
```

We cannot conclude whether any of these findings are "significant" (except perhaps by bootstrapping the entire analysis). However, the PartialDependence() function has two settings that help visualize the "importance" of a finding: rawdata, which plots the weighted raw data (studies with larger weights are plotted with a larger point size), thereby visualizing the variance around the mean prediction, and pi, which plots a (e.g., 95%) percentile interval of the predictions of individual trees in the model. This is not the same as a confidence interval, but it does show how variable or stable the model predictions are.

The analysis has revealed, for example, that effect sizes tend to be stronger when the dependent variable is in line with the content of the intervention, and that single-site training interventions tend to have bigger effect sizes (Figure 13.4). Because these variables are binary, their effects could also be parsimoniously modeled by a linear regression analysis. Indeed, the original paper reported significant effects for these variables. Non-linear effects, on the other hand, are more easily overlooked in a linear meta-regression.

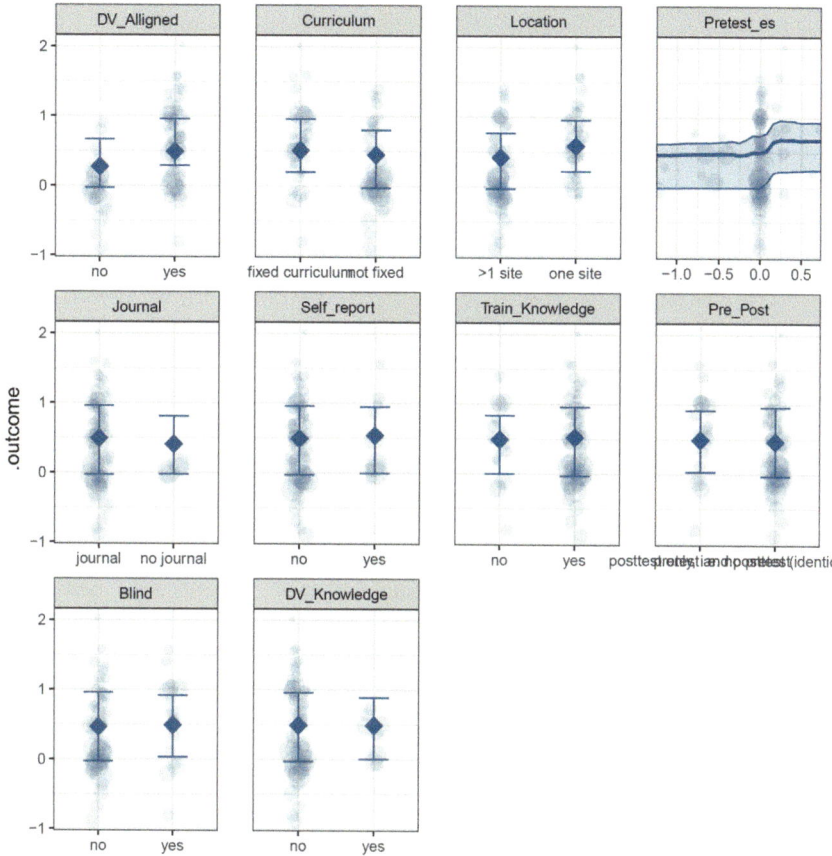

FIGURE 13.5 Marginal relationship of moderators with effect size

This exploratory moderator analysis could be followed with meta-regression, focusing only on the relevant moderators. The binary predictors could be straightforwardly included. For the continuous variables, one might consider a piecewise linear approach: Creating dummy variables at the inflection points identified from the partial dependence plots, and then interacting these dummy variables with the continuous variable itself. However, the exploratory nature of this follow-up analysis should always be emphasized; it is merely a way to look at the same results from the familiar linear regression framework.

What to report

The preceding paragraphs offer a step-by-step instruction on how one might go about conducting a MetaForest analysis on a small sample meta-analytic data set. One could simply apply these steps to a different data set. If readers are concerned with the amount of space required to report and explain this type of analysis in a journal whose readership might be relatively unfamiliar with the machine learning approach, then one might simply report the analysis summary, and cite appropriate publications for MetaForest (Van Lissa, 2017), and random forests in general (e.g., Strobl et al., 2009). Because it is essential that the analysis process is reproducible and transparent, the annotated syntax – and, preferably, the data – can be published as supplementary material on the Open Science Framework (www.osf.io), and referred to in the paper. For example:

> We conducted an exploratory search for relevant moderators using Meta-Forest: a machine-learning-based approach to meta-analysis, using the random forests algorithm (Van Lissa, 2017). Full syntax of this analysis is available on the Open Science Framework, DOI:10.17605/OSF.IO/XXXXX. To weed out irrelevant moderators, we used 100-fold replicated feature selection, and retained only moderators with positive variable importance in > 10% of replications. The main analysis consisted of 10.000 regression trees with fixed-effect weights, four candidate variables per split, and a minimum of three cases per terminal node. The final model had positive estimates of explained variance in new data, $R^2_{oob} = 0.13$, $R^2_{cv} = 0.48$. The relative importance of included moderators is displayed in Figure X. The shape of each moderator's marginal relationship to the effect size, averaging over all values of all other moderators, is illustrated in Figure XX.

Several published studies illustrate ways to apply and report MetaForest analyses. For example, Curry et al. (2018) used MetaForest to examine moderators of the effect of acts of kindness on well-being (full syntax and data available at github.com/cjvanlissa/kindness_meta-analysis). Second, Bonapersona et al. (in press) used MetaForest to identify moderators of the effect of early life adversity on the behavioral phenotype of animal models, with full syntax and data available at osf.io/ra947/. Third, Gao, Yao, and Feldman (2018) used MetaForest to examine moderators of the "mere ownership" effect.

Final thoughts

MetaForest is a helpful solution to detect relevant moderators in meta-analysis, even for small samples. Its main advantages over classic meta-regression are that it is robust to overfitting, captures non-linear effects and interactions, and is robust even when there are many moderators relative to cases. One remaining concern, which cannot be addressed by any statistical solution, is the generalizability of these findings to genuinely new data. When the sample of studies is small, it is unlikely to be representative of the entire "population" of potential studies that could have been conducted. Machine learning techniques, such as MetaForest, aim to optimize a model's performance in "new data" – but the estimates of performance in "new data", based on bootstrap aggregation and cross-validation, are still conditional on the present sample.

What implications might this have? To understand the problem, we might imagine conducting a primary study on the link between father involvement and child well-being, and drawing a sample by selecting one citizen of every country in the European Union. Whether this study will generate any reliable insights that generalize beyond this selective sample depends, in part, on the strength of the effect, and the heterogeneity between our different Europeans. But it also depends on the universality of the phenomenon under study. If father involvement benefits children all around the world, we will be more likely to detect an effect, even in such a heterogeneous sample. If the association is not universal, it might be moderated, and we can measure these moderators and use an inductive approach like MetaForest to identify which ones make a difference.

Another remaining concern is that the cumulative nature of science means that researchers are typically building upon the work of their predecessors. Consequently, we might ask whether it is ever possible for a body of literature to be considered a random sample of the population of all possible studies that "could have been". If the answer is no, then it would be prudent to consider every meta-analysis to be, to some extent, merely a descriptive instrument; a quantitative summary of the published literature.

References

Bonapersona, V., Kentrop, J., Van Lissa, C. J., Van der Veen, R., Joels, M., & Sarabdjitsingh, R. A. (in press). *The behavioral phenotype of early life adversity: A 3-level meta-analysis of rodent studies: Supplemental material.* bioRxiv.

Borenstein, M., Hedges, L. V., Higgins, J. P. T., & Rothstein, H. R. (2009). *Introduction to meta-analysis.* Chichester: John Wiley & Sons.

Breiman, L. (2001). Random forests. *Machine Learning, 45*(1), 5–32.

Crocetti, E. (2016). Systematic reviews with meta-analysis: Why, when, and how? *Emerging Adulthood, 4*(1), 3–18.

Curry, O. S., Rowland, L. A., Van Lissa, C. J., Zlotowitz, S., McAlaney, J., & Whitehouse, H. (2018). Happy to help? A systematic review and meta-analysis of the effects of performing acts of kindness on the well-being of the actor. *Journal of Experimental Social Psychology, 76,* 320–329.

De Jonge, H., & Jak, S. (2018). *A meta-meta-analysis: identifying typical conditions of meta-analyses in educational research.* Retrieved from https://osf.io/zau68/.

Fukkink, R. G., & Lont, A. (2007). Does training matter? A meta-analysis and review of caregiver training studies. *Early Childhood Research Quarterly, 22*(3), 294–311.

Gao, Y., Yao, D., & Feldman, G. (2018). *Owning leads to valuing: meta-analysis of the mere ownership effect.* Unpublished. doi: 10.13140/RG.2.2.13568.33287/1.

Guolo, A., & Varin, C. (2017). Random-effects meta-analysis: The number of studies matters. *Statistical Methods in Medical Research, 26*(3), 1500–1518.

Hastie, T., Tibshirani, R., & Friedman, J. (2009). *The elements of statistical learning: Data mining, inference, and prediction.* Berlin: Springer.

Hedges, L. V., & Vevea, J. L. (1998). Fixed- and random-effects models in meta-analysis. *Psychological Methods, 3*(4), 486–504.

Higgins, J. P. T., & Thompson, S. G. (2002). Quantifying heterogeneity in a meta-analysis. *Statistics in Medicine, 21*(11), 1539–1558.

Higgins, J. P. T., & Thompson, S. G. (2004). Controlling the risk of spurious findings from meta-regression. *Statistics in Medicine, 23*(11), 1663–1682.

Janitza, S., Celik, E., & Boulesteix, A.-L. (2016). A computationally fast variable importance test for random forests for high-dimensional data. *Advances in Data Analysis and Classification, 12*(4), 1–31.

Kuhn, M. (2008). Building predictive models in R using the caret package. *Journal of Statistical Software, Articles, 28*(5), 1–26.

Maxwell, S. E., Lau, M. Y., & Howard, G. S. (2015). Is psychology suffering from a replication crisis? What does "failure to replicate" really mean? *American Psychologist, 70*(6), 487–498.

Strobl, C., Malley, J., & Tutz, G. (2009). An introduction to recursive partitioning: rationale, application, and characteristics of classification and regression trees, bagging, and random forests. *Psychological Methods, 14*(4), 323–348.

Van Den Noortgate, W., López-López, J. A., Marín-Martínez, F., & Sánchez-Meca, J. (2015). Meta-analysis of multiple outcomes: A multilevel approach. *Behavior Research Methods, 47*(4), 1274–1294.

Van Erp, S., Verhagen, J., Grasman, R. P. P. P., & Wagenmakers, E.-J. (2017). Estimates of between-study heterogeneity for 705 meta-analyses reported in psychological bulletin from 1990–2013. *Journal of Open Psychology Data, 5,* 1.

Van Lissa, C. J. (2017). MetaForest: Exploring heterogeneity in meta-analysis using random forests. Open Science Framework. doi:10.17605/OSF.IO/KHJGB.

Van Lissa, C. J. (2018). *Metaforest: exploring heterogeneity in meta-analysis using random forests (version 0.1.2) [R-package].* Retrieved from https://CRAN.R-project.org/package=metaforest.

Wright, M. N., & Ziegler, A. (2015). Ranger: A fast implementation of random forests for high-dimensional data in C++ and R. *arXiv:1508.04409 [stat].*

14

ITEM PARCELS AS INDICATORS

Why, when, and how to use them in small sample research

Charlie Rioux

DEPARTMENT OF EDUCATIONAL PSYCHOLOGY AND LEADERSHIP, TEXAS TECH UNIVERSITY, LUBBOCK, USA

Zachary L. Stickley

DEPARTMENT OF EDUCATIONAL PSYCHOLOGY AND LEADERSHIP, TEXAS TECH UNIVERSITY, LUBBOCK, USA

Omolola A. Odejimi

DEPARTMENT OF EDUCATIONAL PSYCHOLOGY AND LEADERSHIP, TEXAS TECH UNIVERSITY, LUBBOCK, USA

Todd D. Little

DEPARTMENT OF EDUCATIONAL PSYCHOLOGY AND LEADERSHIP, TEXAS TECH UNIVERSITY, LUBBOCK, USA
& OPTENTIA RESEARCH PROGRAM, FACULTY OF HUMANITIES, NORTH-WEST UNIVERSITY, VANDERBIJLPARK, SOUTH AFRICA

Introduction

Researchers frequently use questionnaires with several items measuring the same underlying construct. Because structural equation modeling (SEM) is increasingly used in the behavioral sciences, modeling such scales as latent constructs is both common and advantageous. Advantages include correcting for measurement error, making minimal psychometric assumptions, establishing factorial invariance across time and groups, evaluating model fit, and broad flexibility for confirmatory modeling. When examining the associations among several latent constructs, however, model complexity increases, which can be problematic in small samples. One solution is parceling. Parceling involves making aggregates of two or more item-level indicators by averaging the items, and then using these aggregate-level indicators to represent the latent constructs (Little, Cunningham, Shahar, & Widaman, 2002; Matsunaga, 2008). In this chapter, we provide an overview of (a) the key advantages of parcels, (b) specific advantages for small samples, and (c) methods for building parcels.

Benefits of parceling

Parceling is helpful in addressing several issues stemming from the sources of variance that are commonly found in item-level data, some of which are particularly important when working with small sample sizes. Independent of the desired true source of variance, undesirable item-level variance can come from a number of sources when some but not all items are impacted by effects such as method contamination, acquiescence response bias, social desirability, priming, and item-wording characteristics such as negatively valenced items, subordinate clauses, common parts of speech, and the like (Little, Cunningham, Shahar, & Widaman, 2002). Other problems from item-level data, when compared to aggregate-level data, include lower reliability, lower communality, smaller ratio of common-to-unique factor variance, and greater likelihood of distributional violations, which are particularly problematic with small samples.

Items constructed from scales also have fewer, larger, and less equal intervals between scale points when compared to parcels. A seven-point Likert scale, for example, will have responses at each integer along that scale, while a composite parcel will include values that fall between the points on the continuum, creating a more continuous scale of measurement. Table 14.1 provides a summary of the benefits of parceling (for thorough reviews of the benefits of parceling, see Little, Cunningham, Shahar, & Widaman, 2002; Little, Rhemtulla, Gibson, & Schoemann, 2013; Matsunaga, 2008).

One key benefit of parceling is that it can diminish the impact of sources of variance that emanate from both sampling error and parsimony error. Figure 14.1 shows an item-level solution for two constructs where six items for each construct are available. In the Figure, we have indicated one potential dual loading ($\lambda_{7,1}$) and two correlated residuals ($\theta_{8,6}$ and $\theta_{12,10}$) that arise because of sampling variability around a true value that is essentially zero. These relationships are represented using dashed lines because they are indicated in the data but are errors in that they arise only from sampling variability and are specific to this hypothetical sample. We have also indicated a couple of correlated residuals that are not trivial in the population and should be estimated as part of the true

TABLE 14.1 Some of the key benefits of parceling

Psychometric benefits	*Model estimation and fit benefits*
Parcels (vs. items) have:	Models with parcels (vs. items) have:
Higher reliability	Lower likelihood of correlated residuals
Greater scale communality	Lower likelihood of dual factor loadings
Higher common-to-unique factor variance ratio	Reduced sources of sampling error
Lower likelihood of distributional violations	Reduced sources of parsimony error
More, tighter, and more-equal intervals	

Note. Based on Little, Cunningham, Shahar, and Widaman (2002).

item-level solution for these items ($\theta_{3,1}$, $\theta_{5,2}$ and $\theta_{11,8}$). When correlated residuals and dual factor loadings emerge in a model because of sampling variability, parceling minimizes their impact by reducing the magnitude of the variances leading to these effects. Even when effects are true in the population, parceling can provide a simplified rendering of the information with no loss of generality regarding the means, variances, and covariances among the constructs that are included in a model. An appropriate model at the item level, such as the model in Figure 14.1, would necessitate that the true correlated residuals be estimated. These effects are true in the population and, as such, have a clear theoretically justified reason for these parameter estimates. Normally, such effects would be anticipated a priori and would be expected to emerge across any sample, big or small, when this particular item set is administered. As such, if not specified, the item-level model is mis-specified and all parameters that are associated with each mis-specified model would be biased.

Returning to the dashed-line parameters, which are only resulting from sampling variability, they should be ignored and left unestimated because they are not true in the population. On the other hand, if left unestimated, the model fit would be relatively poorer and the model parameters could also be biased because the magnitudes of these unestimated parameters are sufficiently larger than zero; they cannot be ignored and treated as if they were zero. Here, the unestimated yet untrue parameter reflects a "lose-lose" situation. No theoretical reason other than chance can be offered to explain the observed relationship and, if estimated, the parameter would not be expected to replicate in a new sample.

Parceling explicitly addresses problems of correlated residuals and unexpected dual factor loadings. For example, when items with a correlated residual are aggregated, the effect of the correlation is removed though isolation in the residual term of the new aggregate. Specifically, if Items A1 and A3 are averaged then the shared true parameter ($\theta_{3,1}$) becomes isolated in the residual variance of

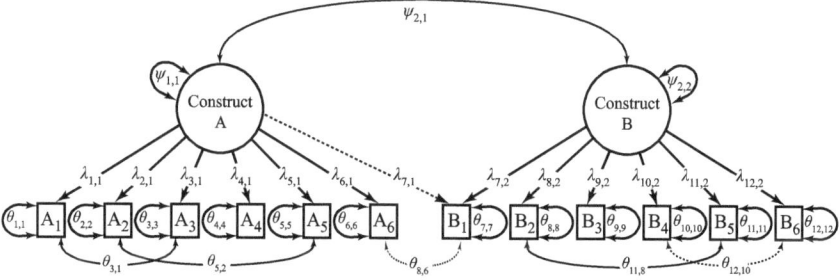

FIGURE 14.1 Item-level solution for two constructs with six items each: Sampling Error and Parsimony Error illustrated. λ = Estimated loading of an indicator on a construct. ψ = Variance of a construct or covariance between two constructs. θ = Residual variance of an indicator or residual covariance between two indicators

the parceled indicator when the parcel-level model is estimated. Similarly, if Items B2 and B5 are averaged into a parcel then the shared true parameter $\theta_{11,8}$ becomes isolated in the residual variance of the parceled indicator. And the same is true if Items A2 and A5 are averaged – the shared true parameter ($\theta_{5,2}$) becomes isolated within the residual term of the parcel. For the dual factor loading, $\lambda_{7,1}$, and the correlated residual labeled $\theta_{8,6}$, parceling has the advantage of significantly reducing the sources of variance that are causing these unintended effects. A6 would be averaged with A4 in this hypothetical example and B1 would be averaged with B3. The shared residual that was associated with A6 and B1 would become one-quarter of its original magnitude. The reduction in the size of the residual correlation would likely render the effect trivially small again, which could then be ignored without introducing any bias.

Even when correlated residuals and cross-loadings are seen in the population, if the phenomenon is unimportant to the model and the parameter estimates are of theoretical interest, the reduction of these effects through parceling can be advantageous – that is, parsimony error is minimized. Reducing the unwanted sources of variance via parceling can reduce bias in the estimated model that occurs when correlated residuals and cross-loadings are omitted. In fact, although the item-level model in the population may have correlated residuals and/or cross-loadings, the parcel model in the population is less likely to have these effects, or at least their magnitude may be reduced to the point of being noninfluential (Little, Rhemtulla, Gibson, & Schoemann, 2013).

To understand the above discussion better, we turn to the traditional factor analytic model of item structure. Specifically, item-level indicators can be represented by three sources of variance. The first is the variance shared between the items that comes from the common factor (i.e., the construct) that the item measures. This "true score" (T) is the variance you are trying to model and is the target component of the item's variance. There is also "specific" variance (s) that is not associated with the true score but is itself a stable and reliable source of variance that comes from the systematic nature of the item itself. This source of variance is, by definition, independent of the true score. The third and final source of variance is the random error (ε) that is unassociated with either the true score or the specific variance.

These latter two elements, s and ε, are also, by definition, uncorrelated with each other and have means of zero. The sum of these two elements is referred to as the item's *uniqueness*. Across all items in a pool of items, the s and ε of each item is assumed to be uncorrelated with all other s and ε elements. Because ε represents the truly random error aspect of measurement, it must, by necessity, be uncorrelated with all other ε's and s's. The s component of a given item, on the other hand, is unlikely to be truly uncorrelated with all other s's. In fact, the common saying that s is assumed to be uncorrelated with all other s's is not quite an accurate statement. The real assumption is that the s's are trivially correlated with other s's such that they can be treated as if they were zero correlated with the other s's. The whole idea behind item parcels is to reduce the size of the s's and thereby reduce the size of any correlation that an s may have with any other s in a given analysis model.

When parcels are computed, the variance that is shared among the items is preserved while the variance that is not shared among the items is reduced. Because items included in parcels tap into the same construct, the T portion is common/shared across items. Because s and ε are either uncorrelated or trivially correlated across items, they are reduced when aggregating items into parcels. The proportion of the "true" score relative to the uniqueness will be higher in the parcel than in the individual items. Thus, for a two-item parcel as illustrated in Figure 14.2, the parcel is expected to include the variance of the true score plus one-quarter of each of the four sources of variance not associated with the common factor: (1) the specific variance of item 1, (2) the specific variance of item 2, (3) the random error of item 1, (4) the random error of item 2 (i.e., the variance of the parcel is now equal to the shared variance of $T + \frac{1}{4}$ of the variance of s_1, s_2, ε_1, ε_2). For complete covariance algebra demonstrating this reduction in specific variance and random error, see Little, Rhemtulla, Gibson, and Schoemann (2013). Figure 14.2 shows that by reducing the effect of specific variance (s_1 and s_2) and random error (ε_1 and ε_2) associated with item-level measurement, parceling allows for a more accurate model of the true construct variance.

Benefits of parceling for small sample size

Small sample size is a concern for researchers in the behavioral sciences, where low-powered studies remain common. Regarding factor structures, subject-to-

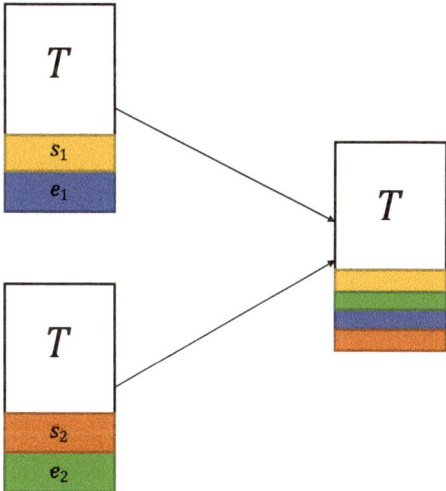

FIGURE 14.2 Variance of parcel composed of two averaged indicators. T = true score; s = specific variance; ε = random error

item ratio rules of thumb persist, the most common being 5:1 or 10:1. However, Barrett and Kline (1981) showed that subject-to-item ratios have no effect on factor stability. Two personality surveys, one with sub-scaled indicators and the other without, were given to respondents in various sized groups. Factor stability held in groups with ratios as low as 3:1 and 1.25:1. While Barrett and Kline (1981) recommend a minimum of 50 observations to exhibit a distinguishable factor pattern, they also emphasize that when using "strong" variables with known factor structures, underlying patterns will be present regardless of sample size. Lastly, they state that when compared to the statistical errors of bad sampling of target populations, the errors due solely to small sample size are minimal. A simulation study by Velicer and Fava (1998) also showed that for any given sample size, strong factor loadings and a minimum of three indicators per factor will have a positive effect on model fit and parameter estimation. Additionally, they concluded that careful variable sampling and strong factor loadings can compensate for low sample size and rules should not exist for sample size as a function of manifest indicators.

Parceling can help meet these recommendations for small sample sizes since factor loadings for the parcels are stronger than for the items. In fact, one common reason for creating parcels is because sample size is small (Williams & O'Boyle, 2008). Although it has been shown that with a small sample size, latent variable models can have lower power than scale-score path models when estimating structural paths, one suggestion to increase power has been to parcel similarly constructed items and constraining the parcel loadings to be equal (if the parcels have similar measurement properties; Ledgerwood & Shrout, 2011). Parcels have also been recommended for small sample sizes because fewer parameters are needed in the model estimation (Bagozzi & Edwards, 1998) and convergence issues are less likely to occur. Likewise, a simulation study by Orçan and Yanyun (2016) showed several advantages of parceling in SEM with a small sample sizes. First, by reducing model complexity, the likelihood of estimation difficulties decreased. Second, parcel-level analysis produced more reasonable Type I error rates for the chi-square test, with rejection rates being too high when analyses were done at the item level. Third, maximum likelihood with robust standard errors (MLR) estimation methods at the item level showed much higher Type I error rates than MLR estimation at the parcel level. Lastly, Orçan and Yanyun (2016) note that since the item-level and parcel-level analyses produce similar structural estimates but the item-level model had increased chances of misfit, common attempts to improve model fit by adding parameters in item-level analyses may lead to overparameterized and, therefore, mis-specified models, particularly in small samples. Thus, parceling may be particularly advantageous in small samples.

Arguments against parceling

Although, as seen above, parceling has numerous advantages, there are also arguments against parceling that have persisted in the literature. It is beyond the scope of this chapter to review all these arguments. Although thorough reviews of the arguments both pro and con with parceling can be found in Little, Cunningham, Shahar, and Widaman (2002) and Matsunaga (2008), we discuss the two main arguments against parceling here. The first is that when constructs are multidimensional, parcels can negatively affect the measurement model by providing biased loading estimates and can make the structural relations in the model more difficult to interpret (e.g., Bandalos, 2002). This argument holds when parcels are randomly or improperly created. On the other hand, when parcels are properly constructed, they can clarify rather than obscure the structure of multidimensional constructs (Graham & Tatterson, 2000). The second main argument against parceling is that it may mask model misspecification. From this point of view, since cross-loadings and residual correlations are more difficult to detect when modeling with parcels, estimates and other model parameters may be biased. Furthermore, since model fit is usually improved with parceling, researchers may falsely believe that misspecification is not present (e.g., Bandalos, 2002; Marsh, Ludtke, Nagengast, Morin, & Von Davier, 2013). Thoughtful parcel creation and careful examination of local misfit of a parcel-level solution easily mitigate this potential problem.

As mentioned above, parceling will also reduce Type II error where researchers would conclude that cross-loadings and residual correlations exist in the population when they do not. A recent simulation study (Rhemtulla, 2016) showed that parceling produces similar or reduced-bias estimates more often than the item-level models. Furthermore, although parcel models had lower power than item models to detect within-factor misspecifications and single cross-loadings, they had higher power to detect multiple cross-loadings and structural model misspecifications (Rhemtulla, 2016). In order to avoid misspecification, it has been recommended to model data at the item level to identify potential sources of misspecification and to inform the choice of a parceling scheme (Bandalos & Finney, 2001; Little, Rhemtulla, Gibson, & Schoemann, 2013; Rhemtulla, 2016). Furthermore, the root mean square error of approximation (RMSEA) and the standardized root mean square residual (SRMR) fit indices can be useful in identifying misspecification as they were found to increase in parcel models compared to item models when there was misspecification (Rhemtulla, 2016).

Building parcels

When parcels are constructed thoughtfully, they are efficient, reliable, and valid indicators of latent constructs (Little, Cunningham, Shahar, & Widaman, 2002; Little, Rhemtulla, Gibson, & Schoemann, 2013). There are several ways in which you could construct a parcel, but first it is essential to gain a thorough understanding of the items and the data. The level of thoughtfulness stems from knowing the items themselves and the ways in which they are constructed, as well as understanding the behavior of the items in a given sample. This knowledge is often accomplished by running an item-level analysis to examine the item-level content, reviewing the matrix of correlations among the items, and running item-level reliability analysis (Little, Rhemtulla, Gibson, & Schoemann, 2013). Once you have a thorough understanding of your items and how they behave, you can decide on the method you will use to construct your parcels.

The first method of parceling items is random assignment, in which one assigns items to a parcel group randomly without replacement, leading to parcels that contain roughly equal "true score" variance (T). This method is predicated on the strong assumption that all items are interchangeable in the population and sampling variability is low. As such, it is best to only use this method when one has a large set of items with high communality (i.e., high loadings in an item-level measurement model) from which to create parcels (Little, Rhemtulla, Gibson, & Schoemann, 2013). Ideally, items should come from a common pool, such as items that share a common scale on a questionnaire. If items come from different scales using different metrics of measurement, the items can be rescaled to be on a common metric prior to creating a parcel (Little, Rhemtulla, Gibson, & Schoemann, 2013). One proposed procedure of using the random assignment parceling method is to take the average model results of hundreds or thousands of item-to-parcel allocations, which has the added benefit of providing an estimate for the amount of parcel-allocation variability within your set of items (Sterba & MacCallum, 2010).

Another method of parceling involves examining the item characteristics of your measure either from existing validation studies or from your own data. This examination is particularly important for items that demonstrate correlated residual variances or are known to cross-load onto two constructs. Items that share these characteristics should be placed in the same parcel, and in the case of cross-loading items, the parcel may need to still allow a cross-loading within the model (Little, Rhemtulla, Gibson, & Schoemann, 2013). If existing empirical information about your items is limited, your own preliminary analysis should inform these decisions.

The third way one could construct parcels is by using the SEM model to inform your parceling. This process begins by specifying a single-construct model that includes all items associated with the construct. Then, the three highest-loading items are used as the anchors with which to create parcels, first by combining the highest-loading item with the lowest-loading item, then the next highest with the next lowest, then the third highest with the third lowest. If more items remain unparceled, the procedure would continue by placing lower-loading items with higher-loading parcels until a balance is achieved (Landis, Beal, & Tesluk, 2000; Little, Cunningham, Shahar, & Widaman, 2002). Note that the number of items in a given parcel does not have to be equal across all parcels for a given construct. In fact, you may find that one item is particularly good and you do not want to parcel it with another item. The other remaining items can be used to create parcels while leaving the one item alone as an indicator of the construct. We strongly recommend averaging in these scenarios so the parcels and the lone item stay on the same scale of measurement (sums of items will change the means and variances to be on different metrics).

For multidimensional items, two methods have been proposed in order to combine items that share specific reliable variance. A first option would be to assign items that correlate the most strongly with each other to the same parcel (Landis, Beal, & Tesluk, 2000; Rogers & Schmitt, 2004). The second option would be to assign items that share secondary facet-relevant content to the same parcel (Hall, Snell, & Foust, 1999; Little, Cunningham, Shahar, & Widaman, 2002).

These above methods are recommended when dealing with already existing data, or data generated from existing item inventories. An alternative method for parcel construction is to design questionnaires that contain an a priori parceling scheme (Little, Cunningham, Shahar, & Widaman, 2002). For example, the Control, Agency, and Means-Ends Interview (Little, Oettingen, & Baltes, 1995) includes parceling instructions. The questionnaire includes six questions, three of which are worded in a positive direction (e.g., "I can try hard"), and three of which are worded in a negative direction (e.g., "I am just not very smart") and then reverse-coded. Instructions are to construct parcels based on one positive item and one negative item, so that the bias associated with question valence can be reduced.

Parceling with missing data

When computing parcels, there may be items with missing data within parcels. Indeed, item-level missing data is common, notably because participants may skip or refuse to answer some items. Item-level missing data may also be intentionally introduced by a researcher through a planned missing-data design (Little & Rhemtulla, 2013; Rhemtulla & Hancock, 2016). Although little research has examined how different missing-data handling procedures influence results with parcels, research on item-level missing data when computing scales can be informative.

When using multiple imputation, one could either impute before or after parceling items. When computing scales, no differences in bias have been found when comparing imputation before and after computing the scales, but imputing items before computing scales had an important power advantage. Indeed, scale-level imputation required a 75% increase in sample size to achieve the same power as item-level imputation (Gottschall, West, & Enders, 2012). If effects were similar with parcels, this power difference means that imputing items before parceling would increase power, which may be particularly important in small samples. However, the ability to impute items simultaneously would depend on the number of variables since the number of cases must exceed the number of variables. Furthermore, the power advantage when imputing items for parcels may be lower than when imputing items for scales. Indeed, item-level imputation is notably advantageous because within-scale correlations are stronger than between-scale correlations, and between-parcel correlations may be closer to within-scale correlations.

A study also examined full information maximum likelihood (FIML) approaches to item-level missing data, where scales are computed without imputing items first (Mazza, Enders, & Ruehlman, 2015). Results showed that simply entering scales with missingness without further information for missing-data handling provided highly biased parameters. Bias was eliminated, and power was equivalent to item-level imputation, *if the individual items were included as auxiliary variables*. A remaining issue is that too many auxiliary variables can lead to convergence issues. One solution that provided the same power and results was to use an average of complete items with the individual incomplete items as auxiliary variables (Mazza, Enders, & Ruehlman, 2015). Thus, although FIML approaches to item-level missingness when using parcels still need to be examined, research on scales suggests that individual items with missingness should be included as auxiliary variables. Note that when using this method, any item missing on the parcel would result in a missing score on the parcel – the technique of proration, where available items are averaged although some are missing, should be avoided (Lee, Bartholow, McCarthy, Pedersen, & Sher, 2014; Mazza, Enders, & Ruehlman, 2015).

Conclusion

Parceling has many benefits, particularly for small sample sizes since they can increase power and reduce estimation difficulties. However, parcels will only be beneficial with thoughtful construction of the parcels based on thorough understanding of the items and data. Furthermore, parcels are not beneficial for all research questions since it is not ideal to fully represent the dimensionality of measurement (Little, Cunningham, Shahar, & Widaman, 2002). Therefore, parceling should be strongly considered by researchers when using latent-variable-based SEM with a small sample size, but always taking into account the goals of their study.

Acknowledgement

Zachary L. Stickley and Omolola A. Odejimi contributed equally to the chapter. Parts of this chapter were supported by the Canadian Institutes of Health Research and the Fonds de recherche du Québec - Santé through fellowships to Charlie Rioux. Todd D. Little is director of the Institute for Measurement, Methodology, Analysis and Policy at Texas Tech University and is the owner of Yhat Enterprises, which runs his international Stats Camps (see Statscamp.org). He is also affiliated with East China Normal University, China and North-West University, South Africa.

References

Bagozzi, R. P., & Edwards, J. R. (1998). A general approach for representing constructs in organizational research. *Organizational Research Methods*, *1*(1), 45–87. doi:10.1177/109442819800100104.

Bandalos, D. L. (2002). The effects of item parceling on goodness-of-fit and parameter estimate bias in structural equation modeling. *Structural Equation Modeling: A Multidisciplinary Journal*, *9*(1), 78–102. doi:10.1207/s15328007sem0901_5.

Bandalos, D. L., & Finney, S. J. (2001). Item parceling issues in structural equation modeling. In G. A. Marcoulides & R. E. Schumacker (Eds.), *New developments and techniques in structural equation modeling* (pp. 269–296). Mahwah, NJ: Lawrence Erlbaum.

Barrett, P. T., & Kline, P. (1981). The observation to variable ratio in factor analysis. *Personality Study and Group Behavior*, *1*(1), 23–33.

Gottschall, A. C., West, S. G., & Enders, C. K. (2012). A comparison of item-level and scale-level multiple imputation for questionnaire batteries. *Multivariate Behavioral Research*, *47*(1), 1–25. doi:10.1080/00273171.2012.640589.

Graham, J. W., & Tatterson, J. W. (2000). *Creating parcels for multi-dimensional constructs in structural equation modeling*. Retrieved from the Methodology Center, Pennsylvania State University, methodology.psu.edu/node/2241.

Hall, R. J., Snell, A. F., & Foust, M. S. (1999). Item parceling strategies in SEM: Investigating the subtle effects of unmodeled secondary constructs. *Organizational Research Methods*, *2*(3), 233–256. doi:10.1177/109442819923002.

Landis, R. S., Beal, D. J., & Tesluk, P. E. (2000). A comparison of approaches to forming composite measures in structural equation models. *Organizational Research Methods*, *3*(2), 186–207. doi:10.1177/109442810032003.

Ledgerwood, A., & Shrout, P. E. (2011). The trade-off between accuracy and precision in latent variable models of mediation processes. *Journal of Personality and Social Psychology*, *101*(6), 1174–1188. doi:10.1037/a0024776.

Lee, M. R., Bartholow, B. D., McCarthy, D. M., Pedersen, S. L., & Sher, K. J. (2015). Two alternative approaches to conventional person-mean imputation scoring of the Self-Rating of the Effects of Alcohol Scale (SRE). *Psychology of Addictive Behaviors*, *29*(1), 231–236. doi:10.1037/adb0000015.

Little, T. D., Cunningham, W. A., Shahar, G., & Widaman, K. F. (2002). To parcel or not to parcel: Exploring the question, weighing the merits. *Structural Equation Modeling: A Multidisciplinary Journal*, *9*(2), 151–173. doi:10.1207/s15328007sem0902_1.

Little, T. D., Oettingen, G., & Baltes, P. B. (1995). *The revised Control, Agency, and Means-Ends Interview (CAMI): A multi-cultural validity assessment using mean and covariance structures (MACS) analyses*. Berlin: Max Planck Institute.

Little, T. D., & Rhemtulla, M. (2013). Planned missing data designs for developmental researchers. *Child Development Perspectives*, *7*(4), 199–204. doi:10.1111/cdep.12043.

Little, T. D., Rhemtulla, M., Gibson, K., & Schoemann, A. M. (2013). Why the items versus parcels controversy needn't be one. *Psychological Methods*, *18*(3), 285–300. doi:10.1037/a0033266.

Marsh, H. W., Ludtke, O., Nagengast, B., Morin, A. J. S., & Von Davier, M. (2013). Why item parcels are (almost) never appropriate: Two wrongs do not make a right – Camouflaging misspecification with item parcels in CFA models. *Psychological Methods*, *18*(3), 257–284. doi:10.1037/a0032773.

Matsunaga, M. (2008). Item parceling in structural equation modeling: A primer. *Communication Methods and Measures*, *2*(4), 260–293. doi:10.1080/19312450802458935.

Mazza, G. L., Enders, C. K., & Ruehlman, L. S. (2015). Addressing item-level missing data: A comparison of proration and full information maximum likelihood estimation. *Multivariate Behavioral Research*, *50*(5), 504–519. doi:10.1080/00273171.2015.1068157.

Orçan, F., & Yanyun, Y. (2016). A note on the use of item parceling in structural equation modeling with missing data. *Journal of Measurement and Evaluation in Education and Psychology*, *7*(1), 59–72. doi:10.21031/epod.88204.

Rhemtulla, M. (2016). Population performance of SEM parceling strategies under measurement and structural model misspecification. *Psychological Methods*, *21*(3), 348–368. doi:10.1037/met0000072.

Rhemtulla, M., & Hancock, G. R. (2016). Planned missing data designs in educational psychology research. *Educational Psychologist*, *51*(3-4), 305–316. doi:10.1080/00461520.2016.1208094.

Rogers, W. M., & Schmitt, N. (2004). Parameter recovery and model fit using multidimensional composites: A comparison of four empirical parceling algorithms. *Multivariate Behavioral Research*, *39*(3), 379–412. doi:10.1207/s15327906mbr3903_1.

Sterba, S. K., & MacCallum, R. C. (2010). Variability in parameter estimates and model fit across repeated allocations of items to parcels. *Multivariate Behavioral Research*, *45*(2), 322–358. doi:10.1080/00273171003680302.

Velicer, W. F., & Fava, J. L. (1998). Effects of variable and subject sampling on factor pattern recovery. *Psychological Methods*, *3*(2), 231–251. doi:10.1037//1082-989x.3.2.231.

Williams, L. J., & O'Boyle, E. H. (2008). Measurement models for linking latent variables and indicators: A review of human resource management research using parcels. *Human Resource Management Review*, *18*(4), 233–242. doi:10.1016/j.hrmr.2008.07.002.

15

SMALL SAMPLES IN MULTILEVEL MODELING

Joop Hox
DEPARTMENT OF METHODOLOGY AND STATISTICSUTRECHT UNIVERSITY, UTRECHT, THE NETHERLANDS

Daniel McNeish
DEPARTMENT OF PSYCHOLOGY, ARIZONA STATE UNIVERSITY, ARIZONA, UNITED STATES OF AMERICA

Introduction

When thinking about sample size in multilevel modeling, it is important to realize that there are potential sample size issues at several distinct levels. The concern is usually about the highest-level sample size, because sampling at the higher level often means sampling organizations or groups, which may be limited by the costs or by having a small population at that level. For example, if the higher-level population is provinces in the Netherlands, there are only 12 provinces and no amount of research effort is going to increase that number. Even if there is a large population within the small number of clusters at the highest level, as in business surveys, obtaining cooperation at the organizational level can be difficult and therefore costly (Snijkers, Haraldsen, Jones, & Willimack, 2013). Small group sizes at the lowest level are problematic with moderate or small higher-level samples sizes, although such issues can dissipate if the sample at the higher level is large enough (McNeish, 2014). For example, data from couples have at most two units in each group, which is a small sample size. If not all members of the couples participate, the average cluster size could be as low as 1.7, which is very small. The same goes for multilevel analysis of repeated measures or panel studies, where the lowest level may be two or three measurement occasions, and some individuals not participating in all waves of data collection. All these are small samples too.

Different estimation methods are available for the parameters of multilevel regression and structural equation models. Maximum Likelihood (ML) estimation is the estimation method of choice for most multilevel models and data. For non-normal data, Weighted Least Squares (WLS) is often used instead of ML. Both ML and WLS are large-sample estimation methods, with sample size requirements that are not absolute but dependent on the size and complexity of the model. Bayesian estimation methods are gaining in popularity, as Bayesian estimation is not a large-sample method. This does not mean that all is well at all sample sizes, but in general Bayesian estimation is expected to be more precise at small sample sizes. The performance of different estimation methods is discussed in the sections on multilevel regression and multilevel structural equation modeling (MSEM).

The current chapter discusses problems that may arise in the presence of small samples and potential remedies for small sample issues. The discussion of small sample sizes in multilevel regression assumes that the reader has some familiarity with multilevel regression, as explained for example in the introductory chapter of Hox, Moerbeek, and Van de Schoot (2018) available online (multilevel-analysis.sites.uu.nl/). This chapter discusses sample size issues and potential solutions in multilevel regression and multilevel structural equation models, with both ML/WLS and Bayesian estimation.

Multilevel regression models

The most straightforward multilevel model is multilevel regression, with a single outcome variable at the lowest level, and predictor variables at all available levels (Hox et al., 2018; Snijders & Bosker, 2012). In this model, two kinds of parameters are estimated: regression coefficients and variances. If we have individuals nested in groups, the regression coefficients for the individual predictor variables are assumed to vary across the groups, so they have variance components at the group level. In ordinary multiple regression, the residual variance is seldom interpreted. Conversely, in multilevel regression, the distribution of the variance of the outcome variable across the different levels is important, and the values of the variances of the regression coefficients is also important. As a consequence, the accuracy of the estimates of both the regression coefficients (commonly called the fixed part of the regression equation) and the variances (commonly called the random part of the regression equation) is important.

An often-suggested rule of thumb is the 30/30 rule (30 lower-level units in 30 clusters), discussed by Bickel (2007, p. 207). There is quite a number of simulation studies investigating the accuracy of parameter estimates and their associated standard errors under a variety of conditions. The seminal study in this area was performed by Maas and Hox (2005), who found that 10 clusters was insufficient with traditional multilevel regression, but that 30 was sufficient. Ferron, Bell, Hess, Rendina-Gobioff, and Hibbard (2009), Baldwin and Fellingham (2013), Stegmueller (2013), and Bell, Morgan, Schoeneberger, Kromrey, and Ferron (2014) extend Maas and Hox (2005) to include different sample size conditions and investigations of corrective procedures, including Bayesian methods (see McNeish & Stapleton, 2016a, for a review of small sample studies in multilevel regression). McNeish and Stapleton (2016b) then conducted a "Battle Royale" simulation to compare the performance of 12 different small sample methods for higher-level samples of under 15 to determine where particular methods break down.

Generally however, there is no applicable rule like 30/30 or any other set of alternative numbers, because minimum sample size requirement fluctuates based on model complexity, the number of random effects, and the intraclass correlation, among other factors. Nonetheless, there are indications when estimates of standard errors become biased, and some suggestions for remedies.

The capability to obtain accurate estimates and standard errors with few clusters is the result of two improvements in estimation and testing. The first improvement is to use Restricted Maximum Likelihood (REML) estimation instead of Full ML (FML). FML estimates the variance components in the model while assuming that the fixed effects (the regression coefficients) are known. With large sample sizes, this works fine. However, with smaller sample sizes the regression coefficients are estimated with a considerable amount of uncertainty. As a result, the variances are also estimated poorly and are generally much too small. The standard errors are also estimated poorly, and generally too small, so the type I error rate for the fixed effects is inflated. REML separates the estimation of the fixed effects and the variance components by removing the fixed effects when the variance components are estimated. As a result, the variance components are estimated more accurately. Subsequently, the fixed effects are estimated conditional on these variance components. With large samples, REML and FML are equivalent. With smaller samples, REML generally leads to much better estimates.

The sampling variance of the fixed estimates (regression coefficients) is generally taken from the Fisher information matrix. In large samples, this is a good indicator of the variability of the estimates. In small samples, it is only a poor approximation of the variability. Consequently, with small samples, calculating the standard normal Z-statistic by dividing an estimate by its standard error does not work well. The problem is not only that this ignores the degrees of freedom, but also with small samples the standard errors are estimated with a negative bias. Several corrections have been proposed for these twin problems. The most promising correction is the Kenward–Roger correction, which consists of two steps; see Chapter 16 (Rosseel) for more details. First, it estimates the small sample bias in the standard errors and adjusts the standard errors for that bias. Second, it estimates the effective degrees of freedom. The degrees of freedom are estimated on the basis of the parameter estimates for the model under consideration, and it is common to obtain fractional values for the degrees of freedom. A similar but less compelling correction is the Satterthwaite correction, which estimates the degrees of freedom, but does not correct the standard errors.

In most multilevel regression software, the variances are tested with a Z-statistic. Even in large samples, this is a poor procedure, because it assumes that the underlying statistic has a normal sampling distribution. The null distribution for variances is skewed because negative variances are not permissible; the skew is magnified with smaller samples. If the software bounds the variance estimates to be non-negative, a 50:50 mixture chi-square distribution is required to obtain proper *p*-values (Savalei & Kolenikov, 2008; Stram & Lee, 1994). Otherwise, the null test value (i.e., whether the variance is equal to 0) is on the boundary of the parameter space (the null test value is the lowest possible number allowed), which can inflate *p*-values.

Table 15.1 gives some rough guidelines for minimal number of clusters in multilevel regression for estimates to be stable and trustworthy. Note that these values should not be used as universal recommendations to determine sample sizes for having power to detect effects, because sufficient sample sizes are heavily influenced by multiple factors. The values in Table 15.1 are based on models used in small sample multilevel regression simulations (see McNeish & Stapleton, 2016a, for an overview), which should serve as a coarse approximation for models with about five or fewer fixed effects, continuous outcomes, no missing data, and one or two variance components. Longitudinal designs need larger sample sizes because they typically have a more complicated covariance structure. Fortunately, in longitudinal designs we have measurement occasions nested within individuals, and the minimum requirements refer to the sample of respondents, and usually obtaining more respondents is simpler than obtaining more clusters in cross-sectional studies.

With small samples at the lowest level (e.g., dyadic data or few repeated measures), estimation of random slopes is severely limited. For example, in a longitudinal model with two measurement occasions, we can specify a random intercept and a random slope for the variable Time. If there is also a covariance between the intercept and the slope for Time, we fully exhaust the degrees of freedom at the lowest level. As a result, the residual variance at the lowest level equals zero, and software that cannot constrain this variance to zero fails. If we have a second predictor variable in addition to Time, a random slope cannot be added because such a model has too few degrees of freedom to be identified and estimation will fail. As a consequence, small samples at the lowest level must assume a simple variance structure. Marginal models to account for clustering that do not use random effects such as generalized estimating equations or cluster-robust errors may be worth considering with small lower-level sample sizes as well (McNeish, 2014).

TABLE 15.1 Some rough guidelines about minimal number of groups

	ML	REML	REML-KR *corr.*
Cross-sectional			
Fixed part	30	20	5–8
Random part	30–40	7–10	—
Longitudinal			
Fixed part	50	20	15
Random part	50–75	25	—

Non-normal outcomes, such as categorical data or counts, require special estimation procedures. Specifically, a generalized linear model must be specified within the multilevel estimation procedure. There are two issues here. First, these outcome variables provide less information than continuous distributions, and consequently require larger sample sizes than models for continuous outcomes (Moineddin, Matheson, & Glazier, 2007). The second issue pertains to estimation. One of two methods are generally used to estimate non-normal outcomes in multilevel regression. The first approximates the nonlinear likelihood with a linear model using Taylor series expansion (Breslow & Clayton, 1993). This method is computationally efficient, but known to be biased. The second method is numerical approximation of the correct likelihood using adaptive Gaussian quadrature (Pinheiro & Bates, 1995). With large samples, simulations have shown that numerical approximation is superior to Taylor expansion (Pinheiro & Chao, 2006). With small samples, however, the advantage is less clear because numerical approximation uses FML, so the more accurate REML method cannot be used, and there is also no available small sample bias or degree of freedom correction such as Kenward–Roger. So, the Taylor expansion approach may be preferable with smaller samples. Additional discussion of sample size for multilevel models with non-normal outcomes can be found in McNeish (2016a) for binary outcomes or McNeish (2019) for count outcomes.

Multilevel structural equation models

A more complicated multilevel model is MSEM. Structural equation modeling is a very general statistical model that combines factor analysis and regression or path analysis. The interest is often on theoretical constructs, which are represented by the latent (unobserved) variables (factors). The relationships between the constructs are represented by regression (or path) coefficients between the factors, while the relationship between the latent variables and the observed variables are represented by factor loadings (which are also regression coefficients). In MSEM, observed and latent variables and a model for their relations can be formulated at all available levels. Just as in multilevel regression, regression coefficients for individual variables may vary across clusters. All this makes MSEM much more complex than multilevel regression, which is actually a special case of the more general MSEM.

In MSEM, all the complexities of SEM can be modeled at two or more levels. Since SEM models are based on relations between variables they are founded on covariance structures between variables (one of the first programs for SEM was called ACOVS, for Analysis of COVariance Structures; Joreskog, Gruvaeus, & Van Thillo, 1970). Some models – for example, growth curve models – can be specified both as a multilevel regression model and a MSEM. In these cases with small samples, a multilevel specification is preferred due to REML estimation and Kenward–Roger corrections. In SEM, we have only FML estimation and large-sample Z-tests (McNeish & Matta, 2018). Essentially, using an MSEM package for these types of models is equivalent to using a multilevel regression approach with the worst possible modeling choices. On the other hand, MSEM has goodness-of-fit measures for the fit of the model and latent variables that allow corrections for measurement error (Wu, West, & Taylor, 2009). For a general introduction to SEM we refer to Kline (2016), who briefly describes multilevel SEM. For an introduction to multilevel SEM we refer to the chapters on SEM in Hox et al. (2018).

There have been many simulations on minimal sample sizes for single-level SEM. Minimal sample sizes depend strongly on the complexity of the model and the type of data, but most simulations point to a minimal sample size of 100 (e.g., Kline, 2016, p. 292), with 50 as a lower limit when the model is relatively simple. This is much higher than the minimal sample sizes suggested for multilevel regression. With small samples, both standard errors for the parameter estimates and the global model test are untrustworthy. In addition, the chi-square statistics used to evaluate the model tends to be too high with smaller samples, leading to an operating Type I error rate that is much higher than the nominal level; i.e., models are rejected too often (Curran, Bollen, Paxton, Kirby, & Chen, 2002). McNeish and Harring (2017) report a simulation of a small growth curve model, with the results showing that 100 subjects are needed for acceptable results, and discuss small sample corrections to the chi-square test for samples as low as 20. These corrections are not implemented in current SEM software, but are easy to compute manually.

Bayes estimation

Bayesian estimation is an entirely different way to approach the estimation problem; see Chapters 2–4 (Miočević, Levy, & Savord; Van de Schoot, Veen, Smeets, Winter, & Depaoli; Veen & Egberts). ML estimation is based on frequentist reasoning: if I could do the analysis on an infinite number of random samples from my population, what would the distribution of my estimates be? If the population value is actually zero, what is the probability of obtaining the estimate that I just found? In Bayesian estimation, the parameter under consideration always has a probability distribution that describes the distribution of possible values. Before data are observed, this distribution is the prior distribution, which describes the prior knowledge or beliefs about the possible parameter values. After the data have been observed, the information in the data is combined with the prior distribution to produce the posterior distribution that describes the possible values after observing the data.

Bayesian estimation has some important advantages over frequentist estimation. Firstly, unlike ML estimation, it does not rely on asymptotic reasoning; Bayesian estimation is valid in small samples. In addition, the estimated values are always in the right range. For example, with ML estimation in small samples, it is quite possible for a variance estimate to be negative, which is an impossible value.

The default priors in most software are chosen to be uninformative; for example, a normal distribution with a very large variance for the regression coefficients, or a wide inverse gamma distribution for the variances. Even uninformative priors provide some information; for example, the information that a variance parameter cannot be negative. With uninformative priors Bayesian estimation tends to be no better with small samples than REML estimation (McNeish, 2016b; Smid, McNeish, Miočević, & Van de Schoot, 2019). With accurately specified informative priors, Bayesian estimation is much better than ML or REML estimation, or Bayesian estimation with uninformative priors (Smid et al., 2019). The disadvantage of informative priors is that an informative prior that is wide of the mark will strongly bias the results (Depaoli, 2014). There must be strong justification for an informative prior; for example, by basing it on previous research, information from experts, or a pilot study. A nice discussion of the use of informative priors with small samples is given by Van de Schoot, Broere, Perryck, Zondervan-Zwijnenburg, and Van Loey (2015). For a comparative review of Bayesian and frequentist methods with small samples in MSEM, see Smid et al. (2019).

Bayesian estimation is attractive in MSEM with small samples. For example, Meuleman and Billiet (2009) carried out a simulation study to evaluate how many countries are needed for accurate MSEM estimates. They specified within-country sample sizes comparable to the within-country samples in the European Social Survey (around 1,200). The number of countries was varied from 20 to 100. They conclude that 20 countries are not enough for accurate estimation. They do not suggest a specific lower limit for the country-level sample size; Hox, Van de Schoot, and Matthijsse (2013) concluded that a sample of 60 countries produces acceptable results, which confirms the suggestion that about 50 clusters is the minimum for accurate estimation in MSEM. Hox et al. (2013) replicate the simulation using Bayesian estimation with uninformative priors. Their main result is that a sample of about 20 countries is sufficient for accurate Bayesian estimation, while a sample size of 10 countries yielded results that were judged inaccurate.

Table 15.1 does not mention Bayesian estimation because suggestions are highly dependent on specification of the prior. With uninformative priors, Bayesian estimation should work with the sample sizes indicated for ML. Bayesian estimation with weakly informative priors roughly corresponds to the REML column, and Bayesian estimation with strongly informative priors is typically appropriate with lower samples than suggested for REML with the Kenward–Roger correction (McNeish, 2016b).

Discussion

Multilevel regression and MSEM are complex models and given that the degree of complexity of the model is one of the determinants of minimal sample size, it is difficult to give firm rules of thumb. This leads to one clear recommendation with smaller samples: keep the model simple. In multilevel modeling, random slopes complicate the model; with small samples these should be specified rarely and with caution. Similarly, MSEM models with latent variables are complex and the number of latent variables must be judiciously monitored.

Some of the approaches described elsewhere in this book can also be used in multilevel analysis. For example, randomization tests can be applied in multilevel data, by constructing a null model where subjects are randomly assigned to groups, and individual predictor variable values are randomly permuted between individuals within groups. Unfortunately, there is no multilevel software that implements this, so this option is only available to researchers that can write their own program.

Bootstrapping is often mentioned as a possible approach to small samples or distributional problems. However, this option is of limited usefulness, since bootstrapping is not a small sample technique. Yung and Chan (1999) discuss bootstrapping in small (single-level) samples. They conclude that existing simulation studies show that the bootstrap generally performs better than asymptotic methods. They do not provide clear recommendations for the minimal sample size for the bootstrap to work, citing simulation studies where the recommended minimal sample size varies from 20 to 400 (Yung & Chan, 1999, p. 100). Given such results, the bootstrap is not the best approach when the problem is small sample sizes. In addition, multilevel bootstrapping is complicated (Preacher & Selig, 2012). The straightforward but naïve notion that we simply bootstrap clusters and subsequently bootstrap individuals within groups is incorrect. Not only will it lead to different sample sizes in different bootstrap samples, it also fails to maintain the dependence structure across bootstrap samples. Most software implements multilevel bootstrapping by only resampling groups. This makes sense only if the multilevel structure consists of repeated measures within subjects. The correct approach to multilevel bootstrapping is the residual bootstrap, where the model is fitted to the data and the residuals are bootstrapped, after they have been adjusted to reflect the estimated covariances exactly (Goldstein, 2011), for a review of the issues in multilevel bootstrapping). A study by Cameron, Gelbach, and Miller (2008) showed that the "wild bootstrap", which is similar to the residual bootstrap, was effective with as few as five clusters, which is even lower that the minimal sample size reported in Yung and Chan (1999). Unfortunately, the residuals bootstrap is not implemented in all software (but is available in MLwiN (Rasbash, Steele, Browne, & Goldstein, 2019) and M*plus* (Muthén & Muthén, 2017); the wild bootstrap can be carried out in the R package clusterSEs (Esarey & Menger, 2018).

Another straightforward remedy if the number of groups is small is a fixed-effect model that includes all possible dummy variables to model the clusters (McNeish & Kelley, 2019). In this approach, we can validly use Ordinary Least Squares procedures for single-level regression, which does not assume large samples, or comparative methods for single-level SEM, some of which work with smaller samples. An important disadvantage of the fixed-effect approach is that there can be no second-level variables in the model, and no random slopes. However, if the interest is only in the fixed effects of the lowest-level variables, these approaches are simple and effective with as few as four clusters (McNeish & Stapleton, 2016b).

Whether ML estimation or Bayesian estimation is used, with small samples convergence problems and inadmissible estimates are likely to occur. With ML estimation, supplying good starting values for the estimation procedure often helps. Some software allows the estimation procedure to be automatically repeated with different starting values, which allows an evaluation of the estimation procedure. If using different starting values leads to different "converged" estimates, all estimates are questionable. With Bayesian estimation, more and longer chains are often needed to converge on the correct posterior distribution. Regarding issues in Bayesian estimation with small samples, we refer to Hox et al. (2013) for a discussion of issues with uninformative priors, and Van de Schoot et al. (2015) for a discussion involving informative priors.

This review of issues in multilevel data with small sample sizes focusses on the accuracy of parameter estimation and standard errors. One important issue has been conspicuously neglected, which is the issue of power. With small samples, the power to reject an incorrect null hypothesis is low. It is difficult to provide general rules here, because we are investigating complex multivariate models, and the power to reject an incorrect null hypothesis will be different for different parameters. Furthermore, the power for a test of a specific parameter also depends on the multilevel structure. Having 20 countries is a small sample, but if the within-country sample size is 1,200, some parameters can still be tested with high power, while other parameters may only be tested with high power if the effect size is very large. The general recommendation is to assess the power for a specific parameter given the model and the data, and the most general approach to do this is simulation (cf. Hox et al., 2018, Chapter 12).

References

Baldwin, S. A., & Fellingham, G. W. (2013). Bayesian methods for the analysis of small sample multilevel data with a complex variance structure. *Psychological Methods*, *18*(2), 151–164. doi:10.1037/a0030642.

Bell, B. A., Morgan, G. B., Schoeneberger, J. A., Kromrey, J. D., & Ferron, J. M. (2014). How low can you go? An investigation of the influence of sample size and model complexity on point and interval estimates in two-level linear models. *Methodology: European Journal of Research Methods for the Behavioral and Social Sciences*, *10*(1), 1–11. doi:10.1027/1614-2241/a000062.

Bickel, R. (2007). *Multilevel analysis for applied research: It's just regression!* New York, NY: Guilford Press.

Breslow, N. E., & Clayton, D. G. (1993). Approximate inference in generalized linear mixed models. *Journal of the American Statistical Association*, *88*(420), 9–25. doi:10.1080/01621459.1993.10594284.

Cameron, A. C., Gelbach, J. B., & Miller, D. L. (2008). Bootstrap-based improvements for inference with clustered errors. *Review of Economics and Statistics*, *90*(3), 414–427. doi:10.1162/rest.90.3.414.

Curran, P. J., Bollen, K. A., Paxton, P. M., Kirby, J. B., & Chen, F. (2002). The noncentral chi-square distribution in misspecified structural equation models: Finite sample results from a Monte Carlo simulation. *Multivariate Behavioral Research, 37*(1), 1–36. doi:10.1207/S15327906MBR3701_01.

Depaoli, S. (2014). The impact of inaccurate "informative" priors for growth parameters in Bayesian growth mixture modeling. *Structural Equation Modeling: A Multidisciplinary Journal, 21*(2), 239–252. doi:10.1080/10705511.2014.882686.

Esarey, J., & Menger, A. (2018). Practical and effective approaches to dealing with clustered data. *Political Science Research and Methods*, 1–19. doi:10.1017/psrm.2017.42.

Ferron, J. M., Bell, B. A., Hess, M. R., Rendina-Gobioff, G., & Hibbard, S. T. (2009). Making treatment effect inferences from multiple-baseline data: The utility of multilevel modeling approaches. *Behavior Research Methods, 41*(2), 372–384. doi:10.3758/brm.41.2.372.

Goldstein, H. (2011). Bootstrapping in multilevel models. In J. J. Hox & J. K. Roberts (Eds.), *Handbook of advanced multilevel analysis* (pp. 163–172). New York, NY: Routledge.

Hox, J. J., Moerbeek, M., & Van de Schoot, R. (2018). *Multilevel analysis: Techniques and applications* (3rd ed.). New York, NY: Routledge.

Hox, J. J., Van de Schoot, R., & Matthijsse, S. (2013). How few countries will do? Comparative survey analysis from a Bayesian perspective. *Survey Research Methods, 6*(2), 87–93. doi:10.18148/srm/2012.v6i2.5033.

Joreskog, K. G., Gruvaeus, G. T., & Van Thillo, M. (1970). ACOVS: A general computer program for the analysis of covariance structures. *ETS Research Bulletin Series, 1970*(1), i-54. doi:10.1002/j.2333-8504.1970.tb01009.x.

Kline, R. B. (2016). *Principles and practice of structural equation modeling* (4th ed.). New York, NY: Guilford Press.

Maas, C. J. M., & Hox, J. J. (2005). Sufficient sample sizes for multilevel modeling. *Methodology: European Journal of Research Methods for the Behavioral and Social Sciences, 1*(3), 86–92. doi:10.1027/1614-2241.1.3.86.

McNeish, D. (2014). Modeling sparsely clustered data: Design-based, model-based, and single-level methods. *Psychological Methods, 19*(4), 552–563. doi:10.1037/met0000024.

McNeish, D. (2016a). Estimation methods for mixed logistic models with few clusters. *Multivariate Behavioral Research, 51*(6), 790–804. doi:10.1080/00273171.2016.1236237.

McNeish, D. (2016b). On using Bayesian methods to address small sample problems. *Structural Equation Modeling: A Multidisciplinary Journal, 23*(5), 750–773. doi:10.1080/10705511.2016.1186549.

McNeish, D. (2019). Poisson multilevel models with small samples. *Multivariate Behavioral Research*, 54(3), 444–455. doi:10.1080/00273171.2018.1545630.

McNeish, D., & Harring, J. R. (2017). Correcting model fit criteria for small sample latent growth models with incomplete data. *Educational and Psychological Measurement, 77*(6), 990–1018. doi:10.1177/0013164416661824.

McNeish, D., & Kelley, K. (2019). Fixed effects models versus mixed effects models for clustered data: Reviewing the approaches, disentangling the differences, and making recommendations. doi:10.1037/met0000182.

McNeish, D., & Matta, T. (2018). Differentiating between mixed-effects and latent-curve approaches to growth modeling. *Behavior Research Methods, 50*(4), 1398–1414. doi:10.3758/s13428-017-0976-5.

McNeish, D., & Stapleton, L. M. (2016a). The effect of small sample size on two-level model estimates: A review and illustration. *Educational Psychology Review, 28*(2), 295–314. doi:10.1007/s10648-014-9287-x.

McNeish, D., & Stapleton, L. M. (2016b). Modeling clustered data with very few clusters. *Multivariate Behavioral Research*, *51*(4), 495–518. doi:10.1080/00273171.2016.1167008.

Meuleman, B., & Billiet, J. (2009). A Monte Carlo sample size study: How many countries are needed for accurate multilevel SEM? *Survey Research Methods*, *3*(1), 45–58. doi:10.18148/srm/2009.v3i1.666.

Moineddin, R., Matheson, F. I., & Glazier, R. H. (2007). A simulation study of sample size for multilevel logistic regression models. *BMC Medical Research Methodology*, *7*(1), 34. doi:10.1186/1471-2288-7-34.

Muthén, L. K., & Muthén, B. (2017). *Mplus version 8 user's guide*. Muthén & Muthén. www.statmodel.com/download/usersguide/MplusUserGuideVer_8.pdf.

Pinheiro, J. C., & Bates, D. M. (1995). Approximations to the log-likelihood function in the nonlinear mixed-effects model. *Journal of Computational and Graphical Statistics*, *4*(1), 12–35. doi:10.1080/10618600.1995.10474663.

Pinheiro, J. C., & Chao, E. C. (2006). Efficient Laplacian and adaptive Gaussian quadrature algorithms for multilevel generalized linear mixed models. *Journal of Computational and Graphical Statistics*, *15*(1), 58–81. doi:10.1198/106186006X96962.

Preacher, K. J., & Selig, J. P. (2012). Advantages of Monte Carlo confidence intervals for indirect effects. *Communication Methods and Measures*, *6*(2), 77–98. doi:10.1080/19312458.2012.679848.

Rasbash, J., Steele, F., Browne, W. J., & Goldstein, H. (2019). *A user's guide to MLwiN, v3.03*. Bristol: Centre for Multilevel Modelling, University of Bristol.

Savalei, V., & Kolenikov, S. (2008). Constrained versus unconstrained estimation in structural equation modeling. *Psychological Methods*, *13*(2), 150–170. doi:10.1037/1082-989X.13.2.150.

Smid, S. C., McNeish, D., Miočević, M., & Van de Schoot, R. (2019). Bayesian versus frequentist estimation for structural equation models in small sample contexts: A systematic review. *Structural Equation Modeling: A Multidisciplinary Journal*. doi:10.1080/10705511.2019.1577140.

Snijders, T. A. B., & Bosker, R. J. (2012). *Multilevel analysis: An introduction to basic and advanced multilevel modeling* (2nd ed.). Los Angeles, CA: SAGE.

Snijkers, G., Haraldsen, G., Jones, J., & Willimack, D. (2013). *Designing and conducting business surveys*. Hoboken, NJ: John Wiley & Sons.

Stegmueller, D. (2013). How many countries for multilevel modeling? A comparison of frequentist and Bayesian approaches. *American Journal of Political Science*, *57*(3), 748–761. doi:10.1111/ajps.12001.

Stram, D. O., & Lee, J. W. (1994). Variance components testing in the longitudinal mixed effects model. *Biometrics*, *50*(4), 1171–1177. doi:10.2307/2533455.

Van de Schoot, R., Broere, J. J., Perryck, K. H., Zondervan-Zwijnenburg, M., & Van Loey, N. E. (2015). Analyzing small data sets using Bayesian estimation: The case of posttraumatic stress symptoms following mechanical ventilation in burn survivors. *European Journal of Psychotraumatology*, *6*(1), 25216. doi:10.3402/ejpt.v6.25216.

Wu, W., West, S. G., & Taylor, A. B. (2009). Evaluating model fit for growth curve models: Integration of fit indices from SEM and MLM frameworks. *Psychological Methods*, *14*(3), 183–201. doi:10.1037/a0015858.

Yung, Y.-F., & Chan, W. (1999). Statistical analyses using bootstrapping: Concepts and implementation. In R. H. Hoyle (Ed.), *Statistical strategies for small sample research* (pp. 82–108). Thousand Oaks, CA: SAGE.

16

SMALL SAMPLE SOLUTIONS FOR STRUCTURAL EQUATION MODELING

Yves Rosseel

DEPARTMENT OF DATA ANALYSIS, GHENT UNIVERSITY, GHENT, BELGIUM

Introduction

Structural equation modeling (SEM) is a statistical modeling procedure that is used in the social and behavioral sciences to study the relationships among latent variables (Bollen, 1989). Usually, a structural equation model can be divided into two parts: The measurement part relates the latent variables to a set of observed variables or indicators, and the structural part represents the hypothesized relationships among these latent variables. A typical model is presented in Figure 16.1.

SEM has a bad reputation when it comes to sample size requirements, which is likely due to a combination of factors. First, structural equation models can become quite large, involving many (observed and latent) variables. As a result, many parameters must be estimated, and a reasonable amount of data is needed to obtain good-quality estimates for those parameters. Second, the statistical machinery behind (traditional) SEM is based on large sample theory, which implies that good performance (of both point estimation and inference) is only guaranteed when the sample size is large enough. Third, some simulation studies in the SEM literature have suggested that huge sample sizes are needed in order to yield trustworthy results. And although these findings were only relevant for specific settings (one infamous example is the so-called "Asymptotically Distribution Free" or ADF estimation method), these studies fueled the now conventional wisdom that SEM can only be used if the sample size is reasonably large (say, $n > 500$) or even very large ($n > 2000$).

For many reasons, however, small sample sizes are simply a reality. When this is the case, many applied researchers hesitate to use SEM and instead employ suboptimal procedures, such as regression or path analysis based on sum scores. Unfortunately, these procedures often lead to biased results and misinformed

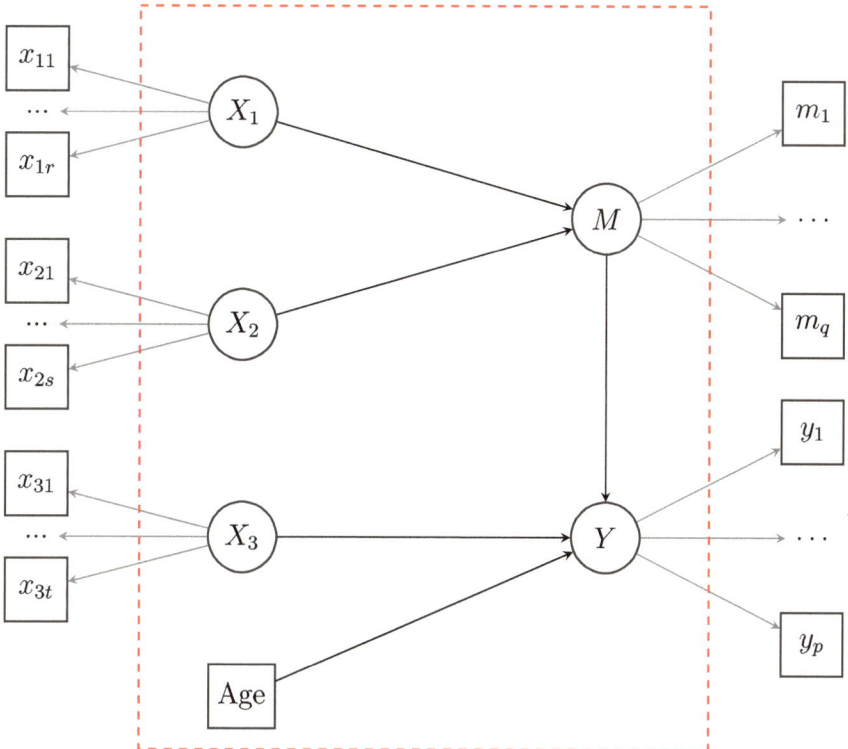

FIGURE 16.1 A typical structural equation model with a structural part (within the dashed box) and multiple measurement models. Age is an observed variable, but X_1, X_2, X_3, M, and Y are latent variables. Each latent variable is measured by a set of observed indicators. For example, X_1 is measured by a set of r indicators: x_{11}, x_{12}, x_{13}, …, x_{1r}.

conclusions. Perhaps a better strategy would be to keep the spirit of SEM but to also look for solutions to handle the small sample problem. In this chapter, I will describe some of these solutions. For readers seeking guidance on choosing an appropriate sample size for their study, I suggest reading Muthén and Muthén (2002) or Wolf, Harrington, Clark, and Miller (2013).

The remainder of this chapter is organized into three sections: First, I discuss some issues that may arise with small sample sizes in SEM. Next, I present four alternative estimation approaches that may be used (instead of traditional SEM) when the sample size is small. Finally, I describe some small sample corrections for test statistics and standard errors.

Some issues with small samples sizes in SEM

Consider a fairly large model similar to the model in Figure 16.1. If all observed variables are continuous, the default estimator in most (if not all) SEM software packages is maximum likelihood. Usually, the maximum likelihood estimator is a good choice because it features many desirable statistical properties. In addition, the maximum likelihood approach can be adapted to handle missing data (under the assumption that data are missing at random), and so-called "robust" standard errors and test statistics have been developed to deal with non-normal data and mis-specified models.

However, if the sample size is rather small (say, $n < 200$), then several problems may arise; this has been well documented in the literature (Bentler & Yuan, 1999; Boomsma, 1985; Nevitt & Hancock, 2004). First, the model may not converge, which means that the optimizer (the algorithm trying to find the values for the model parameters that maximize the likelihood of the data) has failed to find a solution that satisfies one or more convergence criteria. On rare occasions, the optimizer is simply mistaken. In this case, changing the convergence criteria, switching to another optimization algorithm, or providing better starting values may solve the problem. But if the sample size is small, it may very well be that the data set does not contain enough information to find a unique solution for the model.

A second problem may be that the model converged but resulted in a non-admissible solution. This means that some parameters are out of range. The most common example is a negative variance. Another example is a correlation value that exceeds 1 (in absolute value). It is important to realize that some estimation approaches (both frequentist and Bayesian) may—by design—never produce out-of-range solutions. Although this may seem like a desirable feature, it merely masks potential problems with either the model or the data. It is important that users notice negative variances (or other out-of-range parameters; Savalei & Kolenikov, 2008). Negative variances are often harmless, but they can be a symptom of structural misspecification. Several ways to test for structural misspecification are discussed in Kolenikov and Bollen (2012).

A third problem relates to the fact that maximum likelihood is a large sample technique. This implies that working with small sample sizes may lead to biased point estimates, standard errors that are too small, confidence intervals that are not wide enough, and p-values for hypothesis tests that cannot be trusted.

Possible solutions for point estimation

In this section, I briefly describe four alternative approaches to estimate parameters in an SEM framework with small sample sizes. The purpose of this section is not to give an exhaustive overview of all possible solutions, or to compare them under different settings, but to briefly introduce these solutions because they are not widely known among applied users. I limit myself to frequentist methods and solutions that are available in free and open-source software.

Penalized likelihood estimation

Penalized likelihood methods (or regularization methods) have been developed in the (statistical) machine-learning literature and are particularly useful when the sample size is small—compared to the number of variables in the model (Hastie, Tibshirani, & Friedman, 2009). Penalized likelihood methods are similar to ordinary likelihood methods (like maximum likelihood estimation) but include an additional penalty term to control for the complexity of the model. The penalty term can be formulated to incorporate prior knowledge about the parameters or to discourage parameter values that are less realistic (e.g., far from zero). Two popular penalty terms are the l_2 or ridge penalty, and the l_1 or lasso (least absolute shrinkage and selection operator) penalty (Tibshirani, 1996).

To illustrate how this penalization works, imagine a univariate regression model with a large number of predictors. Without any penalization, all the regression coefficients are computed in the usual way. However, the ridge penalty term will shrink (all) the coefficients towards zero, whereas the lasso penalty will additionally shrink tiny coefficients all the way to zero. In the latter approach, only "strong" predictors (for which there is strong support in the data) survive, while "weak" predictors that can hardly be distinguished from noise are eliminated. In general, adding penalty terms leads to models that are less complex, and this is particularly beneficial if the sample size is small. Alternative penalty terms have been proposed to overcome some of the limitations of the ridge and lasso penalties. Two recent penalties are smoothly clipped absolute deviation (SCAD; Fan & Li, 2001) and minimax concave penalty (MCP; Zhang, 2010). Interestingly, penalized likelihood methods are closely related to Bayesian estimation methods. In particular, ridge and lasso penalties correspond to Gaussian and Laplace priors, respectively, whereas both SCAD and MCP correspond to certain improper priors (Huang, Chen, & Weng, 2017).

Although these penalization approaches have been around for a few decades, they have only recently been applied to SEM (Jacobucci, Grimm, & McArdle, 2016; see also Huang et al., 2017). Fortunately, we now have access to several free and open-source R packages that have implemented these methods for SEM. Two examples are the `regsem` package (Jacobucci, Grimm, Brandmaier, Serang, & Kievit, 2018) and the `lslx` package (Huang & Hu, 2018).

A disadvantage of these penalized methods is that the user needs to indicate which parameters require penalization, and how much. In an exploratory analysis, it may be useful and even advantageous to penalize parameters towards zero if little support for them can be found in the data. However, SEM is usually a confirmatory approach, and the user needs to ensure that all parameters that are initially postulated in the model are not removed by the penalization.

Model-implied instrumental variables

Bollen (1996) proposed an alternative estimation approach for SEM based on model-implied instrumental variables in combination with two-stage least squares (MIIV-2SLS). In this approach, the model is translated to a set of (regression) equations. Next, each latent variable in these equations is replaced with its marker indicator (usually the first indicator, where the factor loading is fixed to unity and the intercept is fixed to zero) minus its residual error term. The resulting equations no longer contain any latent variables but have a more complex error structure. Importantly, ordinary least squares estimation is no longer suitable for solving these equations because some predictors are now correlated with the error term in the equation. This is where the instrumental variables (also called instruments) come into play. For each equation, a set of instrumental variables must be found. An instrumental variable must be uncorrelated with the error term of the equation but strongly correlated with the problematic predictor. Usually, instrumental variables are sought outside the model, but in Bollen's approach, the instrumental variables are selected from the observed variables that are part of the model. Several (automated) procedures to find these instrumental variables within the model have been developed. Once the instruments are selected, an estimation procedure is needed to estimate all the coefficients of the equations. Econometricians developed a popular method to accomplish this called two-stage least squares (2SLS).

A major motivation for MIIV-2SLS is that it is robust: It does not rely on normality and is less likely to spread bias (which may arise from structural misspecifications) in one part of the model to other parts of the model (Bollen, 2018). Another attractive feature of MIIV-2SLS is that it is noniterative. Meaning, there cannot be any convergence issues, and MIIV-2SLS may provide a reasonable solution for models where the maximum likelihood estimator fails to converge.

An important aspect of the model-implied instrumental variables approach is the (optimal) selection of instruments when there are a large number of instruments to choose from. Bollen, Kirby, Curran, Paxton, and Chen (2007) found that with small sample sizes (e.g., $n < 100$) it was best not to use a large number of instruments because it led to greater bias. More research is needed to evaluate the performance of this estimator in settings where the sample size is (very) small. The MIIV-2SLS approach is available in the R package MIIVsem (Fisher, Bollen, Gates, & Rönkkö, 2017).

Two-step estimation

In the two-step estimation approach, a strict distinction is made between the measurement part and the structural (regression) part of the model, and estimation proceeds in two steps. In the first step, all the measurement models are fitted one by one. In the second step, the full model is fitted, including the structural part, but the parameters of the measurement models are kept fixed to the values found in the first step. The main motivation for the two-step approach is to separate the measurement model(s) from the structural part during estimation so that they cannot influence each other. In the traditional maximum likelihood framework, all parameters are fitted simultaneously. As a result, misspecifications in the structural model may affect the estimated factor loadings of one or more measurement models, and this may lead to interpretation problems for the latent variables (Burt, 1976; see also Anderson & Gerbing, 1988).

The two-step approach received renewed attention in the latent class literature (Bakk & Kuha, 2018; Bakk, Oberski, & Vermunt, 2014) and was recently implemented within the R package lavaan (Rosseel, 2012); see also Chapter 17 (Smid & Rosseel). For very large models with many latent variables, it may be expected that fewer convergence problems arise because the model is estimated in parts. Encountering convergence issues in the first step allows the researcher to identify the problematic measurement model(s). If convergence issues only occur in the second step, it becomes clear that the problem lies in the structural part of the model.

Factor score regression

The simple but powerful idea of factor score regression is to replace all latent variables with factor scores. Similar to the two-step method, each measurement model is fitted one at a time. Next, factor scores are computed for all the latent variables in the usual way. Once the latent variables have been replaced by their factor scores, all variables are observed. In a final step, the structural part of the model is estimated. This estimation often consists of a regression analysis or a path analysis (as in Figure 16.1). The name "factor score regression" refers to both scenarios.

If used naïvely, factor score regression will likely lead to substantial bias in the estimated parameters of the structural part, even when the sample size is very large (Skrondal & Laake, 2001), because the factor scores have been treated as if they were observed without measurement error. Fortunately, there are various ways to correct for this bias. For example, Croon (2002) devised a correction that removes the bias, and several studies have shown that this method works remarkably well (Devlieger, Mayer, & Rosseel, 2016; Devlieger & Rosseel, 2017). Croon's method works as follows: First, the variance–covariance matrix of the factor scores is computed. Based on the information from the measurement models, the elements of the variance–covariance matrix are corrected in order to approximate the model-implied variances and covariances of the latent variables. This corrected variance–covariance matrix then forms the input of a regular regression or path analysis.

Similar to the two-step method, factor score regression (combined with Croon's correction) may be a useful alternative for fairly large models (with many measurement models) in combination with a relatively small sample size. In addition, it is possible to fit the measurement models using a noniterative estimator (for an example based on instrumental variables, see Hägglund, 1982). For the structural model, depending on whether it is recursive, a single-stage or a two-stage least squares estimator can be used. In short, this method can be made fully noniterative, which would avoid any convergence issues (Takane & Hwang, 2018). Still, Croon's correction may produce a variance–covariance matrix (for the variables belonging to the structural part) that is not positive definite—particularly if the measurement error is substantial. Therefore, Croon's correction is not entirely free from estimation problems. In this case, the only solution may be to create a sum score for each latent variable and to estimate a model where each latent variable has a single indicator (the sum score) with its reliability fixed to a realistic value that is provided by the user (Savalei, 2018).

Discussion

All the methods I have described in this section have advantages and disadvantages. The penalized likelihood approach is perhaps the only method that was specifically designed to handle (very) small sample sizes. The other three methods use a divide-and-conquer approach; they break down the full model into smaller parts and estimate the parameters of each part in turn. Apart from reducing the complexity and being less vulnerable to convergence issues, the latter three methods have the advantage of being good at localizing the problematic parts within a large model.

At the time of writing, it is not clear which method is universally superior when the sample size is (very) small. Instead of picking one method, I would recommend that applied users try all of them. Each method may provide additional insights. If the final results agree across multiple methods, then your confidence in your findings will increase. However, if the results diverge, this may indicate that the sample size is simply too small, given the complexity of the model.

Small sample inference for SEM

In this section, I will assume that a point estimation using maximum likelihood estimation, for example, was successful and resulted in an admissible solution. The next step is to note the inference part of the model: the chi-square test statistic (for overall goodness of fit), the standard errors of the individual model parameters, and the corresponding confidence intervals and/or hypothesis tests. Many authors have documented that when the sample size is small, the chi-square test leads to inflated Type I errors even under ideal circumstances (i.e., correctly specified model, normal data; see Nevitt & Hancock, 2004 and references therein). Similarly, standard errors are often attenuated (too small), and confidence intervals are not wide enough. In the next two subsections, I will briefly discuss a few attempts to tackle these small sample inference issues in SEM.

Improving the chi-square test statistic

Several corrections have been suggested to improve the performance of the chi-square test statistic, such as the Bartlett correction (Bartlett, 1937, 1954). Variations of this correction exist, but the one most studied (Nevitt & Hancock, 2004; see also Fouladi, 2000; Savalei, 2010) is a simplified correction proposed by Bartlett (1950) in the context of exploratory factor analysis. A more general correction is called the Swain correction (Swain, 1975), and even more corrections were described by Yuan, Tian, and Yanagihara (2015).

Herzog, Boomsma, and Reinecke (2007) and Herzog and Boomsma (2009) compared these corrections and concluded that the Swain correction worked best; however, they only looked at complete and normal data. Shi, Lee, and Terry (2018) also compared the various corrections in more realistic settings and concluded that the so-called "empirically" corrected test statistic proposed by Yuan et al. (2015) generally yielded the best performance—particularly when fitting large structural equation models with many observed variables. Still, they warn that when the number of variables (P) in a model increases, the sample size (n) also needs to increase in order to control Type I error. They suggest that, roughly speaking, n should be larger than P^2 (Shi et al., 2018, p. 39). Finally, Jiang and Yuan (2017) proposed four new corrected test statistics aiming to improve model evaluation in nonnormally distributed data with small sample sizes. The results were promising, but they conclude:

> To our knowledge, there does not exist a test statistic that performs well universally. As indicated by our results, the overall model evaluation with small n is rather challenging in SEM. Although the new statistics allow more reliable model evaluation than existing ones under conditions of nonnormally distributed data at small n, their performances are still far from universally optimum.
>
> (Jiang & Yuan, 2017, p. 493)

To evaluate models when the sample size is small, perhaps the chi-square test should be abandoned altogether and alternatives approaches should be explored. One approach is to consider confidence intervals and tests of close fit based on the standardized root mean square residual (SRMR; Maydeu-Olivares, 2017; Maydeu-Olivares, Shi, & Rosseel, 2018). Although these tests were not constructed with small sample sizes in mind, they seem to work well even when n = 100 (the smallest sample size considered in Maydeu-Olivares et al., 2018) and the model is not too large. These tests have been implemented as part of the `lavResiduals()` function of the `lavaan` package.

Yet another approach is to consider local fit measures. This can be based on evaluating just a subpart of the model. For example, one measurement model at a time, as in the two-step and factor score regression approaches, or one equation at a time, as is done using the Sargan test in Bollen's model-implied instrumental variables approach. A different set of local fit measures is based on graphical criteria such as d-separation or trek-separation (Thoemmes, Rosseel, & Textor, 2018).

Better standard errors and confidence intervals

Literature on the performance of standard errors in SEM is limited (Yuan & Bentler, 1997; Yuan & Hayashi, 2006) and is mostly concerned with the effect of nonnormality or model misspecifications on the quality of the standard errors. Small sample sizes, indeed, were not the focus of these studies. But in general, it is well known that if large sample theory is used to construct analytic expressions in order to compute standard errors, they may perform poorly in small samples.

When assumptions underlying analytic standard errors are not met, it is often suggested to use a resampling approach instead. One popular method is the bootstrap (Efron & Tibshirani, 1993): A bootstrap sample is generated (either by randomly sampling rows from the original data set with replacement or by simulating a new data set under the model), and a new set of parameters is estimated for this bootstrap sample. This is repeated a large number of times (say, 1,000), and the standard deviation of a parameter across all replicated bootstrap samples is used as an estimate of the standard error for that parameter. Unfortunately, despite many other advantages (Chernick, 2007), the bootstrap does not appear to be a reliable solution when the sample size is (very) small (Yung & Bentler, 1996). Hence, it may be worthwhile to explore better analytical solutions after all. Small sample corrections for (robust) standard errors have been developed in econometrics (MacKinnon & White, 1985) and have recently been adapted to the SEM context (Dudgeon, Barendse, & Rosseel, 2018). The preliminary results are encouraging, but this is still a work in progress. At the time of writing, this technology is not yet available in SEM software.

Conclusion

In this chapter, we discussed several problems in the context of SEM when the sample size is small and standard (maximum likelihood) estimation methods are used, such as nonconvergence, non-admissible solutions, bias, poorly performing test statistics, and inaccurate standard errors and confidence intervals. As potential solutions to attain better point estimates (or a solution at all), we briefly discussed four alternative estimation approaches: penalized likelihood estimation, model-implied instrumental variables, two-step estimation, and factor score regression. Only the first method was specifically designed to handle small samples. The latter approaches were developed with other concerns in mind, but they may be viable alternatives for estimation when the sample size is small.

For the inference part, I discussed various attempts to improve the performance of the chi-square test statistic for evaluating global fit in the presence of small samples. For the standard errors, I underlined that bootstrapping may not be the solution we are looking for. Unfortunately, to attain better standard errors (and confidence intervals) in the small sample setting, we may need to wait until new technology is available. Admittedly, my selection of topics in this chapter is somewhat biased. I certainly did not present all the solutions that have been proposed in the literature, but interested readers may consult Deng, Yang, and Marcoulides (2018) for an alternative perspective.

In this chapter, I focused on frequentist solutions, but a Bayesian approach is presented in Chapter 17 of this book. A major advantage of the Bayesian approach is that it does not rely on large sample asymptotics. This implies, for example, that getting correct standard errors and credible (confidence) intervals is not an issue in the Bayesian framework. On the other hand, model evaluation in a Bayesian framework requires a new set of skills; this may be intimidating for those who are unfamiliar with the Bayesian framework. The same is true for specifying priors. Choosing adequate priors is an essential ingredient of Bayesian estimation, and you should be prepared to critically reflect on this before you proceed. If you are unwilling to specify any priors, and you rely on software defaults, then you should probably avoid Bayesian SEM altogether (McNeish, 2016). If, on the other hand, you fully endorse the Bayesian approach, and you have a priori knowledge that can be encoded in informative priors, the Bayesian approach is an excellent choice.

A last closing comment: If the sample size is (very) small, it may be that the data simply do not contain enough information to answer the research questions. In that case, one should not expect miracles from statistical technology. Small samples sizes have limitations, and we should accept them.

References

Anderson, J. C., & Gerbing, D. W. (1988). Structural equation modeling in practice: A review and recommended two-step approach. *Psychological Bulletin*, *103*(3), 411.

Bakk, Z., & Kuha, J. (2018). Two-step estimation of models between latent classes and external variables. *Psychometrika*, *83*(4), 871–892.

Bakk, Z., Oberski, D. L., & Vermunt, J. K. (2014). Relating latent class assignments to external variables: Standard errors for correct inference. *Political Analysis*, *22*(4), 520–540.

Bartlett, M. S. (1937). Properties of sufficiency and statistical tests. *Proceedings of the Royal Society of London. Series A*, *160*(901), 268–282.

Bartlett, M. S. (1950). Tests of significance in factor analysis. *British Journal of Statistical Psychology*, *3*(2), 77–85.

Bartlett, M. S. (1954). A note on the multiplying factors for various χ^2 approximations. *Journal of the Royal Statistical Society. Series B (methodological)*, 16, 296–298.

Bentler, P. M., & Yuan, K. H. (1999). Structural equation modeling with small samples: Test statistics. *Multivariate Behavioral Research*, *34*(2), 181–197.

Bollen, K. A. (1989). *Structural equations with latent variables*. New York, NY: Wiley.

Bollen, K. A. (1996). An alternative two stage least squares (2sls) estimator for latent variable. *Psychometrika*, *61*(1), 109–121.

Bollen, K. A. (2018). Model implied instrumental variables (MIIVs): An alternative orientation to structural equation modeling. *Multivariate Behavioral Research*, *54*(1), 1–16. doi:10.1080/00273171.2018.1483224.

Bollen, K. A., Kirby, J. B., Curran, P. J., Paxton, P. M., & Chen, F. (2007). Latent variable models under misspecification: Two-stage least squares (2SLS) and maximum likelihood (ML) estimators. *Sociological Methods & Research*, *36*(1), 48–86.

Boomsma, A. (1985). Nonconvergence, improper solutions, and starting values in LISREL maximum likelihood estimation. *Psychometrika*, *50*(2), 229–242.

Burt, R. S. (1976). Interpretational confounding of unobserved variables in structural equation models. *Sociological Methods & Research, 5*(1), 3–52.

Chernick, M. R. (2007). *Bootstrap methods: A guide for practitioners and researchers* (2nd ed.). Hoboken, NJ: Wiley.

Croon, M. (2002). Using predicted latent scores in general latent structure models. In G. A. Marcoulides & I. Moustaki (Eds.), *Latent variable and latent structure models* (pp. 195–223). Mahwah, NJ: Lawrence Erlbaum.

Deng, L., Yang, M., & Marcoulides, K. M. (2018). Structural equation modeling with many variables: A systematic review of issues and developments. *Frontiers in Psychology, 9*, n.p.

Devlieger, I., Mayer, A., & Rosseel, Y. (2016). Hypothesis testing using factor score regression: A comparison of four methods. *Educational and Psychological Measurement, 76*(5), 741–770.

Devlieger, I., & Rosseel, Y. (2017). Factor score path analysis: An alternative for SEM. *Methodology, 13*, 31–38.

Dudgeon, P., Barendse, M., & Rosseel, Y. (2018). *Leverage-based confidence intervals for structural equation modelling.* Paper presented at the Modern Modeling Methods (M3) conference, Storrs, CT.

Efron, B., & Tibshirani, R. J. (1993). *An introduction to the bootstrap* (Vol. 57). Boca Raton, FL: Chapman & Hall/CRC.

Fan, J., & Li, R. (2001). Variable selection via nonconcave penalized likelihood and its oracle properties. *Journal of the American Statistical Association, 96*(456), 1348–1360.

Fisher, Z., Bollen, K. A., Gates, K., & Rönkkö, M. (2017). MIIVsem: Model implied instrumental variable (MIIV) estimation of structural equation models [Computer software manual] (Version R package 0.5.2). Retrieved from https://CRAN.R-project.org/package=MIIVsem.

Fouladi, R. T. (2000). Performance of modified test statistics in covariance and correlation structure analysis under conditions of multivariate nonnormality. *Structural Equation Modeling: A Multidisciplinary Journal, 7*(3), 356–410.

Hägglund, G. (1982). Factor analysis by instrumental variables methods. *Psychometrika, 47*(2), 209–222.

Hastie, T., Tibshirani, R. J., & Friedman, J. (2009). *The elements of statistical learning: Data mining, inference, and prediction* (2nd ed.). New York, NY: Springer.

Herzog, W., & Boomsma, A. (2009). Small-sample robust estimators of noncentrality-based and incremental model fit. *Structural Equation Modeling: A Multidisciplinary Journal, 16*(1), 1–27.

Herzog, W., Boomsma, A., & Reinecke, S. (2007). The model-size effect on traditional and modified tests of covariance structures. *Structural Equation Modeling: A Multidisciplinary Journal, 14*(3), 361–390.

Huang, P.-H., Chen, H., & Weng, L.-H. (2017). A penalized likelihood method for structural equation modeling. *Psychometrika, 82*(2), 329–354.

Huang, P.-H., & Hu, W.-H. (2018). lslx: Semi-confirmatory structural equation modeling via penalized likelihood [Computer software manual] (Version R package 0.6.4). Retrieved from https://CRAN.R-project.org/package=lslx.

Jacobucci, R., Grimm, K. J., Brandmaier, A. M., Serang, S., & Kievit, R. A. (2018). regsem: Regularized structural equation modeling [Computer software manual] (Version R package 1.2-0). Retrieved from https://CRAN.R-project.org/package=regsem.

Jacobucci, R., Grimm, K. J., & McArdle, J. J. (2016). Regularized structural equation modeling. *Structural Equation Modeling: A Multidisciplinary Journal, 23*(4), 555–566.

Jiang, G., & Yuan, K.-H. (2017). Four new corrected statistics for SEM with small samples and nonnormally distributed data. *Structural Equation Modeling: A Multidisciplinary Journal*, *24*(4), 479–494.

Kolenikov, S., & Bollen, K. A. (2012). Testing negative error variances: Is a Heywood case a symptom of misspecification?. *Sociological Methods & Research*, *41*(1), 124–167.

MacKinnon, J., & White, H. (1985). Some heteroskedasticity-consistent covariance matrix estimators with improved finite sample properties. *Journal of Econometrics*, *29*(3), 305–325.

Maydeu-Olivares, A. (2017). Assessing the size of model misfit in structural equation models. *Psychometrika*, *82*(3), 533–558.

Maydeu-Olivares, A., Shi, D., & Rosseel, Y. (2018). Assessing fit in structural equation models: A Monte-Carlo evaluation of RMSEA versus SRMR confidence intervals and tests of close fit. *Structural Equation Modeling: A Multidisciplinary Journal*, *25*(3), 389–402.

McNeish, D. (2016). On using Bayesian methods to address small sample problems. *Structural Equation Modeling: A Multidisciplinary Journal*, *23*(5), 750–773.

Muthén, L. K., & Muthén, B. O. (2002). How to use a Monte Carlo study to decide on sample size and determine power. *Structural Equation Modeling: A Multidisciplinary Journal*, *9*(4), 599–620.

Nevitt, J., & Hancock, G. R. (2004). Evaluating small sample approaches for model test statistics in structural equation modeling. *Multivariate Behavioral Research*, *39*(3), 439–478.

Rosseel, Y. (2012). Lavaan: An R package for structural equation modeling. *Journal of Statistical Software*, *48*(2), 1–36.

Savalei, V. (2010). Small sample statistics for incomplete non-normal data: Extensions of complete data formulae and a Monte Carlo comparison. *Structural Equation Modeling: A Multidisciplinary Journal*, *17*(2), 241–264.

Savalei, V. (2018). A comparison of several approaches for controlling measurement error in small samples. *Psychological Methods*. Advance online publication. doi: http://dx.doi.org/10.1037/met0000181.

Savalei, V., & Kolenikov, S. (2008). Constrained versus unconstrained estimation in structural equation modeling. *Psychological Methods*, *13*(2), 150–170.

Shi, D., Lee, T., & Terry, R. A. (2018). Revisiting the model size effect in structural equation modeling. *Structural Equation Modeling: A Multidisciplinary Journal*, *25*(1), 21–40.

Skrondal, A., & Laake, P. (2001). Regression among factor scores. *Psychometrika*, *66*(4), 563–575.

Swain, A. J. (1975). *Analysis of parametric structures for variance matrices* (Unpublished doctoral dissertation), University of Adelaide, Department of Statistics.

Takane, Y., & Hwang, H. (2018). Comparisons among several consistent estimators of structural equation models. *Behaviormetrika*, *45*(1), 157–188.

Thoemmes, F., Rosseel, Y., & Textor, J. (2018). Local fit evaluation of structural equation models using graphical criteria. *Psychological Methods*, *23*(1), 27.

Tibshirani, R. J. (1996). Regression shrinkage and selection via the lasso. *Journal of the Royal Statistical Society. Series B (methodological)*, *58*(1), 267–288.

Wolf, E. J., Harrington, K. M., Clark, S. L., & Miller, M. W. (2013). Sample size requirements for structural equation models: An evaluation of power, bias, and solution propriety. *Educational and Psychological Measurement*, *73*(6), 913–934.

Yuan, K.-H., & Bentler, P. M. (1997). Improving parameter tests in covariance structure analysis. *Computational Statistics & Data Analysis*, *26*(2), 177–198.

Yuan, K.-H., & Hayashi, K. (2006). Standard errors in covariance structure models: Asymptotics versus bootstrap. *British Journal of Mathematical and Statistical Psychology*, *59*(2), 397–417.

Yuan, K.-H., Tian, Y., & Yanagihara, H. (2015). Empirical correction to the likelihood ratio statistic for structural equation modeling with many variables. *Psychometrika*, *80*(2), 379–405.

Yung, Y.-F., & Bentler, P. M. (1996). Bootstrapping techniques in analysis of mean and covariance structures. In G. A. Marcoulides & R. E. Schumacker (Eds.), *Advanced structural equation modeling* (pp. 195–226). Mahwah, NJ: Lawrence Erlbaum.

Zhang, C.-H. (2010). Nearly unbiased variable selection under minimax concave penalty. *Annals of Statistics*, *38*(2), 894–942.

17

SEM WITH SMALL SAMPLES

Two-step modeling and factor score regression versus Bayesian estimation with informative priors

Sanne C. Smid

DEPARTMENT OF METHODOLOGY AND STATISTICS, UTRECHT UNIVERSITY, UTRECHT, THE NETHERLANDS

Yves Rosseel

DEPARTMENT OF DATA ANALYSIS, GHENT UNIVERSITY, GHENT, BELGIUM

Introduction

Bayesian estimation is regularly suggested as a beneficial method when sample sizes are small, as pointed out by systematic literature reviews in many fields, such as: organizational science (Kruschke, 2010), psychometrics (Rupp, Dey & Zumbo, 2004), health technology (Spiegelhalter, Myles, Jones & Abrams, 2000), epidemiology (Rietbergen, Debray, Klugkist, Janssen & Moons, 2017), education (König & Van de Schoot, 2017), medicine (Ashby, 2006) and psychology (Van de Schoot, Winter, Ryan, Zondervan-Zwijnenburg & Depaoli, 2017). Similarly, many simulation studies have shown the advantages of applying Bayesian estimation to address small sample size issues for structural equation models (SEMs), instead of using frequentist methods (see, for example, Depaoli, 2013; B. O. Muthén & Asparouhov, 2012; Stegmueller, 2013; Van de Schoot, Broere, Perryck, Zondervan-Zwijnenburg & Van Loey, 2015; Van Erp, Mulder & Oberski, 2018). However, as discussed in McNeish (2016) and echoed in the systematic literature review of Smid, McNeish, Miočević and Van de Schoot (2019), the use of Bayesian estimation with only diffuse default priors can cause extremely biased estimates when samples are small. The specification of informative priors is therefore required when Bayesian estimation is used with small samples.

Besides using Bayesian estimation with informative priors, there are also options for analyzing SEMs with small samples within the frequentist framework. Many studies have shown that the use of maximum likelihood (ML) estimation with small samples can result in convergence problems, inadmissible parameter solutions and biased estimates (see, for example, Boomsma, 1985; Nevitt & Hancock, 2004). Two newly introduced and promising frequentist methods to analyze SEMs with small samples are two-step modeling (two-step) and factor score regression (FSR). A recent development is the implementation of two-step and FSR in the accessible software `lavaan` (Rosseel, 2012), as discussed in Chapter 16 (Rosseel). In two-step, the measurement models for the latent variables are estimated separately as a first step. As a second step, the remaining parameters are estimated while the parameters of the measurement models are kept fixed to their estimated values. Two-step originates from work of Burt (1976) and Anderson and Gerbing (1988), and more recent work can be found in the latent class literature (e.g., Bakk, Oberski, & Vermunt, 2014). In FSR, each latent variable in the model is replaced by factor scores and subsequently path analysis or regression analysis is run using those factor scores. Recent developments in FSR can be found in studies of Croon (2002); Devlieger, Mayer and Rosseel (2016); Devlieger and Rosseel (2017), Hoshino and Bentler (2013), and Takane and Hwang (2018).

No simulation studies were found in which two-step and FSR are compared to Bayesian estimation. Therefore, the goal of this chapter is to examine the performance of the following estimation methods under varying sample sizes: two-step, FSR, ML estimation and Bayesian estimation with three variations in the specification of prior distributions. The remainder of the chapter is organized as follows: next, the statistical model will be discussed, as well as software details, the simulation conditions, and evaluation criteria. Then, results of the simulation study will be described. We end the chapter with a summary of the results, and recommendations on when to use which estimation method in practice.

Simulation design

Statistical model

The model of interest in this simulation study is an SEM in which latent variable X is predicting latent variable Y; see Figure 17.1. Both latent variables are measured by three continuous indicators. The model and population values are similar to the model discussed in Rosseel and Devlieger (2018). The parameter of interest in the current chapter is the regression coefficient β. The standardized regression coefficient, β^Z, is 0.243, which can be considered a small effect according to Cohen (1988).

Software details

Data sets were generated and analyzed in R version 3.4.4. (R Core Team, 2013), using packages `lavaan` version 0.6–1 (Rosseel, 2012) for the analyses of two-step, FSR and ML; and `blavaan` version 0.3–2 (Merkle & Rosseel, 2018) for the analyses of the Bayesian conditions. Example code of the analyses using the six

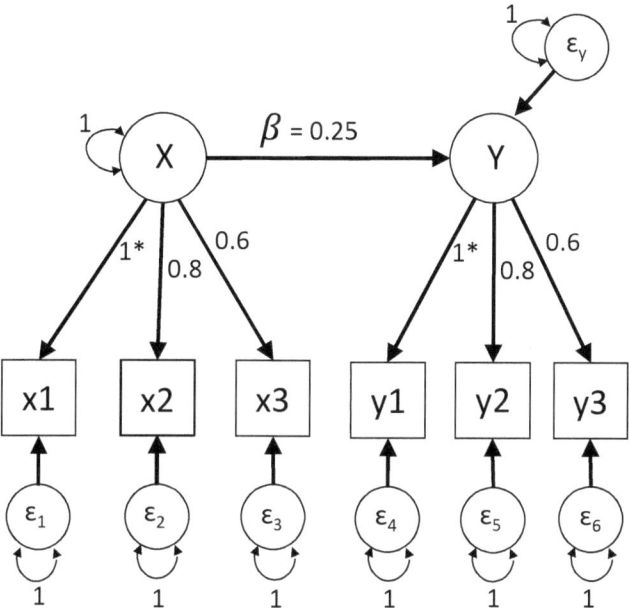

FIGURE 17.1 The model and unstandardized population values used in the simulation study. For scaling, the first factor loading for each factor is fixed to 1 (denoted by 1* in the figure), and the means of the latent variables are fixed to zero (not shown in the figure)

estimation methods can be found in supplemental file S1. All simulation code and supplemental files are available online (osf.io/bam2v/).

Six levels of sample size were examined, and for each sample size 1,000 data sets were generated according to the model and population values shown in Figure 17.1. Each generated data set was analyzed using six estimation methods. Accordingly, a total of 6 (sample size) * 6 (estimation methods) = 36 cells were investigated in the simulation design.

Simulation conditions

Six levels of sample size are studied: 10, 20, 50, 100, 250 and 500 to investigate how sample size influences the performance of the varying estimation methods. For the current model, sample sizes of 10 and 20 are extremely small. A sample size of 50 is considered small, and sample sizes of 100 and 250 are considered medium. The sample size of 500 is considered large and included as a benchmark.

Six estimation methods are considered in the current study: three frequentist estimation methods – two-step, FSR and ML – and Bayesian estimation with three types of prior specifications. For the three frequentist methods, all default settings of the `lavaan` package were used. For the default settings, see the help page for `lavOptions()` in the `lavaan` package. For the Bayesian methods, we used four chains instead of the two default chains. In terms of convergence, we used the Potential

Scale Reduction (PSR) factor, set it to a stricter criterion of 1.01, and used the following minimum number of iterations: a fixed burn-in period of 10,000 iterations (specified in blavaan by adapt = 2,000, burnin = 8,000), and for the sampling period 20,000 iterations (specified in blavaan by sample = 20.000)[1]. As an additional check, we visually assess convergence for two randomly selected data sets for each of the sample sizes and the Bayesian conditions (2 data sets * 6 sample sizes * 3 Bayesian conditions = 36 cases), by inspecting the traceplots for all parameters.

Three variants of prior specifications were examined, and all priors were specified for unstandardized parameters: BayesDefault, BayesInfoI, and BayesInfoII; see Table 17.1. The BayesDefault condition refers to a naïve use of Bayesian estimation, where only blavaan default priors are used. The BayesInfoI and BayesInfoII conditions refer to research situations where weakly prior information is available. In BayesInfoI, weakly informative priors are specified for the factor loadings, and blavaan default priors are specified for the remaining parameters. In BayesInfoII, weakly informative priors are used for both the factor loadings *and* regression coefficient β, in combination with blavaan default priors for the remaining parameters. Weakly informative priors were specified as follows: we set the mean hyperparameter of the normal distribution equal to the population value, and the precision hyperparameter equal to 1.

Evaluation criteria

For each of the estimation methods and sample sizes, the occurrence of convergence problems and warnings will be assessed. For the parameter of interest, regression coefficient β, the following evaluation criteria will be used to evaluate the performance under the varying estimation methods and sample sizes: relative mean bias, relative median bias, mean squared error (MSE), coverage and power. All evaluation criteria will be computed across completed replications[2].

Relative mean bias shows the difference between the average estimate across completed replications and the population value, relative to the population value. Relative median bias shows the relative difference between the median

TABLE 17.1 Specified prior distributions for the three Bayesian conditions

Parameter	BayesDefault	BayesInfoI	BayesInfoII
Factor loadings	$\mathcal{N}(0, 0.01)$	$\mathcal{N}(pop, 1)$	$\mathcal{N}(pop, 1)$
Regression coefficient β	$\mathcal{N}(0, 0.01)$	$\mathcal{N}(0, 0.01)$	$\mathcal{N}(pop, 1)$
Variances latent variables*	$G(1, 0.5)$	$G(1, 0.5)$	$G(1, 0.5)$
Intercepts observed variables	$\mathcal{N}(0, 0.01)$	$\mathcal{N}(0, 0.01)$	$\mathcal{N}(0, 0.01)$
Residual variances observed variables*	$G(1, 0.5)$	$G(1, 0.5)$	$G(1, 0.5)$

Note. The column BayesDefault shows the blavaan default priors (Merkle & Rosseel, 2018).
* Note that in blavaan the default priors are placed on precisions, which is the inverse of the variances.
Abbreviations: $\mathcal{N}$ = Normal distribution with mean μ and precision τ; G = Gamma distribution with shape α and rate β parameters on the precision (which equals an Inverse Gamma prior with shape α and rate β parameters on the variance); *pop* = population value used in data generation.

across completed replications and the population value. The relative mean and median bias are computed by:

$$\text{Relative mean bias} = \left[(\bar{\theta} - \theta)/\theta\right] \times 100,$$

$$\text{Relative median bias} = \left[(\tilde{\theta} - \theta)/\theta\right] \times 100,$$

where $\bar{\theta}$ denotes the mean across completed replications, θ is the population value used for data generation, and $\tilde{\theta}$ denotes the median across completed replications. Values of relative mean and median bias below -10% or above +10% represent problematic levels of bias (Hoogland & Boomsma, 1998).

MSE is a combination of variability and bias across completed replications, where lower values indicate more stable and less biased estimates across replications. The MSE is computed by: $MSE = (\sigma)^2 + (\bar{\theta} - \theta)^2$, where σ is the standard deviation across completed replications, $\bar{\theta}$ denotes the average estimate across completed replications and θ is the population value (Casella & Berger, 2002). A narrower distribution of estimates across replications (i.e., less-variable estimates) leads to a smaller standard deviation across completed replications. Besides, the closer the estimated values are to the population value across completed replications, the smaller the amount of bias. MSE will be lower (and thus preferable) when the standard deviation and amount of bias across completed replications are small.

Coverage shows the proportion of completed replications for which the symmetric 95% confidence (for frequentist methods) or credibility (for Bayesian methods) interval contains the specified population value. Coverage values can range between 0 and 100, and values within the [92.5; 97.5] interval are considered to represent good parameter coverage (Bradley, 1978).

Finally, statistical power is expressed as the proportion of estimates for which the 95% confidence (for frequentist methods) or credibility (for Bayesian methods) interval did not contain zero, across completed replications. Power values can range from 0 to 100, where values above 80 are preferred (Casella & Berger, 2002).

Results

Convergence

With small samples, we encountered severe convergence problems when frequentist methods were used; see Table 17.2. Differences between the three frequentist methods were especially visible when $n < 100$. With $n < 100$, two-step resulted in most non-converged cases, followed by ML, and finally followed by FSR.

The three Bayesian conditions produced results in all 1,000 requested replications under all sample sizes[3]. However, when visually examining trace plots (for 2 randomly selected data sets * 6 sample sizes * 3 Bayesian conditions = 36 cases), severe convergence problems were detected for the smaller sample sizes, such as mode-switching; see Figure 17.2A. Mode-switching is defined as a chain that moves back

TABLE 17.2 Number of completed replications, number of warnings about negative variance estimates, and number of completed replications without negative variance estimates for two-step, FSR and ML under varying sample sizes.

n	Completed replications out of 1,000 requested replications			Number (%) of warnings of the completed replications			Number of completed replications without negative variance estimates		
	Two-step	FSR	ML	Two-step	FSR	ML	Two-step	FSR	ML
10	475	641	533	259 (54.5%)	432 (67.4%)	446 (83.7%)	216	209	87
20	605	797	744	167 (27.6%)	360 (45.2%)	419 (56.3%)	438	437	325
50	809	970	955	41 (5.1%)	202 (20.8%)	217 (22.7%)	768	768	738
100	950	999	997	9 (0.9%)	58 (5.8%)	52 (5.2%)	941	941	945
250	1000	1000	1000	0	0	1 (0.1%)	1000	1000	999
500	999	1000	1000	0	1 (0.1%)	0	999	999	1000

Note. n = sample size, Two-step = two-step modeling; FSR = factor score regression, ML = maximum likelihood estimation.

and forth between different modes (Erosheva & Curtis, 2011; Loken, 2005), such as the chains in Figure 17.2A which move back and forth between values 5 and -5.

To further examine the extent of Bayesian convergence problems, we assessed trace plots for another 25 randomly selected data sets (resulting in 25 data sets * 6 sample sizes * 3 Bayesian conditions = 450 cases). In the assessment of these 25 selected data sets, mode-switching only occurred when BayesDefault was used when $n = 10$ or 20. Mode-switching disappeared when weakly informative priors were specified; see Figures 17.2B and 17.2C. Besides mode-switching, mild spikes were also detected when $n < 100$; see Figure 17.2D. Spikes are extreme values that are sampled during Markov Chain Monte Carlo iterations, and could be seen as severe outliers. The appearance of spikes was reduced by the specification of weakly informative priors; see Figures 17.2E and 17.2F. From $n = 100$ onward, no convergence problems were detected when default priors were used. For more details on the convergence checks and more examples of trace plots, see supplemental file S2 (osf.io/bam2v/).

Warnings

For all small sample sizes, the three frequentist methods lead to a high percentage of warnings within the number of completed replications; see Table 17.2. All warnings were about negative variance parameters[4]. Differences between the three methods were especially present when $n < 100$. For these sample sizes, ML led to the highest percentage of warnings, followed by FSR, and followed by two-step. As can be seen in Table 17.2, the number of warnings decreased when sample size increased. The number of completed replications without warnings about negative variance estimates is higher for two-step and FSR compared to ML, especially when $n < 100$.

For BayesDefault, three warnings about a small effective sample size occurred for $n = 10$, and two for $n = 20$[5]. No warnings occurred in the BayesInfoI and BayesInfoII conditions.

Results for regression coefficient β

In Figure 17.3, the relative mean bias (top) and relative median bias (bottom) are presented for the varying sample sizes and estimation methods. Because of the large discrepancy between the mean relative bias and median relative bias for sample sizes below 100, we plotted the complete distribution of parameter estimates for $β$ across replications; see Figure 17.4. For all estimation methods, an increase in sample size led to: a decrease in the number of outliers; a narrower distribution of estimates (i.e., estimates are more stable across replications); and estimates closer to the population value. With samples as small as 10 and 20, the distributions of estimates are wider and a lot of outliers are present, which are signs of unstable estimates across replications. ML produced the most extreme outliers (up to 37.57 when $n = 10$). FSR and two-step show the narrowest distribution of estimates, indicating relatively stable behavior across replications.

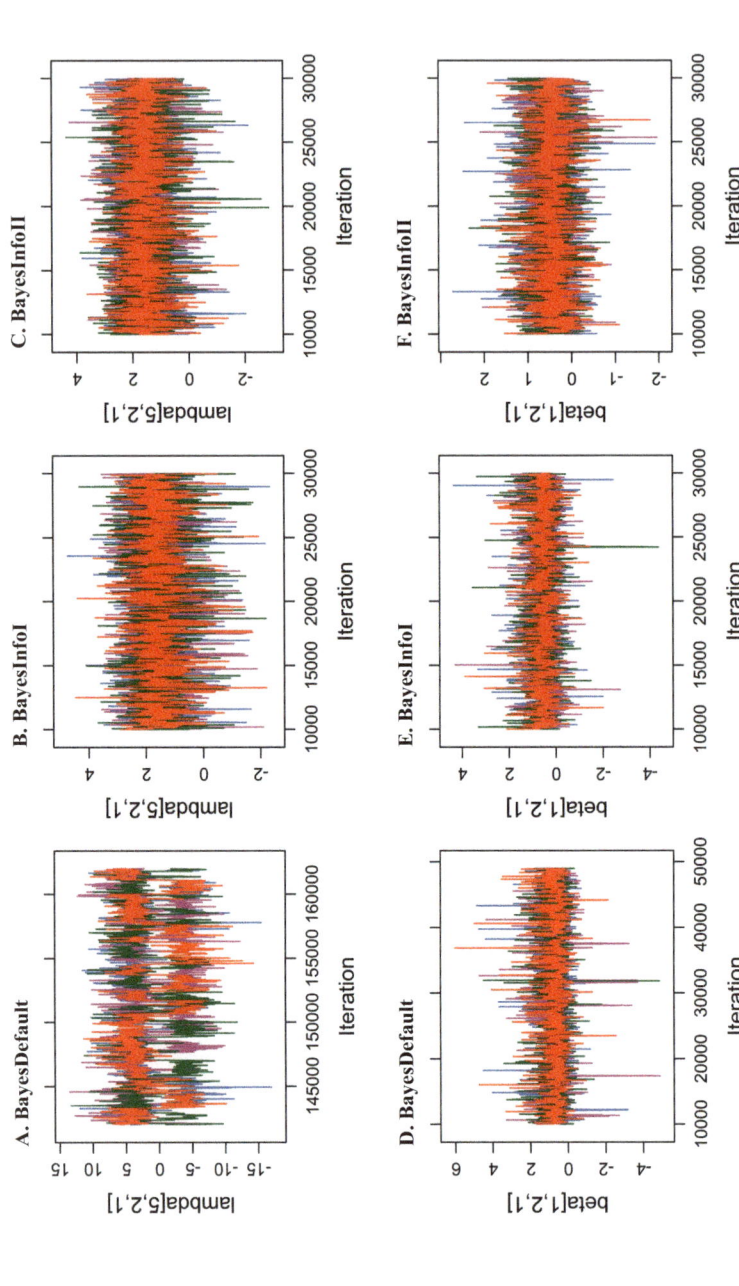

FIGURE 17.2 Trace plots for factor loading 5 (A–C), and regression coefficient β (D–F) after the analysis of BayesDefault, BayesInfoI and BayesInfoII. Trace plots A–C correspond to the analysis of replicated data set 802 (within the simulation study) with a sample size of 10. Trace plots D–F correspond to the analysis of replicated data set 260 (within the simulation study) with a sample size of 20

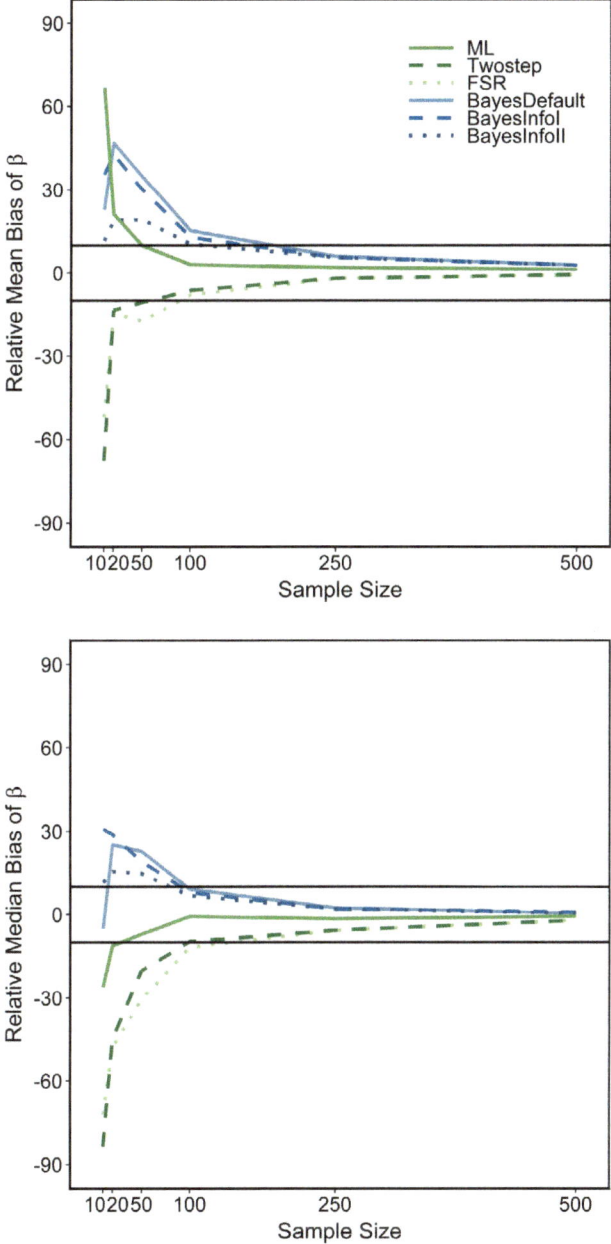

FIGURE 17.3 Relative Mean Bias (top) and Relative Median Bias (bottom) for parameter β, under varying sample sizes and estimation methods. The static black horizontal lines represent the desired ±10% interval

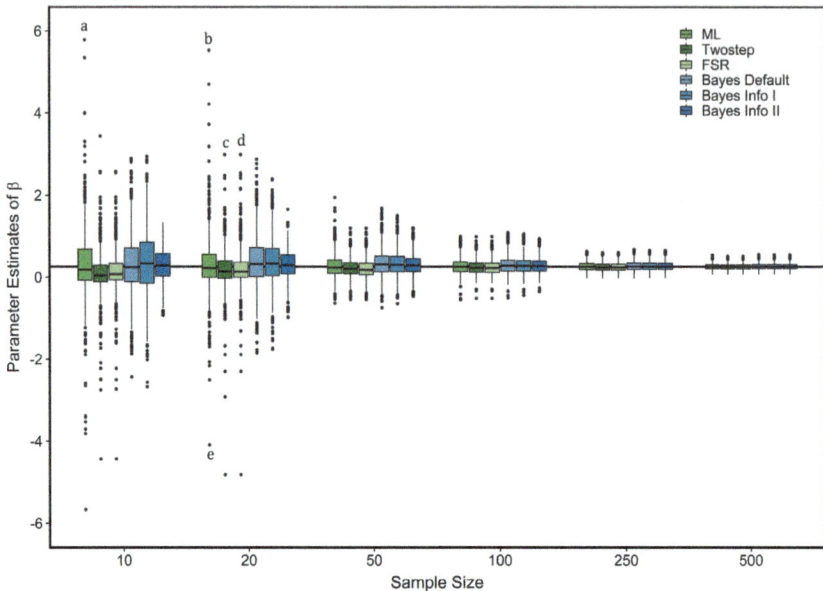

FIGURE 17.4 Distribution of the estimates for parameter β across completed replications, per estimation method and sample size. The static black horizontal line denotes the true population value of 0.25 for β. Outliers are displayed as black circles, and outliers outside the interval [-6; 6] are denoted as follows: [a] denotes 11.39, 11.46, 14.87, 37.57 for ML when $n = 10$; [b] denotes 6.49, 8.89, 9.12 for ML when $n = 20$; [c] denotes 6.86, 6.89 for two-step when $n = 20$; [d] denotes 6.86, 6.89 for FSR when $n = 20$; and [e] denotes -17.76 for ML when $n = 20$

Overall, BayesInfoII offers the best compromise between bias and stability: a narrow distribution of estimates, a mean and median close to the population value, and the smallest number of outliers. When $n = 100$, the differences between estimation methods become smaller; and the estimates become more stable across replications. For sample sizes of 250 and 500, differences between estimation methods are negligible and all estimation methods led to unbiased relative means and medians.

MSE for the regression coefficient β can be found in Figure 17.5A. Results are comparable to those shown in Figures 17.3 and 17.4. Differences between methods are especially visible when sample sizes are below 100. From $n = 100$ onward, MSE values are all close to zero. ML shows the highest MSE values for $n = 10$ and 20. BayesInfoI shows higher MSE than BayesDefault for $n = 10$, which was also visible in Figure 17.4 from the wider distribution of BayesInfoI relative to the distribution of BayesDefault for $n = 10$. The lowest MSE values are reported for BayesInfoII, followed by FSR, two-step, BayesDefault and BayesInfoI at $n = 10$. MSE values for FSR, two-step, BayesDefault and BayesInfoI are similar at $n = 20$, while BayesInfoII keeps the lowest MSE value. When

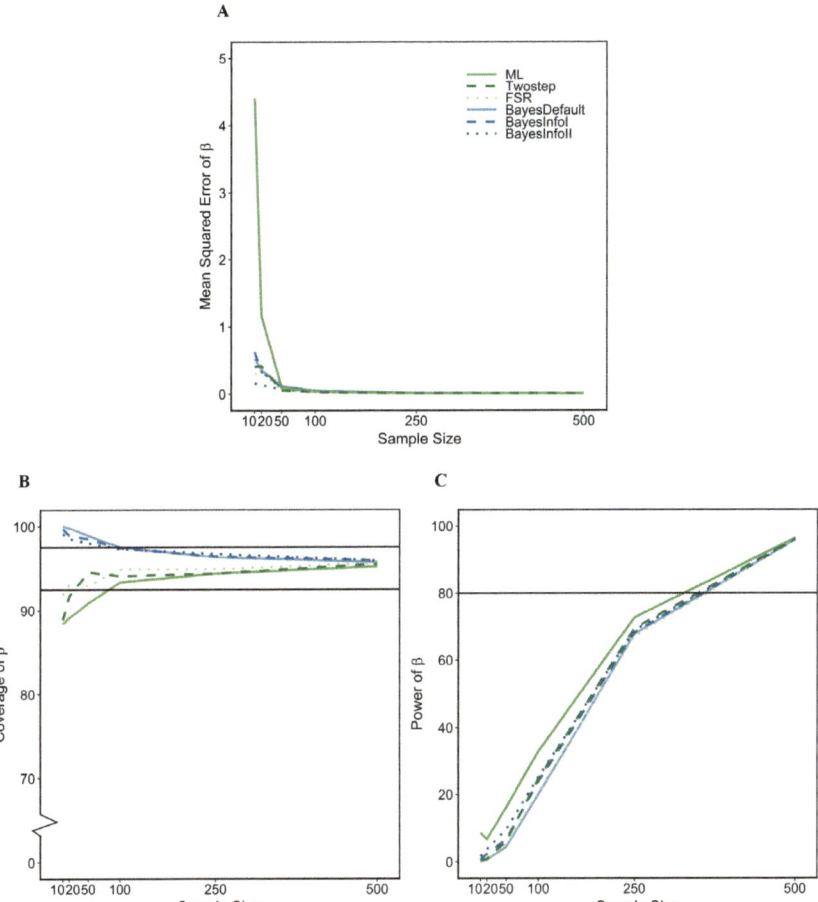

FIGURE 17.5 Mean Squared Error (A), Coverage (B), and Power (C) for parameter β, under varying sample sizes and estimation methods. The static black horizontal lines in subfigure B represent the [92.5; 97.5] coverage interval, and the black horizontal line in subfigure C represents the desired 80% power level

$n = 50$ MSE values are comparable between methods, and from $n = 100$ onward the differences in MSE between methods are negligible.

Coverage results for regression coefficient β can be found in Figure 17.5B. All estimation methods show adequate coverage levels from $n = 100$ onward. For $n < 100$, the three Bayesian conditions show excessive coverage (> 97.50), although this slightly improved under BayesInfoI and BayesInfoII. Within the three frequentist methods, two-step and FSR resulted in higher coverage levels than ML. When $n < 100$, ML shows undercoverage (< 92.50), while FSR only shows slight undercoverage when $n = 10$, and two-step when $n = 10$ and 20.

Results in terms of power can be found in Figure 17.5C. For all estimation methods, power is extremely low when the sample size is small, and only reached the desirable power level when $n = 500$. Across all sample sizes, the highest power levels are found for ML, followed by BayesInfoII, BayesInfoI, and two-step. The lowest power levels are found for FSR and BayesDefault.

Results for remaining parameters

Besides regression coefficient β, 12 remaining parameters are estimated in the model: two variances for latent variables, four factor loadings and six residual variances[6]. In supplemental file S3 (osf.io/bam2v/), the distributions of parameter estimates across replications are displayed for the remaining parameters.

Estimates for these 12 parameters seem similar across estimation methods and have good statistical properties when $n = 250$ and 500. However, with sample sizes of 100 and below, frequentist methods show many (extreme) outliers and wide distributions, indicating unstable results across replications. Bayesian methods show notably fewer outliers and in general narrower distributions than the frequentist methods, especially under BayesInfoI and BayesInfoII conditions, although the medians of the distributions still deviate from the population values when $n < 100$.

Conclusion

In this chapter, we assessed – under varying sample sizes – the performance of three frequentist methods: two-step, FSR and ML estimation; and Bayesian estimation with three variations in prior specification. With sample sizes of 250 and 500, differences between estimation methods are negligible, and all methods led to stable and unbiased estimates. Consistent with existing simulation literature (e.g., Depaoli & Clifton, 2015; Hox & Maas, 2001; Van de Schoot et al., 2015) we found that ML led to severe convergence problems and a large amount of negative variance parameters when sample sizes are small. Compared to ML, both two-step and FSR led to better convergence rates without negative variances. Also, with small samples, two-step and FSR resulted in more stable results across replications and less extreme parameter estimates than ML. When Bayesian estimation was used with default priors, problematic mode-switching behavior of the chains did occur under small samples ($n = 10$, 20), even though the PSR values indicated that the overall model had converged. The presence of mode-switching can be a sign that the model is too complex for the data (Erosheva & Curtis, 2011).

Power is low for all estimation methods and only with a sample size of 500 was the desired level of 80 reached. The use of *weakly informative* priors (i.e., BayesInfoI and BayesInfoII conditions), as well as the specification of blavaan default priors for the remaining parameters, could explain why ML led to slightly higher power levels than Bayesian estimation in the current chapter (as opposed to previous studies; for example, Miočević, MacKinnon & Levy, 2017; Van de Schoot et al., 2015).

Also, the differences in power between default and informative prior conditions were smaller in the current chapter than expected. In previous studies (e.g., Van de Schoot et al., 2015; Zondervan-Zwijnenburg, Depaoli, Peeters & Van de Schoot, 2019), priors with varying precision hyperparameters (e.g., 10 and 1) were compared to Mplus default priors with a precision hyperparameter of 10^{-10} (L. K. Muthén & Muthén, 1998–2017). In the current chapter, the difference in precision hyperparameters between the informative (precision = 1) and default (precision = 0.01) conditions is noticeably smaller. This could explain why the increase in power with informative priors is lower in the current chapter than expected based on previous studies. Note that the level of informativeness of a prior distribution can only be interpreted relative to the observed data characteristics, and is therefore not generalizable to other studies (i.e., a weakly informative prior in one study can act as a highly informative prior in another study that uses different measurement instruments).

In summary, with extremely small sample sizes, all frequentist estimation methods showed signs of breaking down (in terms of non-convergence, negative variances, and extreme parameter estimates), as well as the Bayesian condition with default priors (in terms of mode-switching behavior). When increasing the sample size is not an option, we recommend using Bayesian estimation with informative priors. However, note that the influence of the prior on the posterior is extremely large with relatively small samples. Even with thoughtful choices of prior distributions, results should be interpreted with caution (see also Chapter 4 by Veen and Egberts) and a sensitivity analysis should be performed; see Depaoli and Van de Schoot (2017) and Van Erp et al. (2018) on how to perform a sensitivity analysis. When no prior information is available or researchers prefer not to use Bayesian methods, two-step and FSR are a safer choice than ML, although they can still result in non-convergence, negative variances, and biased estimates.

However, note that by adjusting the implementation of two-step and FSR, non-convergence problems could be circumvented by using an alternative non-iterative estimation method (instead of ML) to estimate the measurement and structural models (see Takane & Hwang, 2018); and as discussed in Chapter 16. In addition, negative variances could be avoided by restricting the parameter space to only allow positive values for variance parameters. Therefore, the preferred approach to implement two-step and FSR in small sample contexts should be further examined. We hope the current chapter is a starting point for future research in those directions.

Acknowledgement

The first author was supported by a grant from the Netherlands Organisation for Scientific Research: NWO-VIDI-452-14-006.

Notes

1 When the PSR criterion is not reached after the specified minimum number of iterations, the number of iterations is automatically increased until the PSR criterion is met. We adjusted the blavaan default for the maximum time that the software uses to increase the amount of iterations to "24 hours" instead of the default "5 minutes".
2 We defined completed replications as replications for which (1) the model did converge according to the optimizer and (2) for which for all parameters standard errors could be computed. If the model did not converge or standard errors were not computed for one or more parameters, we defined the replication as incomplete and excluded the replication from the aggregation of the results. All simulation code can be found in supplemental file S4 (osf.io/bam2v/).
3 Note that the number of iterations in the Bayesian analyses was automatically increased until the PSR criterion of 1.01 was reached.
4 The warning message that occurred for two-step, FSR and ML was: "some estimated ov [observed variables] variances are negative". For two-step and ML, a second message also occurred: "some estimated lv [latent variables] variances are negative".
5 The warning message for BayesDefault: "Small effective sample sizes (< 100) for some parameters". The effective sample size expresses the amount of information in a chain while taking autocorrelation into account; see Chapter 4.
6 Note that when FSR is used, only three parameters are estimated: regression coefficient β, the variance of latent variable X and the variance of latent variable Y.

References

Anderson, J. C., & Gerbing, D. W. (1988). Structural equation modeling in practice: A review and recommended two-step approach. *Psychological Bulletin*, *103*(3), 411.

Ashby, D. (2006). Bayesian statistics in medicine: A 25 year review. *Statistics in Medicine*, *25*(21), 3589–3631. doi:doi.org/10.1002/sim.2672.

Bakk, Z., Oberski, D. L., & Vermunt, J. K. (2014). Relating latent class assignments to external variables: Standard errors for correct inference. *Political Analysis*, *22*(4), 520–540. doi:10.1093/pan/mpu003.

Boomsma, A. (1985). Nonconvergence, improper solutions, and starting values in LISREL maximum likelihood estimation. *Psychometrika*, *50*(2), 229–242. doi:10.1007/BF02294248.

Bradley, J. V. (1978). Robustness? *British Journal of Mathematical Statistical Psychology*, *31*(2), 144–152.

Burt, R. S. (1976). Interpretational confounding of unobserved variables in structural equation models. *Sociological Methods & Research*, *5*(1), 3–52. doi:10.1177/004912417600500101.

Casella, G., & Berger, R. L. (2002). *Statistical inference* (2nd ed.). Pacific Grove, CA: Duxbury.

Cohen, J. (1988). *Statistical power analysis for the behavioral sciences* (2nd ed.). Hillsdale, NJ: Erlbaum.

Croon, M. (2002). Using predicted latent scores in general latent structure models. In G. A. Marcoulides & I. Moustaki (Eds.), *Latent variable and latent structure models* (pp. 195–223). Mahwah, NJ: Lawrence Erlbaum.

Depaoli, S. (2013). Mixture class recovery in GMM under varying degrees of class separation: Frequentist versus Bayesian estimation. *Psychological Methods*, *18*(2), 186–219. doi:10.1037/a0031609.

Depaoli, S., & Clifton, J. P. (2015). A Bayesian approach to multilevel structural equation modeling with continuous and dichotomous outcomes. *Structural Equation Modeling: A Multidisciplinary Journal*, *22*(3), 327–351. doi:10.1080/10705511.2014.937849.

Depaoli, S., & Van de Schoot, R. (2017). Improving transparency and replication in Bayesian statistics: The WAMBS-Checklist. *Psychological Methods*, *22*(2), 240–261. doi:10.1037/met0000065.

Devlieger, I., Mayer, A., & Rosseel, Y. (2016). Hypothesis testing using factor score regression: A comparison of four methods. *Educational and Psychological Measurement*, *76*(5), 741–770. doi:10.1177/0013164415607618.

Devlieger, I., & Rosseel, Y. (2017). Factor score path analysis: An alternative for SEM. *Methodology*, *13*, 31–38. doi:10.1027/1614-2241/a000130.

Erosheva, E. A., & Curtis, S. M. (2011). *Dealing with rotational invariance in Bayesian confirmatory factor analysis*. Technical Report. Seattle, WA: Department of Statistics, University of Washington, 35.

Hoogland, J. J., & Boomsma, A. (1998). Robustness studies in covariance structure modeling: An overview and a meta-analysis. *Sociological Methods Research in Higher Education*, *26*(3), 329–367.

Hoshino, T., & Bentler, P. M. (2013). Bias in factor score regression and a simple solution. In A. De Leon & K. Chough (Eds.), *Analysis of mixed data* (pp. 43–61). Boca Raton, FL: Chapman & Hall/CRC Press.

Hox, J. J., & Maas, C. J. M. (2001). The accuracy of multilevel structural equation modeling with pseudobalanced groups and small samples. *Structural Equation Modeling: A Multidisciplinary Journal*, *8*(2), 157–174. doi:10.1207/S15328007SEM0802_1.

König, C., & Van de Schoot, R. (2017). Bayesian statistics in educational research: A look at the current state of affairs. *Educational Review*, 1–24. doi:10.1080/00131911.2017.1350636.

Kruschke, J. K. (2010). Bayesian data analysis. *Wiley Interdisciplinary Reviews: Cognitive Science*, *1*(5), 658–676. doi:10.1002/wcs.72.

Loken, E. (2005). Identification constraints and inference in factor models. *Structural Equation Modeling: A Multidisciplinary Journal*, *12*(2), 232–244. doi:10.1207/s15328007sem1202_3.

McNeish, D. (2016). On using Bayesian methods to address small sample problems. *Structural Equation Modeling: A Multidisciplinary Journal*, *23*(5), 750–773. doi:10.1080/10705511.2016.1186549.

Merkle, E. C., & Rosseel, Y. (2018). Blavaan: Bayesian structural equation models via parameter expansion. *Journal of Statistical Software*, *85*(4), 1–30. doi:10.18637/jss.v085.i04.

Miočević, M., MacKinnon, D. P., & Levy, R. (2017). Power in Bayesian mediation analysis for small sample research. *Structural Equation Modeling: A Multidisciplinary Journal*, *24*(5), 666–683. doi:10.1080/10705511.2017.1312407.

Muthén, B. O., & Asparouhov, T. (2012). Bayesian structural equation modeling: A more flexible representation of substantive theory. *Psychological Methods*, *17*(3), 313–335. doi:10.1037/a0026802.

Muthén, L. K., & Muthén, B. O. (1998-2017). *Mplus user's guide*. Los Angeles, CA: Muthén & Muthén.

Nevitt, J., & Hancock, G. R. (2004). Evaluating small sample approaches for model test statistics in structural equation modeling. *Multivariate Behavioral Research*, *39*(3), 439–478. doi:10.1207/S15327906MBR3903_3.

R Core Team. (2013). R: A language and environment for statistical computing. R Foundation for Statistical Computing, Vienna, Austria. URL https://www.R-project.org/.

Rietbergen, C., Debray, T. P. A., Klugkist, I., Janssen, K. J. M., & Moons, K. G. M. (2017). Reporting of Bayesian analysis in epidemiologic research should become more transparent. *Journal of Clinical Epidemiology*, *86*, 51–58. e52 10.1016/j.jclinepi.2017.04.008.

Rosseel, Y. (2012). lavaan: An R package for structural equation modeling. *Journal of Statistical Software, 48*(2), 1–36.

Rosseel, Y., & Devlieger, I. (2018). *Why we may not need SEM after all.* Amsterdam: Meeting of the SEM Working Group.

Rupp, A. A., Dey, D. K., & Zumbo, B. D. (2004). To Bayes or not to Bayes, from whether to when: Applications of Bayesian methodology to modeling. *Structural Equation Modeling: A Multidisciplinary Journal, 11*(3), 424–451. doi:10.1207/s15328007sem1103_7.

Smid, S. C., McNeish, D., Miočević, M., & Van de Schoot, R. (2019). Bayesian versus frequentist estimation for structural equation models in small sample contexts: A systematic review. *Structural Equation Modeling: A Multidisciplinary Journal.* doi:10.1080/10705511.2019.1577140.

Spiegelhalter, D. J., Myles, J. P., Jones, D. R., & Abrams, K. R. (2000). Bayesian methods in health technology assessment: A review. *Health Technology Assessment, 4*(38), 1–130.

Stegmueller, D. (2013). How many countries for multilevel modeling? A comparison of frequentist and Bayesian approaches. *American Journal of Political Science, 57*(3), 748–761. doi:10.1111/ajps.12001.

Takane, Y., & Hwang, H. (2018). Comparisons among several consistent estimators of structural equation models. *Behaviormetrika, 45*(1), 157–188. doi:10.1007/s41237-017-0045-5.

Van de Schoot, R., Broere, J. J., Perryck, K. H., Zondervan-Zwijnenburg, M., & Van Loey, N. E. (2015). Analyzing small data sets using Bayesian estimation: The case of posttraumatic stress symptoms following mechanical ventilation in burn survivors. *European Journal of Psychotraumatology, 6*(1), 25216. doi:10.3402/ejpt.v6.25216.

Van de Schoot, R., Winter, S. D., Ryan, O., Zondervan-Zwijnenburg, M., & Depaoli, S. (2017). A systematic review of Bayesian articles in psychology: The last 25 years. *Psychological Methods, 22*(2), 217–239. doi:10.1037/met0000100.

Van Erp, S., Mulder, J., & Oberski, D. L. (2018). Prior sensitivity analysis in default Bayesian structural equation modeling. *Psychological Methods, 23*(2), 363–388. doi:10.1037/met0000162.

Zondervan-Zwijnenburg, M. A. J., Depaoli, S., Peeters, M., & Van de Schoot, R. (2019). Pushing the limits: The performance of ML and Bayesian estimation with small and unbalanced samples in a latent growth model. *Methodology.* doi:https://doi.org/10.1027/1614-2241/a000162.

18

IMPORTANT YET UNHEEDED
Some small sample issues that are often overlooked

Joop Hox

DEPARTMENT OF METHODOLOGY AND STATISTICS, UTRECHT UNIVERSITY, UTRECHT, THE NETHERLANDS

Introduction

When dealing with small samples, the customary approach is to worry which analysis method will work best with our data. With 'best' I mean providing good control of Type I error, and providing the most power, aptly called by Elstrodt and Mellenbergh (1978) 'One minus the forgotten fault'. However, there are other issues associated with small samples. This chapter considers five such issues not discussed in the previous chapters of the book: the accuracy of Ordinary Least Squares estimation, and the importance of assumptions, estimation methods, data characteristics, and research design with small samples.

The missing estimator: Ordinary Least Squares

The requirements for minimal sample sizes in this book are often discussed in the context of Maximum Likelihood (ML; Chapters 6, 7, 11, 13, 14, 16) or Bayesian estimation methods (Chapters 1–5, 8–10, 12) or both (Chapters 15 and 17). This overlooks the existence of Ordinary Least Squares estimation (OLS). OLS is an estimation method for unknown parameters in a model that minimizes the sum of squares of the residuals. OLS includes well-known analysis techniques such as correlation, multiple regression, *t*-tests, (M)ANOVA, and the like, but it is also available in most structural equation modeling (SEM) packages as the Unweighted Least Squares method (Bollen, 1989). Inference methods for OLS estimates have been developed to work with small samples, commonly defined as samples smaller than 30. OLS estimates are unbiased and efficient given some general assumptions (discussed below). There is no assumption of a minimal sample size; inference is based on well-known sampling distributions where the sample size is reflected in the number of degrees of freedom.

An example of OLS estimation is inference about an unknown population mean, when the population variance is also unknown. This points to Student's *t*-test, introduced in 1908 by Gosset, writing under the pseudonym 'Student' (Student, 1908). In the remainder of the chapter I will use a small example, omitting the complications of multivariate data for a moment. Table 18.1 presents test scores of 12 students on algebra and statistics tests; the example is taken from Good (1999, p. 89); see also the Open Science Framework page for code to reproduce the results (osf.io/am7pr/).

In this small data set, the OLS estimate for the correlation is the Pearson correlation between algebra and statistics $r = .677$, with a two-sided *p*-value of .016. We conclude that algebra and statistics are related skills. If we want to estimate a 95% confidence interval for this correlation, we face a serious problem. First, it is known that the sampling distribution of correlations is not normal; large correlations (such as .677) have a markedly skewed distribution (Hedges & Olkin, 1985, p. 225). The usual solution is to use a Fisher-Z transformation. Second, the standard error for Z, which is given by $1/\sqrt{N-3}$, is a large sample estimate. Our sample size is too small to use this approach. If we use this approach anyway, we apply the Fisher-Z transformation, use the standard normal distribution to establish the 95% confidence interval for Z, and transform the endpoints back to correlations.[1] The result is a 95% confidence interval for the correlation *r*, which runs from .151 to .897. Zero is excluded, and the confidence interval informs us that the null hypothesis should be rejected. We can compare the correlation of .677, its *p*-value, and the 95% OLS-based confidence interval to the results of alternative approaches.

In general, we want our estimates to be unbiased, efficient, and consistent. OLS estimation is unbiased if the covariance between the estimates and the error terms are zero, and the mean of the error terms is zero. OLS estimation is efficient and consistent if the observations are independent (an assumption always violated in multilevel modeling) and error terms are homoscedastic. Finally, for statistical inference we must assume (multivariate) normality.

The statement that OLS methods work well with small samples means in fact that, provided these assumptions are met, both estimates and standard errors are unbiased, and as a result the Type I error is under control. In the long run, if we calculate a 95% confidence interval for a parameter estimate, that interval will contain the true population value in 95% of our samples. Of course, as Bayesians like to point out, we will never know if a particular sample at hand is one of these 95% or not.

TABLE 18.1 Algebra and statistics scores of 12 students

| Algebra | 80 | 71 | 67 | 72 | 58 | 65 | 63 | 65 | 68 | 60 | 60 | 59 |
| Statistics | 81 | 81 | 81 | 73 | 70 | 68 | 68 | 63 | 56 | 54 | 45 | 44 |

What is definitively problematic with OLS and small samples is the power of the statistical tests. This was pointed out in the social sciences by Cohen (1962) and elaborated in his handbook on statistical power analysis (Cohen, 1977). Cohen showed that at sample sizes common in social psychology and related fields, the probability to reject a false null hypothesis is small. Translated in terms of 'One minus the forgotten fault', the probability to detect a specific effect (the power of the test) in a small sample reaches an acceptable value only for very large effects. This is also true for most other estimation methods, such as ML. For example, in a bidirectional (two-sided) test of a correlation in a sample of 30 cases, an α (nominal Type I error rate) of .05 and a desired power of .80, the population correlation must be at least .49 to meet these requirements. With a more modest population correlation of .30, and a sample size of 30 cases, the power to reject the null hypothesis at $\alpha = .05$ is only .37, i.e., notably lower than 50%.

In the context of OLS estimation there is little that can be done about the lack of power. One option is to switch to a directional test. In our example, this would reduce the required population correlation to .44, and in the second example power would increase to .50. These are certainly improvements, but they are not impressive. Another option is to increase the reliability of measurement, which is taken up in the section on design. Finally, an option rarely considered is to increase the criterion for the alpha level. Especially in explorative research, employing an alpha level of .10 is a defensible position (also for other estimation methods).

The importance of assumptions of OLS and how to avoid making these assumptions

Common assumptions in OLS-based multivariate data analysis are (multivariate) normality, which includes absence of outliers, linearity, and homoscedasticity. For ordinal data, proportional odds (parallel regression lines) are assumed, and for dichotomous data linearity in the logit. Most techniques also assume independent observations; notable exceptions are multilevel analysis and the MANOVA approach for repeated measures.

These assumptions can be assessed using statistical or graphical techniques. In small samples, most statistical techniques will suffer from the lack of power mentioned in the previous section. Deviations from assumptions have to be very large to be detected. In small samples, graphical methods, such as P–P normal plots for normality, and boxplots for detection of outliers may be superior to formal tests. Assessing bivariate linearity is generally done by scatterplots.

It is important to understand that the assumptions are about characteristics of the data in the population, while they are assessed in the sample. In small samples, large deviations in a sample from the population are to be expected. So, while formal statistical tests suffer from low power, inspecting graphs may lead to overinterpretation of violations of assumptions. Analysts may read too much into deviations that are totally expected in a small sample.

Some violations of assumptions can be overcome by transforming variables or removing outliers. In general, it is often assumed that with large samples the inference techniques are robust to mild violations of assumptions. Even for large samples this may be problematic (Bradley, 1982), but robustness certainly cannot be claimed for small samples based on the argument that it seems to work well for large samples. It should be noted that incomplete data analysis also relies more heavily on the required assumptions, so missing data analysis with small samples, although certainly possible (Graham & Schafer, 1999), should examine the data characteristics very carefully.

On the bright side: small samples are well suited for permutation tests. Permutation tests (also called randomization tests; for a review of the subtle differences between the two see Onghena, 2018) perform null-hypothesis tests by permuting the data. For example, to test the equality of the mean in two groups, the t-test has to make assumptions to justify using a Student distribution as the sampling distribution. A permutation test would calculate the difference of the means for all possible permutations that distribute the total sample into two groups of the given size. If the difference that is observed in the original sample is in the 5% extreme percentile of the permutation differences, it is considered extreme and significant, and the null hypothesis of no difference is rejected. In general, permutation tests have power close to or often exceeding that of their parametric counterparts, while making far fewer assumptions (Bradley, 1968; Edgington & Onghena, 2007). Even with large samples, a permutation test may be advisable if the distribution is not normal. In large samples it may not be possible to enumerate all possible permutations, in which case a large sample of all possible permutations is generated and analyzed.

For our example data involving 12 cases, a permutation test would keep the X constant, and pair these with permuted Y values. There are 12! possible permutations, approximately 480 million, so we sample 5,000 of these. The permuted p-value is .004. Figure 18.1 shows the observed correlation of .68 and its place in the permutation-based null distribution.

When small samples are analyzed, several issues typically arise. This chapter discusses four problem areas and potential solutions. First, multivariate analysis using OLS estimation does not assume large samples, and therefore works well with small samples, although these still lead to tests with low power. Second, analysis of small samples is more vulnerable to violations of assumptions, and data characteristics and analysis choices in estimation become more important. As a result, data cleaning and examination of potential violations of assumptions are crucial. Finally, problems with small samples are ameliorated by using research designs that yield more information.

The example of a permutation test described above tests the null hypothesis of exchangeability (see also Chapter 2 by Miočević, Levy, and Savord), which states that the correlation between the two variables can be fully explained by the random sampling (or random assignment) process that generates the data. Exchangeability can be violated, for example, if the data contain clusters, as in multilevel data (more about these later). Permutation tests are typically used to test a null hypothesis. They can be used to establish a confidence interval, but

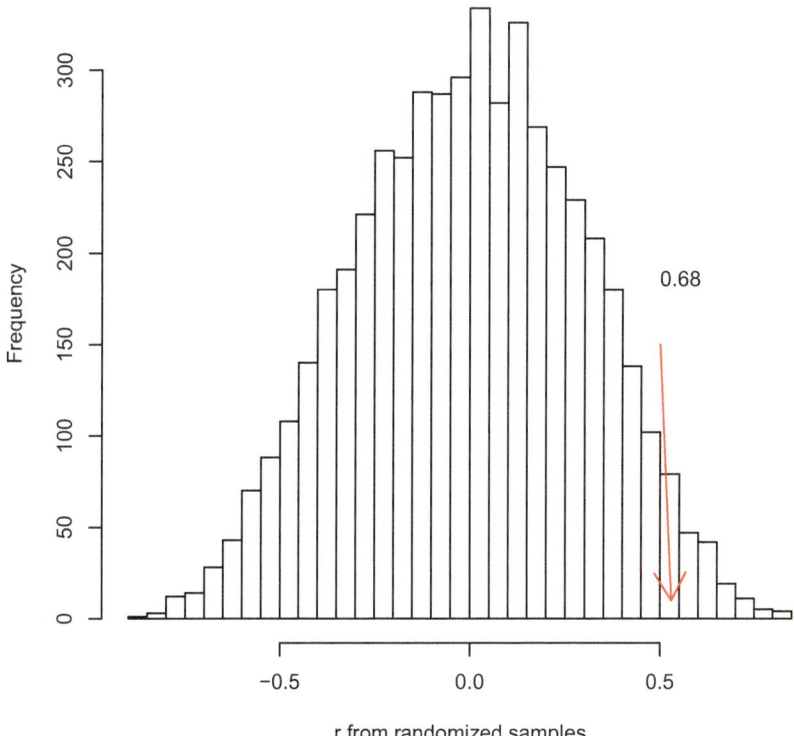

FIGURE 18.1 Permutation-based null distribution and observed *r*

this is more convoluted and computationally intensive. See Garthwaite (1996) for more details on permutation tests.

Permutation tests are similar to bootstrap tests. Bootstrapping estimates the sampling variability by drawing a large number of 'bootstrap' samples from the observed sample. In our example with two groups, bootstrapping would resample with replacement from the 12 cases, keeping the pair of *X-Y* values together, and calculate the correlation for each bootstrap sample. The distribution of the bootstrapped differences is taken as an estimate of the sampling distribution. From the bootstrapped sampling distribution, it is simple to establish a confidence interval. If the observed data are non-normal, it is assumed that this is reflected in the bootstrapped distribution, and therefore non-normality is accounted for. However, since bootstrapping often does not work well with samples smaller than 50 (Good, 2005), it is not really a small sample method. For our example data, the bootstrapped 95% confidence interval is .080–.934, which is much wider than the asymptotic confidence interval of .151–.897. The asymptotic confidence interval clearly underestimates the variability.

The importance of estimation methods and techniques

The parameters of a specific model, say a multilevel logistic regression model, could be estimated using a number of estimation methods. For each estimation method, there are several techniques available to obtain these parameter estimates. For example, in ML estimation we may employ the E–M algorithm or the Newton–Raphson algorithm to maximize the Likelihood. In Bayesian estimation we have not only a choice for different priors (see Chapter 2, and Chapter 3 by Van de Schoot, Veen, Smeets, Winter, and Depaoli), but also a choice of different Markov Chain Monte Carlo (MCMC) generators (see Chapter 3 for a comparison of the Gibbs sampler and the Hamiltonian Monte Carlo sampler). And finally, the same estimation technique may be programmed in different ways, including different defaults to decide when convergence has been reached. For example, popular multilevel analysis software such as HLM (Raudenbush, Bryk, & Congdon, 2011), MLwiN (Rasbash, Steele, Browne, & Goldstein, 2017) and Mplus (Muthén & Muthén, 1998–2017) all include ML as one of the available estimation methods, but all use different techniques to find the maximum of the Likelihood. HLM (version 7.0) uses E–M estimation and decides that the algorithm has converged when the difference between two successive iterations becomes small. MLwiN uses Iterative Least Squares, and Mplus chooses different default estimation methods depending on the model and the data. All this may result in small differences between programs in estimated values. For example, in a review of the three SEM programs AMOS, EQS, and LISREL, Hox (1995) reports almost identical parameter estimates, but some noticeable differences in the chi-square and other goodness-of-fit indices. To facilitate the study of the impact of differences in estimation technique or programming details, Rosseel (2012) developed the R package lavaan that allows the user to mimic the technique used in different SEM programs.

With large data sets, continuous outcomes, and reasonably simple models, these analysis differences generally do not matter much. With small samples and non-linear models, they do matter (Smid, McNeish, Miočević, & Van de Schoot, 2019). For example, multilevel logistic regression can be estimated using linearization (SPSS, HLM, MlwiN) or using numerical approximation (HLM, Mplus, R). With 'nice' sample sizes – for example, 30 groups of average size 30 – numerical estimation is more accurate. However, with small samples, especially a small sample of groups, convergence of the numerical integration algorithm is problematic, and linearization using Restricted Maximum Likelihood estimation is generally more accurate (see also Chapter 15 by Hox and McNeish).

One general issue with ML estimation is that with small samples it typically needs more iterations to converge. It may also converge to a local solution, which means that it converges to a large value for the Likelihood, but not on the largest. One way to approach the problem of local solutions is to repeat the analysis with different starting values, and examine whether the estimated values replicate. In some software this can be done by choosing an option for repeated random starting values.

Bayesian estimation in combination with small samples has two chief advantages. First, unlike ML estimation, it does not assume large samples. Second, the prior distributions for the parameters are generally chosen so that impossible values do not occur (see the explanation of the plausible parameter space in Chapter 3). For instance, an often-used prior for a variance is the Inverse Gamma distribution. This distribution includes only positive values, so a negative variance estimate cannot happen. However, with small samples the data carry little information, and as a result the influence of the prior becomes relatively larger. Also, in most software a larger number of MCMC iterations is needed (see Chapter 3 for an explanation). For our example, the default settings for Bayesian analysis in Mplus (Mplus version 8.0) do not converge. When the setup is changed to specify a large number of iterations, the correlation estimate stabilizes to three decimal places at 1,000,000 MCMC iterations; the correlation is estimated as .68 with a 95% credibility interval 0.160–0.960, which is somewhat wider than the asymptotic confidence interval of .151–.897. Clearly, with this small sample, reliance on the default Bayesian estimation settings is not good enough. For a discussion of sensitivity analyses and choice or priors for small samples, see Van de Schoot, Broere, Perryck, Zondervan-Zwijnenburg, and Van Loey (2015).

The importance of having 'nice' data

Example data in statistical handbooks are generally chosen to be 'nice', meaning that the sample size is sufficient, variables are normally distributed, and there are no outliers or missing data. As discussed in the section on assumptions, with small samples the estimation is less robust, and the impact of problematic data on the estimated values and their standard errors is larger. There are other issues to consider. For instance, when the variables in a multivariate model have widely different scales, estimation becomes more difficult. Thus, if a model contains the variable gender, coded 0–1, with a variance of .25, and an attitude variable that varies from 10 to 100 with a variance of 840, many estimation algorithms will have convergence problems. The simple solution is to divide the attitude scores by 10, or by the number of items in the scale, so they become more in line with the range of the other variables.

Transformation of variables can be helpful to make the data nicer. Skewed variables are commonly made less skewed by a square root or logarithmic transformation. For a general discussion on data cleaning see Tabachnick and Fidell (2013). However, transformations of dependent variables can also be used to simplify the model. For example, a multilevel logistic regression model is complicated, because it involves a nonlinear relation between the observed outcome and the linear predictor of that outcome. If the dependent variable is a proportion, the empirical logit transformation will linearize the outcome, and a multilevel linear model may be used. Similarly, if the dependent variable is a count, instead of using a Poisson model, a logarithmic transformation of the count variable will linearize the relations.

Using a proper nonlinear model is no doubt statistically more elegant, but with small samples it simply may not work.

Much of, if not most, real-world data are incomplete. Missing data are always a problem, not only because they make the analysis more complicated, but also because the missingness may not be random. Simple procedures available in standard software, such as deleting incomplete cases, do not work well with small samples, because they make the sample even smaller. Analysis methods that preserve all available information by incorporating incomplete cases in the analysis are necessary. An often-overlooked advantage of using more sophisticated estimation methods for incomplete cases is that these methods generally make weaker assumptions about the missingness mechanism. Deletion methods must assume that the remaining cases stem from the same population as the deleted cases, which assumes that the deleted cases are Missing Completely at Random. More principled methods to deal with incomplete cases generally assume data are Missing at Random, which is a weaker assumption. For a general discussion of incomplete data and how to deal with them, see Enders (2010). The three main methods to deal with incomplete data are Full Information Maximum Likelihood (FIML), Multiple Imputation (MI), and Bayesian estimation. All three methods have issues with small samples. FIML is a more complicated technique than standard estimation techniques for complete data, and as a result the problems mentioned earlier (convergence problems, local solutions) become worse. MI and Bayesian estimation tend to work better. MI fills the holes in the data set by imputing a plausible value and adding a random prediction error, producing multiple data files that include different errors. With small samples, two problems may arise. Imputations may be model-based or data-based. In model-based imputation, a general model, for example a multivariate normal model, is used to generate imputations. With small samples, there is little information about the model parameters, which makes generating good imputations difficult. Data-based imputation methods replace the missing values for a specific case by matching it to a similar case and filling in the missing values by observed values from the donor. With small samples, there may not be enough donors to produce a good match, and it may be necessary to use donors several times. To some extent, these problems can be addressed by using a large number of imputed data sets, such as 50–100.

In addition, whichever method is used, with a small and incomplete data set it becomes vital to perform sensitivity analyses to evaluate the effect of reasonable changes in the imputation technique or model specification on the resulting estimates, and to address the potential impact on the conclusions in the discussion.

The importance of design

As this volume shows, there are many clever ways to deal statistically with the problem of small samples. There is, however, one problem that no amount of analytical cleverness can eliminate; small samples contain little information. Information can be added by adding cases, but information can also be added in other ways: adding variables adds information, and increasing the reliability of measurement adds information.

Assume that we have a small randomized experiment with an experimental group and a control group. In principle a simple t-test will do. The t-test relies on least squares estimation of means and variances, so it has good Type I error rates in small groups. However, with small groups, the power to detect a real difference is small. One way to increase power is to use a one-sided test. However, one-sided tests have their problems, which have been discussed at length by Cohen (1965), referring to earlier publications by Burke (1953, 1954). One issue is that analysts using a one-sided test should be genuinely unconcerned when they find a hugely 'significant' effect in the unexpected direction. Most analysts would report this effect despite being in the unexpected direction, thereby increasing the actual alpha level to 7.5%. A second issue is that one-sided tests tend to be less robust than two-sided tests against violations of assumptions (Cohen, 1965). I do not recommend totally abandoning one-sided tests, but I do recommend contemplating the scientific wisdom of potentially having to ignore a huge difference in the unexpected direction.

Adding variables will make the data from our experimental design more informative, thereby increasing the power of the statistical test. The simplest and most powerful way to add information is to add a pretest and use this as a covariate. If the pretest is identical to the post-test, the correlation between the two is typically high. Since randomization is used, adding the pretest in an analysis of covariance does not change the expected difference between the groups, but it is likely to greatly reduce the residual error variance. Since the residual error variance determines the variance component in the denominator of the F-ratio, the F-ratio will be larger at the expense of one degree of freedom. Adding more covariates will continue to increase power until the point is reached that the increase in F-ratio is too small to offset the loss of one degree of freedom. Adding more post-tests also increases power, but generally less than adding a pretest does. Adding multiple outcome variables that are weakly correlated increases power; see Tabachnick and Fidell (2013) for a discussion of the question when a Multivariate Analysis of Variance increases power compared to a univariate Analysis of Variance. An extension of the design is to use a pretest, a post-test, and a later follow-up post-test. This still increases power, but the design is mostly used to answer the question whether the experimental effect, if any, persists over time. For a discussion of the various ways in which changes in the design of a study can impact the power of the statistical test, see Venter and Maxwell (1999).

Finally, measurement reliability affects the power of a test by attenuating the statistic being tested. In our algebra-statistics example, the correlation between the two is .677. Assume that the reliability of both tests is .705, which is not bad for an educational test. If we had been able to use the true scores, without error added by unreliability of measurement, the correlation between the two scores would be much higher. How much higher is indicated by the correction for attenuation, which is given by $r_{T_x, T_y} = r_{x,y}/\sqrt{r_{xx}r_{yy}}$, where T_x denotes the true score for x, and r_{xx} is the reliability of measure x, and T_y denotes the true score for y, and r_{yy} is the reliability of measure y. Plugging in the assumed values for our algebra and statistics tests, the correlation between the true scores is estimated to be .90. There is obvious room for improvement. If we manage to increase the reliability of the tests to .90, the observed correlation is expected to be .812, which can be detected more easily by the significance test. Increasing reliability of measurement increases the available information and thus increases the power of the significance test.

Conclusion

A general recommendation for small n studies is to increase the information in the data by using reliable measures and a smart research design. This is useful with all estimation methods. In the context of frequentist statistics, careful examination of potential violations of assumptions is essential. In addition, it is worthwhile to consider methods that rely less heavily on assumptions and large sample methods, such as permutation techniques.

Note

1 $z = \text{arctanh}(r) = 0.5 * \ln\frac{1+r}{1-r}$ and the inverse is $r = \tanh(z) = \frac{e^{2z}-1}{e^{2z}+1}$.

References

Bollen, K. A. (1989). *Structural equations with latent variables*. New York, NY: Wiley.
Bradley, J. V. (1968). *Distribution-free statistical tests*. Upper Saddle River, NJ: Prentice-Hall.
Bradley, J. V. (1982). The insidious L-shaped distribution. *Bulletin of the Psychonomic Society*, *20*(2), 85–88.
Burke, C. J. (1953). A brief note on one-tailed tests. *Psychological Bulletin*, *50*(5), 384–387.
Burke, C. J. (1954). Further remarks on one-tailed tests. *Psychological Bulletin*, *51*(6), 587–590.
Cohen, J. (1962). The statistical power of abnormal-social psychological research: A review. *Journal of Abnormal Social Psychology*, *65*(3), 145–153. doi:10.1037/h0045186.
Cohen, J. (1965). Some statistical issues in psychological research. In B. B. Wolman (Ed.), *Handbook of clinical psychology* (pp. 95–121). New York, NY: McGraw-Hill.
Cohen, J. (1977). *Statistical power analysis for the behavioral sciences*. New York, NY: Academic Press.
Edgington, E., & Onghena, P. (2007). *Randomization tests*. London: Chapman & Hall/CRC Press.
Elstrodt, M., & Mellenbergh, G. J. (1978). Eén minus de vergeten fout. *Nederlands Tijdschrift Voor De Psychologie*, *33*, 33–47.
Enders, C. K. (2010). *Applied missing data analysis*. New York, NY: Guilford Press.
Garthwaite, P. H. J. B. (1996). Confidence intervals from randomization tests. *Biometrics*, *52*, 1387–1393.
Good, P. (1999). *Resampling methods*. Boston, MA: Birkhäuser.

Good, P. (2005). *Permutation, parametric, and bootstrap tests of hypotheses* (3rd ed.). New York, NY: Springer.

Graham, J. W., & Schafer, J. L. (1999). On the performance of multiple imputation for multivariate data with small sample size. In R. H. Hoyle (Ed.), *Statistical strategies for small sample research* (pp. 1–32). Thousand Oaks, CA: Sage.

Hedges, L. V., & Olkin, I. (1985). *Statistical models for meta-analysis*. San Diego, CA: Academic Press.

Hox, J. J. (1995). Amos, EQS, and LISREL for Windows: A comparative review. *Structural Equation Modeling: A Multidisciplinary Journal, 2*(1), 79–91.

Muthén, L. K., & Muthén, B. O. (1998-2017). *Mplus user's guide*. Los Angeles, CA: Muthén & Muthén.

Onghena, P. (2018). Randomization tests or permutation tests? A historical and terminological clarification. In V. Berger (Ed.), *Randomization, masking, and allocation concealment* (pp. 209–228). London: Chapman & Hall/CRC Press.

Rasbash, J., Steele, F., Browne, W. J., & Goldstein, H. (2017). A user's guide to MLwiN, v3.00. Centre for Multilevel Modelling, University of Bristol.

Raudenbush, S. W., Bryk, A. S., & Congdon, R. (2011). *HLM 7.00 for Windows*. Lincolnwood, IL: Scientific Software International.

Rosseel, Y. (2012). lavaan: An R package for structural equation modeling. *Journal of Statistical Software, 48*(2), 1–36.

Smid, S. C., McNeish, D., Miočević, M., & Van de Schoot, R. (2019). Bayesian versus frequentist estimation for structural equation models in small sample contexts: A systematic review. *Structural Equation Modeling: A Multidisciplinary Journal*, 1–31. doi:10.1080/10705511.2019.1577140.

Student. (1908). The probable error of a mean. *Biometrika, 6*, 1–25.

Tabachnick, B. G., & Fidell, L. S. (2013). *Using multivariate statistics* (6th ed.). Boston, MA: Pearson.

Van de Schoot, R., Broere, J. J., Perryck, K. H., Zondervan-Zwijnenburg, M., & Van Loey, N. E. (2015). Analyzing small data sets using Bayesian estimation: The case of posttraumatic stress symptoms following mechanical ventilation in burn survivors. *European Journal of Psychotraumatology, 6*(1), 25216. doi:10.3402/ejpt.v6.25216.

Venter, A., & Maxwell, S. E. (1999). Maximizing power in randomized designs when N is small. In R. H. Hoyle (Ed.), *Statistical strategies for small sample research* (pp. 33–598). Thousand Oaks, CA: Sage.

INDEX

30/30 rule 216–217

a priori parceling 211
adaptive stopping 150–153
All rule 141, *148*, 149
alternation design 90–92
AN(C)OVA 126–127, 128, 157–158, 160–166, 173–184
ANOVAreplication R 181
Any rule 141, 148–149
assumptions 257–259
autocorrelation 8, 35, 38, 41–42, 60

bain 131–133
Bartlett correction 232–233
Bayes factor (BF) 8–10, 127–128, 130–137, 176–179, 183
Bayes' theorem 4–7, 15, 127
BayesDefault 242, 245, *246*, *247*, *248*, *249*, 250
BayesFactor 178
Bayesian statistics 3–10, 114; advantages 220–221, 235, 261; exchangeable datasets 14–19; limitations 223, 235; missing data 262; multiple regression 16–19; penalized regression 71–83
BayesInfoI 242, *246*, *247*, *248*, *249*, 250
BayesInfoII 242, *246*, *247*, *248*, *249*, 250
bayesreg 74, 77–79
binary outcomes 139–153, 198
bootstrapping 189–190, 192, 222, 234, 259
brms 74

causal inference 99–100
chi-square test statistic 232–233

clinical trials 102–110, 139–153
clustered bootstrap sampling 192
Cohen's *d* 164–165, 175–176
collaboration 50–68
Compensatory rule 141, *148*, 149, 153
Completely Randomized Design (CRD) 91–92
confidence intervals 9, 179–180, 233–234
conjugate prior distributions 7, 16–17
constraint syntax 159–160, 161–162, 165, 166, 168–169
convergence 7–8, 34–41, 194, *195*, *197*, 231, 243–245
correlated residuals 204–206
credibility intervals 81–82
Croon's correction 231
cross-validation 190–191

debugging 60–65
decision rules 140–142, 148–149
degrees of freedom 217
dependent data 192
dependent variables 261
descriptive statistics 96
design-based inference 96–97, 100
divergent transitions 58–60
double-exponential prior distributions 73–74
dual factor loading 204–206

effect sizes 164–166, 174, 176–183
efficiency of sampling (ESS) *60*, 60–65, 67
elastic net penalty 76
equivalence test 176

Evidence Rate (ER) 134–136
exchangeable datasets 13–27, 54–56, 258
expert elicitation 113–122

F-ratio 263
factor loadings 204–206, 208
factor score regression (FSR) 231–232, 239–252
False Discovery Rate (FDR) 161
false-positive rates 173–174
Fisher information matrix 217
Fisher-Z transformation 256
fixed-effect model 187
For-all hypothesis 130
frequentist statistics 5, 8–9
full information maximum likelihood (FIML) 212, 262
Full Maximum Likelihood (FML) 217

Gelman–Rubin statistic 38
generalised order-restricted information criterion (GORIC) 164
geometric mean of the product of Bayes factors (gPBF) 134–136
Geweke diagnostic 8, 38–40
Gibbs sampler 34–35
group-level effects 128, 136

Hamiltonian Monte Carlo (HMC) 35, 58–59; *see also* No-U-Turn-Sampler
Hedges' *g* 175–176
heterogeneity 186–201
hierarchical replication 26
horseshoe prior 77, 78, 79, 80
hyperlasso prior 77, 78, 80–82
hyperparameters 5, 34, 78
hypothesis test Type A 158, 165, 166, 167, 169
hypothesis test Type B 158, 163, 165, 166, 167, 169

individual-level effects 126–137
inferential statistics 96
informative hypotheses 126–128, 130, 157–170
informative priors 43, *44*, 45, *46*, 50–68, 221, 239–252
interim analysis 150–153
inverse-gamma distribution 16, 18, 26, 43, 48n1, 261
ipsative z-score 104–105
item-level variance 204, 206–207
item parcels 203–212

JASP 178
Jeffrey's prior 144–145, 146

Kenward-Roger correction 217

lasso prior 71–72, 75–77, 79, 80–82, 229
Latent Growth Model (LGM) 50–68
lavaan 240, 260
Likert scales 204
linear models 157–170, 219
local convergence 40–41, 260
local fit measures 233
log posterior 63
longitudinal designs 218

"Many Labs" replication project 19
marginal posteriors 18
Markov Chain Monte Carlo (MCMC) 7–8, 16, 18, 34–35, 56–65, 73–74, 245, 260
maximum likelihood (ML) estimation 215–216, 220–221, 223, 228–229, 240–241, *247*, *248*, 249, 250, 260
mean squared error (MSE) 243, 248–249
meta-analysis 186–201
meta-regression 187–188
metaforest 186–201
mice 74
minimax concave penalty (MCP) 229
missing data 211–212, 262
misspecification 209
mixed-model analysis 104, 105
mode-switching 250
model-based inference 96–97
model-implied instrumental variables 229–230
moderator variables 187–201
multidimensional constructs 209, 211
multilevel models 97, 215–223
multilevel regression 216–219
multilevel structural equation models (MSEM) 219–220
multiple-baseline design 94, *95*, 104
Multiple Imputation (MI) 262
multiple regression 16–19, 157–158
multivariate studies 139–153

negative variance 228
n1me 105
No-U-Turn-Sampler (NUTS) 35, 51, 57
noise variables 188, 193
non-informative priors 43, *44*, 45, *46*, 221
non-normal outcomes 219
normal distribution 5, 7, 16, 17–18, 26
null hypothesis significance testing (NHST) 8–10, 127, 129, 158, 183, 258
numerical approximation 219

one-sided test 263
optimization 228

order constrained hypothesis testing 127, 158, 160–169
Ordinary Least Squares 222, 255–259
out-of-bag error 191, 192
overfitting 80, 188, 189–190

p-values 9, 99, 180–181, 183
parameter space 32–34
parceling 203–212
parsimony error 204–206
penalization 71–83, 228–229
penalty parameters 73, 229
permutation tests 258
phase design 90, 92–93
population effect 181–183
post-test 263
posterior distribution 4–7, 15, **17**, 35, 42, 114, 145, 220
Potential Scale Reduction factor 8
power 223, 250–251, 257
power priors 26
prediction interval 180
prediction mean squared error (PMSE) 80
preselection 193–194
pretest 263
prior distribution 4–7, 54–56, 114, 220, 235; Bayes factors 131; binary outcomes 144–145; expert elicitation 116–121; limitations 25–27; penalization 72–73; WAMBS checklist 31–34
probability 8–9
publication bias 173–174

quadratic effect 32

random assignment parceling 210
random-effects model 187
random error (ε) 206–207
random forests 189–193
random slope 218
randomization 87–100, 222, 258
Randomized Block Design (RBD) 91–92, 99–100
Randomized Controlled Trial (RCT) 102
ratio of marginal likelihoods *see* BF
regression 126–127, 128
regression coefficients: multilevel regression 216–217; order constraints 166–167; priors 32, *33*, 56; structural equation modeling 245–250
relative mean bias 242–243, *247*
relative median bias 242–243, *247*
Reliable Change Index 105
replication 19–20, 87–100, 173–184
ReplicationBF R 176–178

researcher degrees of freedom 173
residual bootstrap 222
residual error variance 263
Restricted Maximum Likelihood (REML) 217, 260
restricted means 163–164
restriktor 157–170
ridge prior 76–77, 79, 229
rjags 34, 35, *37*, 38–40, *42*
root mean square error of approximation (RMSEA) 209
RStan 34, 35, *37*, 38–40, *42*, 56
rstanarm 74
Rubin model 97

sample sizes 51–53, 148–153, 208, 215, 218, 220, 221, 228–229
sampling error 204–206
Satterthwaite correction 217
sensitivity analysis 42–43, 45, *46*
sequential replication design 94
sequential updating 45
Shiny apps 115, 131, 145
shinystan 62
shrinkage 75–82, 137
simultaneous replication design 94–95
single-case experimental design (SCED) 87–100, 102–110
Single-outcome rule 140–141, *148*, 149
smoothly clipped absolute deviation (SCAD) 229
"specific" variance *(s)* 206–207
spike-and-slab prior 77–78, 79, 80–81
Stability Rate (SR) 135–136
standard deviation *33*
standard error 122–124, 160, 217, 233–234
standardized root mean square residual (SRMR) 209, 233
stopping time 8
structural equation modeling (SEM) 203, 208, 210–211, 219–220, 226–235, 239–252
Student's t-test 77, 78, 256
subject-to-item ratios 207–208
Swain correction 233

t-test 157, 263
tails, heaviness 79
Taylor series expansion 219
test scores 112–124
thinning 8, 10n1
trace plots 8, *37*, 38
tree models 189
"true score" *(T)* 206–207
tuning parameters 190–191, 195–197

two-step estimation 230–231, 239–252, *247*, *248*, *249*
Type I error 151–152, 158, 208, 220

unconstrained model 160
unilevel inference 97–100
uninformative priors 43, *44*, *46*, 221
uniqueness 206–207

variable importance 191–192, *198*

variance hyperparameter 5
visual analysis 96, 104
vote-counting 176

WAMBS checklist 30–48, 50–51
Weighted Least Squares (WLS) 215–216
weighting 187, 190

Z-statistic 217–218, 256